PERVASIVE AND CORE TOPICS

PERVASIVE AND CORE TOPICS

Keir Bamford LLB, Solicitor

Sheila L Bramley LLB, Solicitor

Jane Fraser BA LLM, Solicitor

Richard Halberstadt LLB, Solicitor

Anthony Morgan LLB, Solicitor

Martin Norris LLB, Solicitor

Sarah Pooley BA, MLitt, Solicitor

Robin E Riddett, Solicitor

JORDANS

2001

Published by
Jordan Publishing Limited
21 St Thomas Street
Bristol BS1 6JS

British Library Cataloguing-in-Publication Data
A catalogue record for this book is available from the British Library.

ISSN 1353–3541
ISBN 0 85308 720 2

Printed in Great Britain by Hobbs The Printers Ltd of Southampton

PREFACE

This book is divided into five Parts, the first four Parts each dealing with one of the topics which pervade the syllabus of the Legal Practice Course. These topics are: revenue law, professional conduct, EC law and human rights. Part V deals with the core subject Probate and Administration. The material contained in this book is intended to be an introduction to the pervasive and core topics and is designed for those with little or no previous knowledge of the subjects. It has been written primarily to support and complement the Legal Practice Course undertaken by trainee solicitors. The approach taken to the subjects is essentially practical and is enhanced by worked examples showing the application of the topics in a practical context.

For the sake of brevity, the masculine pronoun is used to include the feminine. To refer to 'he or she' on every occasion when such a reference was necessary would have added many extra pages to an already lengthy book.

We acknowledge with thanks the permission of The Law Society to reproduce the Solicitors' Practice Rules 1990 in Appendix II. We would also like to thank our colleagues at The College of Law for their help in the preparation of this book, particularly Michael Hughes, Jane Chapman, Paula McWhirter and Hellen Revenko, who wrote the first edition of parts of the Revenue section, and the staff at Jordans for their help and support during the production process of the book.

The law is stated as at 26 June 2001.

KEIR BAMFORD
SHEILA BRAMLEY
JANE FRASER
RICHARD HALBERSTADT
ANTHONY MORGAN
MARTIN NORRIS
SARAH POOLEY
ROBIN RIDDETT
The College of Law

CONTENTS

TABLE OF CASES

References are to paragraph numbers.

TABLE OF STATUTES

References are to paragraph numbers and Appendix numbers.

TABLE OF STATUTORY INSTRUMENTS, GUIDANCE AND CODES

References are to paragraph and Appendix numbers.

TABLE OF EUROPEAN LEGISLATION

References are to paragraph numbers. References to the Articles of the EC Treaty are to those in force post-Treaty of Amsterdam. Please see conversion table at 29.4 for pre-Amsterdam numbering.

TABLE OF ABBREVIATIONS

AEA 1925	Administration of Estates Act 1925
APR	annual percentage rate
CFI	Court of First Instance
CGT	Capital Gains Tax
COREPER	Committee of Permanent Representatives
CTM	Community trade mark
CTO	Capital Taxes Office
DIB	discrete investment business
EAT	Employment Appeal Tribunal
ECA 1972	European Communities Act 1972
ECHR	European Convention for the Protection of Human Rights and Fundamental Freedoms 1950
ECJ	European Court of Justice
ECSC	European Coal and Steel Community
ECtHR	European Court of Human Rights
EEA	European Economic Area
EEIG	European Economic Interest Grouping
EFTA	European Free Trade Agreement
EIS	Enterprise Investment Scheme
ESC	Economic and Social Council
EurAtom	European Atomic Energy Community
FSA	Financial Services Authority
HRA 1998	Human Rights Act 1998
ICTA 1988	Income and Corporation Taxes Act 1988
IHT	inheritance tax
IHTA 1984	Inheritance Tax Act 1984
IP	intellectual property
I(PFD)A 1975	Inheritance (Provision for Family and Dependants) Act 1975
ISA	Individual Savings Account
LPA 1925	Law of Property Act 1925
MEP	member of the European Parliament
MEQR	measure equivalent to a quantitative restriction
MIRAS	Mortgage Interest Relief at Source
NCPR 1987	Non-Contentious Probate Rules 1987
non-DIB	non-discrete investment business
OSS	Office for the Supervision of Solicitors
PA	personal allowance
PAYE	Pay As You Earn
PEP	Personal Equity Plan
PET	potentially exempt transfer
PIA	personal investment authority
PR	personal representative
PTP	permitted third party
QLTT	Qualified Lawyers Transfer Test
RPB	Recognised Professional Body
RPI	Retail Prices Index
SIB	Securities and Investment Board
SIBR 1995	Solicitors' Investment Business Rules 1995
SLA 1925	Settled Land Act 1925
SRO	self-regulating organisation
TA 1925	Trustee Act 1925

TESSA	Tax Exempt Special Savings Account
TEU	Treaty on European Union
TIA 1961	Trustee Investments Act 1961
TLATA 1996	Trustees of Land and Appointment of Trustees Act 1996
VATA 1994	Value Added Tax Act 1994
VCT	Venture Capital Trust

PART I

REVENUE LAW

Chapter 1

VALUE ADDED TAX

1.1 INTRODUCTION

1.1.1 Sources of VAT law

The main charging statute relating to Value Added Tax (VAT) is the Value Added Tax Act 1994 (VATA 1994), as amended by later Finance Acts and certain statutory instruments. Detailed provisions implementing the Act are to be found in the VAT (General) Regulations 1995, SI 1995/2518 and other statutory instruments. In addition, HM Customs & Excise issues VAT Notices which, although lacking legal force, express its views on the law. VAT was introduced in 1973 in order to harmonise UK law with European Community law, therefore EC Directives 67/227 and 77/338 are also relevant. The standard practioner's work is De Voil *Indirect Tax Service* (Butterworths, looseleaf).

1.1.2 Charge to tax

Generally, VAT is charged whenever a business supplies goods or services. The business charges the customer VAT at 17.5 per cent on the value of the goods or services. This is known as 'output tax'. The business deducts from the output tax which it collects any VAT it has paid ('input tax') on goods or services received and pays the difference to HM Customs & Excise.

	Value of goods (£)	*VAT charged to buyer (£)*	*VAT paid to C&E (£)*
(1) A manufacturer buys raw material costing £200 plus VAT from a producer	200	35	
Producer pays to C&E			35
(2) The manufacturer sells finished article to a retailer for £1,000 plus VAT	1,000	175	
Manufacturer pays to C&E			140 (175 – 35)
(3) The retailer sells the finished article to a consumer for £2,000 plus VAT	2,000	350	
Retailer pays to C&E			175 (350 – 175)
Total paid to C&E			350

Note: (1) VAT does not cost the business anything as any VAT paid is recouped from VAT charged.

(2) Each business accounts for VAT on the 'value added' to the goods whilst in the possession of the business. The value added by the manufacturer is £800 (£1,000 – £200). 17.5% of £800 is £140, the sum paid to HM Customs & Excise.

(3) The ultimate burden falls on the consumer who pays £2,000 plus £350 VAT for the product. The £350 VAT has been paid to HM Customs & Excise in three stages.

1.2 CHARGE TO VAT

1.2.1 Definition

VAT is 'charged on any supply of goods or services made in the United Kingdom where it is a taxable supply made by a taxable person in the course or furtherance of any business carried on by him' (VATA 1994, s 4(1)). Tax will be charged on the 'value of the supply' (VATA 1994, s 2(1)). The elements of this charge are defined widely, in order both to prevent avoidance and to comply with the Directives, and are dealt with in outline below.

1.2.2 Supply of goods or services

Supply of goods

Any transfer of the whole property in goods is a supply of goods (VATA 1994, Sch 4). As well as more obvious transactions like the sale of consumer goods, this includes a supply of power or heat, the grant of an interest in land and even a gift of goods.

Supply of services

Anything which is not a supply of goods but is done for a consideration is a supply of services (VATA 1994, s 5(2)). This includes the provision of a solicitor's services for a fee but not a gratuitous supply of services.

1.2.3 Taxable supply

Any supply of goods or services (other than an exempt supply) is taxable (VATA 1994, s 4(2)). Exempt supplies are listed in VATA 1994, Sch 9 and include supplies of residential land, insurance, postal services, education and health services.

1.2.4 Taxable person

A taxable person is a person who makes or intends to make taxable supplies and who is or is required to be registered under the Act (VATA 1994, s 3(1)). A person is required to register if he makes taxable supplies in a defined period which have exceeded a limit, which is set each year, or will exceed that limit. Currently, a person must register if the value of his taxable supplies in the preceding 12 months exceeded £54,000.

Any person who makes taxable supplies is entitled to be registered if he so requests (see **1.3.4**). A person who makes only exempt supplies cannot register.

Once registered, a taxable person (individual, partnership or company) receives a VAT number which is issued for all businesses operated by that person.

1.2.5 Course of business

'Business' includes any trade, profession or vocation (VATA 1994, s 94). A supply in the course of business includes the disposal of a business or any of its assets.

1.2.6 Value of supply

VAT is charged on the value of the supply of goods or services. This is what the goods or services would cost were VAT not charged and is often shown as part of the price. For example, a television may be advertised as costing '£400 plus VAT'. £400 is the value of the supply.

If the supply is shown as being for a VAT inclusive amount (eg a television costs '£235'), the value of supply is 'such amount as, with the addition of the tax chargeable, is equal to the consideration' (VATA 1994, s 19(2)). In the case of the television, the value of supply would be £200 and the VAT £35. A price is deemed to include VAT unless the contrary is stated.

If the supply is not for a consideration in money, the value of supply is taken to be its market value (VATA 1994, s 19(3)).

1.2.7 Rate of tax

The standard rate of VAT is 17.5 per cent. However, there is a large category of supplies which are taxed at zero per cent. 'Zero-rated' supplies are listed in VATA 1994, Sch 8 and include food, other than food supplied in the course of catering, water, books and newspapers, transport and construction of dwellings. Domestic fuel attracts a special rate of 5 per cent.

1.2.8 Time of supply

A taxable person must account for VAT one month after the end of each quarter (see **1.3.1**). The time of supply (tax point) determines the accounting period within which a supply of goods or services falls.

In the case of goods, the basic tax point is the time goods are removed or the time they are made available to the person to whom they are supplied. In the case of services, the basic tax point is the time the services are performed (VATA 1994, s 6).

The basic tax point can be varied in a number of cases. For example, it can be brought forward, if the supplier issues a tax invoice (see **1.3.5**) or receives a payment, to the time when the invoice is issued or payment received. It can be delayed, if the supplier issues a tax invoice within 14 days after the basic tax point, to the time when the invoice is issued. Thus the time for accounting for VAT may be brought forward or delayed.

1.3 TAX PAYABLE TO HM CUSTOMS & EXCISE

1.3.1 Introduction

A person who is registered for VAT must send a return to HM Customs & Excise showing the VAT payable by him, together with a cheque for this amount, within one month after the end of each quarter.

The amount payable is the VAT he has charged on all supplies of goods and services in the course of his business ('output tax'), less any VAT he has paid in the course of his business ('input tax'). If input tax exceeds output tax, the person will receive a rebate.

1.3.2 Zero-rated and exempt supplies

Zero-rated and exempt supplies are similar to each other, in that the customer does not pay any VAT. However, a person who makes zero-rated supplies will be able to reclaim the VAT he has paid from HM Customs & Excise. A person who makes only exempt supplies cannot register (see **1.2.4**) and so cannot reclaim VAT.

> *Example*
> A baker and a doctor in private practice are converting premises into a shop and a surgery respectively. They will both pay VAT on the cost of their conversions. The baker, who makes zero-rated supplies of food, will be able to reclaim the VAT while the doctor, who makes exempt supplies of health services, will not be able to do so.

1.3.3 Taxable and exempt supplies

Where a person makes both exempt and taxable supplies, for example a doctor in private practice who also acts as an expert witness in personal injury claims, only part of his input tax will be deductible from the output tax charged on the fees for acting as an expert witness (see the VAT (General) Regulations 1995, SI 1995/2518).

1.3.4 Voluntary registration

A person who makes taxable supplies of less than £54,000 pa is not required to register and charge VAT. This can be an advantage as such a supplier may be able to undercut larger rivals who are obliged to charge VAT.

However, only those people who are registered can reclaim any input tax they have paid. For example, a builder with a small business who bought a van could not reclaim VAT payable on the purchase of the van if he were not registered.

When deciding whether to register voluntarily, people in business must weigh up the advantage of being able to reclaim VAT against the disadvantage that customers might be put off by higher prices.

1.3.5 Tax invoices

A person making a taxable supply to a taxable person must provide him with a tax invoice. A tax invoice is an ordinary invoice or bill which contains specified information about the transaction, such as the VAT number, the tax point, the value of supply and the rate of tax charged.

The tax invoice is important because a person who is claiming to deduct input tax must have tax invoices in respect of all the tax claimed.

1.4 PENALTIES

1.4.1 Introduction

A person who fails to comply with the VAT legislation is liable to a range of criminal and civil penalties in addition to being required to pay any unpaid tax with interest. There are very few defences to these provisions, although, apart from the default surcharge, the civil penalties may be mitigated. A number of these penalties are dealt with in outline below.

1.4.2 Fraudulent evasion of tax

A person knowingly concerned in the fraudulent evasion of tax is liable, on conviction on indictment, to an unlimited fine and imprisonment for a term not exceeding 7 years (VATA 1994, s 72).

1.4.3 Dishonest conduct

A person who dishonestly does any act or omits to take any action for the purpose of evading tax is liable to a civil penalty equal to the amount of tax evaded (VATA 1994, s 60).

1.4.4 Failure to register

Where a person who is liable to register fails to do so, he will be liable to a civil penalty of a percentage of the tax for which he was liable during the period when he should have been registered. This percentage rises from 5 per cent to 15 per cent where the failure lasts more than 18 months (VATA 1994, s 67).

1.4.5 Misdeclarations

Where a taxable person understates his liability or overstates his entitlement to a rebate by a substantial specified amount, he will be liable to a civil penalty of 15 per cent of the tax which would have been lost if the inaccuracy had not been discovered (VATA 1994, s 63). There are further penalties for repeated serious misdeclarations (VATA 1994, s 64).

1.4.6 Breaches of regulations

Regulations impose many obligations on taxable persons. Breach of a regulation will lead to a civil penalty. There is a penalty of £500 for failure to keep certain records. Other breaches attract a penalty calculated at a daily rate over the period of the breach (VATA 1994, s 69).

1.4.7 The default surcharge

A person who fails to send a return (see **1.3.1**) is regarded as being in default. If he is persistently in default he becomes liable to a surcharge rising to 15 per cent of the tax for any period in which he was in default (VATA 1994, s 59).

Chapter 2

INCOME TAX

2.1 INTRODUCTION

2.1.1 The Inland Revenue

Before looking at income tax, it is helpful to have an idea of how the Inland Revenue works.

Treasury

The Treasury is headed by the Chancellor of the Exchequer and is concerned amongst other things with the imposition and collection of taxation.

The Board of Inland Revenue

The statutory Board of the Inland Revenue, comprising a small number of higher civil servants, heads the Inland Revenue and answers to the Treasury Ministers. The Inland Revenue is responsible for the administration of income tax, corporation tax, capital gains tax, petroleum revenue tax, inheritance tax and stamp duties; advice on tax policy; advice on valuation policy and valuation services. The department also collects National Insurance contributions.

Regional Executive Offices

There are ten Regional Executive Offices where staff are engaged in day-to-day operations in assessing and collecting tax.

Local Tax Offices

Taxpayer Service Offices – deal with day-to-day work in settling a taxpayer's liability.

Tax District Offices – handle the main technical and compliance work.

Tax Enquiry Centres – provide assistance for taxpayers who call in.

The Commissioners

The General Commissioners are appointed by the Lord Chancellor to hear appeals against assessments. The Special Commissioners (lawyers of 10 years' standing) are also appointed by the Lord Chancellor and hear appeals involving more difficult statutory provisions.

2.1.2 Sources of income tax law

Statutory basis

The law relating to taxation is based on Acts of Parliament. For income tax, the principal charging Act is the Income and Corporation Taxes Act 1988 (ICTA 1988) as amended by later Finance Acts. References in this chapter are to ICTA 1988 unless otherwise stated.

Income tax is an annual tax renewed each year by Act of Parliament.

Case-law

The meaning and extent of the statutory provisions are decided by the judiciary.

An appeal by a taxpayer against an assessment to tax is heard either by a panel of General Commissioners or by a single Special Commissioner. From the decision of the Commissioners, appeals on a point of law are made to the High Court (certain appeals from decisions of the Special Commissioners may be referred directly to the Court of Appeal). There is a right of appeal from the High Court to the Court of Appeal and, with leave, to the House of Lords. Alternatively, the 'leapfrog' procedure may be used to appeal direct to the House of Lords.

Official statements

There would be an impossible work-load if all questions as to the meaning and extent of tax legislation were taken to court. Official statements made by the Inland Revenue are therefore an important source of information. The two most important types of statement are Extra-Statutory Concessions and Statements of Practice.

EXTRA-STATUTORY CONCESSIONS

These are published by the Inland Revenue. If a taxpayer satisfies the terms of an Extra-Statutory Concession, the Inland Revenue waives its right to collect tax which would otherwise be due.

STATEMENTS OF PRACTICE

These are announced by press release and published in the professional journals. They indicate what view the Inland Revenue will take of particular tax provisions.

Note that these official statements do not bind the courts.

2.1.3 Who pays income tax?

The following are eligible to pay income tax:

(1) individuals;
(2) partnerships (partners are individually responsible for the tax due on their share of partnership profits);
(3) personal representatives (who pay the deceased's outstanding income tax and income tax chargeable during the administration of the estate);
(4) trustees (who pay income tax on the income produced by the trust fund).

Companies pay corporation tax, see LPC Resource Book *Business Law and Practice* (Jordans). Charities are generally exempt from paying tax. There are tax-effective ways of giving money to charities, for example, Give As You Earn and Gift Aid.

2.1.4 Income tax year

The income tax year runs from 6 April to the following 5 April and is called the 'tax year' or the 'year of assessment'. It is referred to by the calendar years which it straddles; for example, the tax year beginning on 6 April 2001 is referred to as the tax year 2001/2002.

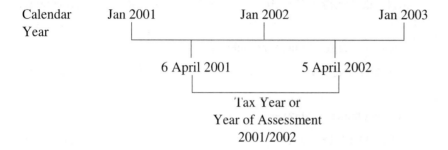

2.1.5 How much tax is payable?

The basic steps to work through to calculate the amount of tax payable are as follows:

Step 1:   Calculate statutory income

Step 2:   Deduct charges on income

The resulting sum is total income

Step 3:   Deduct personal allowances

The resulting sum is taxable income

Step 4:   Charge taxable income to income tax at starting rate, basic rate, higher rate.

Note: Income tax is charged on an individual's taxable income for 2001/2002 at the following rates:

Starting rate at 10%	£0–£1,880
Basic rate at 22%	£1,881–£29,400
Higher rate at 40%	over £29,400

Note: For 2001/2002, the rates of tax applicable to interest received are 10% for income in the starting rate band, 20% for income falling between the starting rate and the basic rate limits and 40% above that. The rates applicable to dividends are 10% for income below the basic rate limit and 32.5% above that (see **2.6**).

2.1.6 Simple income tax calculation

The four steps can be used to do a simple tax calculation. For example, Amy has the following income for 2001/2002: £60,000 salary as an executive and £6,639 from writing learned articles. She is liable to make interest payments of £2,000 pa on a qualifying loan. Amy is a single person. Amy's income tax can be calculated as follows:

		£
	Salary	60,000.00
	Learned articles	6,639.00
STEP 1	STATUTORY INCOME	66,639.00
STEP 2	deduct charges on income (interest)	2,000.00
	TOTAL INCOME	64,639.00
STEP 3	deduct personal allowance	4,535.00
	TAXABLE INCOME	60,104.00
STEP 4	TAX THE TAXABLE INCOME	
	£1,880 at 10%	188.00
	£27,520 at 22%	6,054.40
	£30,704 at 40%	12,281.60
	£60,104	
	INCOME TAX	18,524.00

The calculation above indicates the principles used to establish an individual's liability to income tax. The remainder of this chapter will consider each step of the calculation in more detail.

2.2 STATUTORY INCOME

Remember: Step 1 – Calculate statutory income.

Statutory income is the aggregate of the taxpayer's non-exempt income from all sources. Before you can calculate statutory income, some questions need answering.

2.2.1 When is a sum of money income?

There is no statutory definition of income. A distinction must be made between income and capital profits, the former are subject to income tax, the latter to capital gains tax. Generally, money received will be income if there is an element of recurrence, for example, salary, a share of partnership profits received every month or interest paid on a bank or building society account every quarter.

2.2.2 What income is taxable?

The Schedules

Income is taxable if it comes from a source within one of the Schedules to ICTA 1988. The most important Schedules and their sub-divisions, ie Cases, are listed below.

Schedule	*Source*
A	Rents and other receipts from land in UK
D	
Case I	Profits of a trade in UK
Case II	Profits of a profession or vocation in UK (Cases I and II charge the self-employed and apply to sole traders, trading partnerships, sole practitioners and professional partnerships)
Case III	Interest, annuities and other annual payments, eg income sums paid to a beneficiary by the trustees of a discretionary trust
Case VI	Annual profits or gains not falling under any other Case of Schedule D or any other Schedule
E	
Cases I, II and III	Offices, employments and pensions (Schedule E charges employed as opposed to self-employed persons.) Also chargeable benefits under the social security legislation, eg sick pay and maternity payments
F	Dividends and certain other distributions by companies

How do the Schedules work? If income is shown to be derived from one of the sources, it will be charged to income tax. For example, if an individual receives rent from land he will pay income tax under Schedule A. Income not falling within any Schedule, ie not having a chargeable source, cannot be charged to income tax at all.

Why is it divided into Schedules?

RULES

Each Schedule has its own rules for calculating the amount of income. For example, Schedule A taxes income from land. The charge is on rents and other receipts but the landlord may deduct expenses such as repairs on the property, ie expenses of an income nature. This means that income tax is charged on the profit element rather than the gross income.

Where the Schedules are divided into Cases (Schedules D and E), each is treated as an individual Schedule.

BASIS OF ASSESSMENT

Each Schedule has a basis of assessment which determines how much income is taxable in any tax year. The current year basis applies to all of the Schedules.

2.2.3 Current year basis

Tax is charged in a tax year on the income received in that tax year. For example, in the simple tax calculation above, Amy's salary as an executive falls within Schedule E. Salary received between 6 April 2001 and 5 April 2002 will be charged to tax in the tax year 2001/2002.

2.2.4 Exempt income

Certain items are free of income tax. They include:

(1) certain social security benefits (eg child benefit);
(2) interest on National Savings Certificates;
(3) the first £70 of interest each year from ordinary accounts at the National Savings Bank;
(4) scholarships;
(5) interest on damages for personal injuries or death;
(6) income from investments in an individual savings account (ISA) (see **5.3**);
(7) interest earned in a Tax Exempt Special Savings Account (TESSA) opened before 6 April 1999 (see **5.3**);
(8) dividends paid in a Personal Equity Plan (PEP); no further subscriptions permitted after 5 April 1999 (see **5.3**);
(9) gross income up to a certain limit (£4,250 pa) from letting a room;
(10) annual payments under certain insurance policies, for example, where insurance benefits are provided in times of sickness.

A number of items are exempted from tax because of Extra-Statutory Concessions.

2.2.5 How is the tax collected?

There are two methods of collection of tax.

Direct assessment

Schedule A income is collected by direct assessment under the self assessment procedure. The landlord (taxpayer) receives gross rent from the tenant.

Tax is also assessed directly on the taxpayer under Schedule D Cases I and II, ie profits of a trade or profession which the taxpayer himself has made.

The direct assessment method assumes that the taxpayer has actually received the sum on which he is to pay tax and can send part of it to the Inland Revenue to satisfy his income tax liability. There is a risk that the taxpayer will spend the income received before the Inland Revenue can claim their share.

Under self-assessment, the taxpayer completes an annual tax return form which includes computation pages to enable the taxpayer to calculate his own income tax and capital gains tax liability. The tax returns are issued soon after 5 April. There are different returns for different types of income. Even if a taxpayer does not normally receive a return, there is a statutory obligation to notify the Revenue that he has income that is liable to tax. This must be done within 6 months of the end of the relevant tax year. There is a penalty for default. The tax return and cheque must be filed by 31 January following the tax year to which the return relates, with penalties for default. If the taxpayer would rather have the Inland Revenue calculate his liability he must submit his return by 30 September following the tax year.

The taxpayer is automatically required to make two payments on account towards the income tax due for any year and then a third and final balancing payment to meet any tax still outstanding. The payment scheme covers all income and capital gains tax due.

The first payment on account is due on 31 January in the tax year in question. The second payment on account is due on the 31 July after the end of the tax year. Any balancing payment is due on the next 31 January.

Each payment on account should be approximately one half of the income tax liability for the year. They are calculated by reference to the previous year's income tax liability, and are reduced to give credit for tax deducted at source (see below). No payments on account are required if this 'relevant amount' is below a certain limit. Capital gains tax is included only in the balancing payment.

Example

Josie's income tax liability for 2000/2001 came to £15,000, of which £7,000 was deducted at source. Her return for 2001/2002 will be issued in April 2002 and must be submitted to the Inland Revenue by 30 September 2002, or by 31 January 2003 at the latest. For 2001/2002 she will make interim payments on account of ½ × (£15,000 − £7,000) = £4,000 on 31 January 2002 and 31 July 2002. Her final adjustment for 2001/2002 is due on 31 January 2003.

Taxpayers have the right to claim a reduction or cancellation of payments on account where they have grounds for believing that payments based on the tax liability for the previous year will lead to an overpayment of tax in the current year.

Interest is charged on any amount of tax unpaid at the due date for payment whether that tax is due as a payment on account or as a balancing payment.

Throughout the self-assessment system the onus is on the taxpayer, and there is a statutory requirement to maintain adequate records to support the return, backed up by a penalty for default. The Revenue have extensive powers, for example random audits and specific enquiries, to check the accuracy of any return. Appeals against assessments and determinations are made to the General Commissioners or Special Commissioners.

Deduction at source

For certain types of income, for example interest paid by banks and building societies, salaries and trust income, tax is deducted at source. The payer of the income acts as a tax collector by deducting from the payment an amount of tax and handing it to the Inland Revenue.

Below are some examples of how tax is deducted at source from certain types of income.

Example 1

Interest received is assessable under Schedule D Case III. If the interest is paid by banks and building societies to individuals or personal representatives it is paid after deduction of income tax at 20%, ie the interest is paid net.

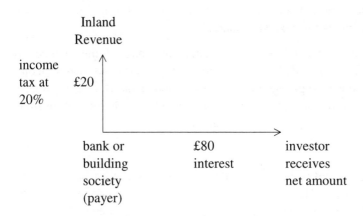

Gross amount £100

Inland
Revenue

income
tax at   £20
20%

bank or   £80   investor
building   interest   receives
society   net amount
(payer)

The investor receives only a net amount (and a written statement showing the gross amount of the payment, the amount of income tax deducted and the actual amount paid to the taxpayer).

If the investor is not liable to income tax (eg he has unused personal reliefs) or he is liable to pay only income tax at 10% (ie his income falls within the starting rate band) he will obtain a repayment from the Inland Revenue. The taxpayer will use the written statement mentioned above to prove to the Inland Revenue the payment and amount of tax deducted. Note that individuals who are not liable to tax may receive their interest gross by lodging the appropriate form with the bank or building society.

For taxpayers whose income from interest falls within the basic rate band, the tax will be deducted at 20% and they will have no more tax to pay on it. Taxpayers who are liable at the higher rate of income tax of 40% have to pay more tax to cover the difference between income tax at 20% and the higher rate (40 – 20 = 20%). Savings income is treated as the top slice of income (see **2.6** for examples of calculations).

Note that interest paid on taxable National Savings investments and government stock (gilts) is paid gross.

Example 2
Salaries are assessable under Schedule E using the Pay As You Earn system (PAYE). Under the PAYE system, the employer deducts from the employee's salary and then pays to the Inland Revenue income tax at starting, basic and higher rates at the time the salary is paid. The PAYE system also takes account of personal allowances. For example, a higher rate taxpayer who receives a salary should have all the tax, including higher rate tax, deducted under the PAYE system.

Gross amount £100

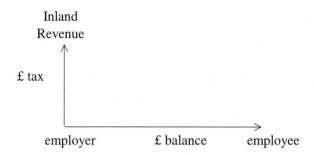

Under the Income Tax (Employments) Regulations 1993, SI 1993/744, the employer is liable for the income tax which has been or should have been deducted.

Example 3

Trust income received by a beneficiary is received after deduction of income tax. The rate of tax deducted depends on the nature of the trust and its income.

Summary

It is important to remember that if tax is collected by direct assessment the taxpayer receives the income gross, whereas if tax is collected by deduction at source the taxpayer receives the income net of tax.

Collection of tax by deduction at source is used wherever possible. It is much easier for the Inland Revenue to require the person making the payment, the payer, to deduct income tax from the payment, and to collect the tax deducted from the payer. This avoids the problem of the money being spent before the taxpayer can be assessed to tax.

2.2.6 Calculating the statutory income

It should now be possible to calculate the statutory income.

The statutory income is the aggregate of income computed according to the rules of the various Schedules and Cases. To work out the statutory income of a taxpayer it is necessary to find out what sources of income he has, calculate the income arising under each source (using the rules of the relevant Schedules and Cases) and then add all the gross income together, for example:

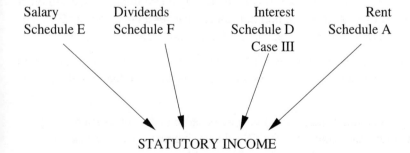

Grossing up

Remember that for certain types of income, tax will have been deducted at source (see **2.2.5**). The payee receives the net amount, not the gross amount.

Any sum received after deduction of tax at source must be grossed up to find the original sum from which the tax was deducted. This gross figure must be entered into the payee's calculation of statutory income. Why? The tax calculation is a way of checking that, overall, the taxpayer pays the right amount of tax.

At the end of the tax calculation the tax that has already been paid will be credited to the taxpayer so that he will owe only the Inland Revenue the outstanding amount.

For example, Barbara receives interest of £800, the equivalent of income tax at 20 per cent has been paid by the building society and handed to the Inland Revenue. She also has income from other sources of £20,000.

To gross up:

$$\text{interest} \times \frac{100}{(100 - \text{rate at which tax deducted})}$$

$$= \quad £800 \times \frac{100}{(100 - 20)}$$

$$= \quad £800 \times \frac{100}{80}$$

$$= \quad £1,000 \text{ gross interest}$$

Tax paid = £200

Barbara's statutory income is:

other sources	£20,000
gross interest (Schedule D Case III)	£ 1,000
Statutory income	£21,000

Another way of grossing up at 20 per cent is to divide the sum received by four and then multiply by five, for example:

$$800 \times \frac{5}{4}$$

= £1,000 gross interest

At the end of the tax calculation when the tax has been worked out, £200 tax can be deducted because this was paid on Barbara's behalf by the building society. In other words, the interest of £800 from the building society carries a tax credit of £200. The amount of the tax credit may be set against Barbara's final liability to income tax.

If a taxpayer's final liability to tax is for less than £200, he can claim a repayment from the Inland Revenue; if it is for more than £200 he will owe the Inland Revenue some money.

Do not gross up Schedule E income in this way because deduction at source may not be just at one single rate. Under the PAYE scheme, income tax at various rates will be deducted from salaries by the employer using tables and information supplied by the Inland Revenue and taking into account the employees' personal reliefs. A certificate of tax paid (P60), showing the gross figure, is given by the employer to the employee on a yearly basis and he can put this figure into his tax return. A taxpayer must complete a tax return if he has other sources of income.

Dividends

Dividends from companies are assessed under Schedule F. The dividend paid to the shareholder carries a tax credit. The rate of credit is determined by reference to the 'tax credit fraction' which is initially fixed at one-ninth. This is equivalent to a tax credit of 10 per cent of the sum of the dividend and the credit, for example, if a company pays a dividend of £900 on 1 June 2001 the credit will be £100 (1/9 of £900) which is 10 per cent of £1,000 (£900 plus the credit of £100).

The Schedule F income assessable is the sum of the dividend and the tax credit (£900 plus the credit of £100).

2.3 CHARGES ON INCOME

Remember: Step 2 – Deduct charges on income.

2.3.1 Total income

Total income is statutory income less certain specified commitments known as charges on income for example interest on qualifying loans. Charges on income are a form of tax relief because they remove sums of money from the income tax calculation.

2.3.2 Interest on qualifying loans

Most interest payments receive no tax relief at all, for example ordinary bank overdrafts, credit card interest and hire purchase interest payments. The borrower pays the interest out of taxed income.

However, in certain cases, tax relief may be available for interest paid on money borrowed. A taxpayer obtains income tax relief for certain interest payments by deducting them from his statutory income as a charge. To obtain tax relief, interest must be payable on a 'qualifying loan'.

Qualifying loans include the following.

A loan to buy a share in a partnership or to contribute capital or make a loan to a partnership

For example, Dawn, a partner, has statutory income of £25,000. She borrows £10,000 to make a loan to the partnership to be used wholly and exclusively for partnership business. The interest rate on the loan is 7 per cent pa. Dawn's total income is:

	£
Statutory income	25,000
Less: charges on income (interest on qualifying loan)	700
Total income	24,300

See LPC Resource Book *Business Law and Practice* (Jordans).

A loan to invest in a close trading company

See LPC Resource Book *Business Law and Practice* (Jordans).

A loan to purchase a main residence

Prior to 6 April 2000, certain interest paid by a borrower on a loan to buy his main residence attracted an element of tax relief known as MIRAS (Mortgage Interest Relief at Source). This has now been abolished.

A loan to personal representatives to pay inheritance tax

See **34.10.6**.

2.4 PERSONAL ALLOWANCES

Remember: Step 3 – Deduct personal allowances.

Personal allowances available at the taxpayer's marginal rate are deducted from total income to obtain the taxpayer's taxable income. This means that a certain amount of income is tax free each year.

Personal allowances available at the taxpayer's marginal rate attract tax relief at whichever rate of tax (starting rate, basic rate, higher rate) the taxpayer pays.

Some personal allowances and reliefs only attract tax relief at 10 per cent. Therefore, these personal allowances cannot be deducted at this stage but will be deducted at the end of the calculation (see **2.7**).

A summary of the personal allowances available for 2001/2002 is set out below:

	£
Personal allowance (PA)	4,535
Aged 65 but under 75	5,990
Aged 75 or over	6,260
Children's tax credit	5,200*
Blind person's allowance	1,450
Income limit for age-related allowances	17,600

* Allowance where relief is restricted to 10 per cent.

It can be seen that the availability of allowances depends not on the type of income involved but on the taxpayer's personal circumstances, for example age, family responsibilities or disability. The taxpayer must claim his allowances each year in his income tax return. If personal allowances exceed the total income of the taxpayer the surplus is unused and cannot be carried forward for use in future years.

The principal allowances available at the taxpayer's marginal rate and deducted at this stage are as follows.

2.4.1 Personal allowance (PA)

This allowance can be claimed by any taxpayer resident in the UK, male or female, adult or child, married or single. It can be set against income of any kind. The personal allowance is increased where the taxpayer is aged 65 or over and has only a limited total income (ie age allowance). It is increased further when the taxpayer is aged 75 or over (subject to the same total income limit).

Married couples

Husband and wife are treated as separate single people. Each spouse is independently liable for tax on his or her own income with his or her own personal allowances.

If a wife is paying a lower tax rate than her husband, a tax saving can be made by transferring investments producing income from the husband's name to the wife. The greatest saving will be made where the wife has an unused personal allowance.

2.4.2 Blind person's allowance

A taxpayer who is a registered blind person receives this relief. If a husband and wife are both registered blind they can each claim the blind person's allowance.

2.5 RATES OF TAX

Remember: Step 4 – Tax the taxable income.

As explained in **2.1.5**, the taxable income is taxed at the appropriate rate or rates, ie starting rate, basic rate and higher rate. These rates are fixed annually.

There are special rates for savings income, which comprises interest received and dividends (see **2.6**).

2.6 SAVINGS INCOME

Interest received is taxed at 10 per cent for income in the starting rate band, at 20 per cent for income falling between the starting rate and the basic rate limits and at 40 per cent above that. Dividends are taxed at 10 per cent for income below the basic rate limit and 32.5 per cent above that.

Savings income is treated as the top slice of taxable income in priority to non-savings income. Dividends are treated as the top slice of savings income in priority to interest received (see diagram below).

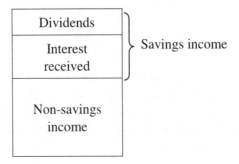

2.6.1 Interest received

To the extent that interest received falls below the starting rate limit, it is taxed at 10 per cent. Interest received which falls between the starting and basic rate limits is taxed at 20 per cent; any excess over the basic rate limit is taxed at the 40 per cent higher rate.

Example 1
An individual with taxable income (after allowances and reliefs) of £1,880 of which £500 is interest (including the tax deducted at source) will be liable to tax:

- at 10% on the first £1,380 of non-savings income; and

- at 10% on the 'top slice' of £500 of savings income.

Example 2
An individual with taxable income (after allowances and reliefs) of £5,000 of which £500 is interest (including the tax deducted at source), will be liable to tax:

- at 10% on the first £1,880 of non-savings income; and
- at 22% on the next £2,620 of non-savings income; and
- at 20% on the 'top slice' of £500 of savings income.

Example 3
An individual with taxable income (after allowances and reliefs) of £30,000, of which £5,000 is interest (including the tax deducted at source), will be liable to tax:

- at 10% on the first £1,880 of non-savings income; and
- at 22% on the next £23,120 of non-savings income.

The savings income will be taxed:

- at 20% to the extent that it falls below the basic rate limit of £29,400, so £4,400 (£29,400 – £25,000) will be taxed at 20%; and
- at 40% on the remaining £600.

Personal allowances and other reliefs are set primarily against an individual's non-savings income.

2.6.2 Dividends

Dividend income is treated as the top slice of taxable income in priority to interest received. To the extent that dividend income falls within the starting rate and basic rate limits, it is taxed at 10 per cent (Schedule F ordinary rate). The liability of starting rate and basic rate taxpayers is met by the tax credit (see **2.2.6**).

Example 1

An individual with taxable income (after allowances and reliefs) of £5,000, of which £500 is dividend income (including the tax credit), will be liable to tax:

- at 10% on the first £1,880 of non-savings income;
- at 22% on the next £2,620 of non-savings income; and
- at 10% on the 'top slice' of £500 of dividends.

To the extent that dividend income exceeds the basic rate limit, it is taxed at 32.5 per cent (Schedule F upper rate).

Example 2

An individual with taxable income (after allowances and reliefs) of £30,000, of which £5,000 is dividend income (including the tax credit), will be liable to tax:

- at 10% on the first £1,880 of non-savings income; and
- at 22% on the next £23,120 of non-savings income.

The dividends will be taxed:

- at 10% to the extent that they fall below the basic rate limit of £29,400, so £4,400 (£29,400 – £25,000) will be taxed at 10%; and
- at 32.5% on the remaining £600.

Higher rate taxpayers get the benefit of the 10 per cent tax credit to reduce their Schedule F upper rate liability:

	£
Net dividend received	4,500
Tax credit (£4,500 × 1/9)	500
Gross Schedule F income	5,000

Income tax liability:		
£4,400 @ 10%	440	
£600 @ 32.5%	195	635
Less: tax credit		500
Income tax still to pay		135

Tax credits on dividends are not reclaimable by shareholders who have no tax liability (eg where there are unused personal allowances).

2.7 ALLOWANCES AND RELIEFS WHERE TAX RELIEF IS RESTRICTED

Some allowances and reliefs only attract tax relief at 10 per cent (see **2.4**). The amount of this tax relief operates as a reduction in the taxpayer's liability to income tax at this stage in the income tax calculation.

The principal allowances where tax relief is restricted are as follows.

2.7.1 Married couple's allowance

Prior to 6 April 2000, an allowance was available to married couples. This allowance has now been abolished. However, it has been retained for couples in which at least one party had reached the age of 65 before 6 April 2000.

2.7.2 Children's tax credit

The children's tax credit was introduced on 6 April 2001. To qualify for this allowance the taxpayer must have one or more 'qualifying' children (broadly, children under the age of 16 at the start of the tax year) living with him for the whole or part of the tax year. A taxpayer will qualify for one allowance only, regardless of the number of qualifying children he may have.

Example 1
Miriam is a single parent living with her two children (aged 8 and 10). She has a gross income of £28,415 pa. Miriam is entitled to the children's tax credit.

Total income	£28,415
Less	
Personal allowance	£4,535
Taxable income	£23,880
Tax the taxable income	
£1,880 @ 10% =	£188
£22,000 @ 22% =	£4,840
£23,880	£5,028
Less	
Children's tax credit	
£5,200 × 10% =	£520
Net income tax liability	£4,508

If the qualifying child lives with a married or cohabiting couple, the partner with the higher total income will be entitled to the relief. If neither partner is a higher rate taxpayer, the couple can choose to share the relief.

Where the taxpayer claiming the relief is a higher rate taxpayer, the relief is withdrawn at the rate of £2 for every £3 of that part of his income.

Example 2
Anthony and Clare are a married couple living with their two children (aged 12 and 14). Anthony earns £35,000 pa and Clare earns £26,000 pa, so Anthony is entitled to the children's tax credit.

Chapter 3

CAPITAL GAINS TAX

3.1 INTRODUCTION

3.1.1 Sources of capital gains tax law

The principal charging statute is the Taxation of Chargeable Gains Act 1992.

3.1.2 The charge to tax

Capital Gains Tax (CGT) is charged on the chargeable gains made by a chargeable person on the disposal of chargeable assets in a tax year.

3.1.3 Chargeable assets

All forms of property are treated as assets for CGT purposes including such things as debts, options, incorporeal property and property created by the person disposing of it. Sterling is excluded from the definition so disposals of cash do not attract CGT liability. The legislation does provide for a limited category of non-chargeable assets, the main example being private motor vehicles. The legislation also provides that certain assets which are not non-chargeable shall be wholly or partly exempt from CGT – see **3.4**.

3.1.4 Who pays CGT?

Chargeable persons are:
(1) individuals;
(2) partners (each partner is charged separately for his share of the partnership gains when there is a disposal of a chargeable partnership asset);
(3) personal representatives (who pay CGT when there is a disposal of the deceased's chargeable assets);
(4) trustees (who pay CGT when there is a disposal of a chargeable asset from the trust fund).

Companies pay corporation tax (see LPC Resource Book *Business Law and Practice* (Jordans)). Charities are generally exempt from paying tax.

3.1.5 How much CGT will an individual pay?

The steps to calculate the amount of CGT payable are as follows:

Step 1: Disposal of a chargeable asset
It is first necessary to identify the disposal of a chargeable asset, for example the sale of land.

Step 2: Calculation of the gain

This, in basic terms, will be the consideration received when the asset is sold less cost.

Note

When calculating the gain, the taxpayer can take an indexation allowance to remove inflationary gains up to April 1998 from the calculation (see **3.3.1**). This allowance is not included in the earlier examples for the sake of simplicity.

Step 3: Consider reliefs

Various reliefs may be available (see **3.4**). Early examples assume that none of these apply for the sake of simplicity.

Step 4: Deduct annual exemption

An individual does not pay tax on all the gains he makes. There is an exemption for the first £7,500 of total net gains made by an individual in a tax year.

Step 5: What is the rate of tax?

The rate of CGT is determined by reference to the individual's income tax position. Individuals are charged to rates of CGT as if the gains were treated as the top slice of savings income. Therefore, it is necessary to consider the taxpayer's income tax position when deciding what rate or rates of CGT to apply. To the extent that gains fall within the basic rate limit, they are charged at 20 per cent (or at 10 per cent if they fall within the starting rate band). If they exceed that limit, they are charged at 40 per cent.

> *Example*
> Sarah sells land for £87,500. The land cost her £40,000. It is her only disposal during the tax year. She pays income tax at the higher rate.
>
> | | | |
> |---|---|---:|
> | Step 1: | Identify the disposal | |
> | | Sale of land | |
> | Step 2: | Calculate the gain | |
> | | Proceeds of disposal | £87,500 |
> | | *Less:* Cost | £40,000 |
> | | | £47,500 |
> | Step 3: | Consider exemptions and reliefs | Nil |
> | Step 4: | Deduct Annual Exemption | £7,500 |
> | | Chargeable gain | £40,000 |
> | Step 5: | What is the rate of tax? | |
>
> As Sarah is a higher rate taxpayer, CGT is charged at 40%.
> CGT at 40% on £40,000 is £16,000.

3.1.6 Assessment and payment of CGT

Because CGT is assessed on the gains of the current tax year, it is necessary to consider all the disposals made during the tax year. Tax for individuals is payable on or before 31 January following the end of the tax year (or 30 days from the making of an assessment if later).

The above example shows the principles used to establish an individual's liability for CGT. The remainder of this chapter will consider each step of the calculation in more detail.

3.2 DISPOSALS

3.2.1 The sale or gift of a chargeable asset

There must be a disposal of a chargeable asset. Disposal is widely defined and includes a sale or a gift. If a gift is made then the Inland Revenue tax the gain the taxpayer is deemed to have made on the disposal. This is done by using the market value of the asset at the time of the gift instead of consideration received.

Example

Barbara makes a gift of a Ming vase worth £267,500. She had bought the vase for £180,000. It is her only disposal during the tax year. She is a higher rate taxpayer.

Step 1:	Identify the disposal	
	Gift of vase	
Step 2:	Calculate the gain	
	Market value of vase	£267,500
	Less: Cost	£180,000
		£87,500
Step 3:	Consider exemptions and reliefs	Nil
Step 4:	Deduct Annual Exemption	£7,500
	Chargeable gain	£80,000
Step 5:	What is the rate of tax?	
	CGT at 40% on £80,000 is £32,000.	

3.2.2 The disposal of part of an asset

A sale of part of an asset or a gift of part of an asset is a disposal, for example the sale of part of a field. This is considered in detail in **3.8**.

3.2.3 The death of the taxpayer

On death there is no disposal by the deceased, so there is no charge to CGT. The personal representatives acquire the deceased's assets at the market value at the date of death. This has the effect of wiping out gains which accrued during the deceased's lifetime so that these gains are not charged to tax.

Example

Christopher dies owning shares worth £150,000. He had bought the shares for £60,000. Since death is not a disposal, there is no charge to CGT when Christopher dies. His personal representatives will acquire the shares at the market value at his death, ie at £150,000. The gain of £90,000 is wiped out and is not charged to tax. The £90,000 is the difference between the cost of the shares and the market value of the shares at the date of death.

3.3 CALCULATION OF GAINS

The gain is generally the consideration for the disposal or the market value if the taxpayer gives away the asset, less the following:

Initial expenditure
(1) The cost price of the asset, or the market value at acquisition (if the asset was given to the taxpayer) plus incidental costs of acquisition, for example legal fees, valuation fees, stamp duty.
(2) Expenditure wholly and exclusively incurred in providing the asset, for example the cost of building a weekend cottage.

Subsequent expenditure
(1) Expenditure wholly and exclusively incurred to enhance the value of the asset which is reflected in the asset at the time of the disposal, for example the cost of building an extension. However, the cost of routine maintenance and insurance cannot be deducted.
(2) Expenditure incurred wholly and exclusively in establishing, preserving or defending title to the asset, for example legal fees incurred in resolving a boundary dispute.

Incidental costs of disposal
Legal fees and estate agent's fees could be incidental costs of disposal.

As these costs are incurred at the time of disposal they will not receive any indexation allowance (see **3.3.1**). As a consequence, it is convenient to deduct them from the proceeds of disposal (to find the net proceeds of disposal) before deducting initial and subsequent expenditure.

Note that expenditure which is deductible for income tax purposes cannot be deducted when calculating a capital gain.

> *Example*
> Paul sells his holiday cottage for £151,500. He bought the cottage for £50,000 and spent £700 on a survey and £1,300 on legal fees when he purchased it. He spent £8,000 improving the cottage. Legal fees when he sells the cottage are £800 and the estate agent's commission is £3,400.
>
> Step 1: Identify the disposal
>   Sale of holiday cottage
>
> Step 2: Calculate the gain
>   Proceeds of disposal   £151,500
>
>   *Less:*
>   Incidental costs of disposal
>   Legal fees   £800
>   Estate agent's commission   £3,400
>   £4,200
>   Net proceeds of disposal   £147,300

Less:
Initial expenditure

Cost	£50,000	
Survey fee	£700	
Legal fees	£1,300	
		£52,000

Subsequent expenditure

Cost of improvements	£8,000	
		£60,000
GAIN		£87,300

After deducting relevant expenditure, the taxpayer may also be entitled to an indexation allowance. This is a further deduction from the proceeds of disposal.

3.3.1 The indexation allowance

The indexation allowance is used when calculating the gain on an asset which has been owned for any period between 31 March 1982 and 5 April 1998. The purpose of the indexation allowance was to remove inflationary gains from the CGT calculation so that a smaller gain is charged to tax. Inflation is measured by reference to the Retail Prices Index (the RPI). The indexation allowance is calculated by applying to the initial and subsequent expenditure the percentage increase in the RPI since the expenditure was incurred, until the date of disposal (or April 1998 if earlier). Tables published by the Inland Revenue express this information as an indexation factor for ease of calculation.

Example (continued)
Since the date of purchase the RPI has increased by 25 per cent up to April 1998, giving an indexation factor of 0.25. Since the date of the improvements the RPI has increased by 10 per cent up to April 1998, giving an indexation factor of 0.1. Paul makes no other disposals in the tax year and he is a higher rate taxpayer.

Step 2 (continued)

GAIN (before indexation)		£87,300

Less:
Indexation allowance

Initial expenditure (0.25 × 52,000)	£13,000	
Subsequent expenditure (0.1 × 8,000)	£800	
		£13,800
GAIN (after indexation)		£73,500
Step 3: Consider reliefs		NIL
Step 4: Deduct annual exemption		£7,500
CHARGEABLE GAIN		£66,000

Step 5: What is the rate of tax?
CGT at 40% on £66,000 is £26,400.

Note that the allowance is applied only to initial and subsequent expenditure incurred between 31 March 1982 and 5 April 1998.

Note also that the indexation allowance cannot be used to create or increase a loss. This is dealt with in **3.7.1**.

3.3.2 Assets owned on 31 March 1982

Where a taxpayer disposes of an asset which he owned on 31 March 1982, special rules are applied. The aim of these rules is to exclude from the tax calculation the part of the gain that accrued before 31 March 1982, so that no CGT is paid on that part of the gain.

In most cases, the indexation allowance for such assets will be based on the market value of the assets on 31 March 1982, rather than actual expenditure.

3.4 RELIEFS

After calculating the indexed gain, the next step is to consider whether any reliefs apply. Generally, reliefs may be available due to the nature of the asset being disposed of. The majority of reliefs are aimed at smaller businesses, to encourage investment in this sector of the economy.

The following is a non-exhaustive list of CGT reliefs.

3.4.1 Tangible moveable property

Wasting assets (ie assets with a predictable life of less than 50 years) are generally exempt. Most consumer goods will fall into this category, for example, televisions and washing machines. Cars are also exempt.

Not all items of tangible moveable property are wasting assets. Some will go up in value, for example antiques. However, they will be exempt from CGT if the disposal consideration is £6,000 or less.

3.4.2 Private dwelling house

A gain on the disposal by an individual of a dwelling house, including grounds of up to half a hectare, will be completely exempt, provided it has been occupied as his only or main residence through his period of ownership (ignoring the last 3 years of ownership).

For most people, their home is their most valuable asset. The effect of this relief is that the house can be sold (or given away) without CGT liability being incurred, see LPC Resource Book *Conveyancing* (Jordans).

3.4.3 Damages for personal injury

The recovery of damages or compensation may amount to the disposal of a chargeable asset, however the receipt of damages for personal injury is exempt.

3.4.4 Hold-over relief

Hold-over relief enables an individual to make a gift of business assets without paying CGT. However, if the donee disposes of the asset, the donee will be charged to tax not only on his own gain but on the donor's gain as well. Because hold-over relief defers the charge to tax until a disposal by the donee, there must usually be an election by donor and donee to claim hold-over relief.

3.4.5 Relief for replacement of business assets ('roll-over' relief)

This relief encourages expansion and investment in business assets by enabling the sale of those assets to take place without an immediate charge to CGT, provided the proceeds of sale are invested in other business assets. The charge to CGT is postponed until the disposal of the new asset.

3.4.6 Roll-over relief on incorporation of a business

This relief again defers a CGT charge. It is applied (subject to conditions) when an individual sells his interest in an unincorporated business (sole trader, partnership) to a company. The indexed gain is rolled over into the shares received as consideration for the interest being sold to the company. The CGT charge is postponed until the disposal of the shares.

3.4.7 Relief for re-investment in certain unquoted shares

To encourage investment in small company shares, it is possible for an individual to defer payment of CGT on any chargeable gain provided the proceeds of sale are re-invested in certain shares in an unquoted trading company. This is dealt with in **5.4**.

3.4.8 Retirement relief

If an individual aged at least 50 years disposes of his business, retirement relief may be available so that he pays either less CGT or possibly no CGT at all.

3.4.9 Taper relief

If none of the above reliefs is available, or there is a gain remaining after available reliefs have been applied, an individual, trustee or a personal representative may be able to claim taper relief. The effect of the relief is to make only a percentage of the gain subject to CGT. The relief came into effect on 6 April 1998.

The amount of taper depends upon two factors:

(1) whether or not the asset is classed as a 'business asset'; and
(2) how long it has been held for. The longer an asset has been owned, the smaller the amount of the gain that is chargeable.

Prior to 6 April 2000 the definition of business assets was more restrictive than that discussed below, and a different rate of taper applied.

Business or non-business asset?

The taper is greater for business assets than for non-business assets. A 'business asset' is one used for the purposes of a trade carried on by the individual, his partnership, or his 'qualifying company'. To qualify the company must be a trading company which is:

- unlisted (eg private companies and those traded on the Alternative Investment Market (AIM)); or
- listed on the Stock Exchange, and the individual is either
    - (a) an employee or officer of the company (there is no requirement for full time involvement); or
    - (b) able to exercise at least 5 per cent of the voting rights.

Shares held by an individual in a qualifying company are also classed as business assets, and are eligible for the enhanced business taper.

Shares held by *officers or employees* of *non-trading* companies are also classed as business assets, provided that he officer/employee does not hold a 'material interest' in the company. A person has a material interest if he holds:

- more than 10 per cent of any class of share of the company; or
- more than 10 per cent of the voting rights in the company; or
- entitlement to more than 10 per cent of the assets of the company on a winding-up.

Any asset which fails the test for a 'business asset' is classed as a 'non-business asset', eg a private investor's small holding of quoted shares. Industrial premises which are let out to tenants would be 'non-business assets'. But if the landlord used them or let them to his own partnership, they would be 'business assets'.

Ownership periods and application of taper

Having identified whether or not an asset is a business asset, the next step is to ascertain how many complete years have elapsed between 6 April 1998 (or acquisition date, if later) and the date of disposal. Non-business assets owned on 17 March 1998 qualify for an additional year's 'bonus'. The gain is then tapered according to the table below, so that a smaller figure becomes chargeable.

Gains on business assets		Gains on non-business assets	
Whole years held after 6 April 1998	**Percentage of gain chargeable**	**Whole years held after 6 April 1998 plus a bonus year if asset held on 17 March 1998**	**Percentage of gain chargeable**
1	87.5	1	100
2	75	2	100
3	50	3	95
4 or more	25	4	90
		5	85
		6	80
		7	75
		8	70
		9	65
		10 or more	60

Example 1

Dawn bought a plot of land in May 1996. She sells it in November 2001, making a gain (after indexation) of £50,000. This is not a business asset. Taper relief will be based on the 3 complete years from April 1998 to November 2001, plus an extra year as Dawn held the land on 17 March 1998, giving 4 qualifying years in total:

£50,000 × 90% = £45,000 tapered gain.

£45,000 (rather than £50,000) worth of gains remain chargeable.

Example 2

In January 1999 Geoffrey paid £4,000 for an initial 40% interest in TrustMe.com Ltd, a software company. In March 2003 MegaSoft plc buy him out for £404,000. No indexation allowance is applicable to his £400,000 gain, but Geoffrey qualifies for taper relief: he has owned a business asset for over 4 years.

£400,000 × 25% = £100,000 tapered gain

Part business usage?

Where an asset has been used only partly for business purposes during its period of ownership (or the last 10 years if shorter), the gain must be apportioned so that part of the gain will attract the business asset taper over the full period of ownership, and the other part will attract the non-business asset taper, again, for the full period of ownership.

Example

Alistair has owned commercial premises for 8 years since April 1998. For the last 3 years they were used by his qualifying company; for the other 5 years he let them commercially. He has just realised a gain of £80,000 on their sale.

Three-eighths of the gain is on a business asset, and attracts business asset taper appropriate to the full 8 years of ownership (though the maximum relief in fact applies after only 4 years):

$^3/_8 \times$ £80,000 = £30,000

£30,000 $\times$ 25% = £7,500 tapered gain

Five-eighths of the gain is on a non-business asset, and attracts non-business asset taper appropriate to the full 8 years of ownership:

$^5/_8 \times$ £80,000 = £50,000

£50,000 $\times$ 70% = £35,000 tapered gain

Alistair's total chargeable gains, after taper, are: £7,500 + £35,000 = £42,500.

3.5 THE ANNUAL EXEMPTION

Where an individual makes several disposals in a tax year, it is necessary to make a separate calculation of the tapered gain (or loss) on each asset disposed of. Any losses are set against the gains (see **3.7.2**) to find the individual's *net* capital gain (or loss).

The annual exemption is then applied, to exempt the first slice of the net capital gain. (It is worth emphasising that, unlike other reliefs, it does not relate to a particular disposal but is rather a general deduction from the overall net gain.) As explained in **3.1.5**, the amount of the exemption for tax year 2001/2002 is £7,500. If an individual has a net gain of less than £7,500 the unused part of the exemption cannot be carried forward to the following tax year.

Personal representatives and trustees of settlements are also entitled to an annual exemption; see Part V: Probate and Administration.

3.6 CGT CALCULATION WHERE THERE IS MORE THAN ONE DISPOSAL IN A TAX YEAR

Example

Gordon made the following disposals during 2003/4. In 2003/2004 he has a taxable income of £24,400. Assume 2001/2002 tax rates still apply.

(1) On 17 May 2003, he sold his 30% holding in Pibroch Ltd, his family's company, for £72,400. He bought it for £40,000 on 16 April 1997. The indexation factor between April 1997 and April 1998 is 0.03.

(2) On 12 August 2003, he sold his holiday cottage, 'Landseer Lodge', for £76,625. He acquired it on his mother's death on 11 January 1990, when its market value was £20,000. The indexation factor between January 1990 and April 1998 is 0.35.

Apart from taper relief, no other reliefs are available on either disposal.

(1) Pibroch Ltd			**(2) Landseer Lodge**		
Step 1: Identify the disposal			Step 1: Identify the disposal		
Sales of shares			Sale of holiday cottage		
Step 2: Calculate the gain		£	Step 2: Calculate the gain		£
Proceeds of disposal		72,400	Proceeds of disposal		76,625
Less:			*Less:*		
Acquisition expenditure		40,000	Acquisition expenditure		20,000
		32,400			56,625
Less:			*Less:*		
Indexation allowance			Indexation allowance		
(40,000 × 0.03)		1,200	(20,000 × 0.35)		7,000
Gain after indexation		31,200	Gain after indexation		49,625
Step 3: Consider reliefs			Step 3: Consider reliefs		
Apply taper relief			Apply taper relief		
(business asset, maximum 4 years)			(non-business asset, 5 + 1 years)		
Tapered gain (31,200 × 25%)		7,800	Tapered gain (49,625 × 80%)		39,700

	£
Aggregate net gains 2003/2004	47,500
Step 4: Deduct annual exemption	7,500
Chargeable gain	40,000

Step 5: What is the rate of tax?

First　　£5,000 × 20% = £1,000

-------------- Basic rate threshold　(£29,400) --------------

Remaining	£35,000 × 40%	= £14,000
CGT payable		£15,000

3.7 LOSSES

3.7.1 Losses

The formula 'consideration received (or market value) less cost' can produce a loss.

Example
Christine bought shares for £10,000 three years ago. She sells them for £9,000. She has made a loss of £1,000.

The indexation allowance can be used to extinguish a capital gain but it cannot be used to create or increase a capital loss. Thus, in the above example Christine cannot use the indexation allowance to increase her loss of £1,000.

Consider the following example.

Example

Barbara bought a portrait for £10,000 five years ago. She sells it for £11,000. There has been a 25 per cent increase in the RPI since she bought the portrait, until 1998, giving an indexation factor of 0.25.

Identify the disposal: sale of portrait

Calculate the gain or loss
Proceeds of disposal	£11,000

Less:
Cost	£10,000
	£1,000

Indexation Allowance	
(limited to £1,000)	£1,000
Capital gain extinguished	nil

Note that the indexation factor of 0.25 applied to the cost of £10,000 gives an indexation allowance of £2,500. However, only £1,000 of the indexation allowance can be deducted, ie enough to extinguish the £1,000 gain. The rest of the indexation allowance cannot be deducted because it cannot generally be used to create (or increase) a loss.

3.7.2 Unabsorbed losses

Losses are normally deductible from other capital gains of the same year, before taper is applied. The 'benefit' of a loss is maximised by setting it against gains which would otherwise attract the least taper. If, on this basis, losses exceed untapered gains in a given year, the unabsorbed loss may be carried forward to future years and then used to the extent necessary to reduce gains to the limit for the annual exemption. Unabsorbed losses can be carried forward indefinitely. The approach should be:

(1) work out the untapered gain or loss on each disposal made during the tax year;
(2) deduct any losses of the current year from gains which would attract the least taper;
(3) taper each remaining gain as appropriate;
(4) deduct the annual exemption from any remaining gains.

If there are any unabsorbed losses from earlier years they should be deducted after step (2) from gains which would attract the least taper; however only so much of an earlier loss is used as is necessary to reduce the remaining gains to the level of the annual exemption.

Example (continued from **3.6***)*

Year of loss

In 2002/2003, the year before the **3.6** scenario, Gordon made gains (before taper) of £30,000, and losses of £50,000. He had no unused losses from previous years.

Gains for the year	£30,000
Less: losses for the year	£50,000
Net loss for the year	£20,000

The £30,000 gain is wiped out, and the unused loss of £20,000 is carried forward to next year.

As there is no net gain for 2002/2003, the annual exemption cannot be used in this year and it cannot be carried forward to later years. Taper relief is not applied.

Year following year of loss

In 2003/2004 Gordon's loss of £20,000 carried forward from 2002/3 would be set against the indexed gain on Landseer Lodge which would be tapered to 80%, rather than against the indexed gain on the Pibroch Ltd shares which would be tapered to only 25% of its original figure. Thus the £49,625 indexed gain on Landseer Lodge is reduced by £20,000 to £29,625. That reduced figure would then be tapered to 80%, producing a net tapered gain of £23,700.

Gordon's CGT position for 2003/2004 would now be:

	£
Landseer Lodge, net tapered gain	23,700
Pibroch Ltd shares, tapered gain	7,800
2003/2004 aggregate net gains	31,500
Less: annual exemption	7,500
2003/2004 taxable gains	24,000

Further example

If Gordon's loss in 2002/2003 had been greater, for example £80,000, it would be carried forward and used in 2003/2004 as follows:

First, £49,625 of the loss is set against the Landseer Lodge indexed gain (which would otherwise be tapered to 80 per cent), thus wiping that gain out; £30,375 of the loss remains unused.

Secondly, £23,700 of the loss is set against the £31,200 Pibroch Ltd indexed gain (which would otherwise be tapered to 25%), thus reducing that gain to £7,500. That reduced gain is covered by Gordon's annual exemption. £6,675 of the original loss remains unused, to be carried forward to future years. There are no outstanding gains for taper to be applied to in 2003/2004.

	Loss carried forward	*2003/4 gains*
	£	£
2002/3 loss	80,000	
Landseer Lodge (potential 80% taper)		49,625
Use part loss	(49,625)	(49,625)
	30,375	nil
Pibroch Ltd (potential 25% taper)		31,200
Use part loss	(23,700)	(23,700)
Balance	6,675	7,500

2003/4 aggregate net gains of £7,500 covered by annual exemption.

3.8 PART DISPOSALS

Where the disposal is of only part of the asset the initial and subsequent expenditure are apportioned when calculating the gain.

Example

Anna bought a large plot of land for £100,000. She sells part of it for £90,000 in October 2001. The RPI has risen by 10 per cent to April 1998, giving an indexation factor of 0.1. The remaining land is worth £360,000. The land is a non-business asset for the purposes of taper relief. She is a higher rate taxpayer and this is her only disposal in the tax year.

Identify the disposal: sale of part of the land.

Calculation of the gain on the land sold:

The consideration received is £90,000.

What is the cost of the part sold?

The total value of the two pieces of land is £450,000, ie £90,000 plus £360,000.

The part sold is worth $^1/_5$ of the total value, ie £90,000 is $^1/_5$ of £450,000.

Therefore, take $^1/_5$ of the cost as the relevant figure for the calculation, ie $^1/_5$ of £100,000, that is, £20,000.

	£
Proceeds of disposal	90,000
Less:	
Apportioned cost	20,000
	70,000
Less:	
Indexation allowance $(0.1 \times 20,000)$	2,000
Gain after indexation	68,000
Consider reliefs:	
Apply taper relief (non-business asset, 3 + 1 years)	
Tapered gain $(68,000 \times 90\%)$	61,200
Deduct annual exemption	7,500
Chargeable gain	53,700

What is the rate of tax?
CGT at 40% on £53,700 is £21,480

Note that the indexation allowance is based on the apportioned cost of £20,000.

3.9 HUSBAND AND WIFE

3.9.1 Disposals between spouses

Where spouses are living together, a disposal by one to the other is treated as being made for such a consideration as to provide neither a gain nor a loss. This means that a spouse can dispose of property to the other without paying CGT on the disposal. The donor's gain is not wiped out but merely deferred. If the donee disposes of the asset, the donee will be charged to tax not only on the donee's gain but on the donor's gain as well.

Taper relief is not applied at the time of the inter-spouse transfer. However, it is given on the ultimate disposal for the spouses' combined period of ownership.

Example
(Assume all ownership periods are after 1998, so there is no indexation allowance.)

David gives a portrait to his wife Jane. David will not pay CGT on this disposal.

The portrait was worth £100,000 at the time of the gift. It cost David £80,000 three years ago.

Usually, when a gift is made the acquisition cost of the donee is the market value at the time of the gift (£100,000) but because the portrait was a gift from her husband, Jane will acquire it with a value of £80,000, ie the amount David paid for the painting.

If Jane disposes of the asset, she will have a lower acquisition cost to set against her gain and she will be charged to tax on both her own gain and her husband's gain.

Assume Jane sells the painting for £150,000, five years later.

The calculation will be:

Consideration received	£150,000
Less: Cost	£80,000
	£70,000

Tapered gain (non-business asset,
8 years' combined ownership): £70,000 × 70% = £49,000

If Jane had not acquired the painting from her husband, so that the ordinary rules applied, the calculation would have been:

Consideration received	£150,000
Less: Cost	£100,000
	£50,000

Tapered gain (non-business asset,
5 years' ownership): £50,000 × 85% = £42,500

A comparison of the above calculations shows that a larger gain is produced on Jane's disposal where she acquired the portrait from her husband but, of course, David avoided any CGT charge at the time of the gift to Jane.

3.9.2 Tax planning points

Using the annual exemptions of both spouses

Husband and wife are each entitled to an annual exemption of £7,500. If, for example, the husband's annual exemption will not be used while the wife's annual exemption will be used in full, it may be beneficial to transfer some assets to the husband so that he disposes of them and makes the gain. The aim is to make use of both annual exemptions so that tax is saved on a further £7,500. As discussed in **3.9.1**, there will be no charge to tax when the assets are transferred to the husband.

Using the lower and basic rate tax bands of both spouses

If one spouse pays income tax at a higher rate than the other spouse and the wealthier spouse wishes to dispose of an asset, it is likely to be beneficial to transfer the asset into the name of the less wealthy spouse so that at least part of the gain will be charged to CGT at a lower rate. The aim is to save tax by using up the basic rate tax bands of both spouses.

Example

Elizabeth is a basic rate taxpayer with a taxable income of £21,400. Her husband Mark pays income tax at 40% and wants to sell some shares. The disposal of the shares will produce a large gain. Elizabeth has made gains which exactly match her annual exemption.

If the shares are transferred to Elizabeth who then sells them, CGT will be charged at only 20% on the first £8,000 of chargeable gain. As discussed in **3.9.1**, there will be no charge to CGT when the shares are transferred to Elizabeth. When Elizabeth sells the shares, she will pay CGT both on any increase in value in the shares while she owns them and on the gain which accrued during Mark's ownership. However, the first part of the chargeable gain will be taxed at 20%, whereas if Mark sold the shares the entire chargeable gain would be taxed at 40%. Tax will be saved by transferring the shares to Elizabeth.

3.10 TAX-EFFICIENT WAYS OF INVESTING

This is dealt with in Chapter 5.

Chapter 4

INHERITANCE TAX

4.1 INTRODUCTION

This chapter explains the basic principles of inheritance tax (IHT).

IHT is governed principally by the Inheritance Tax Act 1984 (IHTA 1984). The Act may be found in the *Butterworths Yellow Tax Handbook 2001–2002* (Butterworths Tax) with explanation in Whitehouse *Revenue Law – Principles and Practice* 19th edn (Butterworths Tax, 2001). Suggestions for further reading are listed in the Appendix to Part I.

There are three main occasions when IHT may be charged.

(1) Death

As its name implies, IHT is primarily a tax which takes effect on death. When an individual dies, IHT is charged on the value of his estate (broadly his assets less his liabilities) subject to various exemptions and reliefs.

(2) Gifts made within 7 years of death

If IHT were limited to a charge on death, one way to avoid tax would be to reduce the size of one's estate by making lifetime gifts. IHT is therefore also charged on certain lifetime gifts or 'transfers' if the donor dies within 7 years of making them. Such gifts are called 'potentially exempt transfers' because at the time when the transfer is made no IHT is chargeable; the transfer is 'potentially exempt'. If the transferor survives for 7 years, the transfer becomes exempt. If he dies within that period, the transfer becomes chargeable.

(3) Gifts into a discretionary trust

IHT might also be avoided by the use of a discretionary trust. A discretionary trust is a trust where the trustees may determine the amount of capital or income which any potential beneficiary shall receive, for example 'for such of my children and grandchildren as my trustees shall think fit'. Such trusts are specially treated for IHT purposes, and gifts into them do not qualify as potentially exempt transfers. A lifetime gift into a discretionary trust is immediately chargeable to IHT at the time when it is made.

4.2 THE MAIN CHARGING PROVISIONS

IHT is charged on 'the value transferred by a chargeable transfer'. The term 'chargeable transfer' is defined as 'a transfer of value which is made by an individual but is not an exempt transfer' (IHTA 1984, ss 1, 2).

This charge may apply in any of the three situations outlined above, because the term 'chargeable transfer' may refer to:

(1) the transfer on death; or
(2) a lifetime transfer which is potentially exempt when it is made but becomes chargeable because the transferor dies within 7 years; or
(3) a lifetime transfer which is immediately chargeable at the time when it is made.

In each case, the method by which tax is calculated is broadly similar, and may be approached by applying a sequence of logical steps.

Step 1: Identify the transfer of value

A lifetime transfer of value is any disposition which reduces the value of the transferor's estate. On death, tax is charged as if the deceased had made a transfer of value of his estate.

Step 2: Find the value transferred

For a lifetime transfer, this is the amount of the reduction in the transferor's estate. On death, it is the value of the estate.

Step 3: Apply any relevant exemptions and reliefs

Some exemptions apply both to lifetime transfers and to the transfer on death (eg transfers to spouse). Others are more restricted, and many apply only to lifetime transfers (eg annual exemption).

The main reliefs are business and agricultural property relief, which may apply both to lifetime transfers of such property and to the transfer on death.

Step 4: Calculate tax at the appropriate rate

Each individual has a 'nil rate band' (currently £242,000) for IHT purposes. This is a sum which, in any given 7-year period, an individual may transfer without payment of IHT, because the rate of tax is 0 per cent. The rate of tax which applies to transfers in excess of the nil rate band varies according to the type of transfer (details are given in context below).

In order to calculate the tax on any transfer, whether during lifetime or on death, one must first look back over the 7 years immediately preceding the transfer. Any chargeable transfers made by the transferor during that period must be taken into account in order to determine how much of the nil rate band is available. This process is known as 'cumulation'.

This chapter will consider the detailed application of the steps outlined above to each of the three types of transfer in turn. Note that, for ease of reference in the examples provided, any mention of the nil rate band assumes that the band has always been £242,000. In fact, it has increased over the years to its current level. In real calculations one may have to identify the previous bands.

4.3 TRANSFERS ON DEATH

The steps outlined at **4.2** above apply as follows.

4.3.1 Step 1: Identify the transfer of value

When a person dies, he is treated for IHT purposes as having made a transfer of value immediately before his death, ie there is a deemed transfer of value. The value transferred is the value of the deceased's 'estate' immediately before his death.

Definition of 'estate'

A person's estate is defined by IHTA 1984, s 5(1) to mean all the property to which he was beneficially entitled immediately before his death, with the exception of 'excluded property'.

Property included within this definition falls into three categories as set out below.

(1) Property which passes under the deceased's will or on intestacy. The deceased was 'beneficially entitled' to all such property immediately before he died.

(2) Property to which the deceased was 'beneficially entitled' immediately before his death but which does not pass under his will or intestacy. This applies to the deceased's interest in any joint property passing on his death by survivorship to the surviving joint tenant.

(3) Property included because of special statutory provisions. By statute, the deceased is treated as having been 'beneficially entitled' to certain types of property which would otherwise fall outside the definition. These rules apply to certain trust property and to property given away by the deceased in his lifetime but which is 'subject to a reservation' at the time of death, as explained below.

Trust property included in the estate for IHT purposes

Section 49(1) provides as follows:

> 'A person beneficially entitled to an interest in possession in settled property shall be treated … as beneficially entitled to the property in which the interest subsists.'

A person has an interest in possession in settled (trust) property if he is entitled to claim the income, or part of the income, as it arises, so that the trustees have no power to withhold it from him. The most common example of a trust with an interest in possession is a life interest trust.

Example

In her will, Gina left all her estate to her executors/trustees, Tom and Tessa, on trust to pay the income to Gina's son, Simon, for life with remainder to Rose absolutely. Both Simon and Rose are over 18 years old.

Tom and Tessa must invest the property to produce income. Simon is entitled to the income during his life. Tom and Tessa must pay it to him. Thus Simon, the life tenant, has an interest in possession.

When Simon dies, his rights under the trust cease. Under the terms of the trust instrument (Gina's will), Rose is now entitled to the trust fund, and Tom and Tessa must transfer all the trust property to her.

For IHT purposes, Simon has an interest in possession. Although he was entitled only to the income from the trust property and had no control over the disposition of the fund on his death, he is treated for tax purposes as 'beneficially entitled' to the whole trust fund. The fund is taxed on his death as part of his estate. The tax on the trust property will be paid from the trust fund.

A person who is entitled to part of the income under a trust is treated for IHT purposes as 'beneficially entitled' to a proportionate part of the capital.

Example
A fund worth £300,000 is held on trust to pay the income to Lisa, May and Nora in equal shares. On Lisa's death, one-third of the fund (£100,000) is treated as part of her estate for IHT purposes.

Property subject to a reservation

The Finance Act 1986 contains provisions designed to prevent people from avoiding tax by giving property away more than 7 years before death but continuing to enjoy the benefit of the property. The rule applies where the deceased gave away property during his lifetime, but did not transfer 'possession and enjoyment' of the property to the donee or was not entirely excluded from enjoying the property. If property is subject to a reservation at the time of the donor's death, the donor is treated as being 'beneficially entitled' to the property.

Example
In 1992, Diana gave her jewellery, worth £100,000, to her daughter Emma, but retained possession of it. Diana dies in 2001, when the jewellery (still in her possession) is worth £120,000. Although the jewellery belongs to Emma, tax is charged on Diana's death as if she were still beneficially entitled to it. The jewellery, valued at £120,000, is taxed as part of Diana's estate. The tax on the jewellery will be borne by Emma.

Property outside the estate for IHT purposes

Property to which the deceased was not 'beneficially entitled' immediately before his death falls outside the definition. Thus if the deceased took out a life assurance policy written in trust for a named beneficiary the proceeds are not part of his estate for IHT purposes. Similarly, a discretionary lump sum payment made from a pension fund to the deceased's family is not part of the estate for IHT purposes.

Excluded property

Certain property which would otherwise be included in the estate for IHT purposes is defined in the IHTA as 'excluded property'. Excluded property is not part of the estate for IHT purposes. One example of excluded property is a 'reversionary interest'. For IHT purposes this means any future interest under a settlement, for example an interest in remainder under a trust.

4.3.2 Step 2: Find the value transferred

Basic valuation principle

Assets in the estate are valued for IHT purposes at 'the price which the property might reasonably be expected to fetch if sold in the open market' immediately before the death (s 160).

This means that the value immediately before death of every asset forming part of the estate for IHT purposes must be assessed and reported to the Inland Revenue. Some assets, such as bank and building society accounts and quoted shares, are easy to value. Others, such as land, may be more difficult. Negotiations may be required (in the case of land, with the district valuer) in order to reach an agreed valuation.

The value of an asset agreed for IHT purposes is known as the 'probate value'.

Modification of the basic valuation principle: s 171

Section 171 provides that, where the death causes the value of an asset in the estate to increase or decrease, that change in value should be taken into account.

> #### *Example*
> Brian has insured his life for £50,000. The benefit of the policy belongs to him (ie the policy is not written in trust). Immediately before Brian's death, the value of the policy to him is its 'surrender value'. This will be considerably less than its maturity value of £50,000. Under s 171, the effect of Brian's death on the value of the policy is taken into account: its value for IHT purposes is £50,000.

Quoted shares

The value of quoted shares is taken from the Stock Exchange Daily Official List for the date of death (or the nearest trading day). The list quotes two prices. To value the shares for IHT, take one-quarter of the difference between the lower and higher price and add it to the lower price.

> #### *Example*
> John died owning 200 shares in ABC plc. On the date of John's death the quoted price per share is 102p/106p. The value of each share for IHT is 103p, and so the value of John's holding is £206.

Debts and expenses

Liabilities owed by the deceased at the time of death are deductible for IHT purposes providing that they were incurred for money or money's worth (s 505). Thus debts such as gas and telephone bills may be deducted. In addition, the deceased may not have paid enough income tax on the income he received before he died; this amount may also be deducted.

Reasonable funeral expenses are also deductible (s 162).

4.3.3 Step 3: Apply any relevant exemptions and reliefs

The main exemptions applicable on death depend on the identity of the beneficiary. Reliefs depend on the nature of the property in the estate. Thus it is important to see who is entitled to the property on death and whether the property qualifies for a relief.

Spouse exemption

Section 18 provides as follows:

> 'A transfer of value is an exempt transfer to the extent that the value transferred is attributable to property which becomes comprised in the estate of the transferor's spouse.'

Any property included in the estate for IHT purposes is exempt if it passes to the deceased's spouse under the deceased's will or intestacy or, in the case of joint property, by survivorship.

The rule applicable to 'interest in possession' trusts is that IHT is charged as if the person with the right to income owned the capital. This rule applies for the purpose of spouse exemption, both on creation of the trust and on the death of a life tenant.

> *Example*
> In his will, Dan leaves his estate worth £300,000 to trustees on trust for his wife, Jane, for life with remainder to their children. Although Jane only has the right to the income from Dan's estate for her lifetime, the trust is treated for IHT purposes as if Jane owned the capital. On Dan's death, his whole estate will be spouse exempt.

Charity exemption

Section 23(1) provides as follows:

> 'Transfers of value are exempt to the extent that the values transferred by them are attributable to property which is given to charities.'

Any property forming part of the deceased's estate for IHT purposes which passes on death to charity is exempt. The exemption most commonly applies to property which passes to charity under the deceased's will. However, if the deceased had a life interest in trust property which passes under the terms of the trust to charity, the charity exemption applies.

A similar exemption applies to gifts to certain national bodies and bodies providing a public benefit, such as museums and art galleries, and to political parties.

Business and agricultural property relief

Business property relief applies to reduce the value transferred by a transfer of 'relevant business property' by a certain percentage, provided that the transferor owned the property for the 2 years immediately before the transfer.

The reduction is 100 per cent for:

(1) a business, or an interest in a business (such as a share in a partnership); and
(2) unquoted shares.

The reduction is 50 per cent for:

(1) quoted shares which gave the transferor control of the company; and
(2) certain land, buildings and machinery owned by the transferor but used in his company or partnership.

Agricultural property relief applies in a similar manner to reduce the agricultural value of agricultural property.

Further details of these reliefs are given in the LPC Resource Book *Business Law and Practice* (Jordans).

4.3.4 Step 4: Calculate tax at the appropriate rate

If the deceased has made no chargeable transfers in the 7 years before death, the rate of tax on the first £242,000 of his estate (the 'nil rate band') is 0 per cent. If his estate exceeds £242,000, IHT is charged on the excess at 40 per cent.

If the deceased did make any chargeable transfers in the 7 years before death the cumulation principle outlined at **4.2** will apply. The effect is that the lifetime transfers use up the deceased's nil rate band first, reducing the amount available for the estate. Most lifetime gifts are potentially exempt from IHT and only become chargeable if the transferor dies within 7 years. Less commonly, the deceased may also have made gifts into a discretionary trust in the 7 years before death. The cumulation principle applies to both types of transfer.

The 'values transferred' by such transfers must be aggregated. This means that any lifetime exemptions or reliefs which operate to reduce the value transferred are taken into account.

Example
In 1998, David made a gift to his daughter. The value transferred (after exemptions and reliefs) was £98,000.

In August 2001, David dies leaving his estate, valued at £150,000, to his son.

The 1998 transfer was potentially exempt from IHT but has now become chargeable. David's cumulative total is £98,000.

		£
The nil rate band applicable to David's estate on death is		242,000
less cumulative total		98,000
		144,000

Tax on David's estate:

£144,000 @ 0% =	nil
£6,000 @ 40% =	£2,400

For further details of the effect of the cumulation principle, see **4.6**.

4.3.5 The estate rate

The term 'estate rate' means the average rate of tax applicable to each item of property in the estate for IHT. When tax on the estate has been calculated, it may be necessary for various reasons to work out how much of the tax is attributable to a particular item of property in the estate. For example:

(1) since tax on certain types of property, such as land, may be paid in instalments, the personal representatives (PRs) must calculate how much of the tax relates to that property;

(2) the PRs may not be liable to pay all the tax on the estate. If the estate for IHT purposes includes trust property, the trustees are liable to pay the tax attributable to that property;

(3) the will may give a legacy 'subject to tax'.

The principle is that tax is divided between the various assets in the estate proportionately, according to their value. This may be applied by calculating the average rate of tax on the estate as a percentage, ie the 'estate rate'. For example, if the deceased's nil rate band was completely used up by lifetime transfers, the 'estate rate' would be 40 per cent. However, it is not strictly necessary to calculate the estate rate as a percentage; instead, the amount of tax on a particular item of property in the estate may be calculated by applying to the value of that property the proportion which the total tax bill bears to the total chargeable estate.

> *Example*
> Graham, who has made no lifetime transfers, leaves a house, valued at £225,000, to Henry, subject to payment of IHT, and the rest of his estate, valued at £75,000 net to Ian.

Tax on Graham's estate:	£242,000 @ 0%	nil
	£58,000 @ 40%	£23,200

$$\text{The 'estate rate' is:} \quad \frac{£23,200}{£300,000} \quad \frac{\text{(total tax bill)}}{\text{(total chargeable estate)}}$$

$$\text{Henry pays tax on the house:} \quad £225,000 \quad \times \quad \frac{£23,200}{£300,000} \quad = \quad £17,400$$

$$\text{Ian pays tax on the residue:} \quad £75,000 \quad \times \quad \frac{£23,200}{£300,000} \quad = \quad £5,800$$

4.3.6 Liability for IHT on death

Meaning of 'liability'

The rules which follow concern the question of who is liable to account to the Revenue for the payment of the tax due as a result of death. The Inland Revenue are concerned with obtaining payment of the tax, and not with the question of who bears the burden of the payment. Payment will usually be obtained from people who are not beneficially entitled to the property but who hold property in a representative capacity, ie PRs and trustees. Those who ultimately receive the property are concurrently liable with such representatives, but in most cases tax will have been paid before the beneficiaries receive the property.

The PRs: tax on the non-settled estate

The PRs are liable to pay the IHT attributable to any property which 'was not immediately before the death comprised in a settlement' (s 200). This includes:

(1) the property which vests in the PRs (ie the property which passes under the deceased's will or intestacy); and

(2) property (other than trust property) which does not pass to the PRs but is included in the estate for IHT because the deceased was beneficially entitled to it immediately before death (eg joint property which passes by survivorship).

Thus the PRs are liable to pay the IHT on joint property even though that property does not vest in them. Their liability is, however, limited to the value of the assets they received, or would have received but for their own neglect or default.

Concurrently liable with the PRs is 'any person in whom property is vested ... at any time after the death or who at any such time is beneficially entitled to an interest in possession in the property' (s 200(1)(c)). This means that tax on property passing by will or intestacy may in principle be claimed by the Inland Revenue from a beneficiary who has received that property. Similarly, the Inland Revenue may claim tax on joint property from the surviving joint tenant. Such tax is normally paid by the PRs and it is relatively unusual for the Revenue to claim tax from the recipient of the property.

The trustees: tax on settled property

If the estate for IHT purposes includes any property which was 'comprised in a settlement' immediately before the death, the trustees of the settlement are liable for IHT attributable to that property. This principle is relevant where the deceased had an interest in possession under a trust. Again, any person in whom the trust property subsequently vests or for whose benefit the trust property is subsequently applied is concurrently liable with the trustees.

Example

Property worth £300,000 is held on trust for Ruth for life with remainder to Arthur. Ruth dies leaving property worth £200,000 which passes under her will to Tessa. The trust fund is taxed as part of Ruth's estate as she had an interest in possession for IHT purposes (see **4.3.1**). She had made no lifetime transfers.

Tax on Ruth's death:

on	£242,000 @ 0%	nil
on	£258,000 @ 40%	£103,200

The trustees are liable to pay the tax on the trust fund (calculated according to the estate rate):

$$£300,000 \quad \times \quad \frac{£103,200}{£500,000} \quad = \quad £61,920$$

Arthur, the remainderman, is concurrently liable if any of the trust property is transferred to him before the tax has been paid.

Ruth's PRs are liable to pay the tax on Ruth's free estate:

$$£200,000 \quad \times \quad \frac{£103,200}{£500,000} \quad = \quad £41,280$$

Additional liability of PRs

Property which the deceased gave away during his lifetime is treated as part of his estate on death if the donor reserved a benefit in the property which he continued to enjoy immediately before death (see **4.3.1**). The donee of the gift is primarily liable to pay tax attributable to the property. However, if the tax remains unpaid 12 months after the end of the month of death, the PRs become liable for the tax.

Where a person dies within 7 years of making a PET, the transfer becomes chargeable and IHT may be payable. The transferee is primarily liable, but again, the PRs become liable if the tax remains unpaid 12 months after the end of the month of death.

In each of the above cases the liability of the PRs is limited to the extent of the assets they actually received, or would have received but for their neglect or default. However, PRs cannot escape liability on the grounds that they have distributed the estate and so they should ideally delay distribution until IHT on any such lifetime gifts has been paid.

4.3.7 Time for payment of IHT on death: the instalment option

The basic rule is that IHT is due for payment 6 months after the end of the month of death (although PRs will normally pay earlier in order to speed up the administration of the estate).

However, some property, such as land and certain types of business property, attracts the instalment option. Any tax attributable to instalment option property may be paid in 10 equal yearly instalments, the first falling due 6 months after the end of the month of death. Again, the tax on the estate is apportioned using the estate rate to find how much tax is attributable to the instalment option property.

Qualifying property

The instalment option applies to:

(1) land of any description;
(2) a business or an interest in a business;
(3) shares (quoted or unquoted) which immediately before death gave control of the company to the deceased;
(4) unquoted shares which do not give control if either:

    (a) the holding is sufficiently large (a holding of at least 10 per cent of the nominal value of the company's shares and worth more than £20,000); or

    (b) the Inland Revenue is satisfied that the tax cannot be paid in one sum without undue hardship; or

    (c) the IHT attributable to the shares and any other instalment option property in the estate amounts to at least 20 per cent of the IHT payable on the estate.

Interest

Where the instalment option is exercised in relation to tax on shares or any other business property or agricultural land, instalments carry interest only from the date when each instalment is payable. Thus, no interest is due on the outstanding tax provided that each instalment is paid on the due date.

In the case of other land, however, interest is payable with each instalment (apart from the first) on the amount of IHT which was outstanding for the previous year.

Sale

If the instalment option property is sold, all outstanding tax and interest becomes payable.

4.3.8 Example of the application of IHT to an estate on death

Facts

Veronica dies intestate on 3 August 2001 survived by her partner William (to whom she was not married) and their children Brian (19) and Carla (22). She holds the following property:

	£
House (in joint names with William): full value	200,000
Bank a/c (in joint names with William): full value	10,000
Life assurance policies:	
(1) payable to PRs: maturity value	35,000
(2) written in trust for William: maturity value	30,000
Unquoted shares: 15% holding	15,000
Building society account	19,000
Car and chattels	15,000
Life interest under her father's will: value of trust fund	80,000
(the fund passes to the children on Veronica's death)	

There are various debts, including funeral expenses, which total £4,000.

Two years before her death, Veronica made a gift of £158,000 in cash to William.

She made no other substantial lifetime gifts.

Step 1: identify the estate

Property to which Veronica was beneficially entitled immediately before death:

Passing on intestacy (to children):	life assurance policy (1) unquoted shares building society account car and chattels
Passing by survivorship:	interest in house interest in bank account
Included by special statutory provision:	capital of trust fund (Veronica had an interest in possession)

(Life assurance policy (2) is not included in the estate for IHT purposes because Veronica was not beneficially entitled to it immediately before her death.)

Step 2: value the estate

	£	£
Passing on intestacy:		
life assurance policy (1) (full maturity value)	35,000	
unquoted shares (market value)	15,000	
building society account (including interest to date of death)	19,000	
car and chattels	15,000	
		84,000
Joint property:		
interest in the house (£100,000 less discount of, say, 10%)	90,000	
interest in the bank account	5,000	
		95,000
Trust property:		
value of capital in which life tenant's interest subsisted		80,000
		259,000
Less debts (including funeral expenses)		4,000
Value of estate (before reliefs)		255,000

Step 3: apply exemptions and reliefs

No exemptions apply to Veronica's estate as she had no spouse and left no property to charity.

The unquoted shares qualify for business property relief at 100 per cent:

100% of £15,000	15,000
Value of estate for IHT	240,000

Step 4: calculate tax at the appropriate rate

Cumulate the value transferred by chargeable transfers made in the 7 years before death. The gift to William was a PET which has now become chargeable.

	£
Value of gift	158,000
Less 2 annual exemptions (see **4.4.3**)	6,000
Value transferred	152,000

Only £90,000 of Veronica's nil rate band remains available on her death.

Calculate tax on the estate of £240,000:

on £90,000 @ 0%	nil
on £150,000 @ 40%	£60,000

Liability

The PRs are liable for tax on the 'free estate', ie the property passing on intestacy and the joint property.

	£	£	£
Property passing on intestacy		84,000	
Less: debts	4,000		
business property relief	15,000	19,000	65,000
Joint property			95,000
			160,000

Calculate tax on £160,000 by applying the estate rate:

$$£160,000 \quad \times \quad \frac{£60,000}{£240,000} \quad = \quad £40,000$$

The trustees are liable for tax on the trust property (£80,000).

Calculate tax on £80,000 by applying the estate rate:

$$£80,000 \quad \times \quad \frac{£60,000}{£240,000} \quad = \quad £20,000$$

Time for payment of IHT

Assuming that the PRs deliver the Inland Revenue account before 28 February 2002 (6 months after the end of the month of death), they must, on delivery of the account, pay the tax on that part of the free estate which does not attract the instalment option.

	£
Free estate	160,000
Less instalment option property:	
share of house	90,000
Tax payable on delivery of account on	70,000

Calculate tax on £70,000 by applying the estate rate:

$$£70,000 \quad \times \quad \frac{£60,000}{£240,000} \quad = \quad £17,500$$

The PRs must pay £17,500 on delivery of the Inland Revenue account.

Tax on the house is payable in 10 equal annual instalments.

Tax on the house (£90,000):

$$£90,000 \quad \times \quad \frac{£60,000}{£240,000} \quad = \quad £22,500$$

The first instalment is payable on 28 February 2002 (6 months after the end of the month of death).

Subsequent instalments are payable on each succeeding 28 February with interest on the amount outstanding during the previous year.

Burden of IHT

IHT on the property passing on intestacy is a testamentary expense, payable from the property before division between the children.

IHT on the joint property (the house and joint bank account) is borne by William, the surviving joint tenant.

IHT on the trust property is borne by the trust fund.

4.4 LIFETIME TRANSFERS: POTENTIALLY EXEMPT TRANSFERS

A potentially exempt transfer (PET) is defined as 'a gift to another individual or a gift into an accumulation and maintenance trust or a disabled trust' (IHTA 1984, s 3A(1)(c)) or a gift into an interest in possession trust (IHTA 1984, s 49(1)) to the extent in each case that the gift would otherwise be chargeable.

This means that almost all lifetime gifts, whether to an individual or into a trust will be 'potentially exempt' to the extent that no immediate exemption applies.

4.4.1 Step 1: Identify the 'transfer of value'

The term 'transfer of value' is defined to mean any lifetime disposition made by a person ('the transferor') which reduces the value of his estate (IHTA 1984, s 3(1)). In principle, therefore, any lifetime gift falls within the definition.

4.4.2 Step 2: Find the value transferred

The second step is to find the value transferred by the transfer of value. In the case of a lifetime transfer, this is the amount by which the value of the transferor's estate is 'less than it would be but for' the transfer (IHTA 1984, s 3(1)). In other words, the value transferred is the loss in value to the estate of the transferor brought about by the transfer. The transferor's 'estate' is the aggregate of all the property to which he is beneficially entitled (IHTA 1984, s 5).

In practice, the loss to the estate will usually be the market value of the property transferred, although this does not follow in every case.

Example
Vanessa owns a pair of matching bronze statuettes. The market value of the pair together is £80,000, but individually each one is worth £25,000. If Vanessa were to give away one statuette to her son, the loss to her estate would be calculated as follows:

	£
Value of pair	80,000
Less value of remaining statuette	25,000
Loss to estate	55,000

Related property

The related property rules are designed to prevent tax avoidance in relation to a group or set of assets. The rules apply most often to property transferred between husband and wife.

> *Example (continued)*
>
> Suppose Vanessa gives one of the statuettes to her husband Boris (an exempt transfer to spouse). Without the related property rules Vanessa and Boris would each then own one statuette worth £25,000.
>
> However, the two statuettes owned by Vanessa and Boris are related property. Under the related property valuation rule, the value of each statuette is the appropriate portion of the value of the pair, ie half of £80,000 which is £40,000. If either Vanessa or Boris were to give away their statuette, the value transferred would be £40,000.

4.4.3 Step 3: Apply any relevant exemptions and reliefs

As seen at **4.4**, a gift is potentially exempt only to the extent that it would otherwise be chargeable. At the time when a lifetime gift is made it may be clear that an exemption applies. Some lifetime exemptions, however, may apply to only part of a lifetime transfer, so that the excess is potentially exempt.

The main exemptions and reliefs applicable on death apply also to lifetime transfers. In addition, there are some further exemptions which apply only to lifetime transfers.

(1) Spouse and charity exemptions

These exemptions, outlined at **4.3.3**, apply to lifetime transfers as well as to the transfer on death. So any lifetime gift to the transferor's spouse or to charity is exempt, even if the transferor dies within 7 years.

(2) Business and agricultural property relief

The reliefs set out at **4.3.3** apply to reduce the value transferred by transfers of business or agricultural property made during lifetime as well as on death. However, if the transferor dies within 7 years of the transfer, the relief will generally be available only if the transferee still owns the property when the transferor dies (see **4.6.2**).

Spouse and charity exemptions are applied before reliefs, since their effect is to make the transfer wholly exempt. If, for example, a transferor gives relevant business property to his wife, business property relief is academic – the transfer is exempt.

The 'lifetime only' exemptions, however, may apply to only part of a transfer. Since the reliefs apply to reduce the value transferred, they should be applied before such exemptions are considered.

(3) Lifetime only exemptions

THE ANNUAL EXEMPTION

The annual exemption applies to the first £3,000 transferred by lifetime transfers in each tax year. Any unused annual exemption may be carried forward for one year only, so that a maximum exemption of £6,000 may be available. The current year's exemption must be used before the previous year's exemption can be carried forward.

Example

On 1 May 1999, Annie gives £3,000 to her son Ben. The transfer falls within Annie's annual exemption for 1999/00 and is exempt.

On 1 May 2001, Annie gives £7,000 to her daughter Claire. Annie may apply her annual exemption for 2001/2002 and may carry forward her unused annual exemption for 2000/2001. Thus £6,000 of the transfer is exempt at the time of the gift. (The remaining £1,000 will be 'potentially exempt' as explained below.)

If a transferor makes more than one transfer of value in any one tax year, then the exemption is used to reduce the first transfer. Any unused exemption is set against the second and any further transfers until it is used up.

Example

Sarah gives £10,000 to Jessica on 30 April 2001 and £10,000 to Kirsty on 1 May 2001. She has made no previous transfers. The annual exemptions for 2001/2002 and 2000/2001 will be set against the transfer to Jessica and reduce it to £4,000. (The remaining part of Jessica's gift and the whole of Kirsty's gift will be 'potentially exempt' as explained below.)

SMALL GIFTS

Lifetime gifts in any one tax year of less than £250 to any one person are exempt. This exemption cannot be set against a gift which exceeds £250.

NORMAL EXPENDITURE OUT OF INCOME

A lifetime transfer is exempt if it can be shown that:

(1) it was made as part of the transferor's normal expenditure (ie there must be regular payments); and
(2) it was made out of the transferor's income; and
(3) after allowing for all such payments, the transferor was left with sufficient income to maintain his usual standard of living.

Example

Andrew, who is a highly paid company director, has a daughter at drama college. He sends his daughter £100 each month (paid from his income) to assist her with her living expenses. These transfers are exempt as normal expenditure out of Andrew's income (provided Andrew's remaining income is sufficient to support his normal standard of living).

GIFTS IN CONSIDERATION OF MARRIAGE

Lifetime gifts on marriage are exempt up to:

(1) £5,000 by a parent of a party to the marriage;
(2) £2,500 by a remoter ancestor of a party to the marriage (eg a grandparent); and
(3) £1,000 in any other case.

Potentially exempt transfers

As long as the lifetime transfer is not immediately chargeable (see **4.5**), any value remaining after exemptions and reliefs have been applied is potentially exempt. The transfer will only become chargeable if the transferor dies within 7 years. The transferor does not need to take any action at the time when such lifetime transfers are made, and if he survives for 7 years they will automatically become exempt. However, if the transferor dies within the 7 year period, his PRs must check whether he made any lifetime transfers in the preceding 7 years and declare them. If lifetime transfers exceed the transferor's nil rate band, IHT will be payable on them. In any event, the cumulation principle means that the nil rate band available for the transferor's estate will be reduced, or may have been completely used up. (For further explanation of the effect of death within 7 years, see **4.6**.)

Example

On 1 March 2001, Jane gives £130,000 to her brother, Brian. She has made no previous lifetime gifts. The disposition is a transfer of value because the value of Jane's estate is reduced. The value transferred is £130,000, the loss to Jane's estate.

	£
Value transferred	130,000
Less: annual exemptions for 1999/2000 and 2000/2001	6,000
Potentially exempt transfer	124,000

No tax is payable at the time of the gift. Jane has made a PET, not a chargeable transfer, and so her cumulative total is at present unaffected. If Jane survives until 1 March 2008, the PET will become completely exempt. If Jane dies before that date, the PET will become a chargeable transfer.

4.5 OTHER LIFETIME TRANSFERS: IMMEDIATELY CHARGEABLE TRANSFERS

Any lifetime transfer which does not fall within the definition of a PET (see **4.4**) is an immediately chargeable transfer. The definition of a PET is very wide, and only a small minority of gifts will fall outside it. The most common example is a transfer into a discretionary trust. In a discretionary trust, a group or class of beneficiaries is defined (such as the settlor's children and grandchildren) but the trustees can decide how to distribute income and/or capital between them. Since no one beneficiary has a fixed entitlement under the trust, the trust might be used to enable successive generations of a family to enjoy the property while the capital remained in the hands of the trustees (thus avoiding IHT). The charge to IHT on creation of such trusts is part of a wider regime designed to discourage tax avoidance by this means.

Where an individual does make an immediately chargeable transfer, the IHT calculation begins with application of the first three steps as described at **4.4.1**, **4.4.2** and **4.4.3**. Once relevant exemptions and reliefs have been applied, the balance is chargeable to IHT and tax must be calculated by applying step 4.

4.5.1 Step 4: Calculate tax at the appropriate rate

The rates of tax applicable to immediately chargeable lifetime transfers are:

- 0 per cent on the first £242,000 (the nil rate band); and
- 20 per cent on the balance of the chargeable transfer (this rate being half the rate for transfers which are chargeable on death).

However, chargeable transfers made in the 7 years before the current chargeable transfer reduce the nil rate band available to that current transfer. In other words, the value transferred by chargeable transfers made in the 7 years before the current chargeable transfer must be 'cumulated' with that transfer.

The effect of cumulation

Example 1

In this example, it is assumed that Venetia has used up her annual exemptions in each relevant tax year.

On 1 May 2001, Venetia transfers £50,000 to the trustees of a discretionary trust.

She has previously made the following chargeable transfers (after applying relevant annual exemptions):

1 May 1993	£100,000
1 May 1996	£197,000

She has made no other lifetime transfers (and makes no more in the current tax year).

To calculate the IHT due on the chargeable transfer of £50,000, the values transferred by any chargeable transfers made in the 7 years prior to 1 May 2001 must be 'cumulated'.

The transfer of £100,000 was made more than 7 years ago and can be ignored.

Venetia's cumulative total consists of the £197,000 transferred on 1 May 1996 (less than 7 years before the present transfer).

	£
Nil rate band	242,000
less cumulative total	197,000
	45,000

Tax on current chargeable transfer of £50,000:

£45,000 at 0% =	nil
£5,000 at 20% =	£1,000

Example 2

On 1 May 2002, Venetia makes a further transfer of £94,000 to the trustees of the discretionary trust. Assuming that the rates of IHT remain the same as for 2001/2002, her position for IHT would be as follows:

Nil rate band exhausted by transfers of 1 May 1996 and 1 May 2001.

Tax on current chargeable transfer of £94,000:

£94,000 at 20% = £18,800

Example 3

Venetia makes the following further transfer to the trustees of the discretionary trust:

1 July 2003 £103,000

Assuming the rates of IHT remain the same as for 2001/2002, Venetia's position for IHT would be as follows:

The transfer on 1 May 1996 was made more than 7 years ago and can be ignored.

Venetia's cumulative total consists of the £50,000 transferred on 1 May 2001 and the £94,000 transferred on 1 May 2002.

	£	£
Nil rate band		242,000
less cumulative total		
1 May 2000	50,000	
1 May 2001	94,000	144,000
		98,000

Tax on current chargeable transfer of £103,000:

£98,000 at 0% = nil

£5,000 at 20% = £1,000

Note that the effect of death on lifetime transfers is considered at **4.6.3**.

4.5.2 Payment of tax

Trustees pay

The transferor is primarily liable for IHT, although the Inland Revenue may also claim the tax from the trustees. In practice, the trustees often pay IHT out of the property they have been given.

Example

Ahmed gives £146,000 cash to discretionary trustees. His cumulative total is £202,000 and he is entitled to two annual exemptions. Ahmed stipulates that the trustees must pay any IHT.

		£
Value transferred		146,000
Less:	2 annual exemptions	6,000
		140,000
Rate of tax:	Cumulative total £202,000, so £40,000 of the nil rate band is left	
	£40,000 @ 0%	0
	£100,000 @ 20%	20,000
Tax payable by trustees:		20,000

Transferor pays: grossing up

If the transferor pays, the amount of tax will be more than it would be if the trustees paid. This is because IHT is charged on the value transferred, ie the loss to the transferor's estate brought about by the gift (see **4.4.2**). If the transferor pays, the loss is increased by the amount of tax he pays.

Example

Henrietta transfers £80,000 in cash to trustees of a discretionary trust. Earlier in the tax year, she gave them £300,000 in cash. She has made no previous chargeable transfers.

The annual exemptions for this tax year and last have already been used by the gift of £300,000 and her cumulative total stands at £294,000. All the current transfer will be taxed at 20 per cent.

If trustees pay IHT:

The loss to her estate is £80,000. Tax payable is 20 per cent of £80,000, which is £16,000.

If Henrietta pays IHT:

The total loss to her estate (ie the value transferred) is £80,000 plus the IHT payable on that transfer.

Therefore, in order to ascertain the value transferred, it is necessary to calculate what sum would, after deduction of tax at the appropriate rate (ie 20 per cent), leave £80,000 (ie the transfer must be grossed up).

Gross up £80,000 at 20%

$$£80,000 \quad \times \quad \frac{100}{80} \quad = \quad £100,000$$

The gross value transferred is £100,000.

Calculate tax on £100,000:

£100,000 @ 20% = £20,000

The tax payable by Henrietta is more than the tax payable by the trustees. However, if she pays, the trustees are left with the full amount of the property transferred, £80,000, as opposed to £64,000 if they pay.

Time for payment

IHT on immediately chargeable transfers made after 5 April and before 1 October in any year is due on the 30 April in the following year. IHT on immediately chargeable transfers which are not made between those dates is due 6 months after the end of the month in which the chargeable transfer is made.

4.6 EFFECT OF DEATH ON LIFETIME TRANSFERS

4.6.1 Introduction

The death of a transferor may result in a charge to IHT on any transfers of value which he has made in the 7 years immediately preceding his death, whether those transfers were potentially exempt or immediately chargeable when they were made. First, PETs made in that period become chargeable and the transferee will be liable for any IHT payable. Secondly, the IHT liability on lifetime chargeable transfers made in that period is recalculated and the trustees will be liable for any extra tax payable. In either case, as the liability arises on death, the rate of tax, once the nil rate band is exceeded, is 40 per cent.

4.6.2 Effect of death on PETs

PETs are defined and explained in **4.4**. Most lifetime gifts are PETs. There is no liability on a PET at the time of the transfer, and it will become wholly exempt if the transferor survives for 7 years after the transfer. Many gifts will thus escape a charge to IHT.

A PET will become chargeable only if the transferor dies within 7 years of making the transfer. If tax is payable, the transferee will be liable for any IHT.

Steps 1–3

As seen at **4.4**, the first three steps are applied to determine the size of the PET. Business property relief and/or agricultural property relief may apply to reduce the value transferred, provided that the transferee still owns the business or agricultural property (see LPC Resource Book *Business Law and Practice* (Jordans)).

Step 4: Calculate tax at the appropriate rate

The final step is to identify the rate or rates of tax applicable to the transfer in question. The value transferred after exemptions and reliefs is taxed at rates determined by the transferor's cumulative total at the time of the PET. This will be made up of any lifetime chargeable transfers made in the 7 years before the PET, and also of any other PETs made during that period which have become chargeable because of the death of the transferor within 7 years.

The rates of tax applicable to chargeable transfers made within 7 years of death of the transferor are:

- 0 per cent on the first £242,000 (the nil rate band); and
- 40 per cent on the balance.

Example 1

On 5 May 1999, Adam gives a house worth £256,000 to his daughter, Emma.

On 21 September 2001, Adam dies, leaving his estate (consisting of quoted shares and bank deposits worth £200,000) to his son, Matthew. He made no other significant lifetime gifts.

The transfer on 5 May 1999 was a PET which has now become chargeable as the transferor has died within 7 years.

(1) Tax on the PET	£
Loss to estate	256,000
Less annual exemptions 1999/2000; 1998/1999	6,000
	250,000

Adam had made no chargeable transfers in the 7 years preceding 5 May 1999, so his nil rate band was intact.

Tax on £242,000 @ 0%	Nil
Tax on £8,000 @ 40%	£3,200 (payable by Emma).

(2) Tax on the estate

The cumulation principle means that Adam's nil rate band has been used up by the chargeable transfer made within the preceding 7 years.

Tax on £200,000 @ 40%   £80,000 (payable by Adam's PRs from
                                              the estate passing to Matthew)

Example 2

Gina gave the following gifts of cash to her children:

| 1 September 1995 | £150,000 to Claire |
| 25 June 1999 | £150,000 to James |

Gina died on 30 August 2001 leaving her estate (consisting of her house and bank accounts worth a total of £400,000) to the two children equally. She had made no other significant gifts.

Both gifts were PETs which have now become chargeable as Gina has died within 7 years.

(1) Tax on the 1995 PET	£
Loss to estate	150,000
Annual exemptions 1995/1996; 1994/1995	6,000
	144,000

Gina had made no chargeable transfers in the 7 years before 1 September 1995 so her nil rate band was intact.

Tax on £144,000 @ 0%	Nil.
(2) Tax on the 1999 PET	£
Loss to estate	150,000
Annual exemptions 1999/2000; 1998/1999	6,000
	144,000

Gina's cumulative total of chargeable transfers made in the 7 years up to 25 June 1999 was £144,000 (the 1995 transfer to Claire). Only £98,000 of Gina's nil rate band remains.

Tax on £144,000

£98,000 @ 0%	Nil
£46,000 @ 40%	£18,400 (payable by James)

(3) Tax on Gina's estate

Gina's nil rate band has been used up by the two chargeable transfers in the last 7 years.

Tax on £400,000 @ 40%   £160,000 (payable by Gina's PRs from the
                                              property passing to the children)

Tapering relief

Where a PET has become chargeable tapering relief is available if the transferor survives for more than 3 years after the transfer. The relief works by reducing the tax payable on the PET.

Tax is reduced to the following percentages:

- transfers within 3 to 4 years before death: 80% of death charge
- transfers within 4 to 5 years before death: 60% of death charge
- transfers within 5 to 6 years before death: 40% of death charge
- transfers within 6 to 7 years before death: 20% of death charge

Example

1 January 1995	Leonora makes a gift of £96,000 to Isadora
	Leonora's cumulative total before the gift is made is £250,000
1 July 2001	Leonora dies

Effect of death:		£
Transfer of value		96,000
Less: Annual exemptions 1994/1995; 1993/1994		6,000
PET (which is now chargeable)		90,000

Rate of tax: Cumulative total £250,000 so all £90,000 is in the 40% band

£90,000 @ 40%	36,000

Tapering relief applies. Leonora died within 6 to 7 years of the PET so 20% of this figure is payable

Tax payable by Isadora	20% of £36,000	7,200

4.6.3 Effect of death on lifetime chargeable transfers

If a transferor dies within 7 years of making a lifetime chargeable transfer (eg into a discretionary trust), the IHT payable must be recalculated and more IHT may be payable by the trustees. The tax bill may be increased because the full death rate of IHT will now apply (subject to tapering relief) and also because PETs made before the lifetime chargeable transfer may have become chargeable. They will increase the cumulative total and so reduce the nil rate band applicable to the lifetime chargeable transfer. If the recalculated bill is lower (which may occur if tapering relief is available), no tax is refunded.

IHT is recalculated in accordance with the rates of tax in force at the transferor's death if these are less than the rates in force at the time of the transfer; if not, the death rates at the time of the transfer are applied. If more than 3 years have elapsed between the transfer and the death, tapering relief applies to reduce the recalculated tax as for a PET.

Example 1

On 1 May 1998, George transferred £298,000 into a discretionary trust on condition that the trustees must pay the IHT. He had made no other lifetime gifts.

(a) On 1 May 1998, George made an immediately chargeable transfer.

		£
Value transferred		298,000
Less: Annual exemptions	1998/1999; 1997/1998	6,000
		292,000

Calculate tax.

£242,000 @ 0%	0
£50,000 @ 20%	10,000
Tax payable by trustees	10,000

(b) George dies on 1 September 2001, within 7 years of the immediately chargeable transfer.

Recalculate tax at death rates.

	£
£242,000 @ 0%	0
£50,000 @ 40%	20,000
	20,000

George died between 3 and 4 years after the transfer, so apply tapering relief

	£
80% of £20,000	16,000
Less: tax already paid	10,000
Further tax payable by trustees	6,000

Example 2

Drusilla dies on 1 August 2001. During her lifetime she made only the following transfers of value:

1 July 1995	Gift of £102,000 to Rukhsana
1 July 1998	Gift of £254,000 on discretionary trusts

The consequences are as follows:

(a) On 1 July 1994, Drusilla made a PET:

		£
Value transferred		102,000
Less: Annual exemptions	1995/1996; 1994/1995	6,000
Potentially exempt transfer		96,000

(b) On 1 July 1998, Drusilla made an immediately chargeable transfer:

Charge to tax on 1 July 1998:

			£
Value transferred			254,000
Less: Annual exemptions	1998/1999; 1997/1998		6,000
Potentially exempt transfer			248,000
Rate of tax	Cumulative total zero		
	£242,000 @ 0%		0
	£6,000 @ 20%		1,200
Tax payable by trustees			1,200

(c) Recalculation of tax on death:

Drusilla has died within 7 years of 1 July 1995, so the PET of £96,000 to Rukhsana has become chargeable. There is no IHT on the transfer as it falls within Drusilla's nil rate band, but her cumulative total is now £96,000.

The tax on the transfer of 1 July 1998 must be recalculated.

Rate of tax: Cumulative total £96,000 so £146,000 of nil rate band left

	£
£146,000 @ 0%	0
£102,000 @ 40%	40,800
£248,000	40,800

Tapering relief applies. Drusilla died between 3 and 4 years after the transfer so the recalculated tax is reduced to 80%.

	£
80% of £40,800	32,640
Less: IHT already paid	1,200
Tax payable by trustees	31,440

(d) In the 7 years before her death, Drusilla made two chargeable transfers. Her cumulative total at the time of her death is:

	£
1 July 1995 PET (now chargeable)	96,000
1 July 1998 ICT (immediately chargeable transfer)	240,000
	336,000

This means that, when calculating tax on Drusilla's estate on death, her nil rate band has been used up, and tax on her estate will be charged at a flat rate of 40%.

Chapter 5

TAX-EFFICIENT INVESTMENTS

5.1 INTRODUCTION

An individual with high levels of income or capital gains can reduce his exposure to tax by making tax-efficient investments. Depending on which investment vehicle is chosen, it may be possible to:

(1) obtain income tax relief on the investment (and so pay less income tax in the current year);

(2) ensure that future income or capital gains escape tax;

(3) avoid paying CGT on a capital gain by re-investing it.

The rest of this chapter introduces the main features of some investments which meet these objectives. However, no investor should allow a tax advantage to cloud his judgement as to the merits or risk of any particular investment. The list is not comprehensive, but gives examples of the opportunities available. Fuller treatment of these complex matters can be found in Whitehouse *Revenue Law – Principles and Practice* 18th edn (Butterworths Tax, 2001) and Simon *Simon's Direct Taxes* (Butterworths, loose-leaf).

5.2 INVESTMENTS ELIGIBLE FOR INCOME TAX RELIEF

5.2.1 Enterprise Investment Scheme (EIS)

This relief is designed to encourage investment in smaller (and riskier) companies. An individual is allowed to subscribe up to £150,000 each tax year in the ordinary shares of qualifying unquoted companies. Broadly, this means trading companies which are not listed on The Stock Exchange, so there is no ready market for their shares. Certain asset-based activities, for example share dealing, property development and farming, are excluded. During the 2 years before and 3 years after the subscription, the individual must not be 'connected with' the company. Thus, the combined shareholdings of the investor and his 'associates' (which includes spouse and close family) must not exceed 30 per cent; neither he nor his associates are normally permitted to be paid employees or directors, although there are exceptions to this rule.

The relief is given by deducting a sum equal to 20 per cent of the amount invested from the shareholder's income tax liability for the tax year of the investment (the maximum deduction is, therefore, £30,000) provided he continues to satisfy the personal qualifying conditions throughout the next 3 years. A further attraction is that gains on disposal will be exempt from CGT; conversely, if the enterprise fails, the investor's loss on his shares may be set against his income or capital gains.

5.2.2 Venture Capital Trust (VCT)

A VCT is a quoted company run by professional fund managers as a vehicle to hold shares in a range of unquoted trading companies which match the EIS criteria. Smaller enterprises are thus given access to funds and the investor buying shares in the VCT can invest indirectly in smaller businesses, at the same time reducing the risk attendant on investment in a single unquoted company.

VCTs carry tax advantages similar to EISs, but to qualify, the shares must be held for three years and the maximum investment each tax year is £100,000. As with EISs, a sum equal to 20 per cent of the amount invested can be deducted from the investor's income tax liability (so the maximum tax deduction in any one tax year is £20,000). Gains on disposal are also CGT exempt. The added feature is that dividend income from a VCT is exempt from income tax.

5.3 INVESTMENTS PRODUCING TAX-FREE INCOME OR CAPITAL GAINS

5.3.1 Individual Savings Account (ISA)

This scheme came into effect on 6 April 1999, taking the place of PEPs and TESSAs (see **5.3.2** and **5.3.3**). There are two types of ISA: the Maxi ISA and Mini ISA. Both types of ISA can include three elements – cash, stocks and shares, and life insurance.

In each tax year, an individual aged 18 or over and resident in the UK can put money into either one Maxi ISA or up to three Mini ISAs (one each for cash, stocks and shares, and life insurance). Subscription levels for tax years 1999/2000 to 2005/2006 provide for an overall limit per tax year of £7,000.

Within a Maxi ISA, the whole investment (of up to £7,000) may be in stocks and shares. Alternatively, stocks and shares could be combined with cash (up to a maximum of £3,000) and insurance (up to a maximum of £1,000). In the case of Mini ISAs, a maximum of £3,000 can be invested in both stocks and shares and cash; the limit for insurance is £1,000.

The tax benefits of ISAs are:
- No income tax liability on income produced by the ISA.
- No CGT liability on gains arising from ISA investments.
- Payment into the ISA of a 10 per cent tax credit, until April 2004, in respect of dividends on UK equities.
- Tax relief is not forfeited when money is taken out of the scheme.

5.3.2 Personal Equity Plan (PEP)

PEPs were designed to encourage savers to invest in shares by allowing individuals to invest £6,000 per tax year with an authorised PEP manager, who in turn invested the money in securities listed on the UK Stock Exchange. Although no new PEPs are permitted after April 1999, income and capital gains from existing PEPs continue to be exempt.

5.3.3 Tax Exempt Special Savings Account (TESSA)

This is a special account at a bank or building society, to encourage savers to invest in low risk schemes. The individual could invest up to £9,000 over 5 years. Although no new TESSAs are permitted after April 1999, the interest from existing TESSAs continues to be exempt from income tax, provided the capital is left in the account for the 5 years.

5.3.4 Enterprise Investment Scheme (EIS)

Capital gains are CGT exempt (see **5.2.1**).

5.3.5 Venture Capital Trust (VCT)

Both income and capital gains are exempt (see **5.2.2**).

5.4 INVESTMENT TO ESCAPE A CGT LIABILITY

5.4.1 Deferral relief on re-investment in EIS shares

Unlimited deferral of capital gains arising on the disposal, by sale or gift, of *any* asset is available where an individual subscribes wholly for cash for shares in a company which qualifies under the Enterprise Investment Scheme (EIS). (As the shares must be acquired for cash, this relief will not usually be available to a partner or sole trader who transfers his business to a company, as the shares acquired following such a transfer are usually in return for the non-cash assets of the business.)

(a) This deferral relief is available where the shares acquired meet the requirements of the Enterprise Investment Scheme (see **5.2.1**).
(b) The relief is complex but, in general terms, the individual's chargeable gain on the disposal of the asset (up to the subscription cost of the shares) is deferred until he disposes of the shares at which time taper relief is given against the deferred gain based on the period of ownership of the original asset. The deferred gain is taxed at the rate applicable to the taxpayer in the tax year of the disposal of the EIS shares.
(c) The relief is available where the EIS shares are acquired within one year before or three years after the disposal.
(d) As regards the 'true gain' on the disposal of the EIS shares themselves, a slightly different relief applies. Such gains will be exempt from CGT if held for 3 years, but only if the investor is not 'connected' with the company (see **5.2.1**).

Example
Shares in X Co Ltd (not EIS) have been held by Andrew for 2 years. He sells them and realises a gain (untapered) of £60,000. This gain is deferred when he subscribes for shares in Y Co Ltd (an EIS company) for £100,000. Andrew holds the shares in Y Co Ltd for 4 years and then sells them for £120,000. His deferred gain of £60,000 is now chargeable to CGT but attracts taper relief applicable to the original 2 years' ownership. The 'true' gain of £20,000 on the disposal of the shares in Y Co Ltd will be exempt if all the qualifying conditions are met.

If the 'true gain' on the disposal of the EIS shares is not exempt, it will attract taper relief in the usual way depending upon the period of ownership. If such gains are postponed on re-investment in another EIS company then, on the ultimate disposal, taper relief is calculated for the entire (ie cumulative) period of EIS ownership.

5.4.2 Deferral relief on re-investment in VCT shares

A similar deferral relief to that described for EIS shares is available where the individual invests in VCT shares, though, in this case, the shares must be acquired within one year before or one year after the disposal.

APPENDIX TO PART I

AI.1 SUMMARY OF RATES AND ALLOWANCES FOR 2001/02

Value Added Tax

Rates:	Standard rate	17.5%
Registration threshold:		£54,000

Income Tax

Rates:	Standard rate	£0 – £1,880	10%
	Basic rate:	£1,881 – £29,400	22%
	Higher rate:	over £29,400	40%

	Interest	Dividends
Rates for Savings Income:		
below basic rate limit	20% (or 10%)	10%
above basic rate limit	40%	32.5%

Income Tax Allowances:

Personal allowance	£ 4,535
Aged 65 but under 75	£ 5,990
Aged 75 or over	£ 6,260

Married couple's allowance (relief restricted to 10%)*

Either spouse born before 6 April 1935	£ 5,365*
Either spouse aged 75 or over	£ 5,435*
[Income limit for age-related allowances	£17,600]
Blind person	£ 1,450

* Allowances where relief is restricted to 10%

Capital Gains Tax

Rates:

Individuals: 10%, 20% and/or 40% depending on the individual's income tax position

PRs and
Trustees: 34%

Annual exempt amount:

Individuals:	£ 7,500
Trustees (generally):	£ 3,750

Inheritance Tax

Rates:	(for transfers on or after 6 April 2000)	
	£0 to £242,000	nil %
	over £242,000	40%

Transfers on death

Full rates apply.

Lifetime transfers

(A) POTENTIALLY EXEMPT TRANSFERS

Gifts to individuals, and gifts into accumulation and maintenance trusts or trusts for the disabled or trusts with an interest in possession (not otherwise exempt).

(i)   On or within 7 years of death

On death, the full rates apply with a tapered reduction in the tax payable on transfers as follows:

Years between gift and death	Percentage of full charge
0–3	100
3–4	80
4–5	60
5–6	40
6–7	20

Note: the scale in force at date of death applies

(ii)   More than 7 years before death – gift is exempt therefore NIL tax payable.

(B) CHARGEABLE TRANSFERS

Gifts into and out of discretionary trusts and gifts involving companies.

At the time of gift, half the full rates apply. If the gift also falls within 7 years of death, (A)(i) above applies but the lifetime tax will be credited against tax due on death.

AI.2   FURTHER READING

Yellow Tax Handbook 2001–2002 (Butterworths)

Orange Tax Handbook 2001–2002 (Butterworths)

Greenfield (ed) *Dymond's Capital Taxes* (FT Law & Tax)

Tolley's Value Added Tax 2001–2002 (Tolley)

Tolley's Income Tax 2001–2002 (Tolley)

Tolley's Capital Gains Tax 2001–2002 (Tolley)

Tolley's Inheritance Tax 2001–2002 (Tolley)

Whitehouse *Revenue Law – Principles and Practice* 19th edn (Butterworths Tax, 2001)

Simon *Simon's Direct Taxes* (Butterworths, loose-leaf)

De Voil *Indirect Tax Service* (Butterworths, loose-leaf)

PART II

PROFESSIONAL CONDUCT
AND CLIENT CARE
(INCLUDING FINANCIAL SERVICES)

Chapter 6

THE RULES AND PRINCIPLES OF PROFESSIONAL CONDUCT

6.1 INTRODUCING PROFESSIONAL CONDUCT

Professional conduct is the expression used to denote the code of conduct which governs all members of the solicitors' profession, including student members and trainee solicitors.

A solicitor, through the nature of his work, may handle large sums of other people's money, or be entrusted with a client's business affairs or the secrets of a client's private life. In doing so, a solicitor is expected by the public to be both honourable and beyond reproach. A higher standard of conduct is required of him or her than of the ordinary citizen.

The aim of this chapter is to provide background information about the profession, its make-up, its governing body and the fundamental rules of practice.

6.2 WHAT IS A PROFESSION?

A solicitor is invariably described as being a member of a profession, rather than as having a 'job' or a 'trade'. Other occupations which are also described as 'professions' include those of doctors, architects and accountants.

A profession is said to be different from an ordinary job or trade because it fulfils certain criteria, some of which may be absent from other occupations.

6.2.1 Distinguishing characteristics of a profession

The distinguishing characteristics of a profession are that it is a self-regulating body of people whose members:

(1)   are identifiable by reference to some register or record;
(2)   are recognised as having some special skill or learning in some field of activity in which the public needs to be protected against incompetence;
(3)   hold themselves out as being willing to serve the public;
(4)   voluntarily submit to higher standards of conduct than those required by law of the ordinary citizen; and
(5)   accept personal responsibility for their actions.

6.2.2 Application of these criteria to solicitors

Each item in the above list of characteristics is satisfied in relation to the solicitors' profession. The 'register or record' by which members are identified is called the 'Roll', on which the names of solicitors are entered on admission.

The requirement to have some special skill or learning in a field in which the public needs protection against incompetence is clearly met by the academic standards which need to be satisfied by an entrant to the profession. The standards of learning for admission to the profession and to practise in certain specialised fields (eg child care) are set and regulated by The Law Society itself. The need for the protection of the public has conventionally been demonstrated by the fact that certain areas of work have been reserved to solicitors by statute (eg the preparation of papers for probate), although these reserved areas have now largely been eroded by statutory intervention under the Courts and Legal Services Act 1990. All solicitors subject themselves to the rules of conduct made by The Law Society under statutory powers, which impose on members of the profession higher standards of conduct than are required of the ordinary citizen. The profession is also self-regulating in that the standards of entry and enforcement of discipline are dealt with by the profession itself and not by an outside body.

Solicitors also hold themselves out as being willing to serve the public in that, in exercising their legal skills on behalf of a client, the interests of the client are paramount. Willingness to serve the public does not mean that a solicitor is bound to accept instructions from each and every client who approaches him. Circumstances exist where a solicitor either may, or in some cases must, refuse to accept a client's instructions (see Chapters 8 and 9).

The requirement for personal responsibility is fulfilled in that solicitors are not generally permitted to limit their liability to their clients in contentious business agreements and cannot contract out of liability in negligence.

6.2.3 Other qualities

A solicitor also needs to possess certain personal qualities, some of which may not be present or needed in other occupations. A solicitor is required to accept standards of skill and care in the performance of his duties towards his client. These standards require the solicitor to perform his job to the very best of his ability, which may involve doing work over and above the strict legal duty owed to the client.

The ability to keep the client's affairs secret at all times is a necessary quality because of the duty of confidentiality which is owed to the client (see Chapter 14). A solicitor must possess integrity in that he must be honest in dealing with his client's affairs and his client's money. He must not be a party to anything which is dishonourable in either his professional or private life. The solicitor must be able to retain his independence. He must be free to pursue the best interests of his client, even when the client's interests are in conflict with another person or the state. Independence must not only exist as a personal quality, it must be seen by the public to exist as a fact. Therefore a solicitor should not accept instructions to act where his interests conflict with those of his client, or in circumstances where it might be felt that the solicitor by reason of some personal appointment or connection was able to influence the outcome of a matter, for example, a solicitor should not appear before a court where one of his partners is sitting in a judicial capacity. Integrity is also demonstrated by a solicitor's personal liability to fulfil undertakings given by him or his staff (see Chapter 15).

Apart from accepting personal responsibility in the form of liability to his client in contract and in negligence, a solicitor is also required to exercise proper supervision over the work done by his staff on behalf of a client. He cannot escape responsibility to the client by delegating work to his staff or partners.

A fundamental requirement of the lawyer's job is the ability to communicate effectively with other people. Communication is more than the ability to speak or write clearly, it is the ability to explain a problem clearly, and in language which is appropriate to the client's circumstances. Today's solicitor is more than a lawyer, he is also a businessman, thus management skills and an understanding of financial affairs are qualities which are necessary for him to acquire.

6.3 THE LAW SOCIETY

The Law Society is the governing body of the solicitors' profession. It was formed by Royal Charter in 1845, but owes its origins to an earlier organisation formed in 1739 called the Society of Gentlemen Practisers in the Courts of Law and Equity. The Society's income is derived mainly from the annual practising certificate fees payable by solicitors.

6.3.1 The Law Society's powers

The Society has power under the Solicitors Act 1974 to make rules and regulations governing the training and admission of solicitors, practising certificates and the conduct of professional practice and discipline. The Society is also responsible for the education, training and discipline of solicitors. The Society's power to investigate complaints against solicitors is delegated to a discrete body which, although part of The Law Society, operates under separate management and from separate premises (see Chapter 18). Disciplinary proceedings and the management of the Compensation Fund are also the responsibility of The Law Society.

6.3.2 Membership of The Law Society

Membership of the Society after admission is voluntary. All solicitors, whether or not they are members and irrespective of whether they are engaged in private practice, are bound by the rules of conduct made by the Society. The majority of solicitors do join the Society as members.

6.3.3 The Council of The Law Society

The Society is governed by a Council whose number is limited by its Charter. Council members are elected on a regional basis.

6.3.4 Administration

The administration of the Society is organised through a number of departments which report to the Secretary General. These departments service the various committees which report to the Council. Membership of the committees consists of Council members assisted by co-opted non-council members and, in some cases, lay persons. The non-council members and lay persons who serve on these committees are chosen for their expertise in particular subject fields in order to provide specialist advice and assistance to the committees.

6.3.5 Services provided by The Law Society

The Society has its headquarters in Chancery Lane in London, but some departments have been de-centralised and operate from separate premises. The Society's Hall in London provides library and restaurant facilities for its members. Social and sporting events are also organised by the Society's clubs. The *Law Society's Gazette* is the weekly magazine published by the Society. The Society also runs an appointments registry and provides advice and guidance to the profession and to the public on matters of practice and conduct. The Society runs an insurance advisory service and is trustee of a pension fund run for the benefit of solicitors' staff. Indemnity insurance is also effected through the Society.

6.3.6 Local law societies

Over 100 local law societies exist in England and Wales, some of which were established before the formation of The Law Society itself. These societies are totally independent of The Law Society but regular meetings are held between The Law Society and the secretaries of the local societies in order to promote co-operation and mutual assistance. The views of local law societies are frequently sought by The Law Society before implementing changes in law and practice.

Most local law societies organise lectures and courses for their members on topics of current interest to enable members to fulfil their continuing professional development requirements. Some societies also maintain a library whose facilities are open to its members. Local law societies may provide solicitors for Citizens Advice Bureau legal advice sessions, duty solicitor schemes and legal advice centres. Most societies also operate a complaints system for the informal resolution of complaints made by clients against solicitors. The local societies have no power to discipline their members but many complaints by the public are resolved by use of this procedure. Social events are also organised by local law societies.

6.4 HOW THE PROFESSION REGULATES ITSELF

6.4.1 Solicitors Act 1974

The higher standard of conduct, which applies to a solicitor's private life as well as to his professional life, derives partly from common law principles and partly from statute. The Solicitors Act 1974 (as amended) is the principal statutory provision affecting solicitors. This Act also empowers The Law Society, with the concurrence of the Master of the Rolls, to make rules which regulate the conduct of the profession.

6.4.2 Rules made by The Law Society

A number of rules have been made by The Law Society, the most important of which are the Solicitors' Practice Rules 1990 (set out in full in Appendix 1 to Part II) and the Solicitors' Accounts Rules 1998, which regulate the way in which a solicitor handles money and keeps his accounts. These current rules replace earlier versions of similar rules. The rules are updated regularly and it is important always to refer to only the most recent version of the rules. The Law Society also issues, from time to time, recommendations and Council Directions. Recommendations are statements of preferred practice but are not binding in the same way as a practice rule. Failure to follow a recommendation could however be construed as evidence that a solicitor had failed to carry out his duty towards his client. Council Directions are regarded as mandatory in that failure to observe a Direction will almost certainly lead to disciplinary action being taken against the solicitor.

6.4.3 A voluntary code of conduct

Compliance with the code of conduct is said to be 'voluntary', in so far as no one is compelled by law to become a solicitor. However, having made the decision to join the profession, a solicitor is automatically deemed to have agreed to submit to the code of conduct and to the jurisdiction of The Law Society which has power to discipline offenders. The code therefore binds all solicitors, whether or not they are in private practice and irrespective of whether they are members of The Law Society.

6.4.4 Aim of the code of conduct

The aim of the professional conduct rules and other principles is to provide a safe and efficient foundation for the solicitor's practice as well as providing adequate safeguards to protect the public when dealing with members of the profession and maintaining the integrity of the profession in the public perception.

Viewed in this light, it is understood that members of the profession are expected to honour the spirit as well as the letter of the code. It is possible for there to be a breach of the code of conduct (resulting in a charge of unprofessional conduct being brought against the solicitor) even in circumstances where a practice rule has been observed to the letter. For example, the Solicitors' Practice Rules 1990, Rule 13 (see Chapter 7) lays down the minimum standards of supervision required of a solicitor's office. It would be possible for a solicitor to comply with the wording of Rule 13 and yet still be held to be guilty of unprofessional conduct for not having exercised proper supervision over his staff in the handling of clients' affairs.

6.4.5 Disciplinary powers of The Law Society

The Law Society's disciplinary powers for breach of the code of conduct range from giving a reprimand to striking a solicitor off the Roll (the Roll is the list on which a solicitor's name is entered on his admission as a solicitor) and so depriving him of earning his living (see Chapter 18).

6.4.6 The pervasive nature of conduct

Conduct cannot be viewed in isolation. It pervades all aspects of a solicitor's life and work. The topics covered in this book are of general application. Matters which are specific to a particular subject (eg contract races which relate to conveyancing only) are dealt with in the LPC Resource Book appropriate to that subject.

6.5 DIFFERENT ASPECTS OF PRACTICE

Most solicitors practise in partnership with one or more other solicitors but other types of practice also exist.

6.5.1 The sole principal

A small number of solicitors choose to practise on their own, sometimes employing a few assistant solicitors and auxiliary staff to assist in the running of the practice. While the sole practitioner was until recently a common phenomenon of practice in the small town High Street, the practitioner being to some extent a 'jack of all trades', this method of practice is now less popular than in the past, with the exception of 'niche' practices which specialise in one specific area of law, and current trends seem to indicate a move to larger rather than smaller practices.

The demise of the sole practitioner has been caused by a number of disparate factors. The increase in volume of the law itself has meant that there is increased pressure on a solicitor to specialise in one or two areas rather than to try to have a general working knowledge of all aspects of the law. The decrease in the volume of residential conveyancing work over a number of years has also forced some sole practitioners whose income was heavily dependent on this area of work to merge their practices with larger firms having a broader client base.

When a sole principal is absent from his office for whatever reason (holiday, sickness, etc), he owes a continuing duty to his clients to ensure that his practice will be carried on with the minimum interruption to his clients' business. Consequently, he must make adequate arrangements for his practice to be administered during his absence.

Whether he practises on his own or in partnership, a solicitor needs to have access to research materials (eg *Halsbury's Laws*) and to sophisticated electronic office equipment; the cost of providing these resources may be prohibitive to a sole practitioner, but is less burdensome when shared among partners. Law Society rules, such as those relating to the supervision of offices, also militate against the sole practitioner, and prevent a solicitor from setting up in practice on his own account until he has been qualified for at least 3 years.

6.5.2 Partnerships

Most solicitors practise in partnership with one or more other solicitors. Some firms, notably in the city of London and other major cities, may have in excess of 100 partners, but the ordinary firm in the High Street is more likely to have between four and ten partners.

Every partner is responsible for breaches of the Solicitors' Accounts Rules 1998. Liabilities for breaches of conduct other than those arising under those rules will depend upon whether or not a partner knew or ought to have known of the breach.

6.5.3 Incorporated practices

The Solicitors' Incorporated Practice Rules 1988 (as amended) were made by The Law Society pursuant to the Administration of Justice Act 1985, s 9. These rules permit solicitors to practise either as a company limited by shares or as an unlimited company. An incorporated practice which has been approved by The Law Society is called 'a recognised body'.

A recognised body must be managed and controlled by solicitors or other recognised bodies, although the company secretary need not be a solicitor. The directors of the recognised body must all be solicitors holding a practising certificate and the shareholders must either be solicitors holding practising certificates or recognised bodies.

All the rules, principles and requirements of professional conduct which apply to individual solicitors apply equally to recognised bodies. A recognised body must make contributions to the Solicitors' Indemnity Fund (compulsory insurance) and must also take out top-up insurance in a minimum sum prescribed by The Law Society. The benefits of limited liability as enjoyed by trading companies are to a degree eroded in the case of recognised bodies by the requirement that individual shareholders enter into covenants with the Compensation Fund (a fund run by The Law Society to compensate the victims of solicitors' dishonesty), although this covenant is necessary in order to protect the interests of the fund. The taxation disadvantages of incorporation may also deter solicitors' firms from incorporating their practices.

Recognition of a recognised body lasts for 3 years.

6.5.4 Employed solicitors

The expression 'employed solicitor' refers to a solicitor who is employed by a non-solicitor employer. A number of solicitors work in central and local government and in the legal departments of commercial companies or charitable organisations. A solicitor who is employed by a lay employer is subject to the same principles of professional conduct as a solicitor in private practice. The Solicitors' Practice Rules 1990, Rule 4 deals with employed solicitors and provides that such solicitors must comply with the Employed Solicitors' Code 1990.

6.5.5 Law centres

A law centre is a place where legal advice is given to the public and case work is undertaken on behalf of clients. Normally the service provided to clients is free or subject to only the client's legal aid contribution. A solicitor may be employed by a law centre and must comply in all respects with the Solicitors' Practice Rules 1990 and other principles of conduct.

An organisation must not be described as a law centre unless it is a member of the Law Centres Federation and the organisation effects insurance cover reasonably equivalent to that available to solicitors from the Solicitors' Indemnity Fund.

Law centres are frequently located where there is a scarcity of solicitors in private practice, such as inner city areas.

6.5.6 Legal advice centres

A legal advice centre is a centre where the public may attend for legal advice but where no case work is undertaken.

In many parts of the country legal advice centres are operated by the Citizens Advice Bureau and solicitors will attend the centre to give free legal advice either as an honorary legal adviser or on a rota scheme.

6.5.7 Multi-national partnerships

Under Solicitors' Practice Rules 1990, Rule 7, a multi-national practice consisting of solicitors and registered foreign lawyers may be formed and may operate in England and Wales. At least one principal (partner) in the firm must be a solicitor who has been admitted for 3 years or, in the case of firms who do not undertake any litigation or advocacy in England and Wales, be a registered foreign lawyer who has been qualified in his own jurisdiction for 3 years. Foreign lawyers who wish to become 'registered foreign lawyers' must make application to The Law Society for inclusion on the list of registered foreign lawyers maintained by it.

Registration is renewable annually (by 31 October in each year), failing which The Law Society may cancel the registration. Registration is automatically suspended if the registered foreign lawyer is suspended or struck off in his own jurisdiction or has a bankruptcy or equivalent order made against him in this or another jurisdiction.

Once registered, the foreign lawyer becomes subject to the Solicitors' Practice Rules 1990, and all the other rules and principles of conduct which affect solicitors. This includes the provisions relating to indemnity insurance and the disciplinary powers of the Disciplinary Tribunal.

A registered foreign lawyer has no right to conduct litigation or advocacy in England and Wales.

6.5.8 Multi-disciplinary partnerships

Solicitors are prohibited from entering into partnership with anyone who is not either a solicitor or a registered foreign lawyer. A solicitor qualified in England and Wales cannot therefore be in partnership with, for example, an accountant or an estate agent. The reason for this rule is to preserve the independence and integrity of the solicitor's profession. If a solicitor were allowed to enter into partnership with a non-lawyer, the interests of his non-lawyer partner might influence the solicitor into giving advice to a client which was not wholly in that client's best interests. The rule is reflected in the Solicitors' Practice Rules 1990, Rule 7 which prevents a solicitor from sharing his fees with non-lawyers (see Chapter 11).

The question of whether to allow multi-disciplinary partnerships is now under consideration by The Law Society.

6.6 THE FUNDAMENTAL RULE OF PRACTICE

Rule 1 of the Solicitors' Practice Rules 1990 provides:

> 'A solicitor shall not do anything in the course of practising as a solicitor, or permit another person to do anything on his or her behalf, which compromises or impairs or is likely to compromise or impair any of the following:
>
> (a)   the solicitor's independence or integrity;
> (b)   a person's freedom to instruct a solicitor of his or her choice;
> (c)   the solicitor's duty to act in the best interests of the client;
> (d)   the good repute of the solicitor or of the solicitors' profession;
> (e)   the solicitor's proper standard of work;
> (f)   the solicitor's duty to the Court.'

This rule embodies the basic principles of conduct governing the professional practice of solicitors.

6.6.1 Effect of Rule 1

A solicitor must not do anything which would infringe Rule 1; to do so would be professional misconduct. Rule 1 is deliberately drafted in wide terms in order to allow a certain amount of flexibility and discretion in its operation. It is expected however that solicitors will observe the spirit as well as the letter of the rule so that a charge of misconduct may still lie even where the technical wording of the rule has been honoured. Rule 1 is fundamental to the operation of a solicitor's practice. No act which offends this rule can be done. The rule must be regarded as the cornerstone on which the structure of other rules and regulations rest. Breach of any of the other practice rules and regulations will frequently also result in a breach of Rule 1. Conversely, compliance with the wording of another practice rule will still be an offence if in so doing Rule 1 is breached. For example, a solicitor may in certain circumstances act for two parties in the same transaction within Rule 6, but, if carrying out those instructions would involve the solicitor in a conspiracy to defraud (a breach of the law which would impair the solicitor's integrity and bring the profession into disrepute), the instructions must be declined as being in breach of Rule 1.

6.6.2 Reason for the Rule

It is essential to the relationship between solicitor and client that the solicitor is able to give the client impartial and unbiased advice free from constraints imposed by the influence of a third party. The client must have chosen to instruct the solicitor of his own free will and the solicitor must not be under pressure (financial or otherwise) from a third party which might influence the nature of the advice given to the client. Thus a client may be persuaded by his financial adviser to seek advice from a particular solicitor, the implication being that the client will be able to obtain only the loan which he seeks if this particular solicitor is instructed. Such instructions would be tainted because the client was not in a position to instruct the solicitor of his choice, and accordingly they must be declined. In the converse situation, a solicitor who is regularly instructed by a particular bank may fear harming his relationship with that bank if he gives another client advice which conflicts with the bank's policies. The solicitor is not in a position to give the client impartial and uninhibited advice, and the instructions to act for that client must be declined to avoid breach of Rule 1.

6.7 WHAT IS MEANT BY PROFESSIONAL MISCONDUCT?

6.7.1 Grey areas in conduct

Professional conduct is unlike conventional law subjects in that in very few cases do the rules contain an absolute prohibition on an action or course of conduct (a notable exception to this being the Solicitors' Accounts Rules 1998, which relate to the handling of clients' money). In most cases the rules and principles are drafted with a certain amount of flexibility in their wording, allowing discretion in their application. In some ways this flexibility is more difficult to live with than an absolute rule since it becomes a matter of judgment as to whether a particular action will or will not offend the rules. Conduct is therefore full of grey areas, and issues are made more complex by the appreciation that the same course of conduct taken by the same solicitor but in two different client contexts may produce different results. In one situation the course of action might result in a breach of the rules, in another it might not. A pertinent illustration of this difficulty relates to the rules on advertising, which provide (inter alia) that any advertising placed by a solicitor to publicise his practice 'must be in good taste'. An advertisement placed in a local newspaper may satisfy this criterion, but an identically worded advertisement appearing on the side of the local undertaker's hearse might not be viewed in the same light.

6.7.2 Professional misconduct, unbefitting conduct or breach of duty?

Owing to both the grey nature of professional conduct and to the expectation of high standards of behaviour, it is, perhaps, unwise to attempt to define conduct which would amount to either professional misconduct, unbefitting conduct or breach of duty.

None the less, to facilitate a feel for the subject, the following broad-brush definitions are presented.

6.7.3 Professional misconduct

'Professional misconduct' is generally taken to mean breaches of the conduct rules and principles committed in the course of practising as a solicitor, for example, breaches of Rules 1 and 15.

6.7.4 Unbefitting conduct

This may generally be defined as conduct by a solicitor which is such as to render him unfit to be an officer of the court (*Re Southerton* (1805) 6 East 126). Conduct which is not necessarily criminal in character, nor related to the solicitor's professional status, is within this definition. Any conduct which would be regarded by fellow members of the profession as disgraceful or dishonourable may be the subject of disciplinary proceedings. Unbefitting conduct includes failure to advise on legal aid, giving false references, obstructing complaints, writing offensive letters and offensive behaviour.

6.7.5 Breach of duty

'Breach of duty' is one that gives rise to an action of law, for example, in contract or tort.

6.7.6 Overlapping definitions

There is an overlap between all of the above categories. Failure to advise a client on the availability of legal aid is both unbefitting conduct and could give rise to an action in negligence. A solicitor has, for example, a duty to disclose all relevant information to his client. Failure to do so in the absence of one of the permitted exceptions could give rise to an action for breach of contract and professional misconduct (Rule 1: duty to act in best interests). The best practice approach is to abide by the spirit of the rules, as well as the letter.

6.7.7 Behaviour outside of legal practice?

Whether practising or not, situations in private life or activities outside legal practice may give rise to disciplinary action, particularly in situations which bring the profession into disrepute.

6.8 CHAPTER SUMMARY

(1) Professional conduct rules exist to protect the public and to regulate the profession itself. A higher standard of behaviour is expected of solicitors than of the public at large.

(2) The requirements of professional conduct are in addition to the requirements under the general laws of contract, tort, crime, etc. A solicitor may thus be liable to disciplinary action for professional misconduct even though there has been no breach of the general law.

(3) Rule 1 of the Solicitors' Practice Rules 1990 sets out the basic principles of conduct. The principles stem from the ethical duties imposed on solicitors by the common law.

(4) A solicitor is an officer of the court and should conduct himself or herself appropriately.

(5) The conduct principles affect student members of The Law Society as well as admitted solicitors. Student members/trainees who commit a breach may be prevented from entering the profession.

(6) The Law Society is established under Royal Charter. It is a voluntary body representing solicitors. It is authorised by statute, primarily the Solicitors Act 1974, to regulate the conduct of solicitors, ie it is both the governing body and regulatory body of the profession.

(7) Membership of the Society is voluntary, but all solicitors are bound by the rules of conduct made by it.

(8) It can be difficult to decide which behaviour will amount to a breach of the rules and general principles of conduct. This is attributable to the 'grey' nature of the subject and to the fact that there is a lot of overlap between what is meant by 'unbefitting conduct', 'professional misconduct' and 'breach of duty'. The best practice approach is to abide by the spirit of the rules, as well as the letter.

Chapter 7

THE REQUIREMENTS OF PRACTICE

This chapter will look at:

- the need to hold a practising certificate;
- the structure of a solicitor's business;
- the authority to regulate the profession;
- discrimination;
- supervision and responsibility;
- money laundering;
- employed solicitors.

7.1 PRACTISING CERTIFICATES

7.1.1 Requirement to hold a certificate

Section 1 of the Solicitors Act 1974 states:

'No person shall be qualified to act as a solicitor unless—

(a)   he has been admitted as a solicitor, and

(b)   his name is on the roll, and

(c)   he has in force a certificate issued by the [Law] Society … authorising him to practise as a solicitor (in this Act referred to as a "practising certificate").'

The effect of this section is that any person (whether admitted as a solicitor or not) who does not hold a current practising certificate falls within the definition of an 'unqualified person' in s 87 of the Solicitors Act 1974 and is therefore prohibited from undertaking certain acts such as conducting litigation as a solicitor.

7.1.2 Persons who need a certificate

The following persons must hold a current practising certificate:

(1)   a solicitor who is a partner in a firm;

(2)   any solicitor who appears in court as an advocate (a certificate may not be required for appearance before certain tribunals);

(3)   a solicitor who administers an oath;

(4)   all assistant solicitors in private practice.

7.1.3 Annual enrolment

A solicitor who does not hold a practising certificate (eg a solicitor who is employed as a legal adviser to a company and who does not actively participate in case work) must pay an annual fee to The Law Society to maintain his name on the Roll (Solicitors (Keeping of the Roll) Regulations 1989, as amended).

7.1.4 Issue of certificates

Practising certificates are issued by The Law Society on an annual basis and must be renewed by 31 October in each year. A compulsory contribution to the Compensation Fund is normally also payable with the practising certificate fee (see Chapter 18). In most cases, one application form is submitted on behalf of each firm. This form (RF1) contains a joint application for practising certificates on behalf of all solicitors in the firm. The form also contains an application for an investment business certificate (see Chapter 20).

7.1.5 Solicitors Act 1974, s 12

Where s 12 of the Solicitors Act 1974 applies, The Law Society has a discretion to grant or refuse an application for a certificate, or to impose such conditions on the issue of a certificate as it thinks fit. Conditions may also be imposed by The Law Society on a current certificate. The provisions of s 12 apply (inter alia) where:

(1) a solicitor is applying for a practising certificate for the first time;
(2) a period of 12 months or more has elapsed since the solicitor last held a practising certificate;
(3) a solicitor has been asked by The Law Society to give an explanation in respect of any matter relating to his conduct or has failed to give a satisfactory explanation and has been notified by the Society that he has so failed; or
(4) the solicitor has been the subject of disciplinary proceedings.

Although The Law Society has a discretion to impose such conditions as it thinks fit on the issue of a practising certificate, s 12(4A) suggests that the conditions must be 'conducive to [the solicitor] carrying on an efficient practice'. Thus, a solicitor who has been found to be in breach of the Solicitors' Accounts Rules 1998 could be required, as a condition of the issue of his certificate, to deliver twice-yearly accountant's reports, or may be required to practice in partnership only with certain named individuals.

7.1.6 Refusal of certificate

Except where s 12 applies, if The Law Society refuses or neglects to issue a practising certificate, an application may be made to the High Court or to the Master of the Rolls who may make such order as is just. An appeal against the imposition of a condition on a practising certificate may be made to the Master of the Rolls, whose decision is final, within one month.

7.1.7 The Post-Admission Training Regulations 1990

The Training Regulations 1990 (as amended) require all solicitors to obtain 48 hours of continuing professional development during each consecutive 3-year cycle of practice. Hours may be collected by the attendance at courses run by a list of recognised providers published by The Law Society. A prescribed percentage of the required hours can be satisfied by undertaking a distance learning course, by reading prescribed journals, by studying from videos or by writing learned articles.

7.2 A SOLICITOR'S PRACTICE

Solicitors may practise as:

- a sole practitioner;
- a partnership;
- a company limited by shares or as an unlimited company, known as a recognised body.

7.2.1 Partnership

Most solicitors practise in partnership, ie as an unincorporated body, the size of which may vary from two to two hundred partners. There is no legal maximum on the number of partners which a firm may have.

7.2.2 The law of partnership

A solicitors' partnership, like any other partnership, is governed by the Partnership Act 1890; thus the partners are jointly and severally liable in contract and tort. Every partner has implied authority to bind his co-partners in all matters which relate to the firm's business. All partners are required to hold current practising certificates. Where a partner does not hold a practising certificate the partnership is illegal, and is thus automatically dissolved under the Partnership Act 1890, s 34 (see *Hudgell Yeates and Co v Watson* [1978] 2 WLR 661).

7.2.3 Multi-disciplinary practice

A solicitor must not enter into a partnership with any person other than a solicitor, a registered foreign lawyer, or a recognised body (Solicitors' Practice Rules 1990, Rule 7(6)), and there is a similar rule for recognised bodies.

7.3 CAREER STRUCTURE

Having completed his training contract and having been admitted as a solicitor, the newly qualified solicitor will usually obtain a job as an assistant solicitor (sometimes called an 'associate'), employed by a firm and paid a salary for his services. The Solicitors' Practice Rules 1990, Rule 13 (see **7.8**) prevents the newly qualified solicitor from setting up in practice on his own for 3 years after admission. After a period of time the assistant may aspire to become a partner in the firm. On appointment as a partner, he will accept responsibility for and participate in the firm's management. Partnership may initially be salaried, ie the solicitor is a partner in the firm but still has no share in the firm's profits. After a further period of time the partner may be offered an equity partnership when he will be entitled to share in the profits of the firm. In some cases, he may have to buy his share in the firm by contributing to the firm's capital.

7.4 STRUCTURE OF A TYPICAL FIRM

Most firms now work on a departmental basis, each department is run by one or more of the partners and will specialise in a particular area of law. Each department may then have a staff of assistant solicitors, legal executives, clerks and trainee solicitors who carry out the work of the department under the supervision of the department head. All of these staff are 'fee earners' in that they have client contact and the work which they do earns money for the firm. A number of ancillary staff will be employed to support the fee earners; although they are not direct fee earners, their presence is vital to the smooth running of the firm. Ancillary staff include secretaries, typists, receptionists and telephonists. Most firms employ accounts staff to control the bookkeeping side of the business. Larger firms will employ a range of other non-legal staff such as training officers, librarians, research assistants, messengers and print room operators. Some larger firms also employ consultants, who may be retired partners of the firm or specialists from other professions, to assist in the specialised work of particular departments (eg accountants to assist in taxation matters).

The management of larger firms is sometimes delegated to an administration partner or management committee rather than being the responsibility of all the partners. In such a case the structure and organisation more closely resembles a company than a traditional partnership. While the firm retains its unincorporated status, it is still in law a partnership, and the joint and several liability of the partners for the acts and defaults of the firm remains unaffected by this delegation of management functions.

7.5 RULES

The Solicitors Act 1974 authorises the Council of the Law Society to make rules regulating the professional practice, conduct and discipline of solicitors, and rules relating to the keeping of accounts.

7.6 ACCOUNTANT'S REPORT

Where a solicitor holds client money, he will have to deliver an accountant's report with his practising certificate application form (Solicitors Act 1974, s 34).

This report is made by a qualified accountant who is independent of the solicitor's firm; 'independent' means that the accountant cannot be an employee of the solicitor's firm or an employee of a connected business. Although the report can be signed in the name of the firm for whom the accountant works, the name of the individual who prepared the report must be stated on the form.

The report certifies that the solicitor has complied with the Solicitors' Accounts Rules 1998. If the certifying accountant finds that there has been a breach of the Accounts Rules, he may decline to provide a certificate or may provide a qualified certificate. The Accounts Rules also require the reporting accountant to check that the solicitor's accounts comply with the Solicitors' Investment Business Rules 1995 (SIBR 1995) relating to work connected with financial services.

The report must be delivered once during each practice year (year ending 31 October) and, although it is normally submitted with the application for renewal of a practising certificate, it is a separate requirement from the requirement to hold a practising certificate. In a partnership it is sufficient to submit one report for the firm. An accountant's report is not required for a solicitor who does not hold a practising certificate, nor for a solicitor who does not hold client money. A requirement to submit an accountant's report more than once each year is one of the sanctions which can be imposed by The Law Society following disciplinary proceedings against a solicitor.

7.7 FEE SHARING

Rule 7 of the Solicitors' Practice Rules 1990 provides that a solicitor is not permitted to share or agree to share his professional fees with any person except:

(1) a practising solicitor (including an incorporated practice);
(2) a person who is entitled to practise as a lawyer in any country other than in England and Wales and has his principal office in that other country;
(3) the solicitor's bona fide employee, which provision shall not permit a partnership with a non-solicitor under the cloak of employment; or
(4) a retired partner or predecessor of the solicitor or the dependants or personal representatives of a deceased partner or predecessor.

Rule 7(2) permits a solicitor who instructs an estate agent as his sub-agent for the sale of a property to remunerate the agent on the basis of a proportion of the solicitor's professional fee.

Exceptions set out in the Employed Solicitors' Code also operate as exceptions to Rule 7 but to permit fee sharing only with the solicitor's employer.

Rule 7 prevents a solicitor from entering into partnership with any person except another qualified solicitor, since he may not share his fees with such a person. The exceptions contained in the rule allow solicitors to maintain profit-sharing or bonus schemes for their employees and also to pay a pension or annuity to a retired partner or his dependants.

7.8 DISCRIMINATION

Under the Solicitors' Anti-Discrimination Rules 1995, solicitors must not discriminate on grounds of race, sex or sexual orientation, and must not discriminate unfairly or unreasonably on the grounds of disability in their professional dealings with clients, staff, other solicitors, barristers or other persons. Firms must have policies to deal with the avoidance of such discrimination.

7.9 SUPERVISION OF THE OFFICE

A solicitor is responsible for exercising proper supervision over both his admitted and unadmitted staff. This general principle of conduct, supplemented by the Solicitors' Practice Rules 1990, Rule 13 (as amended) provides (inter alia) that every firm must have at least one principal (ie sole practitioner or partner) who is qualified to supervise and that every office of the firm (ie main office or branch office) must have at least one solicitor who is similarly qualified and for whom that office is their normal place of work. Solicitors will be qualified to supervise only if they have held a practising certificate for at least 3 of the last 10 years and if they have completed appropriate management training specified by The Law Society.

If proper supervision of an office cannot be maintained for any reason (eg sickness, staff holidays), the office should be closed until such time as compliance with Rule 13 can be guaranteed.

7.10 RESPONSIBILITY

As a matter of conduct, a partner is prima facie responsible for the acts or omissions of his firm, and this extends to the acts or omissions of his staff. If there is a breach of the Solicitors' Accounts Rules 1998, (relating to the handling of money by the solicitor), all partners are liable to disciplinary action regardless of whether they knew of or were a party to the breach. Where one partner is guilty of misconduct other than a breach of the Accounts Rules, The Law Society has discretion in deciding whether to institute disciplinary proceedings against all or only some of the partners. Thus a partner who is innocent of the breach committed by another partner may escape penalty. Where the composition of the firm alters (eg on the retirement of a partner), the clients must be notified promptly. The Law Society must be informed of any change in the address of the practice.

7.11 MONEY LAUNDERING

In certain circumstances, a solicitor may commit a criminal offence under the Criminal Justice Act 1988 (as amended), the Drug Trafficking Act 1994 or the Prevention of Terrorism (Temporary Provisions) Act 1989, for example, if the solicitor:

- assists any person to retain or control the proceeds of criminal activity, drug trafficking or terrorism, knowing or suspecting that such person carries on these activities and is benefiting from them;
- fails to disclose knowledge or suspicion of money laundering in relation to drugs or terrorism;
- knowing or suspecting that a disclosure has been made or that a constable may be acting in an investigation into the laundering, passes on information to a client which is likely to prejudice an investigation.

Solicitors who conduct investment business within the meaning of the Financial Services Act 1986 must also comply with the Money Laundering Regulations 1993. These require solicitors, in certain circumstances, to obtain evidence of a client's identity before proceeding.

7.12 EMPLOYED PERSONS

Solicitors employed in private practice or in any other employment by a lay employer are subject to the same general principles of professional conduct as apply to principals in private practice.

7.13 CHAPTER SUMMARY

(1) Practising certificates:

(a) Solicitors Act 1974, s 1 states:

'No person shall be qualified to act as a solicitor unless—

  (a) he has been admitted as a solicitor, and

  (b) his name is on the roll, and

  (c) he has in force a certificate issued by the [Law] Society ... authorising him to practise as a solicitor (in this Act referred to as a "practising certificate").'

(b) Every solicitor who is a principal in private practice or who is employed in private practice in connection with the provision of any legal services must hold a practising certificate (Solicitors Act 1974, s 1A). This would therefore include assistant solicitors in private practice.

(c) Practising certificates are issued by The Law Society and are renewable annually.

(d) The Law Society has a discretion to grant or refuse an application for a Practising Certificate, or to impose such conditions as it thinks fit under s 12 of the Solicitors Act 1974. These provisions apply where, for example:

– the solicitor has been the subject of disciplinary proceedings;

– the solicitor has been asked to give an explanation in respect of any matter relating to conduct, has failed to give a satisfactory explanation and has been notified that he has so failed.

(2) Solicitors are subject to compulsory Continuing Professional Development.

(3) Solicitors may practise as:

- a sole practitioner;
- a partnership; or
- a company limited by shares or as an unlimited company, known as a recognised body.

(4) A solicitor must not enter into partnership with any person other than a solicitor, a registered foreign lawyer or a recognised body (Solicitors' Practice Rules 1990, Rule 7(6)) and there is a similar rule for recognised bodies.

(5) The Solicitors Act 1974 authorises the Council of The Law Society to make rules regulating the professional practice, conduct and discipline of solicitors and rules relating to the keeping of accounts.

(6) Every solicitor who handles client money must produce an annual report by a qualified accountant showing that the solicitor has complied with the Solicitors' Accounts Rules 1998 and the record-keeping provisions contained in the Solicitors' Investment Business Rules 1995 (SIBR 1995).

(7) Solicitors must not discriminate on grounds of race, sex or sexual orientation, and must not discriminate unfairly or unreasonably on the grounds of disability in their professional dealings with clients, staff, other solicitors, barristers or other persons. Firms must have policies to deal with the avoidance of such discrimination.

(8) Supervision of a solicitor's office:

- Sole principal: a solicitor must have been admitted for 3 years or more before he is entitled to practise on his own and supervise his own office.
- A solicitor is responsible for exercising proper supervision over both admitted and unadmitted staff. A solicitor cannot escape responsibility for work carried out in the office by leaving it entirely to his or her staff, however well qualified.
- This general principle is supplemented by Rule 13 of the Solicitors' Practice Rules 1990 which lays down minimum standards of supervision in relation to a solicitor's office.

(9) As a general principle of conduct, a partner is prima facie responsible for acts or omissions of the firm and this extends to the acts or omissions of staff.

- Every partner is responsible for breaches of the Solicitors' Accounts Rules 1998. The penalty imposed will depend upon the facts of the particular case.
- Liability for breaches of conduct, other than those arising under the Accounts Rules, will depend upon whether or not a partner knew or ought to have known of the act of unbefitting conduct.

(10) In certain circumstances, a solicitor may commit a criminal offence under the Criminal Justice Act 1988 (as amended), the Drug Trafficking Act 1994 or the Prevention of Terrorism (Temporary Provisions) Act 1989, for example if the solicitor:

- assists any person to retain or control the proceeds of criminal activity, drug trafficking or terrorism knowing or suspecting that such person carries on these activities or is benefiting from them;
- fails to disclose knowledge or suspicion of money laundering in relation to drugs or terrorism;
- knowing or suspecting that a disclosure has been made or that a constable may be acting in an investigation into laundering passes on information to a client which is likely to prejudice an investigation.

(11) Solicitors who conduct investment business within the meaning of the Financial Services Act 1986 must also comply with the Money Laundering Regulations 1993.

(12) Solicitors employed in private practice or in any other employment by a lay employer are subject to the same general principles of professional conduct as apply to principals in private practice.

Chapter 8

OBTAINING INSTRUCTIONS

8.1 INTRODUCTION

Traditionally, a solicitor obtained his instructions through his own reputation. An existing client would recommend his friends and colleagues to the solicitor and so on, leading to a client base made up from personal contacts. Much of a solicitor's business is still obtained in this way, but in recent years a more commercial approach to the organisation and running of solicitors' practices has been adopted and solicitors are now permitted to advertise their services in much the same way as any commercial organisation does.

8.2 GENERAL PRINCIPLE

It is fundamental to the relationship which exists between solicitor and client that a solicitor should be able to give impartial and frank advice to the client, free from any external or adverse pressures or interests which would destroy or weaken the solicitor's professional independence or the fiduciary relationship with the client. This general principle of obtaining instructions will always apply.

8.3 SOLICITORS' PRACTICE RULES 1990, RULE 1

Although solicitors are now generally free to decide how they wish to obtain their business, this freedom must be exercised within the constraints of the Solicitors' Practice Rules 1990, Rule 1.

8.3.1 Freedom of choice to instruct any solicitor

A prospective client must have a free choice as to whom to instruct. Thus it would be wrong for a solicitor to stipulate that a particular solicitor should be his or her opponent. Equally, a solicitor must not accept instructions knowing that a third party has stipulated that the solicitor must act.

There would be a breach of Rule 1 if, for example, a solicitor acting for a landlord required a prospective tenant not to instruct a named solicitor for advice about the lease, because the landlord's solicitor knew that the named solicitor had already given advice to another prospective tenant suggesting that the lease was drawn in unfavourable terms. This situation might also be regarded as unprofessional conduct on the part of the landlord's solicitor.

A breach would also occur if, for example, a solicitor acting for the defendant in litigation offered a settlement on the terms that the plaintiff's solicitor should agree not to act for the plaintiff in future litigation against the client of the defendant's solicitor.

8.3.2 Claims assessors

To preserve the independence and integrity of the solicitor and the profession, a solicitor is not permitted to obtain instructions through a claims assessor (Rule 9). A claims assessor is a person (not a solicitor) who works on behalf of a 'client' to obtain compensation for that client (usually in a personal injury action) from a third party. A claims assessor is usually paid a percentage of the damages recovered (a contingency fee) and thus may be motivated to pursue a possibly worthless claim to its limits in the hope of recovering his fee. To accept instructions from such a person might involve the solicitor in giving advice to the claimant which was not wholly in the claimant's interests, because of the solicitor's relationship with the claims assessor.

8.3.3 Fee-sharing

To permit a solicitor to share his fees with a non-solicitor might similarly involve the solicitor in being influenced by his fee-sharer into giving advice which was not in a particular client's best interests in order not to offend the fee-sharer. For this reason the solicitor is (subject to limited exceptions) prohibited by Rule 7 from sharing his fees with any person who is not a solicitor or a registered foreign lawyer. This latter restriction will be relaxed if provisions permitting multi-disciplinary partnerships are introduced.

8.3.4 Duty to the court

As an officer of the court, the solicitor owes a duty to the court and instructions must not be obtained or accepted in any circumstances which would prejudice the solicitor's duty to the court. Instructions should therefore be declined in any situation where it is apparent that the client intends to commit perjury in giving his evidence to the court.

8.3.5 Law Society Guidelines

Guidance issued by The Law Society relating to the interpretation of Rule 1 stresses that where two or more of the Rule 1 principles come into conflict the determining factor in deciding which principle should take precedence must be the public interest and especially the interests of the administration of justice.

8.4 INDIRECT INSTRUCTIONS

Where instructions are received not from a client but from a third party on behalf of that client, a solicitor should obtain written instructions from the client that he wishes him to act or see the client in order to obtain instructions directly from him.

It is a general principle of professional conduct that a prospective client who is seeking a solicitor must have a free choice as to whom to instruct. The solicitor who obtains instructions indirectly must therefore expressly confirm those instructions with the client himself.

Example

A friend gives you instructions to sell a house on behalf of his mother who is the owner of the house. The 'client' is the mother, not the friend, and the mother's instructions to act in the sale must be confirmed directly with her to ensure that she wishes the sale to go ahead and is not being pressurised into the sale by her son.

8.5 ADVERTISING

Rule 2 of the Solicitors' Practice Rules 1990 permits a solicitor to advertise his practice provided that the advertisement complies with the Solicitors' Publicity Code 1990.

Advertisements must:

(1) not breach the Solicitors' Publicity Code 1990 or the Solicitors' Practice Rules 1990;
(2) be in good taste;
(3) not be inaccurate or misleading;
(4) comply with the general law.

8.5.1 The Solicitors' Publicity Code 1990

The Solicitors' Publicity Code 1990 generally forbids:

(1) unsolicited visits or telephone calls to the general public;
(2) comparisons with other identifiable firms.

Subject to the constraints listed above, a solicitor is free to advertise his practice in any way in which he thinks fit. If he wishes he can use direct mail shots to the general public, sponsor events at sporting competitions or advertise in newspapers, on television or radio.

The Solicitors' Publicity Code 1990 and the Solicitors' Practice Rules 1990 lay down limits to what is acceptable by way of advertising. The requirement that an advertisement must not be inaccurate or misleading can be judged objectively as a matter of fact, but the rule that an advertisement must be in good taste can only be viewed subjectively, and an advertisement which may be perfectly in order when appearing in a local cinema may not be in good taste if it appears in another context, for example, if it is displayed on the side of a home delivery pizza van.

Example

Two young solicitors have just set up a practice in a quiet seaside town where the population largely consists of elderly people. Being anxious to corner the wills/probate market in the town, the practice decides to advertise the firm in the following ways:

(1) by erecting a large advertisement hoarding adjacent to the local hypermarket;
(2) by sponsoring the gorgeous grandma competition at the local carnival;
(3) by holding an expensive party at the Hotel Splendide to which all the doctors, funeral directors and bank managers will be invited;

(4) by paying the local newsagent to deliver the firm's promotional literature with the morning newspapers;

(5) by paying the local health authority to display the firm's name address and telephone number on the side of their ambulances and in the outpatients' department of the local hospital.

Subject to the constraints outlined above, it would appear that (1)–(4) inclusive would all be permitted advertising, although the advertisement hoarding may need planning permission. Displaying advertisements on the side of an ambulance would probably not be considered to be in good taste, although a similar advertisement on the side of a bus would not offend the Code. Whether an advertisement is in good taste is a matter of judgment in the circumstances of each case – some firms do advertise in hospital casualty departments, other firms might consider that this offends the Code.

8.5.2 Purpose of advertising

An advertisement which publicises the services offered by a local firm of solicitors does not fulfil the same function as an advertisement for a new brand of washing powder. The average client does not need the services of a solicitor as regularly as he needs washing powder. Professional and effective advertising is expensive and a firm first needs to consider what it hopes to achieve from its advertising campaign, and then how its budget can most effectively be utilised to fulfil that purpose. Advertising by solicitors does not generally yield new clients in the same way that the advertising of a consumer product may enhance the sales of that product. Possibly the main benefit of solicitors' advertising is that it raises the public profile of the particular firm, so that, when eventually a prospective client needs a solicitor, the name of the firm which has been advertising springs to mind, leading him to instruct the firm whose name he is familiar with, rather than hunt through the telephone directory for the names of other firms. Most firms take advertisements in Yellow Pages and trade directories. Many firms have brochures, promotional literature and newsletters which describe their services. Some firms use marketing devices such as pens and key fobs bearing the firm's logo, others advertise in local papers or in theatre programmes, but at present only a minority of firms actively advertise their services on a regular basis.

Another purpose of advertising is to heighten public awareness of what solicitors do, and to reduce the fear and mystique surrounding the legal profession which may inhibit the client from going to see a solicitor. This function of advertising can sometimes best be fulfilled by 'group advertising'; a group of solicitors' firms, or perhaps the local law society, join together to fund an advertising campaign to make the public aware of the existence of solicitors in the locality.

8.5.3 Responsibility for advertising

It is the responsibility of the solicitor to ensure that all publicity for his services, whether issued by the solicitor or by another person on the solicitor's behalf, complies with the provisions of the Code. The responsibility cannot be delegated. Where a solicitor becomes aware that any publicity issued by him or on his behalf is in breach of the Code, he must use his best endeavours to have the publicity corrected or withdrawn as appropriate.

Example

A solicitor asks his trainee to draft an advertisement for the firm which is to appear in the local newspaper. When the advertisement is published it is found that the advertisement directly compares the firm's conveyancing charges with those of other firms in the same town. The advertisement as drafted is in breach of the Code which forbids a comparison of fees. Steps must immediately be taken to withdraw the advertisement or to amend it by deleting the references to the fees comparison. In theory the solicitor should not act for any client who had come to the firm as a result of reading the incorrect advertisement because the instructions obtained in this way would be tainted by breach of Rule 2. This problem could have been avoided if the solicitor had checked the contents of the trainee's draft advertisement before sending it to the newspaper.

8.6 INTRODUCTIONS AND REFERRALS

Rule 3 of the Solicitors' Practice Rules 1990 permits a solicitor to enter into an arrangement with a third party for the introduction of clients to the solicitor by the third party or for the referral of the clients to the third party by the solicitor. In this way a solicitor may have an arrangement with a local estate agent to act for clients of the estate agent who do not already have a solicitor acting on their behalf. Similarly, an arrangement could be made so that, if one of the solicitor's clients needed a mortgage, the solicitor would refer that client to a local building society with whom he had an arrangement. Arrangements must not contravene Rule 1 of the Solicitors' Practice Rules 1990, nor any other practice rules, and must comply with the Solicitors' Introduction and Referral Code 1990 (as amended), which applies only to introductions between solicitors and third parties; it does not affect arrangements for the introduction or referral of clients between one solicitor and another, so that where a solicitor finds that he cannot act for a client in a particular situation, the referral of that client to another solicitor for advice is not restricted by the Code.

8.6.1 Payment for introductions

Although a solicitor is permitted to enter into an arrangement with, for example, an estate agent or insurance broker for clients to be referred to him by the agent or broker, the solicitor is not permitted to pay the third party for the introduction. Where a client is referred to the third party by the solicitor, any commission received by the solicitor for effecting the introduction is subject to the Solicitors' Practice Rules 1990, Rule 10 which restricts the circumstances in which the solicitor is entitled to retain the commission.

8.6.2 Best interests of the client

A solicitor must always give his client advice which is independent and in the best interests of the client concerned. Where a solicitor is dependent on a limited number of sources for the introduction of his business, a conflict may arise between the interests of an individual client and the interests of the solicitor in not offending the person who introduced the business. The Solicitors' Introduction and Referral Code stresses that the interests of the individual client are always paramount. A solicitor who recommends a client to a third party must do so in good faith, judging what is in the client's best interests. Any agreement entered into where the solicitor recommends clients to a third party must not restrict the solicitor's freedom to recommend clients to other third parties if this would be in the best interests of the client.

8.6.3 Record-keeping

Firms are required to keep a record of agreements for the introduction of work and should check at six-monthly intervals:

(1) that the provisions of the Solicitors' Introduction and Referral Code have been complied with;
(2) that referred clients have received impartial advice; and
(3) the income arising from each agreement for the introduction of business.

Where more than 20 per cent of a firm's income during a period under review has been obtained from a single source of introduction, the firm should consider whether steps should be taken to reduce that proportion in order to retain the independence of the firm and the impartiality of the advice given to clients.

8.6.4 Payment by a third party

A solicitor may enter an arrangement with a third party to provide legal services for customers of the third party, the solicitor being paid for those services by the introducer. For example, the solicitor may agree to do conveyancing work for the clients of an insurance company, where the company agrees to pay the solicitor's bill for the work done. This type of arrangement is not confined to non-contentious business (non-court work) but is not permitted where the introducer is a seller or his agent and conveyancing work is to be carried out for the buyer. Such an agreement must be in writing and a copy of it must be available for inspection by The Law Society or the Office for the Supervision of Solicitors (OSS).

Any agreement between the introducer and his customer for the provision of the legal services by the solicitor must:

(1) expressly mention the independence of the solicitor's professional advice;
(2) provide that control of the legal advice given to the customer lies solely with the solicitor;
(3) provide that information revealed to the solicitor by the customer will not be disclosed to the introducer without the customer's consent.

In the situation where the solicitor is being paid for his services by the introducer rather than the client, there is a danger of a conflict of interests arising, and the solicitor must decline to act if such a conflict arises or is likely to arise.

8.6.5 Advertisements placed by an introducer

Advertisements placed by the introducer advertising the introducer's services and mentioning that the legal work will be undertaken by the solicitor must comply with the Solicitors' Introduction and Referral Code which, in particular, places stringent requirements on the way in which the pricing of the introducer's services is stated in the advertisement. The introducer must also give his client a notice in writing detailing the services which are to be offered and the price which the client is to pay for them.

8.7 DISCRIMINATION

The Solicitors' Anti-Discrimination Rules 1995 provides that 'solicitors must not discriminate on grounds of race, sex or sexual orientation, and must not discriminate unfairly or unreasonably on grounds of disability, in their professional dealings with clients, staff, other solicitors, barristers or other persons'. This rule is supplemented by the Solicitors' Anti-Discrimination Code. Principal solicitors in private practice must operate a policy dealing with the avoidance of discrimination and, in the absence of a specific policy, will be deemed to have adopted the model policy published by The Law Society.

Discrimination amounts to professional misconduct and may therefore be the subject of disciplinary action against a solicitor who is in breach of the Solicitors' Anti-Discrimination Rules 1995.

Unlawful discrimination may also lead to proceedings under the Race Relations Act 1976, the Sex Discrimination Act 1975, or the Disability Discrimination Act 1995.

8.8 CHAPTER SUMMARY

(1) The general principle of obtaining instructions means that the solicitor should always be independent and impartial when giving advice to a client.
(2) A client has complete freedom to choose any solicitor he or she wishes.
(3) If instructions are received not from the client but from a third party, the solicitor should take steps to confirm the instructions from the client direct.
(4) There are Rules and Codes of Conduct governing publicity and referrals.
(5) Rule 7 of the Solicitors' Practice Rules 1990 broadly states that a solicitor cannot share fees with a non-solicitor. The purpose of Rule 7 is to safeguard the solicitor's independence and his ability to give impartial advice to clients. There are exceptions contained in Rule 7 itself.
(6) Rule 9 of the Solicitors' Practice Rules 1990 essentially forbids solicitors from taking on personal injury work introduced by claims assessors who themselves obtain the work on a contingency fee basis.
(7) Solicitors must adhere to the Solicitors' Anti-Discrimination Code.

Chapter 9

THE RETAINER

9.1 INTRODUCTION

The contract between the solicitor and his client is called 'the retainer'. Although some special rules apply to the solicitor/client relationship, the retainer is governed by the normal principles which apply to English contract law.

9.2 ACCEPTANCE OF INSTRUCTIONS

A solicitor is generally free to decide whether or not to accept instructions from any particular client. Instructions which are received from a third party acting on behalf of a client (eg instructions to draw up a will which are received from the testator's relative) must be confirmed directly with the client to ensure that the client, of his own free will, does wish those instructions to be carried out by that solicitor and that there is no breach of Rule 1 of the Solicitors' Practice Rules 1990 (see Chapter 8).

9.3 DECLINING INSTRUCTIONS TO ACT

The solicitor should decline to accept the instructions in the following circumstances.

(1) To accept the instructions or to continue to act would involve the solicitor in a breach of the law (eg the client wants to perpetrate a fraud on a third party).

(2) To accept the instructions or to continue to act would involve the solicitor in a breach of the rules of conduct (eg acting for both parties in a conveyancing transaction in breach of the Solicitors' Practice Rules 1990, Rule 6 (as amended)).

(3) The solicitor is asked to bring an action against the client's former solicitor, and the solicitor or one of his partners is a friend or colleague of the potential defendant (because of the potential conflict of interests which would exist in this situation).

(4) There is or is likely to be a conflict of interest between the solicitor and his client or between two clients of the solicitor (see Chapter 13).

(5) The solicitor is not competent to act (eg because he lacks expertise in the particular area of law relating to the client's instructions).

(6) The solicitor is unable to devote sufficient time to the client's affairs (eg because he has too much work in hand already from other clients).

(7) The solicitor has reason to believe that the instructions are tainted by duress or undue influence (eg an elderly client is 'persuaded' by her relatives to sell her stocks and shares and give the money to the relatives).

(8) The solicitor, or one of his partners, employees or close relatives, holds some office or appointment which might lead to a conflict of interest or which might give the impression to the public that the solicitor is able to make use of such appointment for the advantage of the client. The term 'near relative' means

spouse, parent, child, brother or sister, or the spouse of any of these persons. Offices or appointments affected by this principle include:

(a)   recorder and assistant recorder;
(b)   magistrate and clerk to the magistrates;
(c)   chairman of a tribunal;
(d)   member of the Gaming Board;
(e)   coroner;
(f)   member of a police authority;
(g)   member of a Legal Aid Committee;
(h)   member of the Criminal Injuries Compensation Board.

For example, a solicitor who is a member of the local authority planning committee must not act for a client in relation to a planning application which is to be decided by that authority since his membership of the committee might affect, or be thought to affect, the way in which he advised the client, or the way in which he casts his vote on the committee. Most solicitors would act with complete impartiality in this situation, irrespective of any connection with the committee. This restriction is therefore in part a reflection of the principle that justice must not only be done, it must also be seen to be done.

(9)   The instructions involve an agreement precluding the investigation by The Law Society of the conduct of a solicitor or his employee.

(10) The instructions would involve the solicitor acting as advocate for the client in circumstances where the solicitor or a member of his firm will be called as a witness on behalf of the client (unless his evidence is purely formal such as citing his name, address and occupation only) (this restriction is again directed at impartiality and the public conception of justice being seen to be done).

(11) The client's action is malicious or vindictive (eg a libel case which is brought by the client with the sole purpose of creating adverse publicity for the defendant).

(12) Another solicitor is already acting for the client in respect of the same matter. This restriction applies until either the first retainer has been determined by the client, or the first solicitor has consented to the second solicitor acting in his place. Where the second solicitor is instructed after the client has terminated the retainer with the first solicitor, there is no duty on the second solicitor to inform the first solicitor of the fact that he has been instructed, except in litigation matters where the first solicitor is on the record. This does not prevent the second solicitor from giving the client a second opinion on a matter before the first solicitor's retainer has been determined.

Example 1

A client instructs his solicitor to lodge an appeal against a tax assessment. It is discovered that the client has been making fraudulent tax returns. Is it possible to act for him? The solicitor may act provided that the client agrees that he will reveal the true facts to the Inland Revenue. If the client refuses to allow this to be done, the solicitor must decline the instructions because to accept them would involve him in both fraud and conspiracy.

Example 2

A solicitor is instructed to represent a client at an industrial tribunal. Another partner in the same firm is an industrial tribunal chairman in the area where the case is to be heard. Can the instructions be accepted? If the solicitor appeared at the tribunal hearing where his partner was sitting as chairman, it might appear to the public that the solicitor had some influence over the proceedings because of his connections with the chairman. Although the solicitor can act in this situation, he and his partner must ensure that the hearing takes place before a tribunal on which the partner is not sitting. The partner (the chairman) cannot appear in front of any tribunal in the area in which he sits as chairman, and therefore could not take over this case if the hearing took place when the instructed solicitor was away from the office on holiday.

9.3.1 Unacceptable reasons for refusing instructions

Subject to **9.2**, the solicitor cannot decline to act:

(1) on the basis of the colour, race or national or ethnic origins of the client (Race Relations Act 1976);

(2) on the basis of the sex or marital status of the client (Sex Discrimination Act 1975);

(3) on the basis of the client's disability (Disability Discrimination Act 1995).

9.4 DUTY TO CLIENT DURING RETAINER

A solicitor who has accepted instructions on behalf of a client is bound to carry out those instructions with diligence and must exercise reasonable care and skill. This duty in conduct is supplementary to the statutory duty to carry out work with reasonable care and skill which is implied in a contract to supply services by the Supply of Goods and Services Act 1982, s 13 (as amended). The statutory duty does not apply to a solicitor who is acting in his capacity as an advocate, but the common law duty of care would still apply to this situation (see the Supply of Services (Exclusion of Implied Terms) Order 1982). Breach of this duty may give rise to an action by the client for breach of contract or in negligence.

9.4.1 Taking instructions

To establish and maintain a good relationship with the client, it is vital to take proper instructions at the outset. These instructions should be clarified with the client and confirmed in writing. The client should be told the issues in the case and how they will be dealt with. The client should have a clear understanding as to exactly what, if any, action is to be taken by both the solicitor and the client – see Chapter 10 for further information.

9.4.2 The client's authority

The solicitor must carry out his instructions within the area of the client's express or implied authority. When taking instructions the solicitor should ensure that the client understands and consents to any actions which the solicitor proposes to take on the client's behalf, and that the extent of the solicitor's authority is clearly understood by both the client and the solicitor. A written retainer is advisable but not legally necessary except in certain circumstances, for example where financial services are involved.

9.4.3 Confidentiality

A duty to keep the client's business and affairs confidential at all times is owed by the solicitor and his staff to the client. It is the solicitor's responsibility to ensure that his staff observe this rule (see Chapter 14).

9.4.4 Observing the rules of conduct

It is an implied term of the retainer that the solicitor will observe the rules of conduct. The solicitor's obligation to observe the rules of conduct prevails over his duty to the client and the client must accept the limitations imposed on the solicitor's freedom to carry out the client's wishes. If the client insists that the solicitor carries out a course of action which would involve the solicitor in a breach of the rules of conduct, the solicitor must cease to act.

9.4.5 Taking advantage of the client

A solicitor must not take advantage of the age, inexperience, lack of education or business experience or ill health of the client.

9.4.6 Keeping the client informed

During the retainer, the solicitor is under a duty to keep the client properly informed (Solicitors' Practice Rules 1990, Rule 15, as amended). This includes informing the client about the costs of the transaction and of recent or impending changes in the law where such changes would affect the client's affairs.

The solicitor must comply with the client's reasonable requests for information concerning his affairs. The solicitor should at regular intervals report to the client on the progress of the client's case or transaction.

There is a general duty for the solicitor to pass on to his client all information which is material to the client's business regardless of the source of that information, except where the imparting of the information to the client could be harmful to the client's physical or mental condition. If, for example, medical reports disclosed that the client was suffering from a terminal illness, the solicitor would be able to use his discretion in deciding whether to reveal this information to the client. A solicitor should, where possible, decline to accept from a third party information which is to be treated as confidential, since he will be in breach of his duty to his client if he does not pass the information on, but may be in breach of his duty of confidentiality to the third party if he does so.

9.4.7 Authority to bind the client

In certain circumstances, a solicitor has implied authority to bind his client (eg to compromise proceedings), but reliance should not normally be placed on the existence of implied authority to perform an act. The solicitor should obtain the client's express authority unless the matter is urgent and the client's consent cannot be obtained. If the solicitor exceeds his authority, he may be liable to a third party for breach of warranty of authority (see *Suleman v Shahisavari* [1989] 2 All ER 460).

9.4.8 Duty to the court

As an officer of the court the solicitor owes a duty to the court as well as to his client and there may be circumstances when these two obligations conflict. In particular, the solicitor, while owing a duty to do the best for his client in litigation, must never mislead or deceive the court.

9.4.9 Avoiding delay

The solicitor owes a duty to the client to deal with the client's affairs promptly. This includes dealing promptly with correspondence relating to the client's affairs and responding to telephone calls received.

9.4.10 Costs

At the beginning of the transaction or matter the solicitor is required to give the client certain information relating to costs and he must keep the client informed as to costs as the matter progresses.

9.4.11 File management and review

The solicitor should adopt appropriate file management methods. Full and accurate attendance notes, checklists, sub-files and diary notes of critical dates and deadlines will all serve to protect the interests of the client. An appropriate file review system, where every file is checked, say, every two weeks, will also help to prevent delay on the part of the solicitor or, indeed, the client, if a response by the client is awaited.

9.4.12 Client care

A solicitor is required to inform clients about the firm's complaints-handling process (see Chapter 10). If the above points are observed, however, the solicitor should give his clients a good service.

9.5 FIDUCIARY RELATIONSHIPS

The relationship between a solicitor and his client is fiduciary, leading to a presumption of undue influence in any transaction entered into between the solicitor and his client.

For this reason, great care should be exercised if a solicitor is to buy property from or sell property to one of his own clients. The presumption of undue influence is rebuttable and to ensure that the transaction will not be set aside the following steps should be taken:

(1) the client should receive independent advice (ie from a separate firm);
(2) a fair price, ascertained by an independent valuation of the property, must be paid;
(3) the client must be aware of all the relevant circumstances (ie there is no question of being able to avoid the presumption of undue influence by buying or selling through a nominee).

9.5.1 Other examples of fiduciary relationships

Fiduciary relationships also exist between the following parties:

(1) parent and child (depending on the circumstances, the fiduciary element in this relationship can exist even after the child attains the age of majority);

(2) trustee and beneficiary;

(3) teacher and pupil;

(4) religious adviser and follower;

(5) fiancé and fiancée.

This list is not exhaustive, and a fiduciary relationship may exist in any circumstances where one party exerts a dominant influence over the other (eg *Lloyds Bank Ltd v Bundy* [1975] QB 326). The relationship between husband and wife is not necessarily a fiduciary one, but in any dealings between husband and wife it is sensible to ensure that the parties receive separate independent advice. In any situation where a fiduciary relationship exists or is thought to exist, the same firm of solicitors should not act for both parties, and the solicitors acting should ensure that the client is aware of all the circumstances surrounding the transaction and that the price paid or consideration for the agreement is fair.

Dealings between trustees and beneficiaries, voluntary settlements and gifts are the types of fiduciary situation most likely to be encountered in practice. Voluntary settlements and gifts will additionally be subject to the Insolvency Act 1986 and a declaration of solvency by the donor of the property may be required.

Example
Trustees of a trust for which the firm act have agreed to sell a house which is part of the trust's property to one of the beneficiaries. The beneficiary is also a trustee of the trust. What matters should be checked to ensure the validity of the transaction? This proposed transaction will be affected not only by the fiduciary relationship between trustee and beneficiary, but is also potentially a voidable transaction because it involves the sale of trust property by trustees to one of their number. In no circumstances should the same firm act for both seller and buyer in this situation, and it should be confirmed that a proper valuation of the property has been made and that all material facts are revealed. In addition to these factors which affect the fiduciary element of the transaction, the solicitor should ensure that one of the circumstances which justifies a sale of trust property by trustees to a co-trustee exists. These factors are:

(1) the trustee is entitled to the property as a beneficiary under the terms of the trust (as the proposed transaction here is a sale and not a gift, this exception may not be relevant in the circumstances of this question);

(2) the trustee had a contract or option to buy the property which was entered into before the trust came into being;

(3) all the beneficiaries (being sui juris) consent to the transaction;

(4) the transaction is authorised by a court order or by the trust instrument.

9.6 GIFTS TO SOLICITORS

Where a client intends to make a gift inter vivos or by will to his solicitor, to the solicitor's partner or a member of staff or to the families of any of them, and the gift is of a significant amount, either in itself or having regard to the size of the client's estate and the reasonable expectations of prospective beneficiaries, the solicitor must advise the client to be independently advised as to that gift, and if the client declines, must refuse to act. This principle is strictly interpreted and, except in cases where the gift or bequest is clearly of nominal value only (eg an inexpensive bottle of wine at Christmas), the solicitor has three choices open to him:

(1) to decline the gift or bequest;
(2) to decline to act;
(3) to insist that the client has independent advice.

Since a fiduciary relationship is deemed to exist between a solicitor and his client it follows that any gift made by a client to his solicitor may raise a presumption of undue influence. If the solicitor does not follow one of the three choices, then he will lose the gift and could also face disciplinary proceedings.

Example 1

An elderly client for whom the firm has acted for many years instructs his solicitor to draw up a new will which is to include a legacy of £10,000 to the solicitor. Can the solicitor draw up the will, and can he include in it the gift to himself? The first question to be asked is whether the gift is of a significant amount, either in itself or having regard to the size of the testator's estate and the expectations of the other beneficiaries. If the gift is of a significant amount, the solicitor should not accept it unless the client receives independent advice as to the gift. If the gift is not of a significant amount, the solicitor may accept it provided that he is satisfied that the client does not feel obliged to make such a gift. In this situation there will be no need for the client to be independently advised.

Example 2

A case of whisky is delivered to the solicitor's office by a grateful client for whom the solicitor has just successfully negotiated a large commercial contract. It is not Christmas. Can the solicitor keep this gift or should he return it to the client? Provided the solicitor is satisfied that the size of the gift is nominal in relation to the client's assets, there is no reason why a gift made in these circumstances should not be accepted.

9.7 TERMINATION OF RETAINER

9.7.1 Termination by client

The client may terminate the retainer at any time and for any reason. When instructions are withdrawn the solicitor will be entitled to charge the client for work done on a quantum meruit basis and may have a lien over certain documents belonging to the client until his reasonable charges are paid.

9.7.2 Termination by solicitor

A solicitor must not terminate his retainer with his client except for good reason and on reasonable notice.

Examples of good reasons for termination include:

(1) where the solicitor cannot continue to act without being in breach of the law (eg the client asks the solicitor to do something which would be a criminal offence);
(2) where the solicitor cannot continue to act without being in breach of the rules of conduct (eg a conflict of interest arises between the solicitor and his client);
(3) where the solicitor is unable to obtain instructions from the client (eg having written to the client and having tried to contact the client by telephone on several occasions the solicitor has received no reply from the client);
(4) where there is a serious breakdown in confidence between the solicitor and the client (eg the solicitor having properly and correctly advised the client, the client refuses to follow the solicitor's advice);
(5) where the client refuses to pay an interim bill in a contentious matter.

9.7.3 Termination by operation of law

The retainer may be terminated by operation of law where the solicitor becomes bankrupt or of unsound mind. Unless the solicitor practises on his own these matters will not normally affect the retainer, since the solicitor's partners will take over the work and carry out the client's instructions.

Where the client becomes of unsound mind, the solicitor should consult with the client's relatives and may also contact the Court of Protection or the Official Solicitor for advice.

9.7.4 Effects of termination

On termination a solicitor should, subject to his lien, deliver to the client all papers and property to which the client is entitled or hold them to his order and account for all funds of the client then held by the solicitor.

At the conclusion of the matter the solicitor should:

(1) write to the client confirming completion of the matter;
(2) where necessary summarise the continuing consequences of the resolution of the matter;
(3) subject to any lien which may exist, deliver to the client all papers or property to which the client is entitled (or hold them to the client's order); and
(4) account to the client for funds held by the solicitor.

9.7.5 Return of papers to the client

Documents which were in existence before the retainer began and which the solicitor holds as agent for the client or a third party should, subject to the solicitor's lien, be dealt with in accordance with the client's instructions.

Documents coming into existence during the retainer have the following status.

(1) Documents which the solicitor prepared for the client belong to the client once the solicitor has been paid. Examples of documents within this category include: instructions and briefs, and copies made by the solicitor of letters written by him to third parties. Copies of letters written by the solicitor to his own client belong to the solicitor.
(2) Documents prepared by the solicitor for his own benefit and for which the client was not charged belong to the solicitor. Examples of documents within this

category include inter-office memoranda, attendance notes and accounts book entries.

(3) Documents sent by the client to the solicitor, the ownership of which is intended to pass to the solicitor, belong to the solicitor, but copyright remains in the client unless expressly released. Documents within this category include letters written by the client to the solicitor.

(4) Documents prepared by a third party during the retainer and sent to the solicitor belong to the client. Examples of documents within this category include letters from third parties to the solicitor, experts' reports and counsel's opinions.

9.8 LIENS

At common law, a solicitor has a lien over his client's property until his costs are paid. He may also ask the court to direct that property recovered by the solicitor in an action brought on the client's behalf should be retained by the solicitor as security against the solicitor's costs. A third type of lien exists by virtue of the Solicitors Act 1974, s 73, which empowers the court to make a charging order over real or personal property belonging to the client as security for the solicitor's taxed costs. The common law lien attaches to all deeds, papers and other personal property of the client which come into the solicitor's possession with the client's consent. Such property must have been received by the solicitor in his capacity as solicitor. No lien attaches to a client's will nor to money which the solicitor holds in the capacity of stakeholder. The lien is restricted to costs due to the solicitor in respect of work done on the client's instructions. The solicitor is entitled to retain the client's property until his costs are paid in full. The existence of the lien does not entitle the solicitor to sell or otherwise dispose of the client's property. Despite the existence of a lien, The Law Society has power to order a solicitor to hand over papers to one of its officers where there is an intervention in a solicitor's practice (Solicitors Act 1974, Sch 1) and the court also has power to order papers to be delivered (Solicitors Act 1974, s 68). On termination of the retainer where the client has instructed another solicitor to act for him, the first solicitor should hand over papers and documents to the second solicitor, subject to obtaining a satisfactory undertaking from the second solicitor in respect of payment of the first solicitor's costs. Where a client is legally aided the solicitor's costs are in effect secured by the existence of the legal aid order or certificate and it is in these circumstances inappropriate to call for an undertaking when papers are handed to a new solicitor.

Example

A solicitor is instructed by a client who is seeking to recover damages for injuries sustained in a road traffic accident. More than 2 years ago the client had given instructions to Turgid and Co to start proceedings on her behalf, but as Turgid and Co had not apparently taken any steps to issue a writ she had terminated her retainer with them and wants the new solicitor to act on her behalf in order to pursue the action. The client has asked Turgid and Co to send their papers to the newly instructed solicitor, but they refuse to do this until they are paid for the work which they have done. The client does not want to pay Turgid and Co any costs since she does not believe they deserve any. How should the client be advised?

Since the client has terminated her retainer with Turgid and Co, the new solicitor advises her. Turgid and Co are entitled to a lien on the papers until they are paid their reasonable charges but should release the file to the new solicitor on receipt of a satisfactory undertaking in relation to their costs. The solicitor must obtain the client's permission for such an undertaking to be given and then request the file from Turgid and Co. If Turgid and Co still refuse to hand over the papers after they have been offered a satisfactory undertaking, the solicitor can apply for a court order for Turgid and Co to hand over the papers.

9.9 CHAPTER SUMMARY

9.9.1 Acceptance of instructions

(1) A solicitor is generally free to decide whether to accept instructions from any particular client but any refusal to act must not be based upon the race, sex or sexual orientation, disability or creed of the prospective client.

(2) A solicitor cannot be retained by a client who does not have mental capacity but there is a presumption of capacity unless the contrary is shown.

(3) In working as an advocate (but not in respect of the provision of any other legal services) a solicitor is not permitted to withhold those services on the ground that the nature of the case is objectionable to him personally or to a section of the public; nor on the grounds that the conduct, opinions or beliefs of the prospective client are unacceptable to him or to any section of the public (Courts and Legal Services Act 1990, s 17(3)).

9.9.2 When instructions must be refused

(1) A solicitor must not act or, where relevant, must cease to act further where the instructions would involve the solicitor in a breach of the law or a breach of the principles of professional conduct unless the client is prepared to change his instructions appropriately.

(2) A solicitor must not act or continue to act in circumstances where he cannot represent the client with competence or diligence.

(3) A solicitor must not accept instructions where he suspects that those instructions have been given by a client under duress or undue influence.

(4) A solicitor must refuse to take action which he or she believes is solely intended to gratify a client's malice or vindictiveness.

(5) A solicitor must not act, or must decline to act further, where there is a conflict of interests.

(6) A solicitor must decline to act where either he, his partner, employer, employee or near relative holds some office or appointment which may lead to a conflict of interests or which might give the impression to the public that the solicitor is able to make use of such appointment for the advantage of the client.

(7) A solicitor must not accept instructions to act in a matter where another solicitor is acting for the client in respect of the same matter, until either the first retainer has been determined by the client, or the first solicitor has consented to the second solicitor acting in his place.

9.9.3 Duties owed by a solicitor during the retainer

(1) A solicitor who has accepted instructions on behalf of a client is bound to carry out those instructions with diligence and must exercise reasonable care and skill.

(2) A solicitor should take detailed instructions and confirm them with their client. During the progress of the matter, the solicitor should work in an organised manner and undertake regular file reviews.

(3) A solicitor must keep his client's business and affairs confidential.

(4) It is an implied term of his retainer that a solicitor is under a duty, at all times, to observe the principles of professional conduct.

(5) A solicitor must not take advantage of the age, inexperience, want of education or business experience or ill health of his client.

(6) A solicitor is under a duty to keep his client properly informed and to comply with reasonable requests from the client for information concerning his affairs.

(7) A solicitor is under a duty to consider and advise a client on the availability of legal aid where the client might be entitled to assistance under the Legal Aid Act 1988.

(8) In certain circumstances, the solicitor has implied authority to bind his client but reliance should not normally be placed on the existence of this.

9.9.4 Termination of retainer

(1) A solicitor must not terminate the retainer with his client except for good reason and upon reasonable notice.

(2) A client can terminate a solicitor's retainer for any reason.

(3) The retainer may be determined by operation of law, for example the client's or solicitor's bankruptcy or mental incapacity.

(4) In certain circumstances, a solicitor may retain client's property, including papers, until the solicitor's reasonable costs are paid.

9.9.5 Gifts to solicitors

Where a client intends to make a gift during his lifetime or by will to his solicitor, the solicitor must advise the client to be independently advised as to that gift, and, if the client declines, must refuse to act. This principle applies only where the gift is of a significant amount, either in itself or having regard to the size of the client's estate and the reasonable expectations of prospective beneficiaries. However, the principle does extend to the solicitor's partner, or a member of staff, or to the families of any of them.

Chapter 10

COSTS INFORMATION AND CLIENT CARE

10.1 INTRODUCTION

Rule 15 of the Solicitors' Practice Rules 1990, as amended, requires solicitors to:

(a) give information about costs and other matters; and

(b) operate a complaints handling procedure,

in accordance with a Solicitors' Costs Information and Client Care Code (the Code).

The Code is set out in Appendix 2 to this Part.

This information should ideally be given to the client at a first interview and should be confirmed in writing.

10.2 INFORMATION ABOUT COSTS

Under the Code, clients should be given the best information possible about the cost of legal services, both at the outset and as a matter progresses.

Solicitors are required to give information concerning:

(1) the likely overall costs, including disbursements and VAT;

(2) the basis of the firm's charges;

(3) whether any further payments are required, either to the solicitor or to a third party;

(4) when and how the client will meet the costs and whether legal insurance or a conditional fee agreement is appropriate;

(5) whether the likely outcome of the matter will justify the expense or risk involved, including the risk of having to bear an opponent's costs.

Further guidance is given in the case of legally aided clients and privately paying clients in contentious matters.

The Code obliges solicitors to keep their clients properly informed about costs as a matter progresses.

10.3 INFORMATION ABOUT OTHER MATTERS

The main object of the Code is to make sure that clients are given the information they need to understand what is happening at the outset and as a matter progresses.

10.3.1 The issues in the case

Solicitors are required to tell their clients, in appropriate language, the issues in the case and how they will be dealt with. The immediate steps that will be taken must also be clearly explained.

The client should not be left in any doubt as to the action that will be taken, if any, by the solicitor, or, indeed, the client. The solicitor should clarify any ambiguous instructions and then confirm those instructions in writing.

10.3.2 Importance and relevance of documents

Solicitors should advise their clients fully on important documents, particularly those which may have an onerous or adverse impact on the client.

10.3.3 Progress of the matter

Solicitors should keep clients informed about the progress of the matter. Solicitors must also respond promptly to requests for information.

10.3.4 Time-scale

The likely time-scale of the matter should be discussed at the outset. The client should be told the reasons for any serious delay.

At the end of the retainer, the solicitor should confirm to the client that the matter has been concluded.

10.4 SITUATIONS WHERE IT IS INAPPROPRIATE TO PROVIDE FULL INFORMATION REQUIRED BY THE CODE

Guidance in the Code cites the following as examples of situations where it may be inappropriate to provide the client with the full information required by the Code:

(1) for a regular client for whom repetitive work is done, unless there is a change in circumstances (eg a change in the staff who handle the client's matters);

(2) for major commercial clients who are sufficiently familiar with the conduct of their business;

(3) where particular sensitivity is required in handling the matter (eg a death bed will);

(4) in cases of urgency (eg an emergency injunction);

(5) where the solicitor receives confidential information from a third party, which the solicitor judges would be harmful to the client's mental or physical well being if communicated to him;

(6) where the information received by the solicitor from a third party is privileged.

10.5 COMPLAINTS AGAINST SOLICITORS

Rule 15, as amended, requires every principal in private practice to maintain a written complaints handling procedure which must ensure that clients are told whom in the firm they should approach in the event of their being dissatisfied with the service being provided to them.

A written complaints procedure provides certainty as to the procedures to be followed both from the solicitor's and the client's point of view, and will if necessary provide evidence to the Office for the Supervision of Solicitors (OSS) of the existence and extent of the firm's procedures. All staff in the firm should be aware of the existence and content of the document containing the procedures.

At the beginning of a transaction a client should be informed in writing of the name of the person within the firm to whom problems relating to the standard of service should be addressed. Full details of the complaints procedures need not be given at this stage but must be given on request.

The client should also be told, preferably at the first interview, the name and status of the person who is responsible for the day-to-day management of the client's business and that of the principal who is responsible for its overall supervision.

10.5.1 Complaints procedures

Guidelines issued by The Law Society recommend that a model form of complaints handling procedure should incorporate the following features:

(1) the name of a person with whom the client should initially raise his problem (eg the fee earner who is dealing with the client's matter or the fee earner's supervisor);

(2) the name of a person who is to act as an internal reference point where the client's problem cannot be resolved under (1) above (eg the senior partner);

(3) a procedure for the client's grievance to be dealt with and resolved promptly;

(4) personal contact with the client to resolve the problem;

(5) a procedure for clarifying the issue with the client and for telling him what it is proposed should be done to resolve the matter;

(6) positive response to justified criticism (eg apologise, explain fully to the client, transfer the matter to another fee earner, or make a deduction from the client's bill);

(7) central written records of the complaints received, the steps taken to resolve them and their final outcome;

(8) a letter informing the client in writing of the firm's final response to the complaint and, if the client remains dissatisfied, informing the client about the OSS and how to contact them.

10.6 BREACH OF THE CODE

A material breach of the Code could lead to a finding that the solicitor has provided inadequate professional services or, in a serious or persistent case, a finding of professional misconduct. Unreasonable failure to advise a client properly on some matters, particularly on the risks as to costs in litigation or the availability of legal aid, may give rise to a claim in negligence.

10.7 ACTION TO BE TAKEN BY THE FIRM

10.7.1 Information to be given at first interview

At a first interview, The Law Society recommends that a client should be informed of:

(1) the name and status of the person who will be handling the case and the name of another person in the firm whom the client may contact (particularly if a problem arises);
(2) what action the solicitor will be taking on the client's behalf, including the next immediate step in the case or transaction;
(3) what action (if any) the client has to take;
(4) the likely duration of the matter, including the approximate time when the solicitor will next contact the client;
(5) the likely cost of the matter and how this cost will be funded, whether privately, by legal aid or by legal expenses insurance.

10.7.2 Information to be given during the progress of the matter

(1) Confirm the above points in writing, particularly the information on costs.
(2) Keep the client informed.
(3) If there is a delay, advise the client of the reason.
(4) Explain the importance of the documents to the client.
(5) Keep costs under review.
(6) At the end of the matter, write to the client confirming that the matter has been completed.

10.8 CHAPTER SUMMARY

(1) A solicitor is under a duty to keep his client properly informed and to comply with reasonable requests from the client for information concerning his affairs.
(2) This general principle of conduct is supplemented by Rule 15 of the Solicitors' Practice Rules 1990 and the Code.
(3) A complaints-handling procedure must be maintained by the firm.

Chapter 11

FEES AND COSTS

This chapter will look at:

- the controls which exist over the charges solicitors may make to clients;
- how a client may challenge the charges made by a solicitor;
- the need to account to clients for commissions received.

11.1 INTRODUCTION

Although the contract between the solicitor and his client (the retainer) is primarily governed by the ordinary law of contract, the amount which the solicitor charges his client for work done on the client's instructions is not purely a matter for agreement between the solicitor and the client. Statutory controls exist which affect the amount which the solicitor is entitled to charge and which also, in certain circumstances, allow the client to have the solicitor's bill reviewed by either The Law Society or the court to ensure that the amount of the bill is fair and reasonable.

11.2 CONTENTIOUS AND NON-CONTENTIOUS BUSINESS

The amount which a solicitor is entitled to charge, and the method by which the client can challenge the amount of the solicitor's bill, is largely affected by whether the business carried out for the client is contentious or non-contentious.

11.2.1 Contentious business

Contentious business means business done, whether as solicitor or advocate, in or for the purposes of proceedings begun before a court or arbitrator (Solicitors Act 1974, s 87). By the Supreme Court Act 1981, s 128, 'contentious business' is defined as business done in, or for the purpose of, proceedings begun before a court or an arbitrator appointed under the Arbitration Acts, not being a business which falls within the definition of non-contentious or common form probate business. Business is 'contentious' only where proceedings are begun. Therefore if a solicitor writes a letter before action on behalf of a client, but never issues a writ or summons because the matter is settled out of court, the costs charged to the client will be assessed on a non-contentious basis. Once proceedings have been issued, the business becomes contentious and the client's bill, including charges for work done before the issue of the proceedings, will be assessed on the contentious basis.

11.2.2 Non-contentious business

Non-contentious business means all work done by a solicitor which is not contentious.

Although conveyancing and uncontested probate are the most obvious examples of non-contentious work, the definition of non-contentious business encompasses many other areas of practice such as negotiating and drafting commercial agreements and company work. Business becomes contentious only once proceedings have been issued; thus if a solicitor is instructed to recover a debt on behalf of a client and manages to resolve the matter without the issue of proceedings, the matter will be classified as non-contentious business. Proceedings before all tribunals except the Lands Tribunal and Employment Appeals Tribunal are treated as non-contentious business.

Remuneration for non-contentious business is principally governed by the Solicitors' (Non-Contentious Business) Remuneration Order 1994.

11.3 COSTS PAID BY THE CLIENT AND COSTS PAID BY AN UNSUCCESSFUL LITIGANT

11.3.1 Solicitor and client costs

In relation to contentious work, a distinction has to be drawn between the costs which are payable by the unsuccessful litigant in the action, and the costs which each litigant has to pay to his own solicitor. The latter are known as solicitor and client costs. In the contract between the solicitor and his client, the solicitor undertakes to take reasonable care in carrying out the client's instructions, in return for which the client undertakes to pay a reasonable sum for the solicitor's services. These costs, known as 'solicitor and client costs', are the responsibility of the client notwithstanding the successful outcome of any litigation in which the client is entitled to recover his costs from the other litigant under a court order to that effect.

11.3.2 Costs between the parties

Costs between the parties are the costs which the court orders the unsuccessful party to a litigation action to pay to the successful litigant. The amount is assessed in accordance with detailed rules of court and may not in all cases cover in full the amount which the successful litigant is bound to pay to his own solicitor.

The effect of an order that an unsuccessful litigant shall pay all or part of a successful litigant's costs is that a successful litigant is entitled to be reimbursed by the unsuccessful litigant in respect of such costs as are reasonably incurred. However, the successful litigant is still responsible for paying the full amount of his solicitor's reasonable charges, subject to his right to be reimbursed by the unsuccessful litigant. Thus, if the amount that the unsuccessful litigant has been ordered to pay does not cover the full amount that the successful party's solicitor is entitled to charge, the difference will be borne by the successful party. Furthermore, if some problem arises with enforcing payment by the unsuccessful litigant, the successful litigant may have to bear the full amount of the costs.

11.4 THE SOLICITOR'S BILL

A solicitor is under a duty to render a bill of costs to his client within a reasonable time of concluding the matter to which the bill relates. It is considered to be good practice to submit a bill to the client as soon as possible. It is particularly important to do so where the solicitor is already holding sums of money on his client's behalf and is waiting for the client's approval of the bill before deducting his costs and accounting to the client for the balance, or where the client has asked for the papers and the solicitor is claiming a lien over them until his costs are met.

A solicitor's bill of costs should contain sufficient information to identify the matter to which it relates and the period covered by it.

The form of the bill should comply with the Solicitors Act 1974, s 69 and must be signed by the sole practitioner or by one of the partners in a firm. The signature may be either that of the solicitor signing the bill or made in the name of the firm. Alternatively, the letter which accompanies and refers to the bill should be so signed. Unless this provision is complied with the solicitor will be unable to sue on the bill. Disbursements should be separately itemised in the bill.

11.5 COSTS IN CONTENTIOUS MATTERS

(1) The client is liable to pay the solicitor a reasonable sum for the work done on his instructions. He is generally entitled to insist that a bill for contentious business is assessed by the Court and the amount is then determined in accordance with the Civil Procedure Rules 1998.

(2) The basis of the assessment is known as the 'indemnity basis'. The court will not allow any costs which have been incurred unreasonably nor those which, although incurred reasonably, are unreasonable in amount. Under the indemnity basis, any doubt as to reasonableness is resolved in favour of the solicitor.

(3) Under r 44.5 of the Civil Procedure Rules 1998, the court must have regard to all circumstances in deciding whether costs are reasonable or not, including:

   (a) the conduct of all the parties;
   (b) the amount or value of any money or property involved;
   (c) the importance of the matter to the parties;
   (d) the complexity of the matter, or difficulty or novelty of the questions raised;
   (e) the skill, effort, specialised knowledge and responsibility involved;
   (f) the time spent on the case;
   (g) the place where and the circumstances in which work was done.

11.6 COSTS IN NON-CONTENTIOUS MATTERS

Costs in non-contentious matters are generally governed by the Solicitors' (Non-Contentious Business) Remuneration Order 1994.

11.6.1 Solicitors' (Non-Contentious Business) Remuneration Order 1994, r 3

Rule 3 of the Solicitors' (Non-Contentious Business) Remuneration Order 1994 provides that remuneration shall be 'such sum as may be fair and reasonable having regard to all the circumstances of the case'. The following matters must be taken into account:

(1) the complexity of the matter or the difficulty or novelty of the questions raised;
(2) the skill, labour, specialised knowledge and responsibility involved;
(3) the time spent on the business;
(4) the number and importance of the documents prepared or perused, without regard to length;
(5) the place where and the circumstances in which the business or any part thereof is transacted;
(6) the amount or value of any money or property involved;
(7) whether any land involved is registered land within the meaning of the Land Registration Act 1925;
(8) the importance of the matter to the client;
(9) the approval, express or implied, of the entitled person or the express approval of the testator to: (i) the solicitor undertaking all or any part of the work giving rise to the costs; or (ii) the amount of the costs.

11.7 PAYMENTS ON ACCOUNT

A solicitor may, at the outset of the retainer, require the client to make a payment on account of costs and disbursements to be incurred. Where the matter is non-contentious, the solicitor must make his acceptance of the instructions conditional on the client's advance payment. Unless he does this the solicitor will not be able to justify the termination of the retainer if the client does not make the interim payment. Where, in a contentious matter, the client fails to make an interim payment following a request from the solicitor for a reasonable sum on account of costs, the solicitor is entitled to terminate the retainer.

11.8 CLIENT'S RIGHT TO CHALLENGE A BILL

If a client is dissatisfied with the amount of his solicitor's bill, he can challenge it in two different ways: by asking the solicitor to obtain a remuneration certificate or by applying to have the bill assessed by the court. It is important to note that the client has a right to have an assessment by the court whether the costs are contentious or non-contentious but the remuneration certificate procedure is available only for non-contentious business.

11.8.1 Remuneration certificate

In respect of non-contentious business, a client who is dissatisfied with his solicitor's bill may require the solicitor to apply to The Law Society for a remuneration certificate, which will either state that in the opinion of The Law Society the sum charged by the solicitor is fair and reasonable or what lesser sum would be fair and reasonable. The right to a remuneration certificate arises from r 3 of the Solicitors' (Non-Contentious Business) Remuneration Order 1994. If the sum stated in the remuneration certificate is less than the amount of the bill, the client need pay only the amount stated in the certificate. An application for a remuneration certificate is free of charge to the client but is available only where 50 per cent of the solicitor's bill (plus all VAT and disbursements) has been paid by the client.

The client is not entitled to require a remuneration certificate where:

(1) a period of more than one month has expired after the date on which he was notified of his right to such a certificate; or

(2) a bill has been delivered and paid (otherwise than by deduction without authority); or

(3) the High Court has ordered the bill to be assessed;

(4) the profit costs exceed £50,000.

This procedure is generally available only to the solicitor's own client and to residuary beneficiaries where the only executor(s) is/are solicitor(s). A third party who is responsible for the payment of the solicitor's bill (eg a tenant who is responsible for his landlord's solicitor's costs) cannot use this procedure.

11.8.2 Assessment by the court

In addition to, or as an alternative to, a remuneration certificate, the client may apply to have his bill assessed by the court. Where the matter is contentious business, the solicitor should, as a matter of practice, advise the client of his right to have the bill assessed.

The assessment is made by a 'costs officer', ie a costs judge or a district judge, who will assess the costs under the provisions of the Civil Procedure Rules 1998, Parts 43–48. The solicitor will be entitled to be paid his costs of the assessment proceedings by the client unless the court orders otherwise.

The remuneration certificate procedure applies only to the solicitor's fee (profit costs) and not disbursements, whereas a client can ask for a court assessment of:

* the fees alone;
* disbursements alone; or
* both.

11.9 AGREEMENTS IN RESPECT OF CHARGES

An agreed fee is a quotation which cannot be altered (without the consent of the client), irrespective of the fact that the work turns out to be more expensive for the solicitor to undertake than he had anticipated.

11.9.1 Non-contentious business

Costs in non-contentious business matters are generally regulated by the Solicitors' (Non-Contentious Business) Remuneration Order 1994. Notwithstanding the existence of this order, the Solicitors Act 1974, s 57 allows a solicitor to make an agreement with a client for costs in a non-contentious matter. There is no common law right to make an agreement for costs in non-contentious business. In order to displace the Order and to be enforceable under the Act (and under ordinary contract law), the agreement must comply fully with the provisions of s 57 which requires the agreement to:

(1) be in writing;

(2) embody all the terms of the agreement;

(3) be signed by the party to be charged (ie the client) or his agent; and

(4) be reasonable in amount and be in lieu of ordinary profit costs.

Remuneration may be by a gross sum, commission, percentage, salary or otherwise, and should state whether the agreed remuneration is to be inclusive of disbursements and VAT. Where the agreement complies with s 57, the client cannot rely on the remuneration certificate procedure but assessment by the court is available.

11.9.2 Contentious business

Section 59 of the Solicitors Act 1974 permits a solicitor in certain circumstances to make an agreement with a client relating to costs in a contentious matter. Such an agreement must be in writing and contain all the terms of the bargain. It may provide for the solicitor to be remunerated by a gross sum, salary or otherwise but may not permit the solicitor to receive a contingency fee (Solicitors' Practice Rules 1990, Rule 8). The agreement should be signed by both parties. Such an agreement is not enforceable by action but is enforceable by summary application to the court. On application to the court, the court has power to enforce the agreement or set it aside (see *Clare v Joseph* [1907] 2 KB 369).

11.10 VARIABLE FEES

A solicitor may agree with a client to charge a fee which varies according to the outcome. Thus, the solicitor may agree to charge his normal fee if the matter progresses to a satisfactory conclusion but to charge a reduced fee (say half the normal fee) if the outcome is unsuccessful. In litigation, it is now common to work on a 'no win no fee' basis (ie the solicitor will charge no fee if the client loses); however, it is usual in such cases for the agreement to provide that the client will pay the solicitor more than the normal fee (eg 50 per cent more – known as the 'uplift' or success fee) if the client wins.

The general rule is that solicitors are prohibited from making such an arrangement with a client to 'prosecute or defend any action, suit or other contentious proceeding ... save one permitted under statute or by the common law' (Solicitors' Practice Rules, Rule 8(1)). An arrangement in respect of non-contentious business will not fall foul of Rule 8. Therefore, a solicitor could enter into an agreement with a client to recover debts due to the client, on the basis of a fee which varies according to whether the solicitor is successful or not in recovering the debts, provided the agreement is limited to debts recovered without the need to begin legal proceedings.

Where the matter involves the provision of advocacy or litigation services, s 58 of the Courts and Legal Services Act 1990, as amended by the Access to Justice Act 1999, provides that such an agreement, known as a conditional fee agreement, is unenforceable unless it complies with certain conditions. The agreement must, inter alia, be in writing, signed by the solicitor and the client and can only be made in relation to any civil, non-family case. It is not permitted where the client is receiving financial support from the Community Legal Service Fund.

A 'no win no fee' agreement does not necessarily mean that if the client loses he will pay nothing. The agreement prima facie refers only to the solicitor's fees and not disbursements, for example counsel's fees, court fees and witness fees. It may be possible to find a barrister who is also willing to work on a 'no win no fee' basis, but the other disbursements will still be payable. It may, however, be possible for the client to take out an insurance policy against having to pay these disbursements. If, therefore the client can afford to pay the premium for such a policy, known as 'After the Event' insurance, and he loses, he will not have to pay either the solicitor's fees, covered by the conditional fee agreement, or the disbursements, which will be covered by the insurance policy.

11.11 OVERCHARGING

A solicitor must not take advantage of the client by overcharging for work done or to be done. Overcharging the client may be professional misconduct. If a costs officer allows less than one half of the sum charged in a non-contentious matter he is under a duty to report the matter to The Law Society. The solicitor is responsible for ensuring that the amount of the bill is fair and reasonable and cannot escape liability by delegating the preparation of the bill to a costs draughtsman.

11.12 COMMISSION

Under the Solicitors' Practice Rules 1990, Rule 10, a solicitor must normally account to his client for any commission received by him which exceeds £20. Thus, where the solicitor introduces a client to an insurance company for the purposes of the client obtaining an insurance policy and, as a result of that introduction, the solicitor receives commission from the insurance company, that commission will be subject to Rule 10.

The solicitor is entitled to keep a commission which exceeds £20 only if, having disclosed in writing its receipt and the amount to the client, the client agrees that the solicitor may keep the money. If the amount is not known, the solicitor must have disclosed the basis of the calculation of the commission to the client.

The rule does not apply where the solicitor acts as agent for a building society or other financial institution and a member of the public whom the solicitor has not advised as a client about the investment of the money deposits money with the solicitor.

Stock Exchange commissions fall within the scope of the rule.

Example 1
A client who is buying a house needs advice about the sources of mortgage finance. His solicitor recommends him to a firm of insurance brokers with whom the solicitor has done business for many years. The client decides to take out a mortgage and a life insurance policy through the agency of the brokers. The solicitor receives commission from the brokers for having introduced the client to them. Can the solicitor keep the commission? If the commission exceeds £20 (which it is likely to do), Rule 10 applies and the solicitor may keep the money only if the client consents.

Example 2
A solicitor acts as the local agent for the Zenith Building Society. A client deposits £1,200 with the solicitor, to be credited to her account with the Building Society. Some time later the solicitor receives £35 commission from the building society relating to this deposit. Can he keep the commission?

Provided that the client had not been advised by the solicitor as a client in relation to the investment of the money he may keep the commission; otherwise Rule 10 will apply.

11.13 CHAPTER SUMMARY

(1) The amount which a solicitor is entitled to charge is controlled by statute and the control differs according to whether the work is contentious or non-contentious.

(2) Contentious and non-contentious costs:

(a) Under the Solicitors Act 1974, 'contentious business' means business done, whether as solicitor or advocate, in or for the purposes of proceedings begun before a court or arbitrator.

(b) All other work is 'non-contentious'.

(c) No work is contentious unless proceedings have actually begun. Thus, work which is intrinsically of a contentious nature (eg instructions to counsel to settle proceedings) which is done before proceedings are begun is non-contentious business if, in fact, proceedings are never begun (eg by issue of a writ).

(3) Costs paid by the client and costs paid by an unsuccessful litigant:

(a) It is important to distinguish between costs which belong to the solicitor, ie the amount which the client is liable to pay for work done on his instructions, from costs which belong to the litigant, ie those costs which the unsuccessful litigant has been ordered to pay to the successful litigant.

(b) In the contract (the retainer) between a solicitor and his client, the solicitor undertakes to take reasonable care in the carrying out of the client's business and in return the client undertakes to pay the solicitor a reasonable sum for that work. Under this contract, the client is therefore liable to pay the solicitor for work done on the client's instructions. Such costs are known as 'solicitor and client costs'.

(c) The effect of an order that an unsuccessful litigant shall pay all or part of a successful litigant's costs is that the successful litigant is entitled to be reimbursed by the unsuccessful litigant in respect of such costs as were reasonably incurred. Such costs are assessed in accordance with detailed rules of the court. However, the successful litigant is still responsible for paying the full amount of his solicitor's reasonable charges, subject to his right to be reimbursed by the unsuccessful litigant. Thus if the amount that the unsuccessful litigant has been ordered to pay does not cover the full amount that the successful party's solicitor is entitled to charge, the difference will be borne by the successful party. Furthermore, if some problem arises with enforcing payment by the unsuccessful litigant the successful litigant may have to bear the full amount of the costs.

(4) Bills:

(a) A solicitor is under a duty to render a bill of costs to a client within a reasonable time of concluding the matter to which the bill relates.

(b) The bill of costs should contain sufficient information to identify the matter to which it relates and the period covered.

(5) Amount payable – contentious business:

(a) The client is liable to pay the solicitor a reasonable sum for work reasonably done on the client's instructions.

(b) Under the Solicitor's Act 1974 the client is generally entitled to insist that the bill is assessed by the court and the amount is then determined in accordance with the Civil Procedure Rules 1998.

(c) Under the Civil Procedure Rules 1998, the amount of costs to be allowed is in the discretion of the costs officer. In exercising his discretion, the officer must have regard to all relevant circumstances. The particular matters to which the officer should have regard are set out in the Civil Procedure Rules 1998 and are similar to the factors set out in the Solicitors' (Non-Contentious Business) Remuneration Order 1994 (see below).

(6) Amount payable – non-contentious business:

Under the Solicitors' (Non-Contentious Business) Remuneration Order 1994, a solicitor's remuneration shall be such sum as may be fair and reasonable having regard to all the circumstances of the case.

The Solicitors' (Non-Contentious Business) Remuneration Order 1994 sets out a number of detailed factors which need to be taken into account in deciding whether the charge is fair and reasonable:

(a) the complexity of the matter or the difficulty or novelty of the questions raised;

(b) the skill, labour, specialised knowledge and responsibility involved;

(c) the time spent on the business;

(d) the number and importance of the documents prepared or perused without regard to length;

(e) the place where and the circumstances in which the business or any part thereof is transacted;

(f) the amount or value of any money or property involved;

(g) whether any land involved is registered land;

(h) the importance of the matter to the client; and

(i) the approval (express or implied) of the entitled person or the express approval of the testator to:

   (i) the solicitor undertaking all or any part of the work giving rise to the costs, or

   (ii) the amount of the costs.

(7) Payments on account:

(a) A solicitor may, at the outset of the retainer, require the client to make a payment or payment on account of costs and disbursements to be incurred.

(b) In non-contentious matters, the solicitor must make any requirement for the payment on account of fees to be incurred, a condition of accepting instructions (contrast disbursements).

(c) In contentious matters, where a solicitor requests a client to make a reasonable payment on account of costs incurred or to be incurred, and the client refuses or fails within a reasonable time to make that payment, then the refusal or failure will be good cause for the solicitor to terminate the retainer upon giving reasonable notice (Solicitors Act 1974, s 65(2)).

(8) Client's right to challenge a bill:

(a) A client who is dissatisfied with the amount of his solicitor's bill in both contentious and non-contentious business may apply to have the bill assessed by the court.

(b) In respect of non-contentious business, under the Solicitors' (Non-Contentious Business) Remuneration Order 1994 the client may within one month of being notified of his right to do so require the solicitor to obtain a certificate from The Law Society.

   (i)   The certificate (a 'remuneration certificate') will state either:

      – that the sum charged is fair and reasonable; or
      – what sum would be regarded as fair and reasonable.

   (ii) This right to require a certificate is without prejudice to the right under the Solicitors Act 1974 to have the bill assessed by the court.

   (iii) The solicitor need not obtain the certificate unless and until the client has paid one half of the profit costs, all disbursements and all of the VAT. The solicitor or the Solicitors' Complaints Bureau may waive this payment.

(c) Where the matter is contentious business, the solicitor should, as a matter of good practice, advise the client of his right to have the bill assessed.

(d) The remuneration certificate procedure applies to the solicitor's fees only (profit costs) and not disbursements, whereas a client can ask for an assessment of:

   – the fees alone;
   – disbursements alone or;
   – both.

(9) Agreements in respect of charges:

(a) An agreed fee is a quotation which cannot be altered (without the consent of the client), irrespective of the fact that the work turns out to be more expensive for the solicitor to undertake than he had anticipated.

(b) Non-contentious business
   In order to be enforceable the agreement must comply with s 57 of the Solicitors Act 1974, ie it must:

   – be in writing;
   – embody all the terms of the agreement;
   – be signed by the client or his agent;
   – be reasonable in amount and be in lieu of ordinary profit costs.

(c) Contentious business
   Section 59 of the Solicitors Act 1974 allows a solicitor to make an agreement with the client. The agreement must be in writing and contain all the terms. It must be signed by both parties. The agreement is not enforceable by action but is enforceable by summary application to the court.

(10) Variable fees:

(a) The general rule is that solicitors are prohibited from making an arrangement with a client in relation to contentious business where the fee varies according to whether the action is successful or not '... save one permitted under statute or by the common law' (Solicitors' Practice Rules, Rule 8(1)).

(b) Rule 8 does not apply to non-contentious business.

(c) Further, an agreement for a variable fee where the matter involves the provision of advocacy or litigation services, known as a conditional fee agreement, is unenforceable unless it complies with certain conditions (Court and Legal Services Act 1990, s 58). The agreement must, inter alia, be in writing, signed by the solicitor and the client and can be made in relation to any civil, non-family case except where the client is receiving financial support from the Community Legal Service Fund.

(11) Commission:

A solicitor must account to clients for commission received of more than £20 unless, having disclosed it in writing, the client agrees to the solicitor retaining it.

Chapter 12

RECOVERY OF CHARGES

This chapter looks at:

- when a solicitor can sue a client who fails to pay;
- the recovery of interest on an unpaid bill.

12.1 RECOVERY OF FEES

A solicitor cannot sue a client in respect of unpaid charges until one month has expired after delivery of a bill. The bill must be in the proper form and the bill, or the accompanying letter, must be signed by a partner or sole practitioner. The court may give the solicitor leave to sue within the one-month period under s 69 of the Solicitors Act 1974.

In a non-contentious matter, the solicitor must not sue, or threaten to sue, unless he has informed the client in writing of his right to require a remuneration certificate and of his right to seek assessment of the bill.

In a contentious matter, there is no obligation to inform a client of his right to have a bill assessed but The Law Society suggests that it might be 'prudent' to inform a client in a letter before action.

12.2 INTEREST ON THE BILL

In a non-contentious matter, a solicitor may charge interest on the whole or the outstanding part of an unpaid bill with effect from one month after delivery of the bill, provided that notice of the client's right to challenge the bill has been given to him. The rate of interest chargeable is that which is payable on judgment debts.

In contentious business, a solicitor may charge interest on an unpaid bill:

(a) if the right to charge interest has been expressly reserved in the original retainer agreement; or

(b) if the client has later agreed to pay it for a contractual consideration; or

(c) where the solicitor has sued the client and claimed interest under s 35A of the Supreme Court Act 1981 or s 69 of the County Courts Act 1984.

12.3 CHAPTER SUMMARY

(1) Under the Solicitors Act 1974, a solicitor may not sue a client until the expiration of one month from the delivery of a bill delivered in accordance with the requirements of the Act.

(2) The result is that no charge made by a solicitor for business done by him, whether it is contentious or non-contentious, can be enforced, or even assessed,

unless it is evidenced by a bill of costs in proper form duly delivered to the client.

(3) The bill must be signed by the solicitor or, if the costs are due to a firm, by one of the partners of the firm.

(4) In respect of non-contentious business, before the solicitor can take proceedings to recover costs, he must have informed the client in writing of his right to have the bill assessed by the court and of his right to require the solicitor to obtain a remuneration certificate from The Law Society (Solicitors' (Non-Contentious Business) Remuneration Order 1994). The client may ask the firm to obtain the remuneration certificate within one month of being notified of his right to do so. The time-limit may run concurrently with the time-limit referred to in (1) above.

(5) In non-contentious business, a solicitor may charge interest on all or part of an unpaid bill from one month after delivery of the bill, provided sufficient notice has been given to the client as mentioned at (4) above.

(6) In a contentious matter, a solicitor may claim interest only on an unpaid bill if there is a binding contract to pay interest or, when suing the client, he claims interest.

Chapter 13

CONFLICT OF INTERESTS

13.1 GENERAL PRINCIPLE

A solicitor should not accept instructions to act for two or more clients where there is a conflict or a significant risk of a conflict between the interests of those clients. It follows therefore that a solicitor must never act for both plaintiff and defendant in a contested matter, or for both husband and wife in a matrimonial matter. It is possible to act for co-defendants in an action provided that their interests do not conflict.

13.1.1 Relevant knowledge

If a solicitor or firm of solicitors has acquired relevant knowledge concerning a former client during the course of acting for him, he or it must not accept instructions to act against him in another matter. Knowledge acquired by the solicitor when acting for a client is confidential, and cannot be disclosed without that client's consent. However, a solicitor is also under a duty to inform his client of any matter which may be relevant to that client's claim. These two duties clearly conflict when, for example, a solicitor who has acted in the past for client X is asked by client Y to defend client Y in an action brought by client X. For this reason the solicitor will not be able to act for client Y in this particular matter, but would be able to act for him in other matters where no conflict existed.

Examples of conflict
(1) Having advised a company, the solicitor is asked by one of the directors to bring an action against the company.
(2) Having acted jointly for a family, the solicitor is asked to represent one or more of the family members in a dispute against other family members.
(3) Having acted for both lender and borrower on the creation of a mortgage, the solicitor is asked to act for the lender to take proceedings to enforce payment of the mortgage.

13.2 CONFLICT ARISING DURING THE RETAINER

13.2.1 Is there a conflict?

It can sometimes be very difficult to decide whether a conflict of interest has arisen between two clients. *The Law Society's Guide to the Professional Conduct of Solicitors* gives the following guidance to help identify whether a conflict exists.

If the solicitor were acting for one of the parties only:

– Would the advice be different?
– Do the parties have different interests?

– Has one of the parties given the solicitor a piece of information on a 'confidential' basis that would affect the advice given to other clients, if the solicitor could disclose it?

If these factors apply, a conflict of interest has arisen.

13.2.2 Conflict between two clients

A solicitor or firm of solicitors must not continue to act for two or more clients where a conflict of interests arises between those clients. In civil litigation or criminal litigation matters in particular, a conflict of interest may arise during proceedings, even though there was no apparent conflict of interests at the outset of the matter. In these situations, it is likely that the solicitor will have to cease to act for both clients as the solicitor will probably have acquired relevant information.

In some non-contentious matters, it may be possible to represent both parties, but if a conflict does arise during the transaction the solicitor must cease to act further for both parties unless he can continue to act for one client with the consent of the other. Irrespective of the consent of one client, the solicitor will not be able to continue to act for either client if he has acquired relevant knowledge about one client which would affect the way in which he advised the other client. In practical terms, therefore, it is unlikely that the solicitor can continue to act for either client.

Example 1

A solicitor is acting for two men who have been charged with a fraud. At first both defendants told the same story in their defence and both intended to plead 'not guilty'. During the trial one defendant changes his mind and decides to plead guilty to the charge. He also intends to give evidence at the trial against his co-defendant. Although it was acceptable for the solicitor to act for both defendants initially, a conflict of interests has now arisen between them and the solicitor is unlikely to be able to continue to act for either. The solicitor will probably have acquired relevant information about one defendant which could be used against the other, in which case he may not continue to act for one even with the consent of the other.

Example 2

Adam and his friend Samantha were both injured in a road traffic accident when the car in which they were travelling was hit by a lorry. The solicitor can act for both Adam and Samantha in their action for damages against the driver of the lorry provided that no conflict of interests exists or is likely to arise between them. If there is any possibility that Adam was partly to blame for the accident (so that Samantha would have a claim against him as well as against the lorry driver), the solicitor should decline to act for both, but in this situation he could accept instructions to act for one of them, provided the other was separately represented.

13.3 CONVEYANCING

In conveyancing transactions, the general principle has been supplemented by the Solicitors' Practice Rules 1990, Rule 6, as amended. This Rule is discussed in detail in the LPC Resource Book *Conveyancing* (Jordans).

13.4 CONFLICT BETWEEN SOLICITOR AND CLIENT

A solicitor must not act where his own interests conflict with the interests of a client or a potential client. A conflict might arise in a situation where a solicitor was proposing to buy property from or to lend money to one of his own clients. Apart from conflict of interests, a fiduciary relationship exists between a solicitor and his client, giving rise to a presumption of undue influence in transactions between them.

A solicitor may not make a secret profit but must disclose to a client fully the receipt of any such profit. He may retain it only provided the client agrees (see Chapter 14).

Rule 10 of the Solicitors' Practice Rules 1990 provides that solicitors must inform their clients in writing if they receive any commission exceeding £20. Solicitors cannot keep any such commission unless the client consents.

13.5 PUBLIC OFFICE

A solicitor who holds a public appointment or office (eg as deputy district judge) may also be precluded from acting in particular circumstances. For example, a solicitor who is a member of the planning committee of the local council cannot advise a client in relation to a planning appeal which was lodged against that council because the solicitor's inside knowledge of the council's policy might affect his judgment in advising the client. One of the solicitor's partners who was not on the planning committee could however advise the client.

Apart from the danger of conflict of interests, it is necessary in this type of situation for the solicitor to ensure that justice is seen to be done. The solicitor who acted for a client in circumstances where the solicitor possessed inside knowledge of the workings of the council or court (or as the case may be) might be accused of having used his knowledge to the benefit of his client. The fact that the solicitor had acted with complete impartiality would be irrelevant, his actions would have cast a shadow on the system of justice and could be said to have brought the profession into disrepute in breach of Rule 1 of the Solicitors' Practice Rules 1990.

13.6 CHAPTER SUMMARY

(1) A solicitor must not act, or must decline to act further, where there is a conflict of interest between:

- – the solicitor and the client (or prospective client);
- – the solicitor's firm and the client (or prospective client);
- – two existing clients;
- – an existing client (or former client) and a prospective client.

(2) If a solicitor or firm of solicitors has acquired relevant knowledge concerning a former client during the course of acting for him, he or she must not accept instructions to act against that client.

(3) If a solicitor acts for one client and is asked to act for another in circumstances where there could be a conflict, he must refuse to act for the second client.

(4) If a solicitor has already accepted instructions from two clients in a matter or related matters and a conflict subsequently arises between those clients, the solicitor must cease to act for both clients, unless he or she can without embarrassment and with propriety continue to represent one client, with the other's consent.

A solicitor may continue to represent one client only if not in possession of relevant confidential knowledge concerning the other obtained while acting for the other. Even in such a case the consent should be sought from the other client (usually through his or her new solicitor) and the solicitor should proceed in the absence of such consent only if there is no good cause for its refusal.

(5) Rule 6 of the Solicitors' Practice Rules 1990 contains important further guidance on avoiding conflicts of interest in conveyancing.

(6) Owing to the fiduciary nature of the relationship between solicitor and client, a solicitor must not make a secret profit. Rule 10 of the Solicitors' Practice Rules 1990 contains an exception to this principle.

Chapter 14

CONFIDENTIALITY

14.1 GENERAL PRINCIPLES

A solicitor is under a duty to keep confidential to his firm the affairs of his clients and to ensure that his staff do the same. This principle means that the facts of a client's case, or the details of a client's business transaction or of his private life, must never be discussed by the solicitor with anyone outside the solicitor's own firm except with that client's prior consent. Implicitly, the client will have given consent for his affairs to be discussed by the solicitor with the other party's representative(s) or for details to be given to the court, but only in so far as disclosure is necessary and relevant to the fulfilment of the client's instructions. Where, for example, the solicitor has been instructed to negotiate a commercial loan on behalf of the client, details of the client's financial status might be necessary and relevant to the lender's decision whether or not to grant the loan, but details of the client's marital circumstances, even if known to the solicitor, would not. The duty to keep information about a client and his affairs confidential applies irrespective of the source of the information, so that information obtained about a client from a mutual friend at a party is still subject to the duty of confidentiality.

14.2 DURATION OF THE DUTY

The duty to keep a client's business confidential continues until the client permits disclosure or waives the confidentiality. Thus, the duty endures beyond the end of the retainer and beyond the client's death.

14.3 THE CLIENT'S WILL

The contents of a will must not be disclosed, even after the testator's death, except to or with the consent of the executors, until probate has been granted.

14.4 THE CLIENT'S ADDRESS

Where a solicitor is asked by a third party for the address of one of his clients, he should not disclose the address without the client's consent. He may, as a matter of courtesy, offer to forward a letter from the third party to the client which is sent to the solicitor's address.

14.5 BREACH OF THE DUTY

Breach of the duty of confidentiality may in certain circumstances render the solicitor liable to a civil action at the instigation of the client and may also lead to disciplinary proceedings against the solicitor.

14.6 MISUSE OF CONFIDENTIAL INFORMATION

A solicitor must not make any profit by the use of confidential information for his own purposes. A solicitor who sold the story of a client's private affairs to a newspaper, or who used confidential financial information to make a personal profit on The Stock Exchange would be in breach of this principle. Apart from disciplinary proceedings against the solicitor for breach, an action may also be brought by the client to account for the profit made.

14.7 INADVERTENT RECEIPT OF CONFIDENTIAL INFORMATION

If a letter or papers intended for a non-client (eg addressed to the other party in a litigation matter) is inadvertently received by the solicitor, he should not read the papers nor make use of the information contained in them. The papers should be returned immediately to the party from whom they were received. This principle is discussed further in the LPC Resource Book *Civil Litigation* (Jordans).

14.8 EXCEPTIONS

Information which would normally be regarded as subject to the duty of confidentiality may be disclosed in the following circumstances:

(1) where the client authorises the disclosure;
(2) under a court order;
(3) where the solicitor has reason to believe that a serious crime is about to be committed;
(4) under a warrant from the police for the seizure of documents (but legal privilege may apply here which will obviate disclosure);
(5) in the interests of national security;
(6) in certain circumstances, where money laundering is suspected;
(7) in certain circumstances, where the client is publicly funded.

> *Example 1*
> A client tells his solicitor about an armed robbery which the client is planning to carry out next month. Is this information confidential or is it the solicitor's public duty to inform the police of the plans?
> *The Law Society's Guide to the Professional Conduct of Solicitors* states that communications made to a solicitor by his client before the commission of a crime 'for the purposes of being guided or helped in the commission of it are not confidential since such communications do not come within the ordinary

scope of the professional retainer'. If the information which the solicitor received falls within this exclusion (the solicitor must be certain in his own mind that the information which the client revealed was fact and not fantasy), then it seems that an exception to the duty of confidentiality applies and the solicitor would be able to contact the police. If in doubt as to whether disclosure of the information is appropriate, advice should be obtained from the professional ethics department of The Law Society. The above example relates to information received about a serious crime which is about to be committed in the future. If the information received had related to a crime which had already been committed, the exception allowing disclosure of the information to the police would not have applied and the information would have been subject to the duty of confidentiality.

Example 2

An assistant solicitor with Prestige and Co acted regularly for Interface plc and acquired detailed information relating to the management of the company and its financial resources. When the solicitor moved to another firm, he found that his case load included cases where Interface plc was the potential defendant in actions brought by the new firm's existing clients. The facts which the solicitor possessed about Interface would be very useful to his new clients in pursuing their actions against Interface. What should he do?

The information which the solicitor obtained about Interface is confidential. It remains confidential even though he no longer acts for the company. That information cannot therefore be revealed by the solicitor to his new clients, and cannot be used by him to benefit his new clients.

Information obtained about Interface which was obtained while the solicitor was working for his old firm may also influence the way in which the solicitor handles the claims on behalf of his new client. For these reasons the solicitor should not act personally in cases against Interface, but there is no reason why another solicitor in the firm who has had no connection with Interface should not conduct the case on behalf of the new firm's clients. The information possessed by the solicitor about Interface will only be 'useful' to a third party for a limited period. For example, details of the company's financial situation may alter over a period of time, or the appointment of a new managing director to the company could radically affect the company's methods of conducting business. It is a question of fact in each case as to how long the information held by the solicitor remains relevant. Once the solicitor is sure that such information as he possessed is no longer relevant he can at that stage act against his former clients.

14.9 CONFIDENTIALITY AND PRIVILEGE

The duty to preserve the confidentiality of the client's affairs should not be confused with legal privilege. The latter principle protects and prevents the disclosure even in a court of law of information which has passed between a solicitor and his client.

Legal professional privilege exists for the protection of the client to enable him to discuss his legal affairs freely with his solicitor without fear of disclosure. Oral or written communications which pass directly or indirectly between the client and his solicitor, acting in the capacity of solicitor, are privileged. The documents must exist for the purpose of the client seeking or the solicitor conveying advice. Thus most, but not all, documents passing between the client and his solicitor will be privileged (see *Balabel v Air India* [1988] 2 All ER 246).

Privilege does not attach to communications which are themselves part of a criminal or unlawful proceeding (see *R v Cox and Railton* (1884) 14 QBD 153; *R v Ataou* [1998] QB 798; *Chandler v Church* (1987) 137 NLJ 451). Privilege endures despite the death of the client (*Bullivant v Attorney-General for Victoria* [1901] AC 196).

Anything which a solicitor says in court while acting as an advocate is privileged and cannot be the subject of proceedings, for example, for defamation.

The court has power to decide whether or not a particular item is privileged. Thus, if a solicitor is concerned as to whether or not he should disclose a matter, he can apply to the court for directions.

14.10 CHAPTER SUMMARY

(1) A solicitor is under a duty to keep the affairs of his clients confidential to his firm and to ensure that his staff do the same.

(2) The duty continues forever, even after termination of the retainer or death of the client, unless the client permits disclosure or waives the confidentiality.

(3) The duty to keep information about a client and his affairs confidential applies, irrespective of the source of the information.

(4) The duty to keep a client's confidences can be overridden in certain exceptional circumstances.

(5) The solicitor's duty to keep the client's affairs confidential at all time must be distinguished from legal professional privilege. Legal privilege means that a solicitor can refuse to disclose communications between himself and a client. If the court decides, however, that matters are not privileged, then despite the duty of confidentiality, a solicitor may have to reveal a confidence.

(6) A solicitor is usually under a duty to pass on to the client and use all information which is material to the client's business, regardless of the source of that information. There are, however, exceptional circumstances where the duty does not apply.

Chapter 15

UNDERTAKINGS

This chapter looks at:

- what an undertaking is;
- the effect of giving an undertaking.

15.1 DEFINITION

An undertaking is a promise made by a solicitor, or on his behalf by a member of his staff, to do or to refrain from doing something. Technically, an undertaking is defined as:

> 'any unequivocal declaration of intention addressed to someone who reasonably places reliance on it and made by:
>
> (a)   a solicitor or a member of staff in the course of practice; or
>
> (b)   a solicitor as "solicitor" but not in the course of his practice;
>
> whereby the solicitor becomes personally bound.'
>
> (*The Law Society's Guide to the Professional Conduct of Solicitors*)

15.2 WHY UNDERTAKINGS ARE NECESSARY

Undertakings are often given by solicitors in order to smooth the path of a transaction, or to speed up its progress. They are a convenient method by which some otherwise problematical areas of practice can be avoided. The following are common examples of situations where undertakings are given.

15.2.1 In conveyancing

A buyer's solicitor will accept an undertaking from a seller's solicitor that the latter will, after completion, use part of the proceeds of sale of the property to discharge the seller's mortgage on the property. Without this undertaking the seller would either have to borrow the money to discharge his mortgage before completion or the lender would have to attend personally at completion to give a receipt for the money owing to him. Either of these alternative courses of action would cause delay and expense in the completion of the transaction.

15.2.2 In court proceedings

A solicitor may give an undertaking to the court that he will file an affidavit on behalf of his client. Without the undertaking the proceedings would have to be adjourned until the document had been filed. The adjournment would cause delay and add expense to the proceedings.

15.3 PERSONAL LIABILITY

It is a principle of conduct that an undertaking given by a solicitor is personally binding on him and must be honoured. Failure to honour an undertaking is prima facie evidence of professional misconduct and the Council of The Law Society will require the undertaking to be honoured as a matter of conduct. Where a solicitor in partnership gives an undertaking, all partners are responsible for its performance.

A solicitor will be held personally liable to honour an undertaking given by the solicitor 'on behalf' of a third party unless such liability is expressly and clearly disclaimed in the undertaking itself. An undertaking may, for example, be given by the solicitor 'on behalf of' his client. In such a situation the solicitor retains primary liability for the fulfilment of the undertaking unless personal liability has been clearly and unambiguously excluded in the terms of the undertaking itself.

An undertaking which seeks to exclude personal liability is legally possible but of little value to the recipient who may therefore be reluctant to accept an undertaking in such terms.

A solicitor is bound to honour an undertaking given by a member of his staff, whether admitted or not. In view of this principle, solicitors should make it clear to their staff whether they have authority to give undertakings on behalf of the firm and, if so, in which circumstances and on what terms. Many firms will have a 'house rule' that undertakings are only to be given by the partners of the firm.

15.4 CONSIDERATION FOR THE PROMISE

Consideration for the promise will often be present. For example, an undertaking to stay proceedings if an agreed sum of money is paid to the client demonstrates consideration flowing from both the giver and recipient of the promise.

However, the presence of consideration is irrelevant to the enforceability of an undertaking; an undertaking is enforceable even in the absence of consideration. An undertaking is binding because it has been given; no other justification is needed for its enforcement.

15.5 ORAL AND WRITTEN UNDERTAKINGS

An undertaking is binding whether it is oral or in writing. To avoid misunderstanding over the terms of the promise it is preferable for an undertaking to be given in writing. Where an undertaking is given orally, a written note of what has been promised should be attached to the client's file as soon as possible, and the terms of the oral undertaking should be confirmed in writing to the recipient.

15.6 AMBIGUITY

Any ambiguity in the terms of the undertaking is construed against the party who gave the promise. Normally no terms will be implied into the undertaking and no extraneous evidence considered.

There are some exceptions to the rule that no terms will be implied into an undertaking, for example, if an undertaking is given to pay money out of a specific fund at some specified time, there is an implied warranty that the fund will be sufficient to discharge the liability.

15.7 A PROMISE TO GIVE AN UNDERTAKING

A promise to give an undertaking at some future time is construed as an undertaking if the terms of the undertaking to be given can be sufficiently identified.

15.8 ASSIGNMENT OF LIABILITY

A solicitor cannot assign the burden of an undertaking (and so claim to be released from it) without the express consent of the recipient of the undertaking.

15.9 ACTS OUTSIDE THE SOLICITOR'S CONTROL

An undertaking remains enforceable even if the promise is to do something which is outside the control of the person giving it. For this reason great care should be exercised in giving undertakings to ensure that what has been promised is within the control of the giver to perform or fulfil. Undertakings are not subject to the Limitation Acts, thus a solicitor cannot evade liability on an undertaking by claiming that an action on it would be statute barred (see *Bray v Stuart West and Co* (1989) EG 60). For example, an undertaking to pay a sum of money which the solicitor expects to receive from his client will have to be honoured by the solicitor personally if the client does not put his solicitor in funds.

Where a solicitor is required to give an undertaking in respect of a matter which is not entirely within his own control to fulfil, he may consider using a 'best endeavours' undertaking. For example, an undertaking 'to obtain the client's signature to a document' should not be given without some qualification since the solicitor cannot physically force the client to sign the document. In these circumstances the solicitor might express the undertaking in the following terms: 'to use my best endeavours to obtain my client's signature ... etc'. Clearly, this qualified form of undertaking is of less value to the recipient than an unqualified undertaking and it is a matter of judgment in the circumstances of each case as to whether an undertaking should be accepted and, if so, whether the terms being offered sufficiently protect the interests of the recipient's client.

15.10 RULES APPLY TO ALL SOLICITORS

A solicitor not engaged in private practice, and whether or not holding a practising certificate, is personally liable on an undertaking given by him. The principles relating to undertakings apply to all solicitors without exception.

15.11 CLIENT'S AUTHORITY

An undertaking which has been given must be honoured; liability cannot be avoided even where the performance of the undertaking would put the solicitor in breach of his duty to his client. An undertaking should not therefore be given unless the solicitor has his client's express and irrevocable authority to give it. Once the solicitor has acted to his detriment on the authority, the client may not alter or revoke his authority.

15.12 CHANGE OF CIRCUMSTANCES

Where, after an undertaking has been given, circumstances change so that the undertaking is no longer capable of fulfilment, either wholly or in part, the giver will remain bound to honour the undertaking as originally given unless the recipient agrees to its variation or discharge. Where, for example, an undertaking has been given to discharge a debt on the client's behalf, and it subsequently becomes clear that insufficient funds are available to discharge the debt, the recipient of the undertaking must immediately be informed of the changed circumstances. Unless the recipient otherwise agrees, the solicitor who gave the undertaking will be liable to discharge the whole of the debt, even if this means that he has to use his personal funds to do so.

15.13 THE COURT'S JURISDICTION

The court, by virtue of its inherent jurisdiction over its own officers, also has power of enforcement in respect of undertakings (see *Udall v Capri Lighting Ltd (Re Richard Oxley Whiting, a solicitor)* [1988] QB 907). Where undertakings are given by solicitors to the court, The Law Society takes the view that enforcement of the undertaking is a matter for the court and will not therefore normally intervene in such a situation.

15.14 STANDARD FORMS OF UNDERTAKING

The Law Society has issued a recommended form of wording for use by a seller's solicitor where an undertaking is to be given in respect of the discharge of a building society mortgage. Other approved forms of wording also exist, for example, in relation to the giving of an undertaking for bridging finance. Although these forms of wording have been approved by The Law Society, care should be exercised in every case to ensure that the standard wording is appropriate to meet the situation in the particular case. If the wording is not appropriate to meet the situation in hand, the undertaking should be amended or re-drafted as necessary.

15.15 UNDERTAKINGS TO PAY MONEY

Where an undertaking is given to pay money, the solicitor should make clear in the wording of the undertaking whether it is intended that the promise to pay is unconditional (ie payment will be made in any event) or whether it is only intended that payment should be made out of a specific fund of money, if and when that fund is received by the solicitor (eg payment out of the proceeds of sale of a property when completion has taken place). Where the undertaking is to pay out of a specific fund, it is implied that there will be sufficient money to discharge the liability. Where an undertaking is given to pay money out of the proceeds of sale of a property, no term is implied to the effect that the solicitor will pay only if the proceeds of sale come into the hands of the solicitor who gave the undertaking. If it is intended to restrict the undertaking in this way, a term to this effect must be included in the wording of the undertaking.

15.16 NON-SOLICITORS

Undertakings should not be accepted from an unqualified person. However, licensed conveyancers are bound by rules of conduct relating to undertakings which are similar to those which apply to solicitors. Undertakings may therefore safely be given to or accepted from a licensed conveyancer in the same way that one would be given to or received from a solicitor.

15.17 SIX GOLDEN RULES

An undertaking should never be given lightly or without consideration for its consequences. The penalties, in terms of personal liability and disciplinary proceedings for failure to honour an undertaking, are applied without regard to the solicitor's personal culpability for the default. The guidelines set out below should help the solicitor to avoid problems in connection with undertakings.

(1) Obtain the client's prior authority to give the undertaking.
(2) Be 100 per cent sure that the wording of the promise is capable of fulfilment.
(3) Put the undertaking in writing.
(4) Have an office rule that undertakings are given or authorised only by partners.
(5) Mark the client's file cover clearly as a reminder to every person who is dealing with the file that an undertaking has been given.
(6) When the undertaking has been performed, obtain a written discharge of the undertaking from the recipient and keep this discharge on the client's file.

Example 1
During negotiations for the sale of property the seller's solicitor agreed to obtain an insurance policy to cover defects in the seller's legal title to the property. Inadvertently this matter was overlooked by the buyer's solicitor until completion of the transaction. When at completion the buyer's solicitor asks what has happened to the policy, he is told that the seller had not in fact obtained the policy as promised. On the basis that the seller's solicitor undertakes to obtain the policy as soon after completion as possible, the buyer's solicitor agrees to complete the transaction. Subsequently, the insurance

company refuses to issue a policy because it is not prepared to accept the risk of the defective title. What is the position in relation to the solicitor's undertaking?

The promise by the seller's solicitor to obtain the policy is an undertaking. This is so whether or not the promise was given in writing, regardless of whether the seller's solicitor had his client's authority to give the undertaking, and whether or not the promise was formally expressed as an 'undertaking'. The problem is that the undertaking is (as it turns out) incapable of fulfilment – the solicitor promised to do an act which was not entirely within his control; he cannot force the insurance company to issue the policy. Impossibility of performance is no bar to the enforcement of an undertaking and failure to honour an undertaking is professional misconduct for which the seller's solicitor may face disciplinary action. Clearly, the buyer will not be able to enforce the undertaking to obtain the insurance policy but he would be able to sue the defaulting solicitor for the loss sustained as a result of the default, ie the difference between the value of the property which has the benefit of such an insurance policy, and its lesser value without the policy. The matter should be reported to The Law Society if the seller's solicitors do not honour their promise.

The facts given above demonstrate the danger of giving an undertaking in circumstances where the fulfilment of the promise is dependent on the actions of a third party. An unqualified undertaking should not have been given in these circumstances. A 'best endeavours' undertaking would have afforded better protection for the seller's solicitor, although in this type of situation it is arguable that an undertaking (of whatever type) is not appropriate and that the best course of action would have been for completion to be delayed until the matter had been resolved. Although not relevant to the question of the undertaking, it should also be noted that the problem of the missing policy would not have occurred had the buyer's solicitor acted diligently at an earlier stage in the transaction. If the buyer's solicitor had pursued the question of the insurance policy with the seller's solicitor, the absence of the policy might have come to light earlier and thus have been resolved before completion. On this basis it is possible that the buyer's solicitor has been negligent in his handling of his client's case and might be liable to his own client in damages for the loss.

Example 2

A trainee solicitor is sent to court by his principal to sit behind counsel during a trial. The trainee is given the file but has had no opportunity of reading it since he was told only on the morning of the trial that he was required to attend court and the matter is not one with which he is familiar. During the proceedings the judge enquires why a particular document which forms part of the client's evidence has not been lodged in court. On looking quickly through the file, the trainee is unable to locate the document and makes the assumption that the document must have been left behind in the office. It appears that the trial will have to be adjourned unless the document can be produced. Counsel is reluctant to adjourn the case because of the expense involved in recalling all the witnesses on another day, and so the trainee gives an undertaking to the court to produce the document to the court on the following day. On returning to the office that evening it proves impossible to locate the document, and when the client is contacted he is unsure whether the document in fact ever existed. What will happen when the trainee returns to court on the following day and is unable to produce the document?

The undertaking binds the trainee's firm whether or not the trainee had authority to give it. This is a further example of an undertaking being given to perform an act which is not totally within the control of the giver of the undertaking. An unqualified undertaking should not have been given in these circumstances; a 'best endeavours' undertaking might have been more appropriate. The undertaking was given to the court and so its enforcement lies with the court, although the trainee and the firm both risk being reported to The Law Society for their failure to honour the undertaking. The trainee should have asked counsel to request a brief adjournment of the case to permit the trainee to telephone his principal for instructions. Had this been done, the problem would have not occurred.

Example 3

A client requires bridging finance from his bank in order to fund the deposit on the purchase of his new house. The client's bank asks for an undertaking to repay the bridging finance out of the proceeds of sale of the client's existing property. What points should be borne in mind when giving the undertaking?

Provided that the solicitor giving the undertaking is satisfied as to the client's integrity and financial stability, an undertaking may be given to the bank provided that:

(1) the amount repayable is limited to a specific sum (ie the amount of the bridging finance plus interest);

(2) the solicitor is satisfied that the balance of the proceeds of sale will be sufficient to discharge the liability;

(3) liability to repay is limited to the 'net' proceeds of sale as defined in the terms of the undertaking (eg such proceeds of sale as are left after the discharge of all liabilities including the discharge of the client's existing mortgage(s), payment of solicitor's fees and estate agent's commission etc);

(4) the undertaking is limited to a requirement to pay out of only the proceeds of sale which are actually received by the solicitor – this restriction guards against the possibility of the solicitor never receiving the proceeds of sale (eg because a third party absconds with the money), but still being liable to repay the bank because the sale has been completed.

Ideally, such an undertaking should not be given until contracts for the sale transaction have been exchanged, because until that time there is no certainty that the sale will proceed at a given price or at all.

15.18 CHAPTER SUMMARY

(1) An undertaking is an unequivocal declaration of intention addressed to someone who reasonably places reliance on it and made by a solicitor:

(a) in the course of his practice, either personally or by a member of his staff; or

(b) as 'solicitor', but not in the course of his practice, whereby the solicitor (or, in the case of a member of staff, his employer) becomes personally bound.

(2) A solicitor who fails to honour the terms of a professional undertaking is, on the face of it, guilty of misconduct. Consequently, the Council will require its implementation as a matter of conduct. The Law Society has no power to enforce compliance with an undertaking as such, but may take disciplinary proceedings against a solicitor in respect of a breach.

(3) Where a solicitor in partnership gives an undertaking as a solicitor in the course of his practice, all partners are responsible for its performance.

(4) A solicitor employer is responsible for honouring an undertaking given by a member of his staff, whether admitted or not.

(5) An undertaking does not have to constitute a legal contract to be enforceable in conduct.

(6) An undertaking may be given orally or in writing. For the sake of certainty, it should be made or confirmed in writing.

(7) An ambiguous undertaking is generally construed in favour of the recipient.

(8) Promises to give undertakings at some future date are treated as an undertaking if the terms of the undertaking to be given can be sufficiently identified.

(9) An undertaking is still binding even if it is to do something outside the solicitor's control.

(10) A solicitor will be held liable to honour an undertaking given 'on behalf of' anyone, unless such liability is expressly and clearly disclaimed in the undertaking itself.

(11) The court, by virtue of its inherent jurisdiction over its own officers, has power to enforce undertakings.

Chapter 16

DUTIES OWED TO THIRD PARTIES

This chapter looks at the relationship of solicitors to:

- third parties generally;
- other solicitors;
- barristers;
- the court.

16.1 RELATIONS WITH THIRD PARTIES

A solicitor must not act, whether in his professional capacity or otherwise, towards anyone in a way which is fraudulent, deceitful or otherwise contrary to his position as a solicitor, nor must he use his position as a solicitor to take unfair advantage either for himself or another person.

16.1.1 Dealing with unrepresented parties

Where the solicitor corresponds with an unrepresented third party he should ensure that no retainer arises by implication from the terms of the letter itself.

If an unrepresented third party sends a draft document to the solicitor which is inadequate, the solicitor should amend the document if it can be put right with a reasonable amount of correction. If this is not possible, and to correct the document would involve the solicitor in re-drafting the document from scratch, the solicitor may return the unaltered document to the third party with the recommendation that he should seek the advice of a solicitor to assist in the preparation of the document.

This situation may arise in conveyancing where, for example, the buyer is acting on his own behalf and submits an inappropriate draft purchase deed to the seller's solicitor. The problems associated with unrepresented parties' conveyancing are specifically referred to in *The Law Society's Guide to the Professional Conduct of Solicitors*, which provides that a solicitor acting for the seller of property should not prepare a form of contract which he knows or ought to know will be placed before a prospective buyer for signature before that party has obtained or has had a proper opportunity to obtain legal advice.

16.1.2 Giving references

A solicitor may incur liability under the principle in *Hedley Byrne and Co Ltd v Heller and Partners Ltd* [1964] AC 465 if he gives a reference on behalf of a client or third party which turns out to be untrue (see *Spring v Guardian Assurance plc* [1994] 3 All ER 129, HL). Such conduct may also be regarded by The Law Society as conduct unbefitting a solicitor.

16.1.3 Offensive letters

Offensive letters written by a solicitor to a third party could bring the profession into disrepute and such action is regarded as unbefitting conduct.

16.1.4 Unqualified persons

If a solicitor discovers that the other party is represented by an unqualified person who is undertaking acts prohibited to unqualified persons (ie acts reserved by the Solicitors Act 1974 to 'qualified solicitors') then, subject to the interests of his own client, his proper course is to decline to communicate with the unqualified person. The Law Society has issued guidance notes for solicitors dealing with unqualified conveyancers.

16.1.5 Threats

When writing a letter before action, a solicitor must not demand anything other than that recoverable under the due process of law, nor should a solicitor acting for a creditor threaten the debtor with any action other than court action if the debt is unpaid.

Where a solicitor is instructed to collect a debt he may communicate with the debtor's employer in order to obtain information relating to the debtor's financial circumstances, but must not use the threat of approaching the employer as a means of obtaining payment.

16.1.6 Duty to the world at large

Although a solicitor does not owe a duty to the world at large, circumstances may exist in which he does nevertheless owe a duty to a third party who is not his client (eg *Ross v Caunters* [1980] 1 Ch 297, where a solicitor who failed to warn a testator that the will should not be witnessed by a beneficiary was held liable in negligence to the beneficiary who witnessed the will for damages suffered as a result of the loss of the beneficiary's interest under the will; see also *White v Jones* [1995] 1 All ER 891, HL, where a solicitor who failed to carry out a testator's instructions was liable in damages to the intended beneficiaries).

Where a solicitor acting for a seller is instructed to deal with more than one prospective buyer at the same time, he must comply with Rule 6A of the Solicitors' Practice Rules 1990.

16.1.7 Agents' costs

Unless there is an agreement to the contrary, a solicitor is personally responsible for paying the proper costs of any professional agent or other person whom he instructs on behalf of his client, whether or not he receives payment from his client.

16.2 RELATIONS WITH OTHER SOLICITORS

A solicitor must act towards other solicitors with complete frankness and good faith consistent with his overriding duty to his client.

Any fraudulent or deceitful conduct by one solicitor towards another may be the subject of disciplinary proceedings.

A solicitor must always honour his word, and must observe good manners and courtesy towards other members of the profession and their employed staff. This duty applies to oral communications and to letters written by one solicitor to another.

A solicitor is under a duty to report to the OSS, where necessary after having obtained his client's consent, any conduct on the part of another solicitor which he believes falls short of the proper standard of conduct of the profession. This principle extends to a duty to inform The Law Society of misconduct within the solicitor's own firm (eg theft by a member of the solicitor's staff) as well as to conduct by other solicitors.

16.2.1 Agency

Where a solicitor instructs another solicitor to act as his agent (eg to attend court on his behalf), he is, in the absence of contrary agreement, personally responsible for the payment of the agent's costs. This rule applies irrespective of whether the solicitor has been put in funds by his own client.

16.2.2 Other solicitors' clients

In general, a solicitor should not interview or otherwise communicate with anyone who to his knowledge has retained another solicitor to act in the matter except with that other solicitor's consent. Thus, a solicitor should not write directly to the client of another solicitor unless he has good reason to believe that the other solicitor's retainer has been terminated. If the other party's solicitor fails to respond to letters, the solicitor may, after warning the other solicitor of his intention to do so, write directly to the client of the other solicitor. There is nothing to prevent clients themselves from communicating directly with each other if they wish to do so.

16.2.3 Supply of documents

Subject to there being no breach of the solicitor's duty of confidentiality towards his client, a solicitor should supply information concerning documents in his possession to another solicitor upon satisfactory provision being made for the payment of his proper costs (eg on receipt of an undertaking in respect of costs).

Example 1
The solicitors acting for the defendant in a litigation matter fail to respond to letters sent to them by the plaintiff's solicitors. They also decline to return telephone calls. As a result, the plaintiff's solicitor finds that he is unable to proceed with the matter and his client is becoming anxious as to what will happen. Is it proper for the plaintiff's solicitor to contact the defendant in person? As a general rule the solicitor should not make direct contact with the defendant since he knows that the defendant has instructed a solicitor to act for him. Communications should therefore be made through the parties' solicitors unless there is good reason to believe that the defendant has terminated his retainer with his solicitors. However, in circumstances such as these where the defendant's solicitors are failing to respond to any communications, the plaintiff's solicitor can write directly to the other party, provided that he writes

to the defendant's solicitors first, informing them of his intention to contact their client and the reason for this course of action.

Example 2

A solicitor is instructed to negotiate a commercial agreement on behalf of his client. When the draft agreement, prepared by the other party's solicitor, is received, it is noticed that the draft appears to omit one of the terms which had been specifically agreed between the parties. The omission of this term would be most beneficial to the client. Is the solicitor under any duty to correct the defective draft agreement, bearing in mind that to do so would adversely affect his own client's interests? Although the client would no doubt prefer the agreement to be finalised without amendment, he had agreed to the inclusion of the omitted term, and thus does not stand to lose anything by its inclusion. The solicitor owes a duty of fairness to fellow members of the profession, and thus should return the draft agreement to the other party's solicitors pointing out that the terms of the agreement do not comply with the terms agreed by his client.

Example 3

On taking instructions from a client, a solicitor discovers that the client has already instructed other solicitors to handle this matter on his behalf although he is dissatisfied with their advice and with the progress of the matter generally. Can he act for this client?

A solicitor may not act for a client who is already represented by another solicitor until that other solicitor's retainer has been terminated. The client does not appear to have terminated his retainer with his existing solicitors and the newly instructed solicitor may not act for the client until this has been done, although a second opinion on his case can be given without offending this rule. Once the first retainer has been terminated, the client can be advised by the newly instructed solicitor, who should then request that the first solicitors hand over their papers to him. The first solicitors will have a lien on the papers until their reasonable costs are paid, or they receive a satisfactory undertaking from the second solicitor in relation to the payment of their charges.

There is nothing to prevent a client from instructing one solicitor to handle one type of work on his behalf and a second solicitor to handle other matters. It is quite common for large companies to instruct one firm to handle their property work and a different firm to deal with their litigation. This type of arrangement does not conflict with the principle outlined above.

16.3 DUTY TO COUNSEL

When instructing a barrister, the solicitor is responsible for ensuring so far as practicable that adequate instructions, supporting statements and documents are sent to counsel in good time. The back sheet to the brief must contain the name of the case, the name of the barrister and of instructing solicitors, the court and the fee.

Where necessary and practicable, solicitors should arrange conferences with counsel to enable the barrister to clarify his instructions by direct discussion with the solicitor and/or the lay client, to discuss the facts, evidence and law with the solicitor and to give advice more directly than is possible in writing.

16.3.1 Attending court with counsel

Where counsel has been instructed, the instructing solicitor is generally under a duty to attend or arrange for the attendance of a responsible representative throughout the proceedings. However, attendance may be dispensed with in the magistrates' court or in certain categories of Crown Court proceedings.

The decision to dispense with attendance at court is a matter for the solicitor's own judgment, but the solicitor should attend the Crown Court (inter alia) where the client is a person at risk, for example, a juvenile, or a person with an inadequate command of English.

Where a solicitor has decided not to attend with counsel, the brief should be delivered to counsel at least 7 days before the hearing so that counsel has time to prepare the case.

16.3.2 Duty to the client

A solicitor may not abrogate his responsibility to his client by instructing counsel.

The solicitor should select a barrister of sufficient seniority and experience to handle the client's case. There is a duty to check advice given by counsel to ensure that it contains no obvious errors and to take further advice (from the same or a different barrister) if there appears to be an error or inconsistency in counsel's advice (see *Re A (A Minor) (Costs)* [1988] Fam Law 339).

Under Rule 16B of the Solicitors' Practice Rules 1990, a solicitor must not make it a condition of providing litigation services that advocacy services must also be provided by that solicitor or by the solicitor's firm or the solicitor's agent.

A solicitor who provides both litigation and advocacy services must, as soon as practicable after receiving instructions and from time to time, consider and advise the client whether, having regard to the circumstances including:

(i)   the gravity, complexity and likely cost of the case;
(ii) the nature of the solicitor's practice;
(iii) the solicitor's ability and experience; and
(iv) the solicitor's relationship with the client,

the best interests of the client would be served by the solicitor, another advocate from the solicitor's firm, or some other advocate providing the advocacy services.

16.3.3 Counsel's fees

Except in legal aid cases, a solicitor is personally liable as a matter of professional conduct for the payment of counsel's proper fees, whether or not he has been placed in funds by his client.

A barrister's relationship with his instructing solicitor is not founded in contract; therefore at common law a barrister is unable to sue for his fees. This anomaly was corrected by the Courts and Legal Services Act 1990, s 61, which permits a barrister to enter into a contract for the provision of his services, subject to any restrictions or prohibitions contained in rules made by the General Council of the Bar. Except in legal aid cases, a barrister is entitled to demand payment of the fee with his brief. Counsel's fees in non-legal aid cases should be paid or challenged within 3 months of the delivery of the fee note at the end of the case, irrespective of whether the solicitor has at that time been paid by his client.

16.3.4 Code of Conduct

The Code of Conduct for the Bar of England and Wales regulates the professional conduct of barristers. Under Rule 16A of the Solicitors' Practice Rules 1990, any solicitor who acts as an advocate must comply with The Law Society's Code for Advocacy. The Code sets out the principles and standards to be observed by all solicitor advocates when acting as such. There are a number of 'fundamental principles' in the Code: for example, advocates owe their primary duty to the lay client; advocates must not permit their absolute independence and freedom from external pressures to be compromised; and advocates must not compromise their professional standards in order to please their clients, the court or a third party.

The Code also imposes requirements in the following areas: the organisation of the advocate's practice; acceptance of instructions to appear on behalf of a client; the circumstances when advocates must and may withdraw from a case; duties to the client in the conduct of a case; duties to the court when conducting proceedings; and establishing proper channels of communications with clients.

16.3.5 Immunity for advocacy work

The immunity of an advocate from actions in tort for negligence or for breach of contract has now been abolished by the House of Lords in *Arthur JS Hall & Co (A Firm) v Simons* [2000] 3 All ER 673.

16.3.6 Race relations

Where counsel is to be instructed, the solicitor is under a duty to discuss with the client any request by the client to employ a barrister of a particular race or sex. If the client's request appears to be based on discriminatory grounds, the solicitor must endeavour to persuade the client to modify his instructions. If in such a case the client refuses to modify his instructions, the solicitor should consider whether it is proper to continue to act. There may, however, be situations in which the instruction of a barrister of a particular race or sex will be beneficial to the client's case (eg where the client's case concerns racial discrimination). It might be argued in this situation that the selection of a barrister of a particular race or sex falls within the 'genuine occupational qualification' exception contained in the Race Relations Act 1976.

16.4 DUTY TO THE COURT

As an officer of the court the solicitor is under a duty never to deceive or mislead the court. In this context the word 'court' includes tribunals and inquiries.

It is an implied duty of the retainer that the solicitor will carry out his instructions within the rules of professional conduct. Therefore, if the client's instructions would involve the solicitor in a breach of his duty to the court, the solicitor must either ask the client to modify his instructions or cease to act. A solicitor must not make, or instruct counsel to make, an allegation which is intended only to insult, degrade or annoy the other side, a witness or any other person.

Except when making an application to the court, a solicitor must not discuss the merits of the case with a judge, magistrate or other adjudicator before whom a case is pending or may be heard, unless invited to do so in the presence of the solicitor or counsel for the other side or party.

A solicitor acting for a party may interview and take statements from any witness or prospective witness at any stage in proceedings, whether or not that witness has been interviewed or called as a witness by another party. The solicitor must not make, or order others to make, payments to a witness, contingent upon the nature of the evidence given or upon the outcome of a case.

A solicitor must comply with any order of the court which the court can properly make requiring him or his firm to take or refrain from taking some particular course of action. A solicitor is bound to honour his undertakings given to any court or tribunal.

16.5 PUBLIC OFFICE

A solicitor must never put himself in a position where his interests conflict or may be thought to conflict with those of his client. Therefore, a solicitor who holds a public office should not accept instructions to act in a situation where such a conflict might arise. Where, for example, a solicitor is a member of the local council's planning committee, he should not advise a client on a matter which is to be decided by that committee.

16.6 CHAPTER SUMMARY

16.6.1 Relations with third parties

(1) A solicitor must not act, whether in his professional capacity or otherwise, towards anyone in a way that is fraudulent, deceitful or otherwise contrary to his position as a solicitor, nor must he use his position as a solicitor to take unfair advantage either for himself or another person.

    (a) When dealing with an unrepresented third party, a solicitor must take particular care to make sure that no retainer arises by implication between the solicitor and the third party.

    (b) Where a solicitor is dealing with an unrepresented third party, he should amend any draft document sent to him if it contains errors which could be put right by a reasonable amount of correction, provided that it is in his own client's interest to do so. If it is so badly drawn as to be inappropriate, there is no objection to his returning it to the lay party and advising him to consult a solicitor on its preparation.

    (c) A solicitor acting for the seller or property should not prepare a form of contract which he knows or ought to know will be placed before a prospective buyer for signature before that party has obtained or has had a proper opportunity to obtain legal advice.

(2) When writing a letter before action, a solicitor must not demand anything other than that recoverable under the due process of law.

(3) Where a solicitor acting for a seller is instructed to deal with more than one prospective buyer at the same time, he must comply with Rule 6A of the Solicitors' Practice Rules 1990.

(4) Unless there is an agreement to the contrary, a solicitor is personally responsible for paying the proper costs of any professional agent or other person whom he instructs on behalf of his client, whether or not he receives payment from his client.

16.6.2 Relations with other solicitors

(1) A solicitor must act towards other solicitors with complete frankness and good faith consistent with his overriding duty to his client.

(2) A solicitor is under a duty to report to the OSS, where necessary after having obtained his client's consent, any conduct on the part of another solicitor which he believes falls short of the proper standard of conduct of the profession.

(3) In general, a solicitor who has been instructed in a matter should not interview or otherwise communicate with anyone on a matter who to his knowledge has retained another solicitor to act in that matter, except with that other solicitor's consent.

16.6.3 Relations with the Bar

(1) When instructing a barrister, it is the solicitor's responsibility to ensure so far as practicable that adequate instructions, supporting statements and documents are sent to counsel in good time.

(2) Where necessary and practicable, a solicitor should arrange conferences with counsel to enable the barrister to clarify his instructions by direct discussion with the solicitor and/or the lay client, to discuss the facts, evidence and law with the solicitor and to give advice more directly than is possible in writing.

(3) Where counsel has been instructed, the solicitor is under a duty to attend or to arrange for the attendance of a responsible representative throughout the proceedings.

(4) A solicitor may not abrogate his responsibility to his client by instructing counsel.

(5) Except in legal aid cases, a solicitor is personally liable as a matter of professional conduct for the payment of counsel's proper fees, whether or not he has been placed in funds by his client.

(6) A solicitor must advise his or her client when it is appropriate to instruct counsel. Rule 16 of the Solicitors' Practice Rules 1990 requires a solicitor to consider and advise a client whether it is in his or her interests for the solicitor's firm or some other advocate to provide any advocacy required. In addition, a solicitor who proposes to act as an advocate himself or herself must comply with the Code for Advocacy.

16.6.4 Duty to the court

(1) A solicitor who acts in litigation, whilst under a duty to do his or her best for his or her client, must never deceive or mislead the court.

(2) A solicitor acting for a party may interview and take statements from any witness or prospective witness at any stage in proceedings, whether or not that witness has been interviewed or called as a witness by another party.

(3) A solicitor must not make or order others to make payments to a witness contingent upon the nature of the evidence given or upon the outcome of a case.

(4) A solicitor must comply with any order of the court which the court can properly make requiring the solicitor or the solicitor's firm to take or refrain from taking some course of action.

(5) A solicitor is bound to honour an undertaking given to any court or tribunal.

Chapter 17

INDEMNITY INSURANCE

17.1 REQUIREMENT FOR INSURANCE

Every solicitor who is held out as a principal in private practice is required to be insured against civil liability incurred in connection with his practice or in connection with any trust of which he is or was formerly a trustee. This means that all sole practitioners and every partner in a firm must carry insurance. Assistant solicitors, trainees and other non-solicitor members of the firm's staff are covered by the insurance taken out by their principals and do not have to carry separate insurance cover of their own.

17.2 THE SOLICITORS' INDEMNITY RULES 2000

The Solicitors' Indemnity Rules 2000, made by the Council of The Law Society under s 37 of the Solicitors Act 1974, impose the obligation to insure and contain the detailed requirements of the scheme.

17.3 THE NEW SCHEME

The Solicitors' Indemnity Insurance Rules 2000 put into place new arrangements for compulsory indemnity insurance.

In the past, solicitors had to insure through a scheme run under the aegis of The Law Society. However, under the new scheme, they can now obtain insurance from a qualified commercial provider. The commercial provider has to comply with certain minimum terms, for example a minimum cover of £1 million for each and every claim.

As an alternative to insuring with a commercial insurer, The Law Society has established a managing agency in a joint venture with a commercial insurance company. This agency guarantees to offer cover to all sections of the profession. The agency, however, can refuse to accept a particular firm if its claims record is unsatisfactory.

The result is that a firm of solicitors can insure either with an approved commercial provider of its choice or with the managing agency established with The Law Society. Some firms, however, may be unable to obtain cover with either, for example because of a poor claims record. Such firms will be covered temporarily by an 'assigned risks pool'. Premiums for this are high and firms have to take special steps to reduce the risk of claims. They will only be allowed to stay in this pool for 2 years. The pool is funded by the qualified insurers, including The Law Society's managing agency.

17.4 AMOUNT OF COVER

Whichever type of insurance a firm may have, it must provide the firm with cover of up to £1,000,000 per claim (subject to an excess on each claim). For many firms, this sum is inadequate and in such cases firms voluntarily take out 'top-up' cover to increase the amount of their insurance.

17.5 EMPLOYED SOLICITORS

A solicitor who is not in private practice does not need to carry insurance of the kind described above. He could, none the less, be sued for a negligent act or advice and so should ensure that his employer carries adequate cover to protect against such an eventuality.

17.6 CHAPTER SUMMARY

(1) The Solicitors' Indemnity Rules 2000 (made under the Solicitors Act 1974) require solicitors to take out compulsory insurance cover against the risks of professional negligence or other civil liability claims.

(2) They apply to 'every solicitor who is, or is held out to the public as a principal in private practice in England and Wales', and are enforceable in the same way as the principles of general professional conduct.

(3) Firms can insure either with an approved commercial insurer or with the managing agency established with The Law Society.

(4) Insurance must provide the firm with cover of up to £1 million per claim. Voluntary top-up or excess cover may therefore be required.

Chapter 18

COMPLAINTS AND DISCIPLINE

This chapter will look at:

* complaints against solicitors;
* the role of the Office for the Supervision of Solicitors;
* inadequate professional work;
* negligence;
* the Legal Services Ombudsman;
* discipline and the role of the Solicitors Disciplinary Tribunal;
* the Compensation Fund.

18.1 COMPLAINTS AGAINST SOLICITORS

If a client wishes to complain about a solicitor, he should approach the Office for the Supervision of Solicitors (OSS). The OSS exercises The Law Society's powers in relation to the handling of complaints, including the statutory powers of intervention conferred on The Law Society under the Solicitors Act 1974, Sch 1. Although established by The Law Society, the OSS emphasises its independence and integrity by operating from premises separate from The Law Society itself.

18.1.1 Jurisdiction of the Office

The OSS's jurisdiction extends to matters relating to professional conduct, including alleged breaches of the Solicitors' Practice Rules 1990 and Solicitors' Accounts Rules 1998, and complaints about inadequate professional services ('shoddy work'). There is limited jurisdiction to investigate allegations of negligence following an extension of the OSS's powers granted by the Courts and Legal Services Act 1990, s 93. Compensation not exceeding £5,000 can be awarded to a complainant under these provisions.

18.1.2 Conciliation

A large number of complaints about minor matters such as costs, or a breakdown in communication between solicitor and client, can be quickly resolved by conciliation. As well as an in-house conciliation unit within the OSS, local conciliators exist in all areas of England and Wales. When a complaint is referred to a conciliator he decides what action to take in relation to that complaint and attempts to resolve it by mediation between the parties. This is an informal method of resolving complaints which provides a cheap, effective and quick solution to a large number of them. The conciliation service is supported by a telephone helpline service, staffed by solicitors, who give practical help, but not legal advice, to the public. The OSS has power to review the decision of the conciliator if the complainant is not satisfied with the result of the initial investigation.

18.1.3 Non-conciliation cases

Complaints which are not dealt with by conciliation, or where conciliation has not resolved the dispute, are referred to one of the specialist sections of the OSS. The Assistant Director of these divisions has authority to resolve the dispute and to exercise powers to remedy a problem (eg by ordering the payment of interest to a client under the Solicitors' Accounts Rules 1998).

18.1.4 Powers of the OSS

The powers of the OSS are in most cases delegated to an Assistant Director and include:

(1) calling for a file to investigate a complaint;
(2) ordering an inspection of the solicitor's accounts;
(3) ordering an intervention in a solicitor's practice;
(4) recommending the refusal of or imposition of conditions on a practising certificate or investment business certificate;
(5) controlling the employment of a solicitor;
(6) ordering the payment of interest on clients' money;
(7) ordering a payment to be made from the Compensation Fund;
(8) inviting a solicitor to take certain recommended action (eg to comply with an undertaking);
(9) rebuking the solicitor;
(10) ordering a remission of fees;
(11) ordering a solicitor to rectify a mistake at his own expense;
(12) taking disciplinary proceedings against a solicitor before the Disciplinary Tribunal;
(13) awarding compensation of up to £5,000 in respect of inadequate professional services.

18.1.5 Investigation Accountants

The Investigation Accountant and his staff have power to inspect the books of account of a solicitor where a serious breach of the Solicitors' Accounts Rules 1998 is suspected.

18.1.6 Intervention

The OSS is empowered, when the public is at risk, to take control of a solicitor's client account and files. Matters in hand will be dealt with by the Office staff and the practice is then closed down or sold off as a going concern. Intervention may also occur where a sole practitioner is unable to continue his practice through ill-health or accident or death. Interventions are most common in the case of sole practitioners since, where a solicitor practises in partnership, his partners are usually able to take over the work and responsibility of their colleague.

18.2 INADEQUATE PROFESSIONAL WORK

The expression 'inadequate professional work' relates to the situation where a solicitor has provided services to the client which are substandard, ie are not of the quality which could be reasonably expected of a solicitor. This may arise through the solicitor's incompetence in the area of the client's instructions (ie he lacks expertise in the law), through organisational incompetence, for example, where the solicitor fails to organise his work efficiently and thus causes delay in carrying out the client's instructions, or through the solicitor committing a material breach of the Solicitors' Costs Information and Client Care Code (see **10.6**).

18.2.1 Distinction between inadequate professional work and negligence

If the solicitor is in breach of his duty of care and loss results, the client may have an action in contract or the tort of negligence against the solicitor. If the solicitor's actions or omissions are such as to be dishonourable to the profession he may be guilty of professional misconduct regardless of whether the client has suffered any loss. Where the solicitor carries out his instructions in an incompetent manner but without causing loss to the client, the solicitor may be guilty of inadequate professional work but he is not negligent. In some cases, a solicitor's acts or omissions may be both inadequate professional work and negligence.

Example 1
A solicitor's failure to supervise his staff properly results in delay being caused to the client but ultimately the matter is resolved to the client's satisfaction. Here the solicitor is not negligent because the client has not suffered loss, but he may be guilty of professional incompetence.

Example 2
A solicitor deals with his client's instructions promptly but wrongly advises the client about the law involved in the matter; this results in the client ultimately losing a case which he should have won. There is no evidence of professional incompetence here but the wrong advice will amount to negligence.

Inadequate professional work by a solicitor may result in a complaint being made to the OSS, which has the power to order the solicitor to:

- waive the bill;
- waive the right to recover a fee;
- refund the money that has been paid;
- rectify any mistakes at his own expense;
- compensate the client up to £5,000.

If the OSS considers it appropriate, it can take disciplinary action against the solicitor before the Disciplinary Tribunal.

18.3 NEGLIGENCE

A solicitor is negligent where he is in breach of his duty of care to his client and as a result of that breach loss is caused to the client.

It is an implied term of the retainer that the solicitor will exercise reasonable skill and care in the performance of his instructions (Supply of Goods and Services Act 1982, s 13).

Where a solicitor has been negligent the client must normally seek redress through a civil action against the solicitor.

18.3.1 Insurance

Where a client or third party makes a claim against a solicitor (or gives notice of intention to make such a claim) and the claim is one in respect of which indemnity is provided by the Solicitors' Indemnity Fund, the solicitor must as soon as possible notify the Solicitors' Indemnity Fund and co-operate with them in dealing with the claim. Where the solicitor carries top-up insurance in excess of the cover provided by the Indemnity Fund, the insurance company with whom the policy is held should also, in appropriate cases, be informed of the potential claim.

The solicitor should not admit liability or settle a claim without the consent of his insurers.

18.3.2 Steps to be taken on discovery of a claim

If a solicitor discovers an act or omission which would justify a claim by a client (or third party) against him he should:

(1) contact his insurers;
(2) inform the client (or third party) in order to enable him to take independent legal advice;
(3) seek the advice of his insurers as to any further communication with the client (or third party);
(4) confirm any oral communication in writing.

18.3.3 Independent advice

If a client makes a claim against his solicitor or notifies his intention of doing so, or if the solicitor discovers an act or omission which would justify such a claim, the solicitor is under a duty to inform his client that he should seek independent advice. If the client refuses to seek independent advice the solicitor should decline to act further for the client unless he is satisfied that no conflict of interest exists. Where the solicitor is asked to hand papers over to another solicitor who is giving independent advice to the client about the claim, the solicitor should keep copies of the original documents for his own reference.

> *Example 1*
> A medical expert was instructed on behalf of a client to prepare an expert's report on the client's injuries sustained in a road traffic accident. The report is delivered to the solicitor's office at a time when he is under considerable pressure from other clients and he puts the report in the file without reading it. Had the solicitor read the report he would have discovered that it contained an error prejudicial to the client's case. As a result of that error the client lost the case. Is this inadequate professional work, or negligence, or both?
>
> The solicitor is under a duty to his client to instruct a competent expert to handle the client's affairs and to check work done by the expert to ensure it contains no obvious errors. The expert instructed in this case may have been competent, but the solicitor omitted to check the work, and since loss resulted to the client he is guilty of negligence to the client. Not having enough time to check the report

because of pressure of other work is no excuse for the solicitor's conduct, and this aspect of the situation amounts to inadequate professional work irrespective of whether the client suffered loss as a result of it.

Example 2

During the course of acting for a tenant who is seeking to renew the lease of his shop under the provisions of Part II of the Landlord and Tenant Act 1954, the tenant's solicitor receives a letter from the landlord's solicitor saying that the landlord is not prepared to negotiate for the renewal because the tenant's application, lodged on his behalf by his solicitor, was made out of time. The Landlord and Tenant Act 1954 lays down strict time-limits which cannot generally be extended. The solicitor's failure to serve the application within these limits means that the tenant will lose his right to renew his lease and this will affect the value and saleability of the lease. In this situation, a mistake has clearly been made by the solicitor (failing to observe the time-limits), and this has caused loss to the client. There is no evidence of inadequate professional work, but the solicitor is guilty of negligence.

18.4 THE LEGAL SERVICES OMBUDSMAN

The post of Legal Services Ombudsman was created by the Courts and Legal Services Act 1990, s 21. The Ombudsman, appointed by the Lord Chancellor, holds office for a renewable term of 3 years; he cannot be an authorised advocate, authorised litigator, licensed conveyancer, authorised practitioner or notary. His function is to investigate any allegation which has been made about the manner in which a complaint has been handled by the professional body of an authorised advocate, authorised litigator, licensed conveyancer, registered foreign lawyer or notary or employees of such persons.

Solicitors are 'authorised advocates' and 'authorised litigators' within the meaning of the Courts and Legal Services Act 1990.

18.4.1 Complaints to the Ombudsman

Complaints against solicitors are made to the OSS which, with the Solicitors Disciplinary Tribunal, has power to investigate complaints and to impose sanctions on a solicitor where the complaint is upheld. A complainant who is dissatisfied with the way in which the Office for the Supervision of Solicitors has handled a complaint may refer the matter to the Legal Services Ombudsman.

The Legal Services Ombudsman is thus not a point of first referral for a complaint. His function is to investigate a complaint which has already been made to one of the relevant professional bodies where there is an allegation that the complaint was not properly handled by the professional body itself.

Complaints cannot be investigated by the Ombudsman where the issue which is the subject of the complaint is being or has already been determined by a court, the Solicitors Disciplinary Tribunal, the Disciplinary Tribunal of the Council of the Inns of Court or any other tribunal specified in regulations made by the Lord Chancellor.

The Ombudsman's report may include recommendations to include one or more of the following:

(1) that the professional body concerned should reconsider the complaint;

(2) that the professional body should exercise its disciplinary functions over the person who was the subject of the complaint;

(3) that a specified amount of compensation should be paid to the complainant either by the professional body or by the person who was the subject of the complaint.

When a report is sent to any of the persons listed above, there is a duty on the recipient to have regard to the report's conclusions and recommendations and to notify the Ombudsman within 3 months of the receipt of the report of the action taken or proposed to be taken to comply with the recommendations.

The Ombudsman can, if he thinks it appropriate, order (rather than recommend) the OSS, or the solicitor who was the subject of the complaint, to pay compensation.

18.5 DISCIPLINARY ACTION

18.5.1 Introduction

The Council of The Law Society has a general duty to ensure that no solicitor is guilty of conduct which renders him unfit to remain on the roll (see *Re Hill* (1868) LR 3 QB 543). A solicitor's failure to maintain the required standard of conduct will result in disciplinary action being taken against him by the Solicitors Disciplinary Tribunal. In this context the word 'conduct' covers three main areas:

(1) criminal conduct;

(2) professional misconduct;

(3) improper conduct.

18.5.2 Criminal convictions

The conviction of a solicitor for a criminal offence prima facie makes the solicitor unfit to remain on the roll and striking off is the penalty which may therefore be imposed by the Tribunal. A solicitor who is serving a prison sentence is normally struck off, but every case is reviewed on its own facts. A period of suspension from practice can be ordered as an alternative to striking off but the latter penalty is invariably imposed where the offence involves dishonesty. No distinction is drawn between a criminal conviction relating to the solicitor's professional role and one which affects him in his capacity as a private individual.

18.5.3 Professional misconduct

Professional misconduct covers a wide range of matters most, but not all, of which will be connected with the solicitor's professional activities. Examples of conduct within this category include:

(1) breach of an undertaking;

(2) improperly borrowing money from or lending money to a client;

(3) breach of the practice rules, accounts rules or other rules made by the Council of The Law Society;

(4) inexcusable negligence (a single negligent act will not be misconduct, but there may be circumstances in which negligence also amounts to misconduct);

(5) deliberately misleading the court (eg by withholding evidence);

(6) breach of the duty of confidentiality.

18.5.4 Improper conduct

Improper conduct is sometimes called 'unprofessional conduct' or 'unbefitting conduct'. It may generally be defined as conduct by a solicitor which is such as to render him unfit to be an officer of the court (*Re Southerton* (1805) 6 East 126). Conduct which is not necessarily criminal in character, nor related to the solicitor's professional status, is within this definition. In practice, the distinction between professional misconduct and improper conduct is unclear. Any conduct which would be regarded by fellow members of the profession as disgraceful or dishonourable may be the subject of disciplinary proceedings.

18.6 JURISDICTION OF THE COURT

The court has an inherent jurisdiction to discipline a solicitor because the solicitor is an officer of the court. The court may order a solicitor to pay costs to his own client or to a third party where those costs have been incurred as a result of the solicitor's misconduct in proceedings before a court (see Rules of the Supreme Court 1965, Ord 62, r 11).

18.7 THE SOLICITORS DISCIPLINARY TRIBUNAL

The Solicitors Disciplinary Tribunal hears and determines applications relating to allegations of unbefitting conduct and/or breaches of the rules of professional conduct by solicitors. Most applications to the Disciplinary Tribunal are made on behalf of The Law Society but (except where the Solicitors Act 1974 provides otherwise) any person may make an application directly to the Disciplinary Tribunal without first making a complaint to The Law Society.

The Disciplinary Tribunal was established by s 46 of the Solicitors Act 1974 and is independent of The Law Society. The members of the Disciplinary Tribunal are appointed by the Master of the Rolls. There is no statutory maximum on the number of members of the Disciplinary Tribunal but it normally comprises twelve solicitor members and six lay members. The solicitor members must have been admitted for at least 10 years, and the lay members must be neither solicitors nor barristers. The Disciplinary Tribunal sits in divisions of three members each made up of two solicitors and one lay person. The decisions of the Disciplinary Tribunal may be delivered by a single member.

18.7.1 Tribunal procedure

The Disciplinary Tribunal has power, exercisable by statutory instrument, to make rules governing its procedure and practice. These rules are made with the concurrence of the Master of the Rolls. The Law Society maintains a panel of solicitors in private practice who prosecute applications before the Disciplinary Tribunal on the Society's behalf. In most cases, the panel solicitor will present the case before the Disciplinary Tribunal; in complex cases, counsel may be instructed to present the case.

18.7.2 Application to the Tribunal

An application to the Disciplinary Tribunal must be made in the form specified by the rules and supported by an affidavit sworn by the applicant (this will be the panel solicitor where the applicant is The Law Society). The Disciplinary Tribunal will consider the application and, if satisfied that there is a prima facie case to answer, will fix a hearing date. Either party may be represented at the hearing by a solicitor or counsel. The evidential procedures of the Disciplinary Tribunal are similar to those which apply to the High Court. Evidence is given on oath and witnesses may be called.

The decisions of the Disciplinary Tribunal, called 'Findings' and 'Orders', are usually given 4 to 6 weeks after the hearing. The Findings must be made in writing setting out the facts which the Disciplinary Tribunal has found to be substantiated and must contain its Order. The Findings and Order are then filed with The Law Society and take immediate effect, except where an appeal against the Order has been lodged when the effect of the Order will be suspended until the appeal is determined.

Where (unusually) an application is made directly to the Disciplinary Tribunal, the Tribunal may refer the matter to The Law Society for investigation before proceeding with the application. Where in such a case The Law Society investigates the complaint (through the Office for the Supervision of Solicitors) and finds it to be substantiated, the Society may take over the application on the applicant's behalf.

18.7.3 Powers of the Tribunal

The Solicitors Act 1974, s 47 (as amended by the Courts and Legal Services Act 1990) gives the Disciplinary Tribunal power to make such order as in its discretion it thinks fit, including the following:

(1) striking a solicitor off the Roll;
(2) suspending a solicitor from practice;
(3) imposing a fine not exceeding £5,000 which is forfeit to Her Majesty;
(4) requiring the payment by any party of costs or a contribution towards costs;
(5) in certain cases, requiring payment of the costs of the Investigation Accountant.

18.7.4 Restoration to the Roll

An application for restoration to the Roll is made to the Disciplinary Tribunal.

18.7.5 Appeals

Appeal from a decision of the Disciplinary Tribunal is made to the Divisional Court of the Queen's Bench Division of the High Court and then with leave to the Court of Appeal and to the House of Lords.

18.8 THE COMPENSATION FUND

The Compensation Fund is maintained by The Law Society under s 36 of and Sch 2 to the Solicitors Act 1974. All practising solicitors, except those who are applying for their first three practising certificates after admission, are required to make a compulsory annual contribution to the Compensation Fund.

Payment is made with the annual practising certificate fee. An additional levy may be imposed if the Fund becomes insufficient to meet the claims being made on it. The Fund exists to make grants to persons who have suffered loss as the result of the dishonesty of a solicitor or a solicitor's employee in connection with the solicitor's practice or in connection with a trust of which the solicitor is a trustee. Payment from the Fund is made only where the applicant cannot recover his money by other means. No grant from the Fund would be made where the applicant could recover his loss from another source (eg an insurance policy). The applicant is also expected to have taken appropriate civil and/or criminal proceedings against the defaulting solicitor before making an application to the Fund.

The Law Society has a discretion to refuse a grant out of the Fund which would result in sums exceeding £1 million being paid to or on behalf of an applicant in respect of any individual transaction or matter.

Where payment is made from the Fund, The Law Society is subrogated to the rights of the applicant and can therefore take proceedings against the defaulting solicitor in order to recover the amount paid out by the Fund.

In some cases, a loan from the Fund may be made to the partners of a defaulting solicitor to enable them to settle liability to a client. Such a loan is repayable on settlement of the claim under the firm's negligence policy.

18.9 CHAPTER SUMMARY

(1) The powers of the Office for the Supervision of Solicitors (OSS) have been delegated to it by the Council of The Law Society under s 79 of the Solicitors Act 1974.

(2) The powers:
- the investigation and handling of complaints against solicitors;
- the remuneration certificate procedure for non-contentious costs;
- the imposition of conditions on practising certificates;
- interventions in a solicitor's practice: suspicion of dishonesty or failure to comply with the Solicitors' Accounts Rules 1998.

(3) Inadequate professional services are those which are not of the quality which could reasonably have been expected of a solicitor. In such a case, the OSS can order the solicitor:
- to reduce the bill;
- to waive the right to recover a fee;
- to refund money which has been paid;
- to rectify any mistakes;
- to compensate the client up to £5,000.

If the OSS considers it appropriate, it can take disciplinary action against the solicitor before the Disciplinary Tribunal.

(4) If a solicitor believes that he may have been negligent, he should:
- contact his insurers;

- tell the client to take independent legal advice;
- take copies of any documents before handing them over to new solicitors.

On no account should the solicitor admit liability without the consent of his insurers.

(5) If a complainant is dissatisfied with the OSS, the complainant can ask the Legal Services Ombudsman to examine the way in which the OSS treated the complaint and to decide whether it was investigated fully and fairly. The Ombudsman may recommend that the OSS should reconsider the complaint or use any of its disciplinary or other powers. He may also recommend, or if he considers it appropriate, order:

- the OSS to pay compensation;
- the solicitor who was the subject of the complaint to pay compensation; or
- the OSS or the solicitor (as appropriate) to repay some or all of the money spent in taking the complaint to the Ombudsman.

Before making an order, the Ombudsman must give the OSS or the solicitor (as appropriate) an opportunity to appear before him and make representations.

(6) The Solicitors' Disciplinary Tribunal is wholly independent from The Law Society and is established by s 46 of the Solicitors Act 1974. Its members are appointed by the Master of the Rolls and are either solicitors of not less than 10 years' standing or lay members who must be neither solicitors nor barristers. For the purpose of hearing and determining applications, the Tribunal sits in divisions of three, comprising two solicitor members and one lay member. Pronouncements of the Tribunal, described as findings or orders, may be delivered by a single member.

The principal function of the Tribunal is to hear and determine applications in respect of solicitors, relating to allegations of unbefitting conduct and discipline under the Solicitors Act 1974. The vast majority of applications to the Tribunal are made on behalf of The Law Society but, subject to those instances under the Act where applications are limited to The Law Society alone, it is open to anyone to make an application to the Tribunal without recourse to the Society.

(7) The Tribunal's powers are defined by the Solicitors Act 1974, s 47, as amended by s 92 of the Courts and Legal Services Act 1990. The Tribunal is given discretion to make such order as it thinks fit in respect of most applications. The Tribunal may order:

- the striking off the Roll of the name of the solicitor to whom the application or complaint relates;
- the suspension of that solicitor from practice;
- the payment by that solicitor of a penalty not exceeding £5,000, which shall be forfeit to Her Majesty; or
- the payment by any party of costs or a contribution towards costs in such amount as the Tribunal may consider reasonable.

(8) The Tribunal has jurisdiction to restore to the Roll the name of a former solicitor where that name has been struck off the Roll.

(9) The procedure for appeal from the Tribunal is governed by the Solicitors Act 1974, s 49. Appeals lie to a Divisional Court or the Queen's Bench Division,

and from there, with leave, to the Court of Appeal, and, again with appropriate leave, to the House of Lords.

(10) Compensation fund:

(a) The Law Society maintains a Compensation Fund pursuant to the Solicitors Act 1974, s 36 and Sch 2. The object of the Fund is to enable the Society to make grants to those who have suffered loss by reason of the dishonesty of a solicitor, or an employee, in connection with the solicitor's practice, or in connection with any trust of which the solicitor is a trustee. Grants may also be made in the event of hardship suffered as a result of a solicitor failing to account for monies due.

(b) The Fund is administered as a fund of last resort and no grant will be made where an applicant is otherwise indemnified against loss. If a partner defaults, The Law Society, in an appropriate case, may make a loan to the defaulter's partners so that they can make good the shortfall immediately. In that event, the partners must make a claim under their professional indemnity policy, so as to enable them to repay the loan.

(c) The Fund is made up of the compulsory annual contributions collected from all solicitors in practice. Payment is made at the same time as applications are made for the annual renewal of practising certificates. No payment is required, however, in respect of the first three practising certificates issued after admission.

Chapter 19

FINANCIAL SERVICES

This chapter looks at:

- How a solicitor might engage in the financial services.
- The need for competence before getting involved in this area.
- The possibility of committing a criminal offence in certain circumstances.

From time to time, solicitors engage in financial services work. To do this, they must be sufficiently competent in that area of practice and, in some cases, will need to comply with certain regulations imposed by the Financial Services Authority (FSA) and/or the Law Society.

Such work could arise:

- in conveyancing, if a client needs help in finding a mortgage and a supporting package which could include a life insurance policy;
- in probate, when the executors sell off the deceased's assets;
- in litigation, if helping a successful client to invest damages just won;
- in company work in making arrangements for a client to buy or sell shares in a company.

Under Rule 1 of the Solicitors' Practice Rules 1990, a solicitor would be in breach of his or her duty to act in the client's best interests if he or she did not have sufficient expertise in the area concerned. Therefore, a trainee solicitor should not give investment advice to a client unless the trainee is an expert in that field.

Under the Financial Services and Markets Act 2000 some investments are 'specified' (eg endowment life policies, unit trusts and shares). To give advice on these, or even to make arrangements for clients to acquire or dispose of them, may require the solicitor to be authorised to carry out that activity by the FSA. To do this without authority could involve the commission of a criminal offence. There are, however, certain exemptions available from the need to obtain authority, particularly for solicitors.

Thus a solicitor may be acting in a probate matter for an executor, who also happens to be the residuary beneficiary, and when the administration is finished the client may seek assistance in connection with investing the amount he has inherited. The solicitor needs to be doubly careful before advising such client and assisting them to acquire the appropriate investment. Has he got the necessary skill and knowledge to give the advice and/or make the arrangements? Is the investment concerned 'specified', for example does the client want to acquire shares, and if they are is the solicitor authorised under the Financial Services and Markets Act 2000 or exempted from the need to be authorised? On top of this, whether authorised by the FSA or not, there are likely to be regulations governing such a transaction, prescribed by the FSA and the Law Society, with which the solicitor will have to comply.

Chapter 20

IMPACT OF PROFESSIONAL CONDUCT ON PARTICULAR FIELDS OF PRACTICE

20.1 SOLICITORS' PRACTICE RULES 1990, RULES 1 AND 15

As stated in Chapter 6, the rule that underpins the solicitor's relationship with his or her client is Rule 1 of the Solicitors' Practice Rules 1990. If the spirit of this rule is applied in conjunction with Rule 15 of the Solicitors' Practice Rules 1990 (client care), the client will be well served by the solicitor.

20.2 PARTICULAR FIELDS OF PRACTICE

The general principles and rules of professional conduct apply irrespective of the particular field in which the solicitor practises. Further specific rules and principles for particular areas of practice which supplement the general rules and principles have evolved and must be considered when appropriate. A brief list of these specific conduct issues relevant to the main compulsory LPC subjects are set out below. Full details of the conduct issues can be found in the appropriate LPC Resource Books: *Business Law and Practice*, *Civil Litigation*, *Criminal Litigation* and *Conveyancing* (Jordans).

20.3 INCOME DERIVED FROM LEGAL BUSINESS

Professional conduct issues arising in *Business Law and Practice* include:

– Deciding who the client is in certain situations – is it the company itself or its shareholders?
– Conflict of interests.

Professional conduct issues arising in *Civil Litigation* include:

– Advice on the most appropriate way to fund the legal costs of a client's case including the increasingly important role of conditional fee agreements.
– Duty to the court.
– Undertakings to the court.
– Conflict of interests.
– Choice of advocate.

Professional conduct issues arising in *Criminal Litigation* include:

– The guilty client who wishes to plead not guilty.
– Conflict of interests.
– Prosecution and defence disclosure requirements under the Criminal Procedure and Investigations Act and Code of Practice 1996.

Professional conduct issues arising in *Conveyancing* include:

–   Undertakings: in particular, The Law Society's recommended forms of undertaking to banks and building societies.
–   The Law Society's formulae for telephonic exchange of contracts.
–   The Law Society's code for completion by post.
–   Rule 6 of the Solicitors' Practice Rules 1990 as amended.
–   Rule 6A of the Solicitors' Practice Rules 1990 as amended.

20.4 INCOME DERIVED FROM OTHER SOURCES

Solicitors may derive income not directly related to legal business. For example, a solicitor might derive income from:

*   *Clients' money on general deposit*
    This is permitted provided the Solicitors' Accounts Rules 1998 are complied with. Further details can be found in the LPC Resource Book, *Accounts for Solicitors* (Jordans).

*   *Commissions received*
    The solicitor will have to consider whether Solicitors' Practice Rules 1990, Rule 10 applies.

*   *Investment business*
    The firm will need to be authorised by The Law Society to carry on investment business and will need to comply with the Solicitors' Investment Business Rules 1995 (see Chapter 19).

*   *Property selling and mortgage related services*
    Solicitors' Practice Rules 1990, Rules 5 and 6, in particular, must be complied with.

20.5 SCOPE OF THIS BOOK

This book is not intended as a definitive guide on the subject. Further details of the topics covered, and of other matters not discussed here, are contained in the following source materials.

20.5.1 Statutes

(1) Solicitors Act 1974;
(2) Courts and Legal Services Act 1990 (which amends the 1974 Act in some important respects).

20.5.2 The Code of Conduct

The Guide to the Professional Conduct of Solicitors, published by The Law Society, sets out the Solicitors' Practice Rules 1990 and other relevant rules and the general principles of conduct with an explanatory text. Professional Practice Bulletins are issued by The Law Society from time to time. These should be checked to ascertain whether any rule which is being referred to has been updated. *The Law Society's Gazette*, a weekly publication distributed free to practising solicitors, also contains information relating to revisions of the rules and other statements issued by The Law Society relating to conduct.

20.5.3 Textbooks

Cordery on Solicitors. This is known as the 'bible' on professional conduct.

Handbook of Professional Conduct for Solicitors by Silverman. This is a quick reference guide to the main principles.

20.6 CONCLUSION

(1) Solicitors are bound by the general principles and rules of professional conduct regardless of the type of work they do.
(2) Whether or not a solicitor is in breach under the general law, he or she may fall foul of the professional conduct rules and be liable to disciplinary action.
(3) Specific professional conduct issues arise in particular fields of legal practice.
(4) Even where solicitors receive income from non-legal sources, there are rules and professional conduct principles governing the solicitor's conduct.

APPENDIX TO PART II

AII.1 SOLICITORS' PRACTICE RULES 1990 WITH CONSOLIDATED AMENDMENTS TO 23 DECEMBER 1999

Rules dated 18 July 1990 made by the Council of the Law Society with the concurrence of the Master of the Rolls under section 31 of the Solicitors Act 1974 and section 9 of the Administration of Justice Act 1985, regulating the English and Welsh practices of solicitors, registered foreign lawyers and recognised bodies and, in respect of Rule 12 only, regulating the English and Welsh and overseas practices of such persons in the conduct of investment business in or into any part of the United Kingdom.

Rule 1 (Basic principles)

A solicitor shall not do anything in the course of practising as a solicitor, or permit another person to do anything on his or her behalf, which compromises or impairs or is likely to compromise or impair any of the following:

(a)   the solicitor's independence or integrity;
(b)   a person's freedom to instruct a solicitor of his or her choice;
(c)   the solicitor's duty to act in the best interests of the client;
(d)   the good repute of the solicitor or of the solicitors' profession;
(e)   the solicitor's proper standard of work;
(f)   the solicitor's duty to the Court.

Rule 2 (Publicity)

Solicitors may at their discretion publicise their practices, or permit other persons to do so, or publicise the businesses or activities of other persons, provided there is no breach of these rules and provided there is compliance with a Solicitors' Publicity Code promulgated from time to time by the Council of the Law Society with the concurrence of the Master of the Rolls.

Rule 3 (Introductions and referrals)

Solicitors may accept introductions and referrals of business from other persons and may make introductions and refer business to other persons, provided there is no breach of these rules and provided there is compliance with a Solicitors' Introduction and Referral Code promulgated from time to time by the Council of the Law Society with the concurrence of the Master of the Rolls.

Rule 4 (Employed solicitors)

(1)   Solicitors who are employees of non-solicitors shall not:

(a)   choose an advocate; nor
(b)   exercise any extended right of audience under one of the Law Society's higher courts qualifications; nor
(c)   as part of their employment do for any person other than their employer work which is or could be done by a solicitor acting as such;

in any way which breaches the Employed Solicitors' Code promulgated from time to time by the Council of the Law Society with the concurrence of the Master of the Rolls.

(2) Solicitors who are employees of multi-national partnerships shall not be regarded as 'employees of non-solicitors' for the purpose of this Rule.

Rule 5 (Providing services other than as a solicitor)

Solicitors must comply with the Solicitors' Separate Business Code in controlling, actively participating in or operating (in each case alone, or by or with others) a business which:

(a) provides any service which may properly be provided by a solicitor's practice; and

(b) is not itself a solicitor's practice or a multi-national partnership.

Rule 6 (Avoiding conflicts of interest in conveyancing, property selling and mortgage related services)

(1)   (General)

This rule sets out circumstances in which a solicitor may act for more than one party in conveyancing, property selling or mortgage related services, in connection with:

(i) the transfer of land for value at arm's length;

(ii) the grant or assignment of a lease, or some other interest in land, for value at arm's length; or

(iii) the grant of a mortgage of land.

The rule must be read in the light of the notes.

Notes

(i)   *'Solicitor' (except where the notes specify otherwise)* **means a solicitor, his or her practice, and any associated practice, and includes a SEAL***; and*

   *   'associated practices' are practices with at least one principal in common;

   *   *a 'principal' is a sole practitioner, a partner in a practice (including a registered foreign lawyer partner), a director of a recognised body, a member of or beneficial owner of a share in a recognised body, or a recognised body; and*

   *   *a 'SEAL' (Solicitors' Estate Agency Limited) means a recognised body which:*

      (a)   does not undertake conveyancing;

      (b)   is owned jointly by at least four participating practices which do not have any principals in common and none of which own a controlling majority of the shares; and

      (c)   is conducted from accommodation physically divided from, and clearly differentiated from that of any participating practice; and

   *   *a 'participating practice' means a practice one or more of whose principals is a member of, or a beneficial owner of a share in, the SEAL.*

(ii)   *'Property selling' means negotiating the sale for the seller.*

(iii)   *'Mortgage related services' means advising on or arranging a mortgage, or providing mortgage related financial services, for a buyer; and*

     *   *'seller' and 'buyer' include lessor and lessee.*

(iv)   *Whether a transaction is 'at arm's length' will depend on the relationship between the parties and the context of the transaction, and will not necessarily follow from the fact that a transaction is at market value, or is stated to be on arm's length terms.*

     A transaction would not usually be at arm's length, for example, if the parties are:

     *   *related by blood, adoption or marriage;*

     *   *the settlor of a trust and the trustees;*

     *   *the trustees of a trust and its beneficiary or the beneficiary's relative;*

     *   *personal representatives and a beneficiary;*

     *   *the trustees of separate trusts for the same family;*

     *   *a sole trader or partners and a limited company set up to enable the business to be incorporated;*

     *   *associated companies (ie, where one is a holding company and the other is its subsidiary within the meaning of the Companies Act 1985, or both are subsidiaries of the same holding company); or*

     *   *a local authority and a related body within the meaning of paragraph 6(b) of the Employed Solicitors' Code 1990.*

(v)   *'Mortgage' includes a remortgage.*

(vi)   *Nothing in the rule allows a solicitor to act in breach of Rule 6A(5) (acting for seller and one of two prospective buyers), or any other rule or principle of professional conduct.*

(2)   *(Solicitor acting for seller and buyer)*

(a)   A solicitor must not act for seller and buyer:

     (i)   without the written consent of both parties;

     (ii)   if a conflict of interest exists or arises; or

     (iii)   if the seller is selling or leasing as a builder or developer.

(b)   Otherwise, a solicitor may act for seller and buyer, but only if:

     (i)   both parties are established clients; or

     (ii)   the consideration is £10,000 or less and the transaction is not the grant of a lease; or

     (iii)   there is no other qualified conveyance in the area whom either the seller or the buyer could reasonably be expected to consult; or

     (iv)   seller and buyer are represented by two separate offices in different localities, and:

         (A)   different solicitors, who normally work at each office, conduct or supervise the transaction for seller and buyer; and

         (B)   no office of the practice (or an associated practice) referred either client to the office conducting his or her transaction; or

     (v)   the only way in which the solicitor is acting for the buyer is in providing mortgage related services; or

(vi)   the only way in which the solicitor is acting for the seller is in providing property selling services through a SEAL.

(c)   When a solicitor's practice (including a SEAL) acts in the property selling for the seller and acts for the buyer, the following additional conditions must be met:

   (i)   different persons must conduct the work for the seller and the work for the buyer; and if the persons conducting the work need supervision, they must be supervised by different solicitors; and

   (ii)   the solicitor must inform the seller in writing, before accepting instructions to deal with the property selling, of any services which might be offered to a buyer, whether through the same practice or any practice associated with it; and

   (iii)   the solicitor must explain to the buyer, before the buyer gives consent to the arrangement:

      (A)   the implications of a conflict of interest arising; and
      (B)   the solicitor's financial interest in the sale going through; and
      (C)   if the solicitor proposes to provide mortgage related services to the buyer through a SEAL which is also acting for the seller, that the solicitor cannot advise the buyer on the merits of the purchase.

Notes

(i)   *If a builder or developer acquires a property in part exchange, and sells it on without development, he or she is not, for the purpose of this rule, selling 'as a builder or developer'.*

(ii)   *The test of whether a person is an 'established client' is an objective one; that is, whether a reasonable solicitor would regard the person as an established client.*

   *   *A seller or buyer who is instructing the solicitor for the first time is not an established client.*
   *   *A person related by blood, adoption or marriage to an established client counts as an established client.*
   *   *A person counts as an established client if selling or buying jointly with an established client.*

(iii)   *The consideration will only count as £10,000 or less if the value of any property given in exchange or part exchange is taken into account.*

(iv)   *Even where none of the other exceptions apply, a SEAL may act for the seller, and provide mortgage related services to the buyer; one of the participating practices may do the buyer's conveyancing, and another participating practice may do the seller's conveyancing.*

(v)   *'Solicitor'*

   *   *in paragraph (2)(b)(iv)(A), means any individual solicitor conducting or supervising the matter; and*
   *   *in paragraph (2)(c)(i), means the individual solicitor supervising the transaction.*

(3) *(Solicitor acting for lender and borrower)*

(a) A solicitor must not act for both lender and borrower on the grant of a mortgage of land:

 (i) if a conflict of interest exists or arises;

 (ii) on the grant of a private mortgage of land at arm's length;

 (iii) if, in the case of an institutional mortgage of property to be used as a private residence only, the lender's mortgage instructions extend beyond the limitations contained in paragraphs (3)(c) and (3)(e), or do not permit the use of the certificate of title required by paragraph (3)(d); or

 (iv) if, in the case of any other institutional mortgage, the lender's mortgage instructions extend beyond the limitations contained in paragraphs (3)(c)and (3)(e).

(b) A solicitor who proposes to act for both lender and borrower on the grant of an institutional mortgage of land, must first inform the lender in writing of the circumstances if:

 (i) the solicitor or a member of his or her immediate family is a borrower; or

 (ii) the solicitor proposes to act for seller, buyer and lender in the same transaction.

(c) A solicitor acting for both lender and borrower in an institutional mortgage may only accept or act upon instructions from the lender which are limited to the following matters:

 (i) taking reasonable steps to check the identity of the borrower (and anyone else required to sign the mortgage deed or other document connected with the mortgage) by reference to a document or documents, such as a passport, precisely specified in writing by the lender;

 following the guidance in the Law Society's 'green card' warning on property fraud and 'blue card' warning on money laundering;

 checking that the seller's solicitors or licensed conveyancers (if unknown to the solicitor) appear in a current legal directory or hold practising certificates issued by their professional body;

 and, in the case of a lender with no branch office within reasonable proximity of the borrower, carrying out the money laundering checks precisely specified in writing by the lender;

 (ii) making appropriate searches relating to the property in public registers (eg local searches, commons registration searches, mining searches), and reporting any results specified by the lender or which the solicitor considers may adversely affect the lender; or effecting search insurance;

 (iii) making enquiries on legal matters relating to the property reasonably specified by the lender, and reporting the replies;

(iv)   reporting the purchase price stated in the transfer and on how the borrower says that the purchase money (other than the mortgage advance) is to be provided; and reporting if the solicitor will not have control over the payment of all the purchase money (other than a deposit paid to an estate agent or a reservation fee paid to a builder or developer);

(v)   reporting if the seller or the borrower (if the property is already owned by the borrower) has not owned or been the registered owner of the property for at least six months;

(vi)   if the lender does not arrange insurance, confirming receipt of satisfactory evidence that the buildings insurance is in place for at least the sum required by the lender and covers the risks specified by the lender; giving notice to the insurer of the lender's interest and requesting confirmation that the insurer will notify the lender if the policy is not renewed or is cancelled; and supplying particulars of the insurance and the last premium receipt to the lender;

(vii)   investigating title to the property and appurtenant rights; reporting any defects revealed, advising on the need for any consequential statutory declarations or indemnity insurance, and approving and effecting indemnity cover if required by the lender; and reporting if the solicitor is aware of any rights needed for the use or enjoyment of the property over other land;

(viii) reporting on any financial charges (eg improvement or repair grants or Housing Act discounts) secured on the property revealed by the solicitor's searches and enquiries which will affect the property after completion of the mortgage;

(ix)   in the case of a leasehold property, confirming that the lease contains the terms stipulated by the lender and does not include any terms specified by the lender as unacceptable; obtaining a suitable deed of variation or indemnity insurance if the terms of the lease are unsatisfactory; enquiring of the seller or the borrower (if the property is already owned by the borrower) as to any known breaches of convenant by the landlord or any superior landlord and reporting any such breaches to the lender; reporting if the solicitor becomes aware of the landlord's absence or insolvency; making a company search and checking the last three years' published accounts of any management company with responsibilities under the lease; if the borrower is required to be a shareholder in the management company, obtaining the share certificate, a blank stock transfer form signed by the borrower and a copy of the memorandum and articles of association; obtaining any necessary consent to or prior approval of the assignment and mortgage; obtaining a clear receipt for the last payment of rent and service charge; and serving notice of the assignment and mortgage on the landlord;

(x)   if the property is subject to a letting, checking that the type of letting and its terms comply with the lender's requirements;

(xi)   making appropriate pre-completion searches, including a bankruptcy search against the borrower, any other person in whom the legal estate is vested and any guarantor;

(xii) receiving, releasing and transmitting the mortgage advance, including asking for any final inspection needed and dealing with any retentions and cashbacks;

(xiii) procuring execution of the mortgage deed and form of guarantee as appropriate by the persons whose identities have been checked in accordance with any requirements of the lender under paragraph (3)(c)(i) as those of the borrower, any other person in whom the legal estate is vested and any guarantor; obtaining their signatures to the forms of Undertaking required by the lender in relation to the use, occupation or physical state of the property; and complying with the lender's requirements if any document is to be executed under a power of attorney;

(xiv) asking the borrower for confirmation that the information about occupants given in the mortgage instructions or offer is correct; obtaining consents in the form required by the lender from existing or prospective occupiers of the property aged 17 or over specified by the lender, or of whom the solicitor is aware;

(xv) advising the borrower on the terms of any document required by the lender to be signed by the borrower;

(xvi) advising any other person required to sign any document on the terms of that document or, if there is a conflict of interest between that person and the borrower or the lender, advising that person on the need for separate legal advice and arranging for him or her to see an independent conveyancer;

(xvii) obtaining the legal transfer of the property to the mortgagor;

(xviii) procuring the redemption of (A) existing mortgages on property the subject of any associated sale of which the solicitor is aware, and (B) any other mortgages secured against a property located in England or Wales made by an identified lender where an identified account number or numbers or a property address has been given by the lender;

(xix) ensuring the redemption or postponement of existing mortgages on the property, and registering the mortgage with the priority required by the lender;

(xx) making administrative arrangements in relation to any collateral security, such as an endowment policy, or in relation to any collateral warranty or guarantee relating to the physical condition of the property, such as NHBC documentation;

(xxi) registering the transfer and mortgage;

(xxii) giving legal advice on any matters reported on under this paragraph (3)(c), suggesting courses of action open to the lender, and complying with the lender's instructions on the action to be taken;

(xxiii) disclosing any relationship specified by the lender between the solicitor and borrower;

(xxiv) storing safely the title deeds and documents pending registration and delivery to or as directed by the lender;

(xxv) retaining the information contained in the solicitor's conveyancing file for at least six years from the date of the mortgage.

(d)   In addition, a solicitor acting for both lender and borrower in an institutional mortgage of property to be used as a private residence only:

    (i)   must use the certificate of title set out in the Appendix, or as substituted from time to time by the Council with the concurrence of the Master of the Rolls ('the approved certificate') and

    (ii)   unless the lender has certified that its mortgage instructions are subject to the limitations contained in paragraphs (3)(c) and (3)(e), must notify the lender on receipt of instructions that the approved certificate will be used, and that the solicitor's duties to the lender are limited to the matters contained in the approved certificate.

(e)   The terms of this rule will prevail in the event of any ambiguity in the lender's instructions, or discrepancy between the instructions and paragraph (3)(c) or the approved certificate.

Anti-avoidance

(f)   A solicitor who is acting only for the borrower in an institutional mortgage of property must not accept or act upon any requirements by way of undertaking, warranty, guarantee or otherwise of the lender, the lender's solicitor or other agent which extend beyond the limitations contained in paragraph (3)(c).

Notes

(i)   *An 'institutional mortgage' is a mortgage on standard terms, provided by an institutional lender in the normal course of its activities; and*

    *   *a 'private mortgage' is any other mortgage.*

(ii)   *A solicitor will not be in breach of paragraphs (3)(a)(iii)-(iv) or (c) if the lender has certified that its mortgage instructions are subject to the limitations set out in paragraphs (3)(c) and (e), and certifies any subsequent instructions in the same way. If there is no certification, a solicitor acting in an exclusively residential transaction must notify the lender that the approved certificate of title will be used and that the solicitor's duties to the lender will be limited accordingly (see paragraph (3)(d)(ii)). In other types of transaction, the solicitor should draw the lender's attention to the provisions of paragraphs (3)(c) and (e) and state that he or she cannot act on any instructions which extend beyond the matters contained in paragraph (3)(c).*

(iii)   *'Solicitor' in paragraph (3)(b)(i) means any principal in the practice (or an associated practice), and any solicitor conducting or supervising the transaction, whether or not that solicitor is a principal; and*

    *   *'immediate family' means spouse, children, parents, brothers and sisters.*

(iv)   *The lender must be informed of the circumstances, in accordance with paragraph (5)(b) so that the lender can decide whether or not to instruct the solicitor.*

(v)   *A lender's instructions may require a wider disclosure of a solicitor's circumstances than paragraph (3)(b) requires; and a solicitor must assess whether the circumstances give rise to a conflict. For example, there will be a conflict between lender and borrower if the solicitor becomes involved in negotiations relating to the terms of the loan. A conflict might arise from the relationship a solicitor has with the borrower - for example, if the solicitor is the borrower's creditor or debtor or the borrower's business associate or cohabitant.*

APPENDIX CERTIFICATE OF TITLE

TO: (*Lender*)
Lender's Reference or Account No:
The Borrower:
Property:
Title Number:
Mortgage Advance:
Completion Date:
Conveyancer's Name & Address:
Conveyancer's Reference:
Conveyancer's bank, sort code and account number:

WE THE CONVEYANCERS NAMED ABOVE CERTIFY as follows:

(1)   If you have provided any photograph(s) and/or specimen signature(s), we have checked the identity of the Borrower against them.

(2)   Except as otherwise disclosed to you in writing:

(i)   we have investigated the title to the Property and, upon completion of the mortgage, the Borrower will have a good and marketable title to the Property and to its rights free from prior mortgages or charges and from onerous encumbrances which title will be registered with absolute title;

(ii)   if you have provided a plan, we have compared the extent of the Property shown on your plan against relevant plans in the title deeds, and in our opinion there are no material discrepancies;

(iii)   if the Property is leasehold the terms of the lease accord with your instructions, including any requirements you have for covenants by the Landlord and/or a management company for the insurance, repair and maintenance of the structure, exterior and common parts of any building of which the Property forms part;

(iv)   the buildings insurance is in place, or will be on completion, for the sum required by you;

(v)   if the Property is to be purchased by the Borrower:

(a)   the contract for sale provides for vacant possession on completion;

(b)   the seller has owned or been the registered owner of the Property for not less than six months;

(c)   we are not acting on behalf of the seller;

(vi)   we have made a local search (which is not more than three months old) and such other searches as are appropriate to the Property, the Borrower and any guarantor;

(vii) nothing has been revealed by our searches and enquiries which would prevent the Property being used by any occupant for residential purposes;

(viii) neither any principal nor any other solicitor in the practice giving this certificate nor any spouse, child, parent, brother or sister of such a person is interested in the Property (whether alone or jointly with any other) as seller, buyer or Borrower.

WE:

(a) undertake, prior to use of the mortgage advance, to obtain the execution by the Borrower of a mortgage and by any guarantor of a guarantee, each in the form of the draft supplied by you, and to obtain consents in the form required by you from any existing or prospective occupier(s) of the property specified by you;

(b) have made or will make such Bankruptcy, Land Registry or Land Charges Searches as may be necessary to justify certificate no (2)(i) above;

(c) will within the period of protection afforded by the searches referred to in paragraph (b) above:

(i)   complete the mortgage;

(ii) arrange for stamping of the transfer if appropriate;

(iii) deliver to the Land Registry the documents necessary to register the mortgage in your favour and any relevant prior dealings;

(iv) effect any other registrations necessary to protect your interests as mortgagee;

(d) will despatch to you the Charge Certificate and any other relevant deeds relating to the Property with a list of them in the form prescribed by you within ten working days of receipt by us from the Land Registry;

(e) will not part with the mortgage advance (and will return it to you if required) if it shall come to our notice prior to completion that the Property will at completion be occupied in whole or in part otherwise than in accordance with your instructions;

(f) will not accept instructions, except with your consent in writing, to prepare any lease or tenancy agreement relating to the Property or any part of it prior to despatch of the Charge Certificate to you;

(g) will not use the mortgage advance until satisfied that any existing mortgage on property the subject of an associated sale of which we are aware, will be discharged prior to or contemporaneously with the transfer of the Property to the Borrower;

(h) will notify you in writing if any matter comes to our attention before completion which would render the certificate given above untrue or inaccurate and, in those circumstances, will defer completion pending your authority to proceed and will return the mortgage advance to you if required.

OUR duties to you are limited to the matters set out in this certificate and we accept no further liability or responsibility whatsoever. The payment by you to us (by whatever means) of the mortgage advance or any part of it constitutes acceptance of this limitation and any assignment to you by the Borrower of any rights of action against us to which the Borrower may be entitled shall take effect subject to this limitation.

Subject to the above limitation we confirm that we have complied with your instructions.

Previous disclosures have been made to you under paragraph (2) above	*Yes/No
No disclosures under paragraph (2) above accompany this report	*Yes/No

Delete as appropriate

SIGNED on behalf of THE CONVEYANCERS...

NAME of Authorised Signatory...

QUALIFICATION of Authorised Signatory...

DATE of Signature..

Rule 6A (Seller's solicitor dealing with more than one prospective buyer)

(1) This rule applies to the conveyancing of freehold and leasehold property. The rule is to be interpreted in the light of the notes.

Notes

(i) *Rule 6A replaces the Council Direction of 6th October 1977 and Principle and Commentary 24.04 in the 1993 edition of 'The Guide to the Professional Conduct of Solicitors' with effect from 1st March 1995. As was the case with the Council Direction, it applies to all conveyancing of land, whether the transaction is of a 'commercial' or 'domestic' nature.*

(ii) *The Council Direction did not and Rule 6A does not set terms for a contract race. It lays down requirements which must be met when a solicitor is instructed to deal with more than one prospective buyer. The rule imposes no obligation on the seller's solicitor to exchange contracts with the first buyer to deliver a signed contract and deposit. It will be a matter of law whether or not the seller has entered into a contractual obligation to exchange with the buyer 'first past the post', or whether the whole matter remains 'subject to contract'.*

(iii) *References to 'solicitor' throughout the rule include a firm of solicitors, a multi-national partnership or a recognised body.*

(2) Where a seller instructs a solicitor to deal with more than one prospective buyer, the solicitor (with the client's consent) shall immediately disclose the seller's decision, if possible by telephone or fax, to the solicitor or other conveyancer acting for each prospective buyer or direct to the prospective buyer if acting in person. Such disclosure, if made by telephone, shall at once be confirmed by letter or fax. If the seller refuses to authorise disclosure, the solicitor shall immediately cease to act. Each prospective buyer must be notified each time a decision is taken to deal with any further prospective buyer.

Notes

(i) *It is the seller's decision to deal with more than one prospective buyer which must be notified. The seller's solicitor must not wait until contracts are actually submitted but must notify the appropriate parties immediately upon receiving instructions to deal with a prospective buyer (other than the first).*

(ii) A solicitor will have been instructed to deal with a prospective buyer where the solicitor is asked to submit a draft contract or to provide any other documentation or information (eg a plan or a note of the Land Registry title number) in order to facilitate the conveyancing of the premises to the prospective buyer. The rule does not, however, cover activities normally performed by an estate agent, such as issuing particulars of sale, showing prospective buyers round the property, and negotiating the price.

(iii) the rule will apply where the contracts are to contain non-identical terms (eg where one contract is to include additional land). It will also apply where the contracts are to relate to different interests in the same property where the sale of one such interest would affect the sale of the other. For example, a party negotiating to take a lease of premises will be affected by another party negotiating to buy the freehold with vacant possession, since the sale of one precludes the sale of the other. On the other hand, the rule would not apply where the seller is proposing to grant a lease and to effect a simultaneous sale of the freehold reversion subject to that lease, since neither transaction precludes the other.

(iv) Where a prospective buyer has retained an unqualified conveyancer, solicitors are reminded to consult the Council guidance on dealing with unqualified conveyancers. However, so far as rule 6A is concerned, the obligations in paragraph (2) will be met by disclosure either to the prospective buyer direct or to the unqualified conveyancer.

(3) The obligations in paragraph (2) of this rule apply where a seller client, to the solicitor's knowledge, deals (whether directly or through another solicitor or other conveyancer) with another prospective buyer (or with that buyer's solicitor or other conveyancer).

Note

'Deals with another prospective buyer' should be interpreted in the light of note (ii) to paragraph (2).

(4) A solicitor shall not act for more than one of the prospective buyers.

Notes

(i) 'Prospective buyers' should be interpreted in the light of note (ii) to paragraph (2).

(ii) This part of the rule recognises the inevitable conflict of interest which makes it impossible for a solicitor to act for more than one of the prospective buyers.

(5) A solicitor shall not act for both the seller and one of the prospective buyers, even in a case which would fall within Rule 6(2) of these rules.

Notes

(i) 'Prospective buyers' should be interpreted in the light of note (ii) to paragraph (2).

(ii) Clearly a solicitor must not act for both where it is known at the time of taking instructions on behalf of the buyer that there is more than one prospective buyer. In addition, this part of the rule does not permit a solicitor to continue to act for both in a case falling within Rule 6(2), where another prospective buyer is introduced during the course of the transaction because of the significant inherent conflict; the solicitor would find it impossible to reconcile the interests of both clients if, for example, it was in the seller's best interests to exchange with the other prospective buyer.

(6) For the purposes of this rule a prospective buyer shall continue to be treated as such until either the prospective buyer or the seller gives written notice (either by letter or by fax) of withdrawal from the transaction, such notice to be

between solicitors or other conveyancers save where such notice is given by or to a prospective buyer acting in person.

Notes

(i) *Solicitors should take particular care where a contract has been submitted but nothing has been heard from the prospective buyer's solicitor for some time. If the seller decides to deal with another buyer, the rule must still be complied with unless the seller's solicitor has already given notice of withdrawal.*

(ii) *Where a prospective buyer has retained an unqualified conveyancer, the provisions of paragraph (6) should be interpreted in the light of note (iv) to paragraph (2).*

(7) This rule does not apply to a proposed sale by auction or tender. The rules does, however, apply to require disclosure to a prospective buyer by private treaty of instructions to offer the property by auction or tender.

Rule 7 (Fee sharing)

(1) A solicitor shall not share or agree to share his or her professional fees with any person except:

   (a) a practising solicitor;

   (b) a practising foreign lawyer (other than a foreign lawyer whose registration in the register of foreign lawyers is suspended or whose name has been struck off the register);

   (c) the solicitor's **bona fide** employee, which provision shall not permit under the cloak of employment a partnership prohibited by paragraph (6) of this rule; or

   (d) a retired partner or predecessor of the solicitor or the dependants or personal representatives of a deceased partner or predecessor.

(2) Notwithstanding paragraph (l) of this rule a solicitor who instructs an estate agent as sub-agent for the sale of properties may remunerate the estate agent on the basis of a proportion of the solicitor's professional fee.

(3) The exceptions set out in paragraphs 2 to 9 of the Employed Solicitors' Code shall where necessary also operate as exceptions to this rule but only to permit fee sharing with the solicitor's employer.

(4) A solicitor who works as a volunteer in a law centre or advice service operated by a charitable or similar non-commercial organisation may pay to the organisation any fees or costs that he or she receives under the legal aid scheme.

(5) For the purposes of sub-paragraph (1)(d) above, the references to a retired or deceased partner shall be construed, in relation to a recognised body, as meaning a retired or deceased director or member of that body, or a retired or deceased beneficial owner of any share in that body held by a member as nominee.

(6) (a) A solicitor shall not enter into partnership with any person other than a solicitor, a registered foreign lawyer or a recognised body.

   (b) A recognised body shall not enter into partnership with any person other than a solicitor or a recognised body.

   (c) In this paragraph, 'solicitor' means a solicitor of the Supreme Court of England and Wales.

(7)   A solicitor shall not practise through any body corporate except a recognised body, or save as permitted under Rule 4 of these rules.

Rule 8 (Contingency fees)

(1) A solicitor who is retained or employed to prosecute or defend any action, suit or other contentious proceeding shall not enter into any arrangement to receive a contingency fee in respect of that proceeding, save one permitted under statute or by the common law.

(2) Paragraph (l) of this rule shall not apply to an arrangement in respect of an action, suit or other contentious proceeding in any country other than England and Wales to the extent that a local lawyer would be permitted to receive a contingency fee in respect of that proceeding.

Rule 9 (Claims assessors)

(1) A solicitor shall not, in respect of any claim or claims arising as a result of death or personal injury, either enter into an arrangement for the introduction of clients with or act in association with any person (not being a solicitor) whose business or any part of whose business is to make, support or prosecute (whether by action or otherwise, and whether by a solicitor or agent or otherwise) claims arising as a result of death or personal injury and who in the course of such business solicits or receives contingency fees in respect of such claims.

(2) The prohibition in paragraph (1) of this rule shall not apply to an arrangement or association with a person who solicits or receives contingency fees only in respect of proceedings in a country outside England and Wales, to the extent that a local lawyer would be permitted to receive a contingency fee in respect of such proceedings.

Rule 10 (Receipt of commissions from third parties)

(1) Solicitors shall account to their clients for any commission received of more than £20 unless, having disclosed to the client in writing the amount or basis of calculation of the commission or (if the precise amount or basis cannot be ascertained) an approximation thereof, they have the client's agreement to retain it.

(2) Where the commission actually received is materially in excess of the amount or basis or approximation disclosed to the client the solicitor shall account to the client for the excess.

(3) This rule does not apply where a member of the public deposits money with a solicitor who is acting as agent for a building society or other financial institution and the solicitor has not advised that person as a client as to the disposition of the money.

Rule 11 (Names used by a firm)

(1) A firm must not use a name which:

  (a) is misleading; or
  (b) brings the profession into disrepute.

(2) A firm name appearing on any letterhead (or fax heading, or heading used for bills), if the name does not itself include the word 'solicitor(s)', must be accompanied by either:

(a) a word 'solicitor(s)'; or

(b) the words 'regulated by the Law Society'.

(3) This rule must be interpreted in the light of the notes.

Notes

(i) *The rule applies to any name used by a firm (which includes a sole practitioner or a recognised body – see rule 18(2)(d)) for its practice or part of its practice.*

(ii) *The rule would allow, for example*

    (a) *a non-conventional name, such as 'The Legal Clinic', 'XYZ Solicitors' or 'Briefcase Legal Services';*

    (b) *a name with a geographical reference, eg, 'Brown and Son (Chancery Lane)' or 'Guildford Solicitors' – but not a name that would breach note (iii)(e);*

    (c) *a name including a field of practice, such as 'Smith & Co Conveyancers' or 'Redditch Conveyancing Service';*

    (d) *a firm name consisting of the names of solicitors or foreign lawyers who are or were principals in the firm or a predecessor firm, such as 'Lewis & Smith', even though Lewis and Smith have died and Browne is now the sole principal;*

    (e) *a firm name which includes the name of an historical character unconnected with the practice, or the name of a fictional character, or an invented name, or a name selected at will - but not a name that would breach note (iii)(c);*

    (f) *the use of '& Co.' or 'Solicitors', even for a sole practitioner.*

(iii) *The rule would not allow:*

    (a) *a name which uses the words 'Law Centre';*

    (b) *a name which implies a connection with a business other than a legal practice, for example 'Safeway Solicitors Group';*

    (c) *a firm name which includes the name of, or refers to, any actual person unless that person is either:*

        (A) *a solicitor or foreign lawyer who is or was a principal in the firm or a predecessor firm; or*

        (B) *an historical character unconnected with the practice; for example, 'Jones and Co' or 'JMJ Financial and Legal Services', where JM Jones is a financial adviser employed in the firm;*

    (d) *a name which implies that a firm is bigger than it is (eg, 'French & Partners', if French is a sole practitioner), unless the name is permitted by note (ii)(d);*

    (e) *a name which uses the definite article together with a geographical reference, for example 'The Chancery Lane Solicitors' or 'The Reddich Property Centre'.*

(iv) *If the name of a multi-national practice includes the word 'Solicitor(s)', the name must also include:*

    (a) *words denoting the countries or jurisdictions of qualification of the foreign lawyer principals and their professional qualifications; or*

     (b)   *the words 'Registered Foreign Lawyer(s)'; and the categories of lawyers must appear in order, with the largest group of principals first.*

  (v)   *Compliance with rule 11(2)(a) in the case of a solicitors' practice will be satisfied by, for example:*

     (a)   *adding after the name a description of the firm which comprises or includes the word 'solicitor(s)'; or*

     (b)   *the appearance of the word 'solicitor(s)' against a list of the partners (or directors); or*

     (c)   *a statement that the partners (or directors) are solicitors.*

  (vi)   *A firm which wishes to comply with rule 11(2)(b), and which uses a statement of authorisation under rule 21 of the Solicitors' Investment Business Rules, may adopt the formula 'regulated by the Law Society; authorised by the Society to conduct investment business'.*

  (vii)   *The notepaper of a multi-national practice has to comply with paragraph 7(b) of the Publicity Code (naming and describing partners and staff), which will ensure compliance with rule 11(2). (The notepaper could, in addition, bear the words 'regulated by the Law Society'.)*

  (viii)   *'Principal' in the case of a recognised body means a director, registered member or beneficial shareowner.*

  (ix)   *Rule 11 applies to private practice only.*

Rule 12 (Investment business)

(1) Without prejudice to the generality of the principles embodied in Rule 1 of these rules, solicitors shall not in connection with investment business:

    (a) be appointed representatives; or

    (b) have any arrangement with other persons under which the solicitors could be constrained to recommend to clients or effect for them (or refrain from so doing) transactions in some investments but not others, with some persons but not others, or through the agency of some persons but not others; or to introduce or refer clients or other persons with whom the solicitors deal to some persons but not others.

(2) Notwithstanding any proviso to Rule 5 of these rules, solicitors shall not by themselves or with any other person set up, operate, actively participate in or control any separate business which is an appointed representative.

(3) Where a solicitor, authorised to conduct investment business, is required by the rules of the relevant regulatory body to use a buyer's guide, the solicitor shall use a buyer's guide in a form which has been approved by the Council of the Law Society.

(4) This rule shall have effect in relation to the conduct of investment business within or into any part of the United Kingdom.

(5) In this rule 'appointed representative', 'investment' and 'investment business' have the meanings assigned to them by the Financial Services Act 1986.

Rule 13 (Supervision and management of a practice)

In this rule, words in italics are defined in the notes.

(1)   The *principals* in a practice must ensure that their practice is supervised and managed so as to provide for:

(a) compliance with principal solicitors' duties at law and in conduct to exercise proper *supervision* over their admitted and unadmitted staff;

(b) adequate *supervision* and direction of clients' matters;

(c) compliance with the requirements of sections 22(2A) and 23(3) of the Solicitors Act 1974 as to the direction and *supervision* of unqualified persons;

(d) effective *management* of the practice generally.

(2) Every practice must have at least one *principal* who is a solicitor *qualified to supervise*.

(3)

(a) Except as provided in (b) below, every office of the practice must have at least one solicitor *qualified to supervise*, for whom that office is his or her normal place of work.

(b) Without prejudice to the requirements of paragraph (1) of this rule, an office which undertakes only property selling and ancillary mortgage related services as defined in rule 6 of these rules, survey and valuation services, must be managed and supervised to the following minimum standards:

(i) the day-to-day control and administration must be undertaken by a suitably qualified and experienced office manager who is a fit and proper person to undertake such work; and for whom that office is his or her normal place of work; and

(ii) the office must be supervised and managed by a solicitor *qualified to supervise*, who must visit the office with sufficient frequency and spend sufficient time there to allow for adequate control of and consultation with staff, and if necessary consultation with clients.

(4) This rule is to be interpreted in the light of the notes, and is subject to the transitional provisions set out in note (k).

(5)

(a) This rule applies to private practice, and to solicitors employed by a law centre.

(b) The rule also applies to other employed solicitors, but only:

(i) if they advise or act for members of the public under the legal scheme; or

(ii) if, in acting for members of the public, they exercise any *right of audience* or *right to conduct litigation*, or supervise anyone exercising those rights.

Notes

(a) Principals' responsibility for the practice

Principals are responsible at law and in conduct for their practices, and compliance with the rule does not derogate from this responsibility. Under rule 6 of these rules, property selling or mortgage related services to one party to a conveyance, and conveyancing services for the other party, may not be supervised by the same solicitor.

(b) 'Supervision' and 'management'

(i) 'Supervision' refers to the professional overseeing of staff and the professional overseeing of clients' matters.

(ii) 'Management' is a wider concept, which encompasses the overall direction and development of the practice and its day-to-day control and administration.

Management functions include business efficiency as well as professional competence.

(iii) Operationally, supervision and management may be delegated within an established framework for reporting and accountability. However, responsibility under paragraph (1)(a) of the rule, and the responsibility referred to in note (a) above, remain with the principals.

(iv) 'With sufficient frequency' in paragraph (3)(b)(ii) would normally mean daily but if the office is open at weekends it may be possible to defer consultations with clients until a weekday and be available only at need to staff.

(c) Evidence of effective supervision and management

Where a question arises as to compliance with paragraph (1) of the rule, principals will be expected to be able to produce evidence of a systematic and effective approach to the supervision and management of the practice. Such evidence may include implementation by the practice of one or more of the following:

(i) guidance on the supervision and execution of particular types of work issued from time to time by the Law Society including:

(A) guidance on solicitors' responsibilities for the supervision of clerks exercising rights of audience under section 27(2)(e) of the Courts and Legal Services Act 1990; and

(B) good practice guidelines on the recruitment and supervision of employees undertaking investment business;

(ii) the practice's own properly documented management standards and procedures;

(iii) practice management standards promoted from time to time by the Law Society;

(iv) accounting standards and procedures promoted from time to time by the Law Society;

(v) external quality standards such as BS EN ISO 9000 or Investors in People; and

(vi) in the case of solicitors employed by a law centre, any management standards or procedures laid down by its management committee.

(d) 'Qualified to supervise'

A solicitor is qualified to supervise if he or she:

(i) has held practising certificates for at least 36 months within the last ten years; and
(ii) has completed the training specified from time to time by the Law Society for the purpose of the rule.

(e) 'Normal place of work'

(i) A solicitor's 'normal place of work' is the office from which he or she normally works, even though the day-to-day demands of practice may often take the solicitor out of the office.

(ii)   If a solicitor normally works from a particular office for a part of the working week, that office is his or her 'normal place of work' for that part of the week. The solicitor may have a different 'normal place of work' for another part of the week.

(iii) A solicitor who has a different 'normal place of work' for different parts of the week could be the sole solicitor qualified to supervise at different offices at different times in the week. However, no solicitor can be the sole solicitor qualified to supervise at two different offices for the same part of the week.

(iv)   For compliance with paragraph (3) of the rule, an office must, for every part of the working week, have a solicitor qualified to supervise for whom that office is his or her 'normal place of work' for that part of the week. This could be a different solicitor for different parts of the week.

(v)   The working week of an office includes early mornings, late evenings and weekends if work is carried on, and if so the office must have a solicitor qualified to supervise for those times. However, it is not required that the solicitor qualified to supervise normally works at those times, provided that he or she:

   (A)   is available for emergency consultation; and
   (B)   pays occasional visits to the office during such times.

(f) Working away from the office

It is particularly important that systems of supervision and management encompass the work of:

(i)   those persons from time to time working away from the office   eg at home, visiting clients, at court, at a police station, at a consulting room open only for a few hours per week, or staffing a stand at an exhibition;

(ii)   any person who normally works away from the office, such as a teleworker or homeworker.

(g) Absence of solicitor qualified to supervise, or office manager

(i)   When the solicitor qualified to supervise at an office is away on holiday, on sick leave, etc., suitable arrangements must be in place to ensure that any duties to clients and others are fully met. A similar standard applies to the absence of an office manager with responsibility for the day-to-day control and administration of a property selling office.

(ii)   If the solicitor qualified to supervise will be away for a month or more, the arrangements will normally need to include the provision of another solicitor qualified to supervise at that office. A similar standard applies to the absence of an office manager with responsibility for the day-to-day control and administration of a property selling office.

(h) 'Right of audience' and 'right to conduct litigation'

'Right of audience' and 'right to conduct litigation' are to be interpreted in accordance with Part II and section 119 of the Courts and Legal Services Act 1990.

(i) Recognised bodies

'Principal', in relation to a recognised body, means a director of that body.

(j) Registered foreign lawyers

(i)   A registered foreign lawyer who is a principal in the practice may fulfil the role of a 'solicitor qualified to supervise' for the purpose of paragraph (2) of the rule provided that:

   (A)   the practice has at least one principal who is a solicitor; and
   (B)   the practice does not exercise or assume responsibility for any right of audience or any right to conduct litigation; and
   (C)   the registered foreign lawyer has practised as a lawyer for at least 36 months within the last ten years; and
   (D)   he or she has completed the training specified under note (d)(ii) above.

(ii)   A registered foreign lawyer who is a principal in the practice may fulfil the role of a 'solicitor qualified to supervise' for the purpose of paragraph (3) of the rule or note (k)(ii)(C) below, provided that:

   (A)   no right of audience or right to conduct litigation is exercised or supervised from that office; and
   (B)   the registered foreign lawyer has practised as a lawyer for at least 36 months within the last ten years; and
   (C)   he or she has completed the training specified under note (d)(ii) above.

(k) Transitional provisions

For a period of 10 years from 23rd December 1999:

(i)   a solicitor or registered foreign lawyer who would not satisfy the requirements for a solicitor qualified to supervise can nevertheless fulfil that role for the purpose of paragraph (2) of the rule or note (k)(ii)(C) below, provided that:

   (A)   immediately before 12th December 1996 he or she was qualified to supervise an office (under practice rule 13(1)(a) as it then stood, or any waiver of that rule); and
   (B)   any requirements of that rule or of any waiver continue to be met;

(ii)   a person who would not satisfy the requirements for a solicitor qualified to supervise can nevertheless fulfil that role for the purpose of paragraph (3) of the rule, provided that:

   (A)   immediately before 12th December 1996 he or she was managing or employed to manage an office in compliance with practice rule 13(1)(b) as it then stood, or any waiver of that rule; and
   (B)   any requirements of that rule or of any waiver continue to be met; and
   (C)   the office is attended on a daily basis by a solicitor qualified to supervise.

Rule 14 (Structural surveys and formal valuations)

Solicitors may not provide structural surveys or formal valuations of property unless:

(a)   the work is carried out by a principal or employee who is a chartered surveyor or who holds another professional qualification approved by the Council; and

(b)   the appropriate contribution has been paid to the Solicitors' Indemnity Fund.

Rule 15 (Costs information and client care)

Solicitors shall:

(a)　give information about costs and other matters, and

(b)　operate a complaints handling procedure,

in accordance with a Solicitors' Costs Information and Client Care Code made from time to time by the Council of the Law Society with the concurrence of the Master of the Rolls, but subject to the notes.

Notes

(i)　*A serious breach of the code, or persistent breaches of a material nature, will be a breach of the rule, and may also be evidence of inadequate professional services under section 37A of the Solicitors Act 1974.*

(ii)　*Material breaches of the code which are not serious or persistent will not be a breach of the rule, but may be evidence of inadequate professional services under section 37A.*

(iii)　*The powers of the Office for the Supervision of Solicitors on a finding of inadequate professional services include:*

　(a)　*disallowing all or part of the solicitor's costs; and*

　(b)　*directing the solicitor to pay compensation to the client up to a limit of £1,000.*

(iv)　*Non-material breaches of the code will not be a breach of the rule, and will not be evidence of inadequate professional services under section 37A.*

(v)　*Registered foreign lawyers, although subject to Rule 15 as a matter of professional conduct, are not subject to section 37A. However, solicitor partners in a multi-national partnership are subject to section 37A for professional services provided by the firm.*

Rule 16 (Cross-border activities within the European Community)

(1)　In relation to cross-border activities within the European Community solicitors shall, without prejudice to their other obligations under these rules or any other rules, principles or requirements of conduct, observe the rules codified in articles 2 to 5 of the CCBE Code of Conduct for Lawyers in the European Community adopted on 28 October 1988, as interpreted by article 1 (the preamble) thereof and the Explanatory Memorandum and Commentary thereon prepared by the CCBE's Deontology Working Party and dated May 1989.

(2)　In this rule:

　(a)　'cross-border activities' means:

　　(i)　all professional contacts with lawyers of member states of the European Community other than the United Kingdom; and

　　(ii)　the professional activities of the solicitor in a member state other than the United Kingdom, whether or not the solicitor is physically present in that member state; and

　(b)　'lawyers' means lawyers as defined in Directive 77/249 of the Council of the European Communities dated 22 March 1977 as amended from time to time.

Rule 16A (Solicitors acting as advocates)

Any solicitor acting as advocate shall at all times comply with the Law Society's Code for Advocacy.

Rule 16B (Choice of advocate)

(1) A solicitor shall not make it a condition of providing litigation services that advocacy services shall also be provided by that solicitor or by the solicitor's firm or the solicitor's agent.

(2) A solicitor who provides both litigation and advocacy services shall as soon as practicable after receiving instructions and from time to time consider and advise the client whether, having regard to the circumstances including:

    (i)   the gravity, complexity and likely cost of the case;

    (ii) the nature of the solicitor's practice;

    (iii) the solicitor's ability and experience;

    (iv) the solicitor's relationship with the client,

the best interests of the client would be served by the solicitor, another advocate from the solicitor's firm, or some other advocate providing the advocacy services.

Rule 17 (Waivers)

In any particular case or cases the Council of the Law Society shall have power to waive in writing any of the provisions of these rules for a particular purpose or purposes expressed in such waiver, and to revoke such waiver.

Rule 18 (Application and interpretation)

(1)   *(Application to solicitors)*

These rules shall have effect in relation to the practice of solicitors whether as a principal in private practice, or in the employment of a solicitor or of a non-solicitor employer, or in any other form of practice, and whether on a regular or on an occasional basis.

(1A)   *(Application to registered foreign lawyers)*

    (a)   For the avoidance of doubt, neither registration in the register of foreign lawyers, nor anything in these rules or in any other rules made under Part II of the Solicitors Act 1974 or section 9 of the Administration of Justice Act 1985, shall entitle any registered foreign lawyer to be granted any right of audience or any right to conduct litigation within the meaning of Part II and section 119 of the Courts and Legal Services Act 1990, or any right to supervise or assume any responsibility for the exercise of any such right.

    (b)   A registered foreign lawyer shall do nothing in the course of practising in partnership with a solicitor which, if done by a solicitor would put the solicitor in breach of any of these rules or any other rules, principles or requirements of conduct applicable to solicitors.

(c)   A registered foreign lawyer shall do nothing in the course of practising as the director of a recognised body which puts the recognised body in breach of any of these rules, or any other rules, principles or requirements of conduct applicable to recognised bodies.

(2)   (Interpretation)

In these rules, except where the context otherwise requires:

(a)   'arrangement' means any express or tacit agreement between a solicitor and another person whether contractually binding or not;

(b)   'contentious proceeding' is to be construed in accordance with the definition of 'contentious business' in section 87 of the Solicitors Act 1974;

(c)   'contingency fee' means any sum (whether fixed, or calculated either as a percentage of the proceeds or otherwise howsoever) payable only in the event of success in the prosecution or defence of any action, suit or other contentious proceeding;

(d)   'firm' includes a sole practitioner or a recognised body;

(da)   'foreign lawyer' means a person who is a member, and entitled to practise as such, of a legal profession regulated within a jurisdiction outside England and Wales;

(db)   'multi-national partnership' has the meaning given in section 89 of the Courts and Legal Services Act 1990;

(e)   'person' includes a body corporate or unincorporated association or group of persons;

(ea)   'principal in private practice' includes a recognised body;

(f)   'recognised body' means a body corporate for the time being recognised by the Council under the Solicitors' Incorporated Practice Rules from time to time in force;

(fa)   'registered foreign lawyer' means a person registered in accordance with section 89 of the Courts and Legal Services Act 1990; and 'register' and 'registration' are to be construed accordingly;

(g)   'solicitor' means a solicitor of the Supreme Court of England and Wales and, except in Rules 7(6) and 15(2A)(b) of these rules, also includes a firm of solicitors or a recognised body; and

(h)   words in the singular include the plural, words in the plural include the singular, and words importing the masculine or feminine gender include the neuter.

Rule 19 (Repeal and commencement)

(1) The Solicitors' Practice Rules 1988 are hereby repealed.

(2) These rules shall come into force on 1 September 1990.

AII.2 SOLICITORS' COSTS INFORMATION AND CLIENT CARE CODE

1. Introduction

(a) This code replaces the written professional standards on costs information for clients (see paragraphs 3–6) and the detail previously contained in Practice Rule 15 (client care) (see paragraph 7).

(b) The main object of the code is to make sure that clients are given the information they need to understand what is happening generally and in particular on:

(i)   the cost of legal services both at the outset and as a matter progresses; and
(ii) responsibility for clients' matters.

(c) The code also requires firms to operate a complaints handling procedure.

(d) It is good practice to record in writing:

(i)   all information required to be given by the code including all decisions relating to costs and the arrangements for updating costs information; and
(ii) the reasons why the information required by the code has not been given in a particular case.

(e) References to costs, where appropriate, include fees, VAT and disbursements.

2. Application

(a) The code is of general application, and it applies to registered foreign lawyers as well as to solicitors. However, as set out in paragraph 2(b), parts of the code may not be appropriate in every case, and solicitors should consider the interests of each client in deciding which parts not to apply in the particular circumstances.

(b) The full information required by the code may be inappropriate, for example:

(i)   in every case, for a regular client for whom repetitive work is done, where the client has already been provided with the relevant information, although such a client should be informed of changes; and
(ii) if compliance with the code may at the time be insensitive or impractical. In such a case relevant information should be given as soon as reasonably practicable.

(c) Employed solicitors should have regard to paragraphs 3–6 of the code where appropriate, e.g. when acting for clients other than their employer. Paragraph 7 does not apply to employed solicitors.

(d) Solicitors should comply with paragraphs 3–6 of the code even where a client is legally aided if the client may have a financial interest in the costs because contributions are payable or the statutory charge may apply or they may become liable for the costs of another party.

(e) The code also applies to contingency fee and conditional fee arrangements and to arrangements with a client for the solicitor to retain commissions received from third parties.

3. Informing the client about costs

(a) Costs information must not be inaccurate or misleading.

(b) Any costs information required to be given by the code must be given clearly, in a way and at a level which is appropriate to the particular client. Any terms with which the client may be unfamiliar, for example 'disbursement', should be explained.

(c) The information required by paragraphs 4 and 5 of the code should be given to a client at the outset of, and at appropriate stages throughout, the matter. All information given orally should be confirmed in writing to the client as soon as possible.

4. Advance costs information – general

The overall costs

(a) The solicitor should give the client the best information possible about the likely overall costs, including a breakdown between fees, VAT and disbursements.

(b) The solicitor should explain clearly to the client the time likely to be spent in dealing with a matter, if time spent is a factor in the calculation of the fees.

(c) Giving 'the best information possible' includes:

(i)   agreeing a fixed fee; or
(ii)   giving a realistic estimate; or
(iii) giving a forecast within a possible range of costs; or
(iv)   explaining to the client the reasons why it is not possible to fix, or give a realistic estimate or forecast of, the overall costs, and giving instead the best information possible about the cost of the next stage of the matter.

(d) The solicitor should, in an appropriate case, explain to a privately paying client that the client may set an upper limit on the firm's costs for which the client may be liable without further authority. Solicitors should not exceed an agreed limit without first obtaining the client's consent.

(e) The solicitor should make it clear at the outset if an estimate, quotation or other indication of cost is not intended to be fixed.

Basis of firm's charges

(f) The solicitor should also explain to the client how the firm's fees are calculated except where the overall costs are fixed or clear. If the basis of charging is an hourly charging rate, that must be made clear.

(g) The client should be told if charging rates may be increased.

Further information

(h) The solicitor should explain what reasonably foreseeable payments a client may have to make either to the solicitor or to a third party and when those payments are likely to be needed.

(i) The solicitor should explain to the client the arrangements for updating the costs information as set out in paragraph 6.

Client's ability to pay

(j) The solicitor should discuss with the client how and when any costs are to be met, and consider:

   (i) whether the client may be eligible and should apply for legal aid (including advice and assistance);

   (ii) whether the client's liability for their own costs may be covered by insurance;

   (iii) whether the client's liability for another party's costs may be covered by pre-purchased insurance and, if not, whether it would be advisable for the client's liability for another party's costs to be covered by after the event insurance (including in every case where a conditional fee or contingency fee arrangement is proposed); and

   (iv) whether the client's liability for costs (including the costs of another party) may be paid by another person eg an employer or trade union.

Cost-benefit and risk

(k) The solicitor should discuss with the client whether the likely outcome in a matter will justify the expense or risk involved including, if relevant, the risk of having to bear an opponent's costs.

5. Additional information for particular clients

Legally aided clients

(a) The solicitor should explain to a legally aided client the client's potential liability for the client's own costs and those of any other party, including:

   (i) the effect of the statutory charge and its likely amount;

   (ii) the client's obligation to pay any contribution assessed and the consequences of failing to do so;

   (iii) the fact that the client may still be ordered by the court to contribute to the opponent's costs if the case is lost even though the client's own costs are covered by legal aid; and

   (iv) the fact that even if the client wins, the opponent may not be ordered to pay or be capable of paying the full amount of the client's costs.

Privately paying clients in contentious matters (and potentially contentious matters)

(b) The solicitor should explain to the client the client's potential liability for the client's own costs and for those of any other party, including:

   (i) the fact that the client will be responsible for paying the firm's bill in full regardless of any order for costs made against an opponent;

   (ii) the probability that the client will have to pay the opponent's costs as well as the client's own costs if the case is lost;

   (iii) the fact that even if the client wins, the opponent may not be ordered to pay or be capable of paying the full amount of the client's costs; and

   (iv) the fact that if the opponent is legally aided the client may not recover costs, even if successful.

Liability for third party costs in non-contentious matters

(c)   The solicitor should explain to the client any liability the client may have for the payment of the costs of a third party. When appropriate, solicitors are advised to obtain a firm figure for or agree a cap to a third party's costs.

6. Updating costs information

The solicitor should keep the client properly informed about costs as a matter progresses. In particular, the solicitor should:

(a)   tell the client, unless otherwise agreed, how much the costs are at regular intervals (at least every six months) and in appropriate cases deliver interim bills at agreed intervals;

(b)   explain to the client (and confirm in writing) any changed circumstances which will, or which are likely to affect the amount of costs, the degree of risk involved, or the cost-benefit to the client of continuing with the matter;

(c)   inform the client in writing as soon as it appears that a costs estimate or agreed upper limit may or will be exceeded; and

(d)   consider the client's eligibility for legal aid if a material change in the client's means comes to the solicitor's attention.

7. Client care and complaints handling

Information for clients

(a)   Every solicitor in private practice must ensure that the client:

   (i)   is given a clear explanation of the issues raised in a matter and is kept properly informed about its progress (including the likely timescale);

   (ii)   is given the name and status of the person dealing with the matter and the name of the principal responsible for its overall supervision;

   (iii)   is told whom to contact about any problem with the service provided; and

   (iv)   is given details of any changes in the information required to be given by this paragraph.

Complaints handling

(b)   Every principal in private practice must:

   (i)   ensure the client is told the name of the person in the firm to contact about any problem with the service provided;

   (ii)   have a written complaints procedure and ensure that complaints are handled in accordance with it; and

   (iii)   ensure that the client is given a copy of the complaints procedure on request.

PART III

EC LAW

Chapter 21

SOURCES OF EC LAW

21.1 INTRODUCTION

The time has passed when EC law could be seen as an area for specialists only. Every solicitor now needs to appreciate the potential application of EC law to a wide variety of work.

The Treaty on European Union (the 'Maastricht Treaty') took the EC into a new stage of development, with more ambitious objectives, in order, in the words of the preamble to the Treaty, 'to continue the process of creating an ever closer union among the peoples of Europe'.

The European Union is founded on the European Community and, according to Article 3 (formerly C) of the Treaty on European Union, the Union is to be served by a single institutional framework which is that of the Community. Insofar as legislation is passed by the institutions in relation to their EC responsibilities (ie under the EC Treaty), it is still appropriate to refer to that as EC law. No legislation has yet been made under the provisions of the Maastricht Treaty. In the following chapters, the term 'EC law' is used throughout, as only EC law has the characteristics of direct effect and supremacy.

Both the EC Treaty and the Maastricht Treaty have recently been amended by the Treaty of Amsterdam. The most obvious change that this Treaty has made is the renumbering of both the EC and Maastricht Treaties. Where the new numbering is used, it is denoted by the suffix 'EC'. When the pre-Amsterdam numbering is used, it is followed by the words 'of the EC Treaty'. There is a full conversion table at **29.4**.

The substantive changes bought in by the Treaty of Amsterdam involve new provisions in the field of immigration, employment and social policy.

The sources of EC law are:

(1) the Treaties;
(2) Regulations;
(3) Directives;
(4) the jurisprudence of the European Court of Justice.

The principal treaty is the EC Treaty (as amended by, eg, the Maastricht and Amsterdam Treaties). It states in broad outline the objectives of the European Community.

Regulations and Directives are secondary legislation made under Article 249 EC. How these sources of law become part of English law will be discussed in Chapter 23. A selection of materials from these texts appears in the LPC Resource Book *Business Law and Practice: Legislation Handbook* (Jordans).

Article 249 EC also provides for the making of Decisions, Recommendations and Opinions. Of these, only Decisions are legally binding and they bind only the person (Member State, company or individual) to whom they are addressed.

The European Court of Justice has been highly influential in developing both substantive areas of EC law (eg the free movement of goods) and general principles of EC law, such as proportionality.

At an Intergovernmental Conference in Nice in December 2000 a draft Treaty of Nice was agreed which, in particular, includes changes to the system of voting in the Council and changes to the make-up of the Commission and the Parliament, in preparation for enlargement of the Union. At the time of writing, it is still in draft form.

21.2 THE TREATIES

21.2.1 The Treaty of Rome 1957 (The EC Treaty)

The primary aim of the Treaty of Rome was to create a European Economic Community, a common market, for the original six signatories: France, West Germany, Italy, The Netherlands, Belgium and Luxembourg. This common market required not only the abolition of customs duties and quotas for goods passing between the six, but also a recognition on the part of the Member States that their populations had a right to share directly in the benefits of the new system. In particular, the Member States had to recognise the right of workers to move freely throughout the Community, and the right of individuals and companies to set up in business or to provide services throughout the Community.

From its very beginning, it was apparent that the Community was more than a mere free trade zone. One of the stated objectives in the preamble to the Treaty was 'to lay the foundations of an ever closer union among the peoples of Europe'. It is also central to an understanding of the Treaty to remember that it created supra-national institutions, not least the European Court of Justice (see Chapter 22). The result was, in the words of the European Court itself in *Van Gend en Loos v Nederlandse Belastingadministratie* [1963] ECR 1, a 'new legal order of international law for the benefit of which the States have limited their sovereign rights, albeit within limited fields, and the subjects of which comprise not only Member States but also their nationals' (see Chapter 23).

The most important provisions, as far as the achievement of a common market is concerned, are those dealing with free movement, in particular of goods, persons and services, and competition law. These will be considered at Chapters 25–28. Space does not permit consideration of all the provisions of the Treaty of Rome. It should be noted, however, that:

(i)   free movement of capital is an objective of the Treaty; and
(ii) Article 141 EC provides that men and women should receive equal pay for equal work.

21.2.2 The Merger Treaty 1965

Since the Treaty of Paris 1951, there had existed a European Coal and Steel Community (ECSC), created by the original six signatories of the Treaty of Rome. That Treaty had also established supra-national institutions, including a High Authority, the equivalent of the EC Commission.

In 1957, at the same time as the European Economic Community was established, the same signatories created the European Atomic Energy Community (EurAtom). The European Economic Community and EurAtom shared with the ECSC only the Court and the Assembly set up under the Treaty of Paris. In 1965, the institutions of the three Communities were merged. The Merger Treaty is therefore concerned with their integration within a single organisational structure.

21.2.3 The Accession Treaties

In 1973, the UK, the Republic of Ireland and Denmark joined the Community, followed in 1981 by Greece and in 1986 by Spain and Portugal. Sweden, Finland and Austria joined on 1 January 1995.

21.2.4 The Single European Act 1986

The Single European Act 1986 saw further significant developments in the Community. It formalised as an objective the completion of the single European market envisaged in the Treaty of Rome, and set a date for its achievement: 31 December 1992. This required enormous legislative activity by the Community in an attempt to overcome remaining barriers to trade, not least the problem of varying trading standards. In order to make this a manageable task, the Single European Act introduced a streamlined legislative process. When single market measures came to the Council for approval, unanimity was not to be required. Instead, only a qualified majority would be needed (see Chapter 22). The Single European Act also extended the areas which would be expressly within the Community's competence, including areas such as environment and health and safety of workers.

21.2.5 The European Economic Area Treaty 1992

The effect of the European Economic Area Treaty was to create a 'European Economic Area' (EEA) consisting of the Member States of the EC and the EFTA countries (Sweden, Norway, Finland, Austria and Iceland, but not Switzerland which decided in referendum not to ratify the Treaty). Within this area, EC law relating to free movement and to competition law will apply, together with all the related Regulations and Directives. The European Economic Area came into effect on 1 January 1994. However, on 1 January 1995, Sweden, Finland and Austria all joined the European Union leaving just Norway, Iceland and Liechtenstein as members of the EEA, but not of the EU. Switzerland, which rejected EEA membership in a referendum, remains in EFTA.

21.2.6 The Treaty on European Union 1992 ('the Maastricht Treaty')

The Treaty on European Union (TEU), signed at Maastricht, came into force on 1 November 1993. It officially renamed the 'EEC' the 'EC' and founded, on the base of the European Community, a European Union. It also renamed the Treaty of Rome the EC Treaty. It made a number of important amendments to the Treaty, in particular:

(1)   the EC undertakes to act in any given area only if Community action is a better means of achieving the desired end than action by the individual Member States (the principle of subsidiarity) (Article 3b of the EC Treaty (now Article 5 EC));

(2) every EC national becomes a citizen of the European Union (Article 8 of the EC Treaty (now Article 17 EC);

(3) the EC now specifically assumes responsibility for developing policies in areas such as public health (Article 129 of the EC Treaty (now Article 152 EC)), consumer protection (Article 129b of the EC Treaty (now Article 154 EC)) and education (Article 126 of the EC Treaty (now Article 149 EC)). These had previously been dealt with primarily as issues affecting free movement;

(4) the European Parliament is given greater powers (Article 189b of the EC Treaty (now Article 251 EC)) (co-decision);

(5) the Council will take decisions on a qualified majority basis on a wider range of matters, such as consumer protection, using the co-decision procedure in Article 189b of the EC Treaty (now Article 251 EC);

(6) free movement of capital is clarified by directly applicable rights in Articles 73b–73g of the EC Treaty (now Articles 56–60 EC).

The Maastricht Treaty did not just amend the Treaty of Rome. It also set out Union objectives, the most important being the promotion of economic and social progress to be achieved by economic and monetary union. The Union also agreed to develop a common foreign and security policy and to co-operate in the fields of justice and home affairs. Importantly, the Union also undertook expressly (in TEU Article 6.2 (F2)) to respect fundamental rights, as guaranteed by the European Convention on Human Rights. Previous ECJ case-law had already shown, however, that Member States must respect human rights law when acting on a Community matter.

Despite the Treaty of European Union, it is nevertheless still correct to talk of EC legislation since it is only in relation to Community matters that the institutions have powers to create rights with direct effect. The TEU is primarily an instrument for inter-governmental co-operation.

21.2.7 The Amsterdam Treaty

In June 1997, the latest Treaty was adopted; the Amsterdam Treaty. The Treaty entered into force at the beginning of May 1999. The Treaty paves the way for EU enlargement. It also provides for greater co-operation in employment matters and for incentive measures to help boost employment. It incorporates into the EC the TEU Social Chapter, which means that all Member States are bound by its provisions. The Treaty also establishes a new section on freedom, security and justice which brings some areas into the framework of the EC Treaty from the 'third pillar' (Justice and Home Affairs) of the Maastricht Treaty. It also strengthens provisions relating to environmental protection. There is a strengthening of public health and consumer protection, and the principle of subsidiarity has been clarified. Finally, there has been an increase in the number of matters to be decided under qualified majority rules and a substantial increase in the use of the co-decision procedure. In the TEU, there is a revised section on common foreign and security policy.

21.3 REGULATIONS

Article 249 EC envisages that secondary legislation is needed to put its broad objectives into effect. It provides that the Council and the Commission 'shall, in accordance with the provisions of this Treaty make Regulations...'. It goes on to state that a Regulation shall have general application (ie it will apply throughout the EU in exactly the terms in which it is made). Further, Article 249 EC states that a Regulation shall be directly applicable in all Member States, ie no Member State need pass any implementing measure to make the contents of the Regulation form part of its own national law, except in the unusual situation when the Regulation itself expressly requires the Member State to do so. In fact, according to the European Court in *Variola sPA v Amministrazione Itialiana della Finanze* [1973] ECR 981, it would ordinarily be wrong for a Member State to disguise the EC origin of the measure by introducing national legislation to enact it.

Many important EC legal measures have taken the form of Regulations, for example, Regulation 1612/68, which sought to make a reality of the free movement of workers provisions in the Treaty, and the Merger Regulation, Regulation 4064/89, under which big multi-national mergers are vetted by the EC Commission for their effect on competition.

21.4 DIRECTIVES

Article 249 EC also gives the Council and the Commission power to issue Directives. It is clear from that Article, however, that their legal effect is quite different from that of Regulations. A Directive is stated to be 'binding, as to the result to be achieved, upon each Member State to which it is addressed, but shall leave to the national authorities the choice of form and methods'. Unlike Regulations, Directives therefore do need a response from each Member State. Unless the national law of the Member State already achieves the objective of the Directive, the Member State must implement it within the specified time-limit. The form of implementing measure may vary from State to State, as may the precise words used to give effect to the Directive. This means that, unlike Regulations, Directives are not of general application throughout the EC in the terms in which they are drafted.

Directives have been issued across a wide range of areas, for example, Directive 76/207, known as the Equal Treatment Directive, the several Company Law Directives, the Environmental Protection Directive (85/337) and the Product Liability Directive (85/374). In order to bring the Single Market into being, the Commission drafted over 200 separate Directives.

21.5 THE JURISPRUDENCE OF THE EUROPEAN COURT

The fundamental principles of EC law found in the EC Treaty are set out in outline only, so the European Court has inevitably played a leading role in developing EC law. The Court has not been reluctant to assume this role and has made a major contribution to the evolution of the EC. By interpreting the Treaty and secondary legislation according to the overall purposes of the EC, the Court has often pushed governments further than they might have initially intended to go. Judgments of the Court are now vital to an understanding of the freedoms upon which the EC is based and to the principles of competition law (another major field of EC activity). In addition, the Court has developed certain general principles of EC law, of which the most important are proportionality (see Chapter 27), legal certainty and respect for fundamental rights (see Chapter 30). As far as the latter is concerned, the Court's approach can be seen in *Nold (J) KG v EC Commission* [1974] ECR 491, where it stated that fundamental rights, derived from the constitutional traditions common to the Member States and from the international treaties to which they are signatories (in particular, the European Convention on Human Rights), form an integral part of the general principles of EC law. In applying 'legal certainty' the Court has sometimes ruled that its more surprising interpretations of the Treaty should be non-retrospective, for example in *Defrenne (Gabrielle) v SABENA* [1976] ECR 455 and *Barber v Guardian Royal Exchange Assurance Group* [1991] 1 QB 344 (see **23.3.1** and **29.1.2**) where direct claims for equal pay and equal pensions were allowed under Article 141 EC. To have held otherwise would have had serious financial consequences in the Member States.

21.6 OTHER EC MEASURES

Apart from the measures already indicated, there exist two other EC measures which have only limited legal effect under Article 249 EC.

EC Decisions are binding only on the parties to whom the Decision is addressed (Article 249 EC). The best examples are Commission Decisions under the competition rules in Articles 81 and 82 EC. Their Decisions that an agreement or conduct infringes Article 81 or 82 EC, that an exemption should be given under Article 81(3) EC), or that fines be imposed are all subject to review by the Court of First Instance (CFI). Subject to this, they bind the parties and must be given effect by national courts. Thus, a Decision that an agreement is exempt will (subject to review) validate the agreement before a national court.

The least effective measure of all is a Council recommendation. This is certainly not legally binding and cannot create any Community rights, but is still worth referring to as 'persuasive opinion' on a particular issue. A good example is the *Code of Practice on Sexual Harassment* set out at 1992 OJ L 49/1. This can be referred to for guidance to determine whether employers who have allowed such conduct are guilty of sex discrimination under the Sex Discrimination Act 1975 (see *Wadman v Carpenter Farrer Partnership* [1993] 3 CMLR 93 (EAT)).

21.7 CONCLUSION

If a client has a problem which has an EC dimension, this could be because it clearly raises questions of substantive EC law, perhaps in relation to one of the freedoms such as free movement of goods or workers. In this case, a solicitor must, of course, pay careful attention to the EC Treaty itself. It will often be necessary to look at the secondary legislation which supplements that particular area of the Treaty as well as at decided cases on the subject.

On the other hand, a client's problem may have an EC aspect because of the ever increasing pervasiveness of EC law, for example a business client may be concerned about the significance of the recent Directives on workplace safety. In this case, a detailed consideration of the relevant legislation will be vital, including an appreciation of how it can interact with relevant domestic law (see further Chapter 23).

For information as to how to research a problem of EC law and how to use the possible sources, see Chapter 6 of the LPC Resource Book *Skills for Lawyers* (Jordans).

21.8 OVERVIEW OF THE EC TREATY

(1) To create the common (single) market, it guarantees four freedoms:

- free movement of goods (Articles 28–30 EC);
- free movement of services (Article 49 EC);
- free movement of persons, ie   workers (Article 39 EC)
  firms (Article 43 EC – right of establishment);
- free movement of capital (Article 56–60 EC).

(2) To create the customs union, it imposes a common external tariff and prohibits internal custom duties (Article 25 EC).

(3) To prevent distortion in the market, it:

- prohibits anti-competitive practices by undertakings (Articles 81 EC, 82 EC);
- prohibits discrimination against EC nationals, both generally (Article 12 EC) and under particular Articles (eg on free movement) or in indirect taxes (Article 90 EC);
- guarantees equal pay between men and women (Article 141 EC).

(4) To provide a framework for future integration, it enables the Council of Ministers to make legislation (ie Directives or Regulations).

(5) Most legislation is passed by qualified majority vote, for example:

- single market measures;
- health and safety at work measures (Article 138 EC).

(6) Some legislation needs unanimity (ie can be vetoed), for example:

- some aspects of social security and employment measures (Article 137(3) EC);
- tax measures (Article 95(2) EC);
- some aspects of immigration measures (Article 95(2) EC).

Chapter 22

THE INSTITUTIONS

22.1 INTRODUCTION

The Treaty of Rome established the following institutions of the Community:

(1) the Council (Articles 145–154 of the EC Treaty (now Articles 202–210 EC));

(2) the Commission (Articles 155–163 of the EC Treaty (now Articles 211–219 EC));

(3) the Parliament (originally known as the 'Assembly') (Articles 137–144 (now Articles 189–201 EC));

(4) the Court (Articles 164–188 of the EC Treaty (now Articles 220–245)).

The Single European Act renamed the Assembly the European Parliament and created the Court of First Instance. The Treaty on European Union made the already existing Court of Auditors into a fifth institution. Although they do not have the status of institutions, mention will be made below of the Committee of Permanent Representatives (COREPER), the Economic and Social Council and the Committee of the Regions (see **22.8–22.10**). There will also be a brief explanation of how EC law is made.

22.2 THE COUNCIL

22.2.1 What is its membership?

The Council consists of one government representative from each Member State. The representative need not be the same person at every Council meeting: it depends on the matters on the agenda at that particular meeting. If, for example, the Council were discussing the environment, the representatives would be the ministers responsible for the environment. When the representative is the Head of State or government, the Council is referred to as the 'European Council'.

Each Member State takes it in turn to be the President of the Council; the Presidency rotates every 6 months. The European Council is required to meet at least twice a year.

22.2.2 What is its role?

The Treaty of Rome gave the Council responsibility for ensuring that the Treaty's objectives were attained. The Council ensures the co-ordination of policies and, above all, takes decisions within the Community. This means that it is the Council rather than the Commission which is responsible for the final decision as to whether a Regulation should be made or a Directive should be issued, although the Commission does have some decision-making powers.

22.2.3 How does it take decisions?

Although the Treaty of Rome envisaged that the Council would normally take decisions on a simple or qualified majority basis, it became clear that, in practice, unanimity would be required. This practice, though, was modified by the Single European Act. In order to facilitate the establishment of the Single Market, the Act provided that, on most matters relating to the internal market, a qualified majority of votes would suffice to pass a particular measure. Under this voting system, each Member State is allocated a certain number of votes, dependent on its size. France, Germany, Italy and the UK have ten votes, Spain has eight, The Netherlands, Belgium, Portugal and Greece have five, Sweden and Austria have four, Denmark, Ireland and Finland have three and Luxembourg has two. In order for a measure to be passed, 62 votes must be cast in favour out of a possible 87. Thus, 26 votes against a measure would be sufficient to defeat it. This system of voting will change when the Treaty of Nice is ratified. In order to pass a qualified majority vote, 258 votes out of 342 will be needed (thus 89 are required to block). In addition, in order to pass a qualified majority vote, 62 per cent of the population of the EU must live in Member States voting in favour. Under the new system, Germany, Britain, France and Italy would have 29 votes, Spain 27, The Netherlands 13, Belgium, Portugal and Greece 12, Sweden and Austria 10, Denmark, Ireland and Finland 7 and Luxembourg 4. New candidates (upon joining) will have: Poland 27, Romania 14, Czech Republic and Hungary 12, Bulgaria 10, Slovakia and Lithuania 7, Slovenia, Latvia, Estonia and Cyprus 4 and Malta 3.

22.3 THE COMMISSION

22.3.1 What is its membership?

There are 20 EC Commissioners, each of whom is responsible for a particular area of Community competence. The Commission is divided into 23 Directorates-General which are responsible for such matters as the environment (Directorate-General XI) and competition law (Directorate-General IV). The Commissioners are appointed by the Member States, but once appointed they must be independent of national loyalties. They cannot be recalled by their appointing State. They hold office for a fixed term of 5 years, although this is subject to renewal. The larger Member States (Germany, France, the UK, Italy and Spain) appoint two Commissioners each; the smaller countries appoint only one each. Each Commissioner's appointment must be approved by all Member States and, since Amsterdam, by the President and by the European Parliament. The President of the Commission is appointed by the Member States after consultation with the European Parliament. The appointment is for a fixed term of 2 years, although this also is renewable. The Commission is based in Brussels.

22.3.2 What is its role?

The Treaty of Rome required the Commission to pursue infringements of EC law. It can, for example, take action before the European Court against Member States which breach EC law. It is also responsible for enforcing EC competition policy and has the power to exact fines for any breach. Above all, however, the Commission is responsible for initiating EC policy and legislation. It has some delegated powers of law making, particularly in the field of competition law, where (under the authority of an enabling Council Regulation 19/65) it has issued Block Exemption Regulations under Article 81(3) EC (see Chapter 28).

22.3.3 How does it reach its decisions?

Within the Commission, decisions are taken on a simple majority basis.

22.4 THE PARLIAMENT

22.4.1 What is its membership?

Following the 1994 elections and the accession of Austria, Finland and Sweden, there are 626 members of the European Parliament (MEPs) (this will change to 738 upon enlargement), all of whom are directly elected, although the voting systems throughout the Community are not uniform. The number of MEPs which each State has depends on its size; for example, Germany has 99, the UK has 87, The Netherlands has 31 and Luxembourg has 6. The MEPs sit in the Parliament according to their political sympathies (political groups) rather than according to national origin. MEPs are elected for a 5-year term. The Parliament holds plenary sessions in Strasbourg for one week per month. Much of its work is, however, done in committees (and plenary sessions) in Brussels. It is organised by an Executive (including a President, ie Speaker) based in Luxembourg.

22.4.2 What is its role?

The Parliament's role was traditionally a consultative one. In a number of areas, the Treaty of Rome provided that, once the Commission had initiated a proposal for legislation and the Council had given its preliminary approval to it, the Parliament had to be given an opportunity to comment. It had to respond to the proposal within a reasonable time and the Council had to take its responses into account, although it was not bound by them.

The Single European Act developed the role of the Parliament by introducing a co-operation procedure in certain areas, for example single market legislation. This meant that, if the Council did not wish to accept the Parliament's comments, the Parliament had to be given a second opportunity to respond. If it continued to object to the Council's version of the measure, the Council could adopt it in its original form only if it did so unanimously within 3 months. The Single European Act also increased the number of matters on which the Parliament had to be consulted so as to include most matters relating to the Single Market.

The Treaty on European Union further increased the role of the Parliament. In certain limited areas, there is a new 'co-decision' procedure (Article 251 EC) which involves the Parliament further in the legislative process. If the Parliament proposes amendments to draft legislation and these amendments are not accepted by the Council, the Parliament can veto the legislation. This procedure applies to measures intended to develop the single market.

The Amsterdam Treaty has greatly extended the areas in which the co-decision procedure will be used. It has also streamlined this procedure.

The Parliament has the right to ask questions of the Commission and, in the last resort, it has the power to remove the whole Commission, though not individual Commissioners. (This almost happened at the beginning of 1999. The Commission actually resigned around 4 weeks after the threat of censure.) The Council, too, must report to the Parliament.

22.5 THE COURT

22.5.1 What is its membership?

There are 15 judges of the European Court, each of whom must be eligible for appointment to the highest judicial office in the country from which he or she comes. There must be at least one judge from each Member State. Each judge is appointed for 6 years at a time. Their appointments are staggered, so they do not all retire at once. There is no retirement age for a judge nor can one be recalled by the Member State which made the appointment. He or she can be removed only by the unanimous resolution of the other judges and Advocates-General. The judges elect one of their number to be President of the Court for a 3-year term.

In addition to the 15 judges, there are also eight Advocates-General. Their task is to assist the judges in reaching their decision. One Advocate-General will be assigned to each case and will hear the evidence and read the papers available to the Court. He will then prepare a reasoned opinion indicating the conclusion to which he would come in that case. The Court is not bound to follow that opinion. When the case is reported, the Advocate-General's opinion is reported, together with the decision of the Court. The Court sits in Luxembourg.

22.5.2 What is its role?

The Treaty of Rome required the Court to ensure that EC law is observed throughout the Community. The three usual ways in which a case may come before it are:

(1) as a result of a reference by a national court under the Article 234 EC procedure (see **23.7**);

(2) as a result of an action brought by the Commission against a Member State pursuant to its powers under Article 226 EC;

(3) as a result of an action brought by one Member State against another under Article 227 EC.

If a Member State fails to comply with a judgment of the European Court, the Treaty on European Union now allows the Court to impose a fine on that Member State.

22.5.3 How are such cases heard?

The European Court usually sits in chambers and consists of three, five or seven judges. In particularly important cases, a full plenary session will hear the case. The procedure is largely by means of written submissions, following a typical civil law (as distinct from common law) pattern. There is very limited scope for oral argument. Barristers and solicitors have a right of audience before the European Court, although if a solicitor wishes to appear in the European Court following an Article 234 EC reference (see **23.7**) he can do so only if he had a right of audience before the court or tribunal which made the reference.

The working language of the court during deliberations is French, although, at hearings, the parties present their arguments in their own language (with simultaneous translation). Each case will have its own official language. One judge (*le juge rapporteur*) puts together a draft judgment synthesising judicial opinions on which the judges then vote.

When the Court has reached a decision, it delivers a single, succinct judgment. No dissenting judgments are delivered.

22.5.4 The nature of EC legal reasoning

The Treaty of Rome was drafted by States which shared a civil law heritage. The original judges of the European Court had been trained in civil law systems which, although they might diverge significantly in their substantive provisions, shared a similar approach to legal reasoning. In particular, such judges were familiar with legislation which provided a framework of principles and which was not intended to be interpreted in an exclusively literal way. They were therefore accustomed to drawing inspiration from the spirit behind legislation. This approach was particularly necessary when interpreting the Treaty of Rome, which is very much a framework treaty. In addition, the early judges of the Court were conscious of the role entrusted to them by the Treaty and the accompanying responsibility to ensure that EC law was a uniform body of legal principles which took effect in the same way throughout the entire Community.

Thus, from a very early stage, it is possible to recognise the purposive approach adopted by the European Court. This entailed the Court interpreting the Treaty of Rome, and later subordinate legislation, in accordance with the ethos of the Treaty of Rome. In doing so it had to bear in mind the fundamental freedoms upon which the Community was expressly stated to be based and, in particular, Article 12 EC which prohibits discrimination on the grounds of nationality.

22.5.5 Precedent

In accordance with the civil law tradition, there is no use of precedent as such in the European Court. However, although the Court is not bound by its own previous decisions, it has tended to develop a body of consistent case-law. The European Court may cite earlier cases in its judgment, and the Advocate-General is likely to discuss earlier decisions in his opinion.

Decisions of the European Court are reported in an official set of reports, the *European Court Reports* (ECR). There is also a commercial series of reports called the *Common Market Law Reports* (CMLR). The *All England Reports* also produce their own EC series cited as [*year*] All ER (EC).

22.6 THE COURT OF FIRST INSTANCE

The Court of First Instance was established by the Single European Act because of the heavy work-load faced by the European Court. Many of the cases before the European Court concerned disputes between Community institutions and their employees. These staff cases were assigned to the Court of First Instance, as were competition law cases (ie appeals from Commission decisions banning agreements, imposing fines, etc). As a result of provisions in the Treaty on European Union, the Council has now transferred to the Court of First Instance all of the European Court's jurisdiction apart from Article 234 EC references and cases involving infringement proceedings against Member States. Appeals on points of law lie to the European Court itself.

22.7 THE COURT OF AUDITORS

The Court of Auditors is responsible for auditing the accounts of the Community and its institutions. It has 15 members appointed by the Council.

22.8 THE COMMITTEE OF PERMANENT REPRESENTATIVES (COREPER)

The Committee of Permanent Representatives (COREPER) was created by the Merger Treaty. It comprises ambassadors of the Member States. They undertake much of the detailed analysis of Commission proposals on behalf of the Council. If COREPER can agree a response to such a proposal, that response will be automatically approved by the Council. Only if there is disagreement at COREPER level will a matter be actively discussed in the Council.

22.9 THE ECONOMIC AND SOCIAL COUNCIL (ESC)

The Economic and Social Council (ESC) is a body which comprises representatives of different sectional interests throughout the Community. There are 222 representatives, for example, of business, of the trade unions and of consumers. The ESC's role is purely consultative.

22.10 THE COMMITTEE OF THE REGIONS

The role of this Committee is purely advisory. It is to consist of 222 members appointed by the Council.

22.11 EC LEGISLATIVE PROCESS

The EC legislative process (somewhat simplified) can be illustrated as follows.

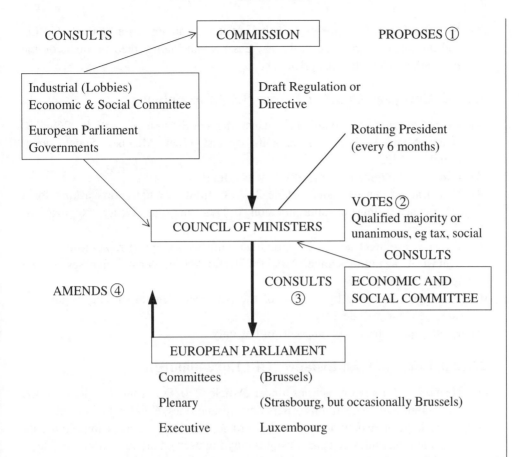

CONSULTS   COMMISSION   PROPOSES ①

Industrial (Lobbies)
Economic & Social Committee

European Parliament
Governments

Draft Regulation or
Directive

Rotating President
(every 6 months)

COUNCIL OF MINISTERS

VOTES ②
Qualified majority or
unanimous, eg tax, social

CONSULTS

AMENDS ④

CONSULTS
③

ECONOMIC AND
SOCIAL COMMITTEE

EUROPEAN PARLIAMENT

Committees	(Brussels)
Plenary	(Strasbourg, but occasionally Brussels)
Executive	Luxembourg

(Matters requiring a qualified majority vote under the co-decision procedure of Article 251 EC may involve amendment or rejection of the 'common position' taken by the Council, by Parliament voting by majority.)

22.12 OVERVIEW OF THE ROLES OF THE COMMISSION AND COURT

22.12.1 Commission's policing role

(1) Ensures Member States' conformity with Treaty rules and implementation of Directives:

– proceedings to enforce before ECJ (Article 226 EC).

(2) Ensures firms' conformity with competition rules (Articles 81, 82 EC):

– Directorate-General IV investigates;
– can by decision ban agreements or practices (or grant exemption);
– can fine up to 10 per cent of worldwide turnover.

(3) Ensures that Member States do not distort competition by giving State aids to nationalised industries and other favoured firms. State aids must be notified in advance and approved by the Commission on certain objective criteria (Article 87 EC). Unapproved State aids must be repaid by firms following a Commission decision.

(4) Negotiates trade agreements on behalf of the Community, for example GATT, and investigates firms (eg in the Far East) which 'dump' their products on the EC market at less than the price at home.

22.12.2 European Court of Justice (ECJ Luxembourg)

(1) Hears Commission's complaints against Member States under Article 226 EC.
(2) Hears Member States' complaints against other Member States under Article 227 EC.
(3) Can fine governments which disobey its rulings.
(4) Can hear references under Article 234 EC from national courts asking for a preliminary ruling on interpretation of EC law (eg Treaty, Regulations, Directives).
(5) Provides no direct access for individual citizens, except in relation to actions against EC institutions under Articles 230 and 288 EC. Most such cases now go to the CFI (see below).
(6) All rulings preceded by opinion of the Advocate-General (usually a guide to how the Court will decide).
(7) Hears appeals from CFI on points of law only.

22.12.3 Court of First Instance (CFI Luxembourg)

(1) Hears judicial review actions under Article 230 EC from decisions of the Commission in competition matters (ie bans and fines on individual firms).
(2) Hears judicial review actions under Article 230 EC from decisions imposing anti-dumping duties, ie extra Customs duty imposed on products from outside the EC by a Council Regulation following investigation by the Commission (see above).

22.13 SUMMARY

The four main institutions have the following primary responsibilities:

(1) the Commission develops policy and proposes legislation;
(2) the Parliament has an advisory role, subject to the limited ability to veto legislation;
(3) the Council is the decision-making body;
(4) the Court ensures that the law which emerges from these three institutions is interpreted correctly and consistently.

Chapter 23

THE RELATIONSHIP BETWEEN EC LAW AND NATIONAL LAW

23.1 INTRODUCTION

The primary source of EC law is the EC Treaty (as amended). Under English law, international treaties are not automatically part of national law, so, when the UK joined the EC, the Treaty of Rome (as it was then known) had to be incorporated into English law. This was done by the European Communities Act 1972.

However, the inter-relationship between the EC and the national legal system is not entirely the product of national statute. If it were, there might be a diversity of approach to EC law in the various Member States. The European Court has instead developed two key concepts:

(1) that EC law can, in certain circumstances, be relied on directly in national proceedings; and

(2) that, when it is utilised, it takes priority over any conflicting national law.

Taken together, these two concepts can give a client a right of action and a remedy which otherwise might not be available under national law.

23.2 EC LAW AND THE EC CITIZEN

EC law, as incorporated into English law by the European Communities Act 1972 (ECA 1972), can have two possible effects on the citizen. First, it can have 'direct effect' (see **23.3**), ie it can create rights which can be relied on in national courts directly against the State or another legal person. Secondly, EC law (in particular, Directives) may have 'indirect effect' (see **23.5**) in that courts should comply with EC law when interpreting national legislation.

23.3 THE CONCEPT OF DIRECT EFFECT

In *Van Gend en Loos v Nederlandse Belastingadministratie* [1963] ECR 1 (see **21.2.1**), the European Court recognised the existence of the Community as a 'new legal order'. In that case, an importer of goods from Germany into The Netherlands argued that Article 12 of the EC Treaty (now Article 25 EC), which prohibited any increase in customs tariffs for goods passing from one Member State to another, meant that a reclassification of his products into a higher tariff was unlawful. Consequently, he sought to rely on Article 12 of the EC Treaty (now Article 25 EC) to claim back from the Dutch customs authorities, which had extracted the increased tariff, the money he had paid. The question for the Court was whether the Treaty could be used in that way by an individual citizen of the Community rather than a Member State or the Commission. The European Court held that it could if the provision in question met certain conditions: it would have to be *clear, precise and unconditional* and would have to leave the Member State with no discretion as to how it should be implemented. In other words, if the provision in question is sufficiently clear, precise and unconditional to create an 'enforceable Community right' for the client, as did Article 12 of the EC Treaty (now Article 25 EC), that right can be enforced through the national courts in preference to national law. In *Van Gend en Loos* itself, the Court found that an individual could rely on Article 12 of the EC Treaty directly to recover the extra tax from the government.

23.3.1 Direct effect and the provisions of the EC Treaty

It has now been established that, applying the criteria set out in *Van Gend en Loos*, all the fundamental Treaty provisions have direct effect, in particular:

(1) Article 30 of the EC Treaty (now Article 28 EC) on free movement of goods (*Ianelli and Volpi sPA v Meroni* [1977] ECR 557);
(2) Article 48 of the EC Treaty (now Article 39 EC) on free movement of workers (*Van Duyn v Home Office* [1974] ECR 1337);
(3) Article 52 of the EC Treaty (now Article 43 EC) on freedom of establishment (*Reyners v The Belgian State* [1974] ECR 631);
(4) Article 59 of the EC Treaty (now Article 49 EC) on freedom to provide services (*Van Binsbergen (JHM) v Bestuur van de Bedrijsverenging voor de Metaalnijverheid* [1974] ECR 1299);
(5) Article 85 of the EC Treaty (now Article 81 EC) on anti-competitive agreements (*Belgische Radio en Televisie v SV SABAM* [1974] ECR 313);
(6) Article 86 of the EC Treaty (now Article 82 EC) on abuse of a dominant position (*Garden Cottage Foods v Milk Marketing Board* [1984] AC 130); and
(7) Article 119 of the EC Treaty (now Article 141 EC) on equal pay (*Defrenne (Gabrielle) v SABENA* [1976] ECR 455).
(8) In addition, Articles 6 of the EC Treaty (now Article 12 EC) (discrimination), 73b–73g of the EC Treaty (now Articles 56–60 EC) (capital), 92 of the EC Treaty (now Article 87 EC) (State aids) and 95 of the EC Treaty (now Article 91 EC) (discriminatory indirect taxes on goods) are considered to have direct effect.

23.3.2 Direct effect and Regulations

Regulations are said by Article 249 EC to be 'directly applicable', ie they are part of national law and do not need implementing legislation. They are binding in the form in which they are made. However, they still have to be sufficiently 'clear, precise and unconditional' to create directly effective rights.

23.3.3 Direct effect and Directives

Directives are not of general application throughout the Community but require implementing measures which are likely to vary from one Member State to another. Despite this, the European Court has held, for example in *Van Duyn v Home Office* [1974] ECR 1337 (see **23.3.1**), that in appropriate circumstances even Directives may be directly effective. The reason for this is that Article 189 of the EC Treaty (now Article 249 EC) expressly states that a Directive is to be legally binding on the State to which it is addressed; this would be meaningless unless there was some possibility that Directives themselves could be relied on where the Member State failed to implement them. However, in the case of Directives, any rights they contain can have direct effect only after the time-limit for implementing the Directive has elapsed (see, eg *Pubblico Ministero v Ratti* [1979] ECR 1629). Thereafter, again provided that the rights in the Directive are sufficiently clear, precise and unconditional, they can be relied on *against the State*, even though not implemented in national law.

23.3.4 'Horizontal' direct effect

In the early cases on direct effect, the defending party was always the State or some State agency, such as the customs authorities in *Van Gend en Loos* [1963] ECR 1 ('vertical' direct effect). Subsequent cases have shown that a party may rely on a Treaty provision, or even a Regulation (but not a Directive), where the other party is not a State body ('horizontal' direct effect). So, for example, in *Defrenne v SABENA* [1976] ECR 455 (see **23.3.1**) the plaintiff relied on Article 119 of the EC Treaty (now Article 141 EC) against a private employer.

Again, Directives are different. A Directive can be used only against a Member State or an 'emanation of the State'. This is clear from *Marshall v Southampton and West Hampshire Area Health Authority* [1986] ECR 723. The rationale here is that allowing the use of a Directive against a Member State that is in delay encourages it to implement that Directive. A non-State body, on the other hand, has no power to influence the implementation of a Directive. If it is clear that the defendant is the State or a State body, it is also apparent from *Marshall* that it makes no difference whether or not the State is fulfilling a public function in the circumstances which gave rise to the case. In *Marshall*, the defendant health authority had dismissed the female plaintiff because she had reached the age of 62, although a male employee would not have been dismissed until the age of 65. The plaintiff argued that this breached the Equal Treatment Directive. The defendant conceded that it was a State body but argued that, as it was acting purely as an employer of the plaintiff, the Directive could not be relied upon against it. This argument failed before the European Court.

From cases following *Marshall*, it appears that other emanations of the State for this purpose include a police force (*Johnston v Chief Constable of the RUC* [1986] ECR 1651) and a local authority (*Re London Boroughs* [1990] 3 CMLR 495 and *East Riding of Yorkshire County Council v Gibson* [2000] 3 CMLR 329).

The European Court has subsequently given guidance on the meaning of the term 'emanation of the State'. According to *Foster v British Gas* [1990] ECR I-3133, it must be some body (whatever its legal form) which is carrying out a public service under the control of the State or which has for that purpose special powers. In *Foster*, the English court applied that definition to find that British Gas prior to privatisation was an emanation of the State. On the other hand, it has since been held by the Court of Appeal in *Doughty v Rolls Royce Plc* [1992] IRLR 126 that Rolls Royce was not an emanation of the State when it was in public ownership because it was not providing a public service. By contrast, the High Court has recently ruled that even the *privatised* water boards are sufficiently controlled by State regulators to satisfy the criteria in *Foster* (see *Griffin v South West Water Services Ltd* [1995] IRLR 15). Clearly even the privatised British Gas or British Telecom could be regarded as State bodies if this case is correct. The ECJ appears to support this view in *Kampelmann v Landschaftsverband Westfalen-Lippe* [1998] IRLR 333, where they ruled that private companies carrying out public services at regional level were still emanations of the State.

This distinction between public and non-public bodies inevitably means that some individuals will be protected by the provisions of a Directive while others will not. This is especially evident in the employment field where employees of the State or State bodies will have an advantage over employees of a private employer. The European Court in *Marshall* pointed out that such unfairness is easily countered by the Member State: it can implement the Directive.

Finally, it should be remembered that, even though enforceable only against the State, a directive may still have indirect consequences for private persons. In *R v Durham ex parte Huddleston* [2000] 1 WLR 1484, a developer obtained from a *planning authority* permission to develop a site. An objector objected that the development had not been subjected to an environmental impact assessment as required by Directive 85/337. This had direct effect against the local planning authority (an emanation of the State) which was compelled to reconsider the permission. The effect was financially disastrous for the developer.

23.4 THE SUPREMACY OF EC LAW

The European Court, in the seminal case of *Amministrazione delle Finanze dello Stato v Simmenthal* [1978] ECR 629, held that it was fundamental to EC law that EC law should be supreme over the domestic law of the Member States. In this way, EC law would apply uniformly throughout the EC. According to *Simmenthal*, 'every national court must ... accordingly set aside any provision of national law which may conflict with' EC law. The European Court has reinforced that message on numerous occasions. The courts of individual Member States have, from time to time, found the concept of supremacy difficult to accept. After the European Communities Act 1972, the English courts tended to rely upon interpreting English law to comply with EC law as far as possible. In recent years, however, the courts have been increasingly prepared to give effect to the *Simmenthal* doctrine. This can be seen in the case of *R v Secretary of State for Transport ex parte Factortame (No 2)* [1990] 3 WLR 818, in which some Spanish fishermen challenged the Merchant Shipping Act 1988 as being incompatible with EC law. The House of Lords referred the matter to the European Court under the procedure under Article 177 of the EC Treaty (now Article 234 EC) (see **23.7**). In the meantime, the fishermen sought interim relief to suspend the operation of the Act until the European Court replied to the reference. They argued that if the Act continued to operate, their livelihoods would be so seriously affected that the ruling of the European Court might prove to be academic. The House of Lords refused relief, partly because it had no power to suspend the effect of an Act of Parliament, and partly because under English law an interim injunction could not be granted against the Crown. The House of Lords did, however, refer to the European Court a second question: was it right to refuse relief? The European Court responded that, where an individual seeks to rely on EC law, a rule of national procedure cannot be invoked in the national courts which would effectively deny the individual that right. The English court then granted the interim relief (see further **24.4**).

23.5 THE CONCEPT OF INDIRECT EFFECT

It would therefore seem clear that, when a national court is confronted by national legislation and directly effective EC legislation which conflicts, the court should, under the principle of the supremacy of EC law, apply EC law to the dispute. However, there may be situations in which EC legislation does not have direct effect and a staightforward preference for it cannot be made. This might be the case where a Directive lacks the qualities necessary to give direct effect, as where it is being used against a non-State body.

In such cases, it may be possible to argue that the Directive has indirect effect. The national court is not asked to apply the Directive instead of the national legislation, but is asked to *interpret* the national legislation in the light of the EC Directive.

Accordingly, in *Litster v Forth Dry Dock & Engineering Co Ltd* [1990] 1 AC 546, the House of Lords interpreted the Transfer of Undertakings (Protection of Employment) Regulations 1981 in the light of Directive 77/187, which the Regulations purported to implement, even though that interpretation was contrary to the meaning on the face of the Regulations. In *Marleasing SA v La Comercial Internacional de Alimentacion SA* [1990] ECR I-4135, the European Court took the concept of 'indirect effect' a stage further by ruling that national law should be interpreted, as far as possible, to give effect to an EC Directive, whether or not the Directive predates the national law. The European Court expressly based the latter decision on Article 5 of the EC Treaty (now Article 10 EC), which requires Member States to take all necessary steps to ensure the fulfilment of their Community obligations. Contrary to its earlier ruling in *Duke v GEC Reliance Ltd* [1988] AC 618, the House of Lords has now conceded that, in interpreting the Sex Discrimination Act 1975, it must take account of the Equal Treatment Directive 76/207 and ECJ rulings on its interpretation. See *Webb v EMO Air Cargo (UK)* [1994] IRLR 482 where the House of Lords accepted that (from 1978 onwards) they were obliged to interpret the Act in line with the later Directive, even though, in their view, the result was not what Parliament had intended when passing the Act.

23.6 ACTION AGAINST A STATE FOR FAILURE TO IMPLEMENT A DIRECTIVE

The European Commission has the responsibility of monitoring the implementation rates of Member States and it has the power to bring a State in default before the European Court. An individual cannot take this action. However, following *Francovich and Bonifacti v Italy* [1992] IRLR 84, an individual can, in appropriate circumstances, sue a State for damages for failure to implement a particular Directive. In that case, Italy had failed to implement Directive 80/987 which would have established a fund available to employees dismissed by insolvent businesses which could not pay them their arrears of salary. Although the Directive was sufficiently precise in the rights it set out to create, these rights were conditional on there being a relevant fund. They were thus not directly effective. However, the European Court gave a right of action against the State itself for non-implementation, relying on Article 5 of the EC Treaty (now Article 10 EC), which requires Member States to take all appropriate measures to ensure the fulfilment of their Community obligations. The ECJ said that a right of action arises where three conditions are met:

(1) the Directive confers rights on individuals;
(2) the content of the rights is identifiable from the Directive;
(3) there is a causal link between the failure to implement and the damage.

This is clearly what we would call in English law an action in tort.

The action itself would be brought before the relevant national court in accordance with the appropriate national procedure (in England, this would be a High Court action against the Attorney-General). That procedure would have to ensure an effective remedy for the plaintiff.

In *R v Secretary of State for Transport ex parte Factortame (No 4)* [1996] 2 WLR 506, the ECJ ruled on whether the Spanish fishermen could recover damages for breach of Article 52 of the EC Treaty (now Article 43 EC) for being denied the right to form UK fishing companies (see **24.4–24.5**). The ECJ introduced a further condition for State liability in this type of case, ie damages are recoverable only where the breach of the Treaty is sufficiently serious, ie where the State manifestly and gravely disregards the limits on its own powers. This extra condition has also been applied in a case of an incorrectly implemented Directive. In *R v HM Treasury ex parte British Telecommunications plc* [1996] All ER (EC) 411, it was held that no damages are recoverable against the State if it has made a reasonable mistake in interpreting the Directive when drafting its implementing legislation. This is a very important case for governments because the broad principles of EC law do provide plenty of scope for innocent, non-negligent interpretation. This will not, however, excuse governments which rely on negligent advice from their lawyers, as happened in the *Factortame* case. The British Government was eventually required to pay damages, the House of Lords accepting that the law on establishment and discrimination being clear, there was a sufficiently serious breach (*R v Secretary of State for Transport ex parte Factortame (No 5)* [1999] 4 All ER 906, HL).

However, note that the non-implementation of a Directive will still be assessed under the original *Francovich* test, since non-implementation is a sufficiently serious breach in itself (see *Dillenkofer and Others v Germany* [1996] 3 CMLR 469).

23.7 ARTICLE 234 EC REFERENCE PROCEDURE

23.7.1 What is the purpose of this procedure?

The Article 234 EC reference procedure enables the European Court to give a preliminary ruling to a national court principally on the interpretation of the EC Treaty, although it can also rule on the validity of acts of Community institutions. This means that the European Court will not, as such, rule on the compatibility of national law with EC law or on the application of EC law to particular facts. This is the national court's responsibility. Thus, in *Foster v British Gas* [1990] ECR I-3133 (see **23.3.4**) the European Court explained how an emanation of the State could be recognised, and the English court then applied the definition to British Gas. It may be, however, that in stating the principle, the European Court, in effect, indicates how it must apply to the facts before the national court. The advantage of Article 234 EC is that it provides a mechanism which enables the European Court to ensure that EC law develops along parallel lines throughout the Community.

23.7.2 How does the procedure work?

Article 234 EC distinguishes two situations.

Where the case is being heard before a court from which there is no judicial remedy

In this case, the national court must make a reference if it believes that a clarification of the EC point is necessary in order to decide the case. Where there is a dispute as to how EC law applies, such a court should refuse to make a reference only where it is absolutely clear what the European Court's opinion is on the point (see *CILFIT Srl v Ministro della Sanitro* [1982] ECR 3415).

A particularly striking example of this is the case involving part-timers (*Equal Opportunities Commission v Secretary of State for Employment* [1994] 1 All ER 910 (HL)). This is another illustration of the point that discrimination, here in relation to pay between men and women (Article 141 EC), always includes unjustifiable indirect discrimination. In this context, paying part-timers less than full-timers is indirectly paying women less than men because most part-timers are women. Thus, the House of Lords ruled that legislation requiring part-timers to work 5 years before qualifying for redundancy payments/unfair dismissal compensation (whereas full-timers qualified after 2 years) was unlawful because it was a breach of equal pay under Article 141 EC). There was no objective reason for the discrimination. The House emphatically rejected Government arguments that it would create new jobs by reducing the burdens on business, saying that there was no evidence that this was the case. No reference was made to the ECJ because the position in EC law was clear. The provisions of the Employment Protection (Consolidation) Act 1978, which had stood for 13 years, were declared unlawful without the need for a reference. The Act has since been amended. In the light of subsequent cases (notably *R v Secretary of State for Employment ex parte Seymour-Smith* [1999] 3 WLR 460, ECJ), it is suggested that the House of Lords should have made a reference.

Where the case is being heard before any other court or a tribunal that is exercising a judicial function

In this case, the court or tribunal has a discretion whether to make a reference. Again, the European Court's opinion must be necessary in order for a decision to be reached. Throughout the Community, a wide range of lower courts and tribunals have made references under Article 234 EC, including UK magistrates' courts and social security appeal tribunals.

In either case, the question whether a reference should be made is one for the court rather than the parties to the case. Once the court has decided that a reference should be made, it should then draft the questions to which it requires a reply. In certain cases, the European Court has reformulated these questions so that they more accurately reflect the issue that needs to be addressed. Although the European Court has no discretion, as such, as to whether it replies to a reference, it has refused to respond where there is no genuine dispute between the parties and where the reference was made in order to raise wider political issues (*Foglia v Novello* [1980] ECR 745).

23.8 SUMMARY

If a client seeks advice on a problem where there could be an EC dimension, remember:

(1) EC law can also be used in its own right if it meets the criteria for direct effect (see **23.3**);

(2) if there is EC legislation which has direct effect, an English court or tribunal must prefer it to conflicting domestic law (see **23.4**);

(3) EC legislation can affect the interpretation of domestic law (see *Marleasing SA v La Comercial Internacional de Alimentacion SA* [1990] ECR I-4135 at **23.5**);

(4) in case of doubt as to the meaning of EC law, consider a reference to the Court under Article 234 EC (see **23.7**).

Chapter 24

SEEKING A REMEDY IN NATIONAL COURTS

24.1 INTRODUCTION

This chapter is not intended as a substitute for earlier chapters. It is an attempt to consolidate the rules and think more practically about how they can be applied in English courts when acting for a client. It serves as a warning to English solicitors who believe that they can advise their clients on English law alone. Ignoring relevant EC law is undoubtedly solicitor's negligence. Although there have been no reported cases in England, lawyers have been successfully sued in other States for ignoring the competition rules (and thus putting their client at risk of a fine or void agreements) or for ignoring the Brussels Convention on Civil Jurisdiction and Enforcement of Judgments 1968 (and thus losing their client's case by suing in the wrong jurisdiction). A lawyer who advises on English law alone will thus often give wrong advice on English law, because English law by definition includes Community law, lock, stock and barrel.

24.2 EC LAW AS A DEFENCE

As Community law overrides conflicting national law, directly effective EC law can always be used as a defence to any civil action, prosecution or tax claim that is based on that national law. Thus, for example, since Article 81(2) EC makes restrictive agreements void, a defendant can plead Article 81 EC when sued in a civil action for breach of the agreement. Likewise, if Articles 28, 49, 39 and 43 EC make measures restricting free movement of goods, services and working persons unlawful, a client prosecuted under such national measures can plead the Articles of the Treaty as a defence. In tax claims, a client can plead the VAT Directive or the Treaty provisions on non-discrimination (Article 90 EC). Thus, where an exemption from VAT exists in the Directive but not in the UK tax legislation, a taxpayer can plead the Directive as defence to a demand for tax. VAT is very much an EC tax and cannot be collected in circumstances not allowed for under the Directive.

24.3 EFFECTIVE REMEDIES

In relation to more active remedies, the ECJ has made it plain in cases like *R v Secretary of State for Transport ex parte Factortame (No 2)* [1990] 3 WLR 818, that national courts must provide a sufficient remedy to protect EC rights. In general, this would be the nearest equivalent national remedy. Where no adequate remedy is available under national law, the court must provide one to protect the EC right in question (as they did in *Factortame*). Thus, a client may be better protected by asserting an EC right than he is under national law (examples being *Marshall v*

Southampton Area Health Authority (No 2) [1993] 3 CMLR 293, discussed below at **24.9**, and *R v Secretary of State for Transport ex parte Factortame (No 4)* [1996] 2 WLR 506).

It should also be noted that administrative decisions affecting EC law must be reasoned, 'proportional' and subject to review by a higher tribunal. Neither the duty to give reasons nor 'proportionality' are well established under English administrative law so that once again the client asserting an EC right may be better protected when dealing with administrative institutions.

24.4 INJUNCTIONS/INTERIM INJUNCTIONS

If one thinks of actual remedies available to protect EC rights, probably the first thing one would think of would be an injunction. This is certainly available to be used against a private person to restrain a breach of Article 85 or 86 of the EC Treaty (now Articles 81 or 82 EC) (see *Garden Cottage Foods v Milk Marketing Board* [1986] AC 180). Thus, a client who feels he is being excluded from a particular market because of a restrictive agreement breaching Article 81 EC, or an abuse of a dominant position breaching Article 82 EC, can get an injunction to restrain such unlawful behaviour, and get back into the market.

However, the remedy of injunction or interim injunction is also available against the government to restrain a breach of EC rules despite the fact that under English law interim injunctive relief is not normally available to suspend statutes or statutory instruments (see *R v Secretary of State for Transport ex parte Factortame (No 2)* [1990] 3 WLR 818 (ECJ and HL)).

In *Factortame*, some Spanish fishermen had set up a UK company to operate UK trawlers with the intention of exploiting the UK fishing quota in the North Sea. The Merchant Shipping Act 1988 provided that, in order to qualify as a UK company for this purpose, the company must itself be owned at least 75 per cent by UK nationals who were UK residents. Not surprisingly, the Spanish fishermen who found themselves excluded by this rule complained that the Act was contrary to the Treaty in that it denied their right of establishment as a UK company (Article 52 of the EC Treaty (now Article 43 EC)) and discriminated against them as EC nationals (Article 6 of the EC Treaty (now Article 12 EC)). Faced with this issue, the House of Lords felt obliged to make a reference to the European Court, but the question then arose as to whether the House of Lords would be bound to grant interim relief protecting the fishermen's rights until the European Court could rule on the main issue. This issue, too, was referred to the European Court which replied, somewhat more promptly than normal, that the national court must grant an interim injunction to suspend the Act of Parliament where this is necessary to protect the EC rights pending the ruling from the European Court. Eventually, the ruling came back (*R v Secretary of State for Transport ex parte Factortame (No 3)* [1991] 3 All ER 769) that the 1988 Act did contravene the Treaty and therefore, in relation to EC nationals, the provisions concerned had to be suspended indefinitely.

It should be noted that *Factortame* involved an urgent case where the fishermen's livelihood was being threatened in circumstances where damages (at the time uncertain) would not have been an adequate remedy. The ruling does not mean that in EC cases the court need not follow the normal balance of convenience test when deciding when to grant an interim injunction, nor that the court need not take into account other factors, for example public policy, when exercising its discretion. In two other cases, a reference was made but an interim injunction was refused in the meantime. These cases are *R v HM Treasury ex parte British Telecommunications plc* [1994] 1 CMLR 621, CA and *R v Heritage Secretary ex parte Continental TV (Red Hot TV)* [1993] 2 CMLR 333, CA. Both cases rested on the 'balance of convenience' with the adequacy of damages being a particular fact in the first case and public policy (protecting sensitive viewers from pornographic television) being a factor in the second.

24.5 DAMAGES FOR BREACH OF EC RIGHTS

Again, there seems little doubt that damages are available against private persons for breach of their statutory duty, for example for anti-competitive behaviour under Articles 85 or 86 of the EC Treaty (now Articles 81 and 82 EC). Although there have been no reported court decisions of damages being awarded, the House of Lords in *Garden Cottage Foods v Milk Marketing Board* [1986] AC 130 was certainly of the opinion that damages could be recovered. A large number of cases have been settled on the basis that this is the case. It would seem, however, in the light of *Factortame (No 4)*, that a purely innocent, non-negligent infringement of the competition rules would attract no damages from the national courts just as it would attract no fine from the Commission (see below). Ignorance of the law, however, is no excuse!

Where the defendant concerned is the government, the claim for tort damages under English public law is a little more complicated. According to the Court of Appeal in *Bourgoin SA v Ministry of Agriculture, Fisheries and Food* [1985] 3 WLR 1027, the government cannot be liable for damages for exercising its powers unlawfully unless it is guilty of deliberate abuse of power ('misfeasance in public office'). This may be a true reflection of English public law, but the decision in *Bourgoin* itself (where the court refused to award damages for what was a flagrant breach of Article 30 of the EC Treaty (now Article 28 EC), a ban on importing French turkeys) is now clearly contrary to the European Court rulings in *Factortame* and *Francovich*. The House of Lords suggested as much (obiter) in *Kirklees MBC v Wickes Building Supplies Ltd* [1992] 3 All ER 717, where they suggested that the government would have had to compensate Sunday traders if the Shops Act 1950 was found to be in breach of Article 30 of the EC Treaty (now Article 28 EC), ie the traders would have been entitled to issue writs against the Attorney-General for damages for all the loss sustained through breach of the statutory duty under Article 30 of the EC Treaty (now Article 28 EC). Clarification of the position in regard to damages was given finally by the European Court in *Factortame (No 4)* [1996] 2 WLR 506, where the question was whether the Spanish fishermen were entitled to damages against the Government for the period in which they were prevented from operating their trawlers before they got their interim injunction. The ECJ having given their ruling on EC law that damages can be regarded where the breach is sufficiently serious (see **23.4**), the English courts have now to determine whether this was such a case. The House of Lords recently awarded damages to the fishermen, thus bringing the long saga to an end (*Factortame (No 5)* [1999] 4 All ER 906, HL). The ECJ gave a similar ruling in *R v Ministry of Agriculture, Fisheries and Food ex parte Hedley Lomas* [1996] All ER (EC) 493. An Irish company which was refused a British export licence to export live animals to Spain (in breach of Article 34 of the EC Treaty (now Article 29 EC)) received damages for its loss.

See also **23.6**.

24.6 REPAYMENT OF DISCRIMINATORY TAX/VAT

Again, if the tax has been unlawfully collected in breach of Article 95 of the EC Treaty (now Article 90 EC) or in breach of the VAT Directives, then the requirement that an adequate remedy be given means that this tax must be repaid in full with interest (see the ECJ's ruling in *Amministrazione delle Finanze dello Stato v Spa San Giorgio* [1983] ECR 359). For reasons which will be explained at **24.8**, it may be that the normal time-limit for reclaiming tax under national tax law cannot run to protect the government until such time as the government brings its own tax law into line with EC law. This case does recognise a principle of 'unjust enrichment'. Thus, tax should not be repaid where it has been passed on to a customer who cannot himself be traced.

24.7 STATUTORY REMEDIES

Initially when asserting an EC right, one starts by looking at the nearest equivalent national remedy. Thus, the client who asserts EC rights in the context of employment law, for example equal pay under Article 141 EC, or sex discrimination under the Equal Treatment Directive 1976/207, is effectively asserting statutory employment rights and therefore must take his claim to an employment tribunal where the remedies and procedures he will be seeking will be equivalent to those under the Equal Pay Act 1970 and the Sex Discrimination Act 1975. In two respects, however, time-limits and limits on compensation, the remedies provided for breach of these EC rights may be better than those for the equivalent rights under national law.

24.8 TIME-LIMITS

Although initially the national time-limits will apply to the claim, the ECJ has made it clear that these cannot be used to protect the government where the claim is based on a Directive which the government has failed to implement. In other words, the claimant cannot be deprived of a right by the government delaying implementation for so long that he is out of time. In such circumstances, the government is estopped from relying on its own wrong and therefore the time-limit begins to run only when it has righted that wrong by introducing national legislation that complies with the Directive (see *Emmott v Minister for Social Welfare and Attorney-General* [1991] IRLR 387 (ECJ)). The ECJ seems to have reduced the effectiveness of this ruling in *Johnson v Chief Adjudication Officer (No 2)* [1995] IRLR 187 where it indicates that a time-limit which limits back-payments of social security may be enforceable even where the government is in breach of a Directive. The same rule applies to tax (see now *Edilizia Industriale v Ministero Delle Finanze* [1999] 2 CMLR 995, ECJ. The normal national time-limit will of course be available to protect a private person, for example an employer faced with a claim for equal pay under Article 141 EC. But even these may not start to run until the employee is aware of his rights under Article 141 EC (see *Cannon v Barnsley Metropolitan Borough Council* [1992] IRLR 474 (EAT)). The ECJ has made it clear in the case of *Fischer* [1994] IRLR 662 (ECJ), that the time-limit must not make it impossible to exercise the EC rights which national courts and governments are obliged to protect. There are thus two basic rules that national time-limits must satisfy (see *Comet BV v Produktschap voor*

Siergewassen [1997] ECR 2043). First, they must still leave the applicant with an effective remedy and not make recovery virtually impossible. Secondly, they must be equivalent to time-limits in similar national claims. This second principle of non-discrimination is well-illustrated by the case of *Levez v Jennings* [1999] IRLR 764, EAT, where the two-year time-limit on back pay in equal pay cases was held to be unlawful as in other similar claims for race and disability discrimination there was no such limit. The EAT's ruling followed guidance from the ECJ in *Levez v TH Jennings (Harlow Pools) Ltd* [1999] All ER (EC) 1. The time-limits for making these claims are not however discriminatory. In *Biggs v Somerset County Council* [1996] ICR 364, the Court of Appeal refused to allow a claim brought by a part-time employee for unfair dismissal compensation as equal pay under Article 119 of the EC Treaty (now Article 141 EC), when it was brought 18 years after the dismissal but within 3 months of the House of Lords ruling in *Equal Opportunities Commission v Secretary of State for Employment* [1994] 1 All ER 910, HL (see **23.7.2**).

24.9 LIMITS ON COMPENSATION

As indicated above, EC rules like those protecting against sex discrimination under the Equal Treatment Directive 1976 do require an adequate remedy. Thus, the European Court has ruled that the national limits on compensation under the Sex Discrimination Act 1975 (the maximum until November 1993 was £11,000) cannot be used to protect a State employer in a claim based on an EC Directive. This is the now famous case of *Marshall v Southampton Area Health Authority (No 2)* [1993] 3 CMLR 293. Mrs Marshall, who established her right to compensation for breach of the EC Directive in *Marshall v Southampton and West Hampshire Area Health Authority (Teaching)* then went back to an industrial tribunal where her compensation was assessed at over £20,000. This figure included an assessment of interest. However, both the EAT and the Court of Appeal ruled that the compensation had to be restricted to the limit set by the Sex Discrimination Act 1975, which not only restricted compensation (at the time to £6,000) but also denied the award of interest. On a reference from the House of Lords, the ECJ ruled that compensation must be awarded without limit and that in assessing compensation the tribunal must, to give an adequate remedy, award interest. The Government reacted promptly and commendably to this ruling by removing both the upper limit and the restriction on interest for all discrimination and equal pay claims with effect from November 1993 (see Sex Discrimination and Equal Pay (Remedies) Regulations 1993, SI 1993/2798). It should be noted that in relation to rights under English law which do not implement EC rights, it is perfectly lawful for the law to provide an inadequate remedy. Thus, 'unfair dismissal' compensation is still limited, although it increased to £51,700 for a compensatory award in February 2001.

24.10 A PRACTICAL EXAMPLE OF EC REMEDIES – THE PREGNANT SERVICE WOMEN CASES

This is a particularly striking illustration of the principles on remedies that have just been stated. For example, Client A, who was dismissed in 1985 for pregnancy, claims compensation for sex discrimination of £150,000 by bringing industrial tribunal proceedings in 1995. A lawyer advising on this claim would be immediately confronted with four major obstacles under English national law as it then stood:

(i)   the armed forces were excluded from the Sex Discrimination Act 1975;
(ii) the Sex Discrimination Act does not expressly cover dismissals for pregnancy (pregnant employees were, at the time, protected from unfair dismissal only where they had been employed for 2 years). The House of Lords in *Webb v EMO Air Cargo (UK)* [1994] IRLR 482 has since decided that the Act can be interpreted in line with the Equal Treatment Directive to cover pregnancy dismissals (see below);
(iii) there is a tight time-limit of 3 months for claiming discrimination under the Act, and Client A is therefore well out of time;
(iv) there was a limit on compensation of £11,000 and interest was not awardable.

All these seemingly impenetrable obstacles under national law can be overcome by bringing a claim under the EC Directive to which the Ministry of Defence, as part of the government, is bound. The exclusion of the armed forces under the Act becomes irrelevant because no such exclusion exists under the Directive. The problems about claiming for pregnancy dismissals under the Sex Discrimination Act 1975 disappear when the claim is brought under the Directive, the European Court having ruled in *Dekker v Stichting Vormingscentrum voor Jonge Volwassenen Plus* [1991] IRLR 27 that dismissal of a pregnant employee is, per se, sex discrimination in that only women get pregnant. This decision was confirmed by the ECJ in *Webb v EMO Air Cargo (UK)* [1994] IRLR 482. Likewise (as we have seen) neither the time-limit, nor the limits on compensation, nor the denial of interest can be used to restrict the claim where it is the government's fault that these claims are not provided for under national law.

Thus, Client A, despite all the odds, could succeed in recovering her £150,000 compensation (assuming that this is the amount of her loss). Indeed, this is fairly typical of something like 4,000 service women who were forced out of their jobs by the MoD policy of not employing women service personnel who became pregnant. This is a salutary lesson for all lawyers advising public authorities. One should never think that English law is all that applies.

In *Ministry of Defence v Pope; Ministry of Defence v Lowe* [1997] ICR 296, the EAT recognised that service women who had decided to have an abortion rather than face dismissal could also claim damages for breach of the Directive.

Chapter 25

FREE MOVEMENT OF WORKERS

25.1 INTRODUCTION

The EC Treaty gave the right of free movement within the Community to people who wished to take up offers of employment made from outside their home State. This fundamental Treaty right has been buttressed by a considerable amount of secondary legislation. Further, EC law has developed to the stage where the rights of individuals to move within the EC are not necessarily dependent on the desire to take up employment. Indeed, as a consequence of the Single European Act, from 1 January 1993, internal barriers to movement within the EC should have been removed. Further, Article 17 EC now states that every EC national shall be a citizen of the European Union. Under Article 18 EC, the Union citizen has the right to move and reside freely within the territory of the Member States, subject to the limitations and conditions in the EC Treaty and in other legislation.

25.2 WHAT DOES THE EC TREATY PROVIDE?

Free movement of workers is guaranteed by Article 39 EC, which gives the EC worker the right of entry and residence for the purpose of taking up employment. According to Article 39(2) EC, Member States must abolish:

'... any discrimination based on nationality between workers of the Member States as regards employment, remuneration and other conditions of work and employment.'

'Work and employment' has been interpreted very widely to include sportspeople. Hence, in *Union Royale Belge des Sociétés de Football Association ASBL v Bosman* [1996] All ER (EC) 97, the ECJ made it plain that restrictions on the number of EC nationals in football teams imposed by UEFA and requirements for large transfer fees in cross-border transfers were both illegal.

25.2.1 How is nationality interpreted?

Nationality is entirely a matter for the domestic law of each Member State, which means that, inevitably, rules vary. In particular, not all Member States permit their nationals to hold dual nationality. One result of this was seen in *Micheletti v Delegacion del Gobierno en Cantabria* [1992] ECR I-4238. The case concerned a dual national of Argentina and Italy who sought entry into Spain. Entry was refused because under Spanish law only the nationality of the State in which the person had last been habitually resident was recognised, and in this case that was Argentina. The European Court found, however, that, as he was an Italian national under Italian law, he was an EC migrant worker protected by Article 48 of the EC Treaty (now Article 39 EC), so that entry into Spain could not be denied.

25.2.2 What rights of residence does the EC national obtain under Article 39 EC?

The EC national has an absolute right of residence so long as he remains in work. Further, he is entitled under Directive 68/360, as proof of this, to a 5-year residence permit, automatically renewable after that time. If the worker becomes involuntarily unemployed, this will continue to guarantee him a right to reside in the host State. However, if he becomes voluntarily unemployed his position is changed as (in accordance with most social security systems) he would be disqualified from social security benefits. Under Directive 90/364, he has a right of residence simply by being a citizen of another Member State as long as he has sufficient resources not to be a burden on the host State. If a worker becomes permanently disabled or reaches retirement age, his right of permanent residence continues under Regulation 1251/70.

An individual can claim the rights of a worker as long as he is genuinely employed, even if his work is part time and obtained so that EC rights can be asserted and even if the salary paid is below a minimum wage limit (*Levin v Secretary of State for Justice* [1982] 1 ECR 1035).

25.2.3 What terms of employment is an EC national entitled to expect?

An EC national can claim the same terms as those offered to a national of the host State. Article 39(2) EC expressly refers to the right not to be discriminated against as regards conditions of work. So, in the case of *Allué (Pilar) and Coonan (Mary Carmel) v Università degli Studi di Venezia* [1991] 1 CMLR 283, an Italian law which provided that non-Italians who accepted jobs in Italy to teach a language could only enter into fixed term contracts for one year was contrary to Article 48(2) of the EC Treaty (now Article 39(2) EC). In addition, Regulation 1612/68, Art 7 prohibits discrimination in relation to conditions of employment, dismissal, social and tax advantages, training and union membership.

25.2.4 What about his social security rights?

Social security rights are governed by Regulation 1408/71, which basically guarantees to EC nationals the social security benefits of the host State. However, where the benefits are dependent on contributions, a worker's entitlement will take into account contributions to the equivalent benefit in his home State or other Member States in which he has worked. The Regulation does not provide for harmonisation of benefits or of levels of benefits throughout the Community. Access to council housing and other local authority benefits is to be provided without discrimination under the Migrant Workers Regulation 1612/68.

25.2.5 Does an EC national have a right of entry to look for work?

Article 39 EC has been interpreted to mean that an EC national has a right of entry to look for work and a reasonable period of residence to find it. In the UK, the immigration rules used to allow such a person to be deported if he did not succeed in finding work after 6 months. The European Court held this rule to be consistent with EC law in *R v Immigration Appeals Tribunal ex parte Antonissen* [1991] 2 CMLR 373, although they stressed that the job seeker might still have a right of residence if he had reasonable prospects of finding work. (There is no longer a fixed time-limit for finding work in the UK.) An EC national has a right to remain in the host State as an ordinary citizen if his resources are adequate and he is covered by health insurance by virtue of Directive 90/364 EC on the right to residence for EU citizens.

25.3 WHEN DOES THE EC TREATY ALLOW MEMBER STATES TO DENY ENTRY?

Article 39(3) EC permits derogations on grounds of public policy, public security and public health. Because these are derogations from one of the fundamental freedoms of the Community, the European Court has interpreted them strictly. Further, Directive 64/221 has made it clear that only personal conduct can be taken into account. Even prior criminal convictions will not necessarily entitle the Member State to deny entry. They will do so only where they indicate that the individual represents a current threat to public security. For example, in *Astrid Proll v Entry Clearance Officer* [1988] 2 CMLR 387, the former Baader Meinhoff terrorist was allowed entry into the UK because she did not represent a present threat.

Article 39(4) EC provides that the rights granted earlier in the Article do not apply to employment in the public service. This has been interpreted strictly by the European Court in *Commission of European Communities v Belgium; Re Public Employees (No 1)* [1980] ECR 3881 to mean only 'posts involving the exercise of official authority and functions related to safeguarding the general interests of the State'.

25.4 CAN THE WORKER BRING HIS FAMILY WITH HIM?

Because a worker might be deterred from moving to another Member State if he could not take his family with him, Regulation 1612/68, Art 10 enables him to do so. It does, however, limit the family members who are entitled to entry to the spouse, children under 21 and dependent relatives of the worker. It is not necessary for family members to be EC nationals. The host State can refuse entry to family members only in those circumstances which allow it to refuse entry to the worker himself (see **25.3** above). The rights of a spouse are not dependent on his or her residing with the worker, thus can terminate only if the worker leaves the host State permanently (*Diatta v Land Berlin* [1985] ECR 567) and, although there is no clear ECJ authority, arguably deportation could follow divorce.

Directive 68/360 lays down formal requirements for entry (including visa) and for obtaining residence permits. Thereafter, the family have the same rights as the worker himself to jobs, social security and education.

EC law can even protect the family of a British national who is returning from working elsewhere in the EC (*Surinder Singh* [1992] 3 All ER 798). In that case, a British national was returning from working in Germany and was accompanied by her husband, who was of Indian nationality. The British immigration authorities refused him entry, because he could not prove that the primary purpose of the marriage was not to gain entry into the UK. The European Court found that this application of the immigration rules was in breach of EC law. However, it should be noted that EC law protects only a *migrant* worker. Thus, whereas an immigrant from another EC State or a returning British national has protection for himself and his family under the regulation, there is no protection for a 'static' British worker. Thus,

British immigration authorities are within their rights in refusing entry to the spouse of a British national unless she or he can show that entry was not the 'primary purpose' of the marriage. They would, however, be acting unlawfully if they applied the same rule to the spouse of, say, an Italian worker, or a British worker who was returning from working elsewhere in the EC. The conflict between UK and EC law has now been removed as the new Labour Government immediately reformed the immigration rules by removing the 'primary purpose' rule. In all cases, the UK immigration authorities must now prove that the marriage was not genuine.

25.5 SUMMARY

If an EC national or a family member is refused entry or residence rights by UK immigration authorities, he will be allowed to invoke his EC rights before the appropriate immigration authority or Appeal Tribunal, or as a defence in criminal proceedings where deportation is being considered.

If an EC national believes that he has been discriminated against in relation to employment, he should, as usual, follow the appropriate national procedure in the host State to obtain a suitable remedy. In England, this would mean commencing proceedings before an employment tribunal under the Race Relations Act 1976. It is important to remember that, to comply with EC law, such national procedure must not discriminate, even indirectly, against the EC national and must give an effective remedy for breach of EC law (see **24.9**).

Two changes to the EC Treaty introduced by the Amsterdam Treaty of 1997 may affect this area.

First, the provisions of the Shengen Agreement are incorporated into the EC Treaty and are thus subject to the interpretation of the European Court of Justice. In broad terms, this enables all persons to move freely across frontiers without the need to show passports or identity cards. However, the States will have to harmonise their external immigration rules to ensure that they are equally tight in this department. The arrangements which need implementing measures to create directly effective rights appear in Article 62 EC. The UK has retained its opt-out.

Secondly, the Treaty contains a new Article 13 EC which entitles the institutions to legislate against race, religion, sexual orientation, age and disability discrimination. The UK already has legislation in the areas of race and disability. There is already extensive EC legislation on sex discrimination (see **29.1.2**). The Commission is currently preparing a draft Directive on all forms of discrimination.

Chapter 26

FREEDOM OF ESTABLISHMENT AND PROVISION OF SERVICES

26.1 INTRODUCTION

The freedom of establishment is the right to base one's business in another Member State permanently. This right is guaranteed by the EC Treaty with the important qualification that it cannot give the establishing business greater rights than those enjoyed by businesses operated by nationals of the host Member State. Thus a French business wishing to establish itself in England would have to comply with laws affecting an English business relating, for example, to employment, health and safety and taxes and social security (except to the extent that these might discriminate directly or indirectly against the foreign firm). The governing Article in the EC Treaty is Article 43 EC.

The freedom to provide services guarantees that a business can provide a service across a Community frontier even if that business does not want to be permanently based outside its home State. As with the right of establishment, the right to provide services is granted on the basis that the services will be provided subject to the same conditions as apply to nationals of the State in which the service is supplied (again subject to these rules constituting indirect discrimination). The governing Article in the EC Treaty is Article 49 EC.

Although under both Articles the firm concerned must comply with the same conditions which apply to local nationals, those conditions are likely to be tighter for establishment. In *Gebhard v Consiglio dell'Ordine degli Avvocati e Procuratori di Milano* [1996] All ER (EC) 139 it was held that a German lawyer giving advice on German law in Italy was prima facie 'established' there by virtue of his permanent office and his adoption of the title Advocato. Had he merely been providing services, he could have relied on his home title as a German lawyer and the earlier Directive on free movement of legal services. However, by establishing himself in Italy, he had to requalify as an Italian lawyer.

In the cases taken to the European Court under Articles 43 EC and 49 EC, emphasis has often been successfully placed on Article 12 EC which prohibits discrimination on the ground of nationality, wherever the matter is covered by the Treaty.

Article 12 EC has direct effect so that provisions of UK statutes can be disapplied by UK courts in so far as they directly or indirectly discriminate against other EU nationals. Residence requirements are a good example of indirect discrimination.

26.2 THE RIGHT OF ESTABLISHMENT: ARTICLE 43 EC

Article 43 EC provides that restrictions on the freedom of establishment by nationals of a Member State in the territory of another Member State must be abolished. This freedom is stated to include the right to take up and pursue activities as self-employed persons and to set up and manage undertakings, in particular companies or firms, under the conditions laid down for its own nationals by the law of the country where the establishment is effected.

26.2.1 What is the implication of this Article?

Article 43 EC means that no Member State can, through its legislation or administrative practices, impose a nationality barrier to businesses which wish to be based permanently in another Member State. In *R v Secretary of State for Transport ex parte Factortame (No 3)* [1991] 3 All ER 769, Article 52 of the EC Treaty (now Article 43 EC) was invoked by Spanish fishermen who operated British-registered fishing boats but who were prevented from fishing the British quota because the Merchant Shipping Act 1988 laid down nationality and residence requirements for the owners of shares in companies operating such boats. The European Court held that such legislation was contrary to Article 43 of the EC Treaty (see **24.4**).

26.2.2 Are there any limitations on the kind of undertaking which can benefit from Article 43 EC?

Article 43 EC refers in particular to companies and firms. This phrase is defined in Article 48 EC to mean 'companies or firms constituted under civil or commercial law including co-operative societies'. The meaning of company or firm is really a matter for the law of the home State. A French company wishing to set up a branch or subsidiary in England can do so provided it meets the requirements under French law for being a company. It must not hold itself out as having been incorporated under English law. The only qualification here is that EC law requires that an undertaking wishing to rely on Article 43 EC must be a profit-making body.

It is particularly important to realise, however, that an entrepreneur wishing to set up a company can choose the State with the least regulatory company regime and then establish a branch back in the State he wishes to trade in. In *Centros Ltd v Erhvervs- og Selskabsstyrelsen* [1999] 2 CMLR 551, the ECJ recognised that it was legitimate to set up a company in the UK and trade through a branch in Holland even though the purpose was to avoid the Dutch requirements for a minimum paid-up share capital.

26.3 THE RIGHT TO PROVIDE SERVICES: ARTICLE 49 EC

According to Article 49 EC, restrictions on the freedom to provide services within the Community must be abolished in respect of nationals of Member States who are established in a State of the Community other than that of the person for whom the services are intended. Services for this purpose, according to Article 50 EC, are services normally provided for remuneration. In *Commission of European Communities v France* [1991] OJ C78/5, for example, it was held that a French law which required tourist guides to hold a licence dependent on the passing of an examination in France was contrary to Article 59 of the EC Treaty (now Article 49 EC) as being unnecessary and discriminatory. There are many similar cases. This Article also means that a business providing services in another Member State had the right to bring its own employees into the host State to enable it to perform those services, even where they would not have been entitled to claim rights under

Article 48 of the EC Treaty (now Article 39 EC) (eg because of transitional rules for nationals of new EU Member States or because the workforce includes immigrants from outside the EU) (*Rush Portuguesa v Office National d'Immigration* [1990] ECR I-1417, *Van der Elst* [1994] ECR I-3803). The workers would, of course, need to be lawfully employed in the State where the employer is established and might need visas to enter the host country; they would not need fresh work permits. The European Court of Justice, however, stresses that the host State can impose its own mandatory rules for workers' protection. Since statutory protection for workers in some countries (eg UK) is less than in other countries (eg Germany), this might enable British firms to provide services to Germany using their British workforce at cheaper rates than German firms which have to pay their employees the minimum wage. A Directive on Posted Workers (96/71) was adopted in September 1996 and implemented in the UK by the Equal Opportunities (Employment Legislation) (Territorial Limits) Regulations 1999, SI 1999/3163. Under the Regulations, a UK company posting its workers in another EU State (eg, whilst working on a building contract) will have to comply with local employment laws where the posting is longer (usually) than one month. The employees can enforce these rights in their UK employment tribunal (as well as local courts).

26.4 CONSTRAINTS UNDER ARTICLES 43 EC AND 49 EC

The in-coming business is subject to the laws that would apply to a business operated by nationals of that State. This can create barriers to the business wishing to operate across a frontier. The host State may require, perhaps, that all such businesses obtain the authority of the State before they can start to operate. Professional people may be required to conform to rules of professional conduct, professional qualifications or to the rules of a professional body within the host State.

Article 57 of the EC Treaty (now Article 47 EC) envisaged that a series of Directives would be issued dealing with mutual recognition and harmonisation of professional regulations. In the light of this, the European Commission, recognising the public interest in maintaining standards while wishing to minimise unnecessary barriers to cross-border enterprise, tried to develop uniform codes in certain sectors which would apply throughout the Community. These 'sectoral' Directives apply to medical professions such as doctors, nurses, dentists and vets, but the development of harmonised professional training and qualifications in all professions would have taken many years. So after the European Court held that Articles 52 and 59 of the EC Treaty (now Articles 43 EC and 49 EC) were directly effective (see *Reyners v The Belgian State* [1974] ECR 631 and *Van Binsbergen (JHM) v Bestuur van de Bedrijfsvereniging voor de Metaalnijverheid* [1974] ECR 1299 at **23.3.1**), the Commission changed its approach to one of encouraging mutual recognition of standards. Thus a professional qualified in one State must, in principle, be recognised in another State to the extent that his qualification is equivalent.

A particularly important Directive in this respect is Directive 89/48 on recognition of higher education qualifications. This Directive was required to be implemented by January 1991. The effect of the Directive is that, where entry into a particular profession depends upon the candidate having obtained a 'diploma' which proves that he has completed at least 3 years' professional education and training, a non-national cannot be denied entry to that profession if he holds the equivalent 'diploma' which would entitle him to enter the profession in his home State.

However, if there are substantial differences in the content of the course leading to the diploma in the home State, the Directive allows the host State to require the candidate to follow an adaptation period of no more than 3 years. As an alternative, the candidate could choose to take an aptitude test. The Directive makes special provision regarding entry to the legal profession. It allows a State to specify whether a candidate must take an aptitude test or follow a period of adaptation. Thus, in England and Wales, qualified lawyers from other EC States must pass the Law Society's Qualified Lawyers Transfer Test (QLTT) before they can be admitted as solicitors. Solicitors from Ireland are, however, admitted without a test, as their qualification is equivalent. The more recent establishment Directive of 1998 (98/5) provides for automatic requalification after a period of practice as a foreign lawyer.

In *Van Binsbergen (JHM) v Bestuur van de Bedrijfsvereniging voor de Metaalnijverheid* [1974] ECR 1299, the European Court held that professional rules of conduct regulating the legal profession would not be in breach of Community law provided they did not discriminate against the non-national, they were objectively justifiable and they were not disproportionate to the aim to be achieved. Hence, a lawyer established in France had the right to provide services by representing clients before Belgian tribunals. He could not be forced to establish himself in Belgium. Simply having an address for service in Belgium would be proportional to any need for supervision of his activities. (An EC Directive has now adopted the *Van Binsbergen* line and allows qualified EU lawyers to represent their clients before foreign tribunals within the EU (see Directive 77/249).) A similar approach can be seen in the more recent case of *Commission of European Communities v Germany* [1988] ECR 5427, which was concerned with the regulation of the German insurance sector. In that case, the Court held that restrictions on the right of an insurance company to provide services in Germany would be acceptable only if they were objectively justified, in the general public good and if they applied to all undertakings so far as they were not regulated in their home State.

Finally, it would seem that, if there is only a tenuous link between the services being provided and a particular restrictive provision, the latter will not be in breach of EC law (see *Society for the Protection of the Unborn Child (Ireland) v Grogan (Stephen)* [1991] 3 CMLR 849). That case concerned Irish legislation prohibiting the supply of information on abortion facilities provided outside Ireland. The European Court acknowledged that the overseas clinics provided services within the meaning of Article 59 of the EC Treaty (now Article 49 EC) but went on to hold that, since the information in question was being made available by student unions rather than by the clinics themselves, there was an insufficient link between the restriction and the provision of the services. Had the clinics been advertising directly themselves (or through an advertising agency), the position would have been different. (The ban on these leaflets may raise questions of freedom of speech under Article 10 of the European Convention on Human Rights – see Chapter 30 below).

26.5 CAN THE SELF-EMPLOYED PERSON BRING HIS FAMILY WITH HIM TO THE HOST STATE?

Directive 73/148 requires Member States to abolish restrictions on the movement of certain categories of family member: spouses, children under 21, and dependent relatives. In each case the nationality of the family member is immaterial.

26.6 DEROGATIONS FROM ARTICLES 43 EC AND 49 EC

It is possible to derogate from Articles 43 EC and 49 EC on grounds of public health, public security and public policy (Articles 46 EC and 55 EC). The interpretation of these terms is the same as that under Article 39(3) EC and Directive 64/221 (see **25.4**). Moreover, the right of establishment does not apply to activities involving, even occasionally, 'the exercise of official authority' (Article 45 EC). Thus a number of 'legal professions', for example judges, magistrates, court registrars and notaries (but not lawyers), can be reserved to home nationals.

26.7 RIGHTS OF POTENTIAL RECIPIENTS OF SERVICES UNDER EC LAW

In *Luisi and Carbone v Ministero del Tesoro* [1984] ECR 377, the European Court interpreted Article 59 of the EC Treaty (now Article 49 EC) to mean that potential recipients of services had the right to go to another Member State to receive those services and that tourists qualified as potential recipients of services. This approach was further developed in *Cowan v Le Trésor Public (The Treasury)* [1989] ECR 195, which concerned a British tourist who was the victim of a criminal assault while in France. His claim for compensation from the French Criminal Injuries Compensation Board was denied because he was not a French national. On an Article 234 EC reference, the European Court held that compensation could not be denied to a recipient of compensation services on grounds of nationality.

In a number of cases, the European Court has considered whether this approach entitles a national of a Member State to take advantage of education services elsewhere in the Community. Strictly speaking, State education cannot be 'services' because, under Article 50 EC, services must normally be paid for. In cases such as *Gravier v City of Liege* [1985] ECR 593, however, it was held that students cannot be asked to pay an additional fee for educational courses because they are non-nationals, provided the course represents vocational training, ie it facilitates access to a particular trade or profession. Even if the courses are normally free (ie not 'services') they still relate to a Treaty matter (training) and therefore any discrimination is unlawful under Article 12 EC (see **26.1**).

26.8 SUMMARY AND CONCLUSION

26.8.1 Distinguish between establishment and services

Establishment (Article 43 EC) implies permanence; services (Article 49 EC) are more temporary. Hence, the presence of a permanent office implies establishment under Article 43 EC (see *Gebhard v Consiglio dell'Ordine degli Avvocati e Procuratori di Milano* [1996] All ER (EC) 139 at **26.1**).

26.8.2 Restriction on free movement

Where services are involved, for Article 49 EC to apply there must be a restriction on free movement. However, services may move in four different ways.

(1) The provider of services moves to another Member State to provide services on a temporary basis (the normal case).
(2) The recipient of services moves to receive services (eg as a tourist – see *Cowan v Le Trésor Public* [1989] ECR 195 at **26.7** above).
(3) The provider moves to another Member State to provide services to nationals of his own State (eg a British interpreter/guide/ski instructor who accompanies a party of British tourists abroad).
(4) Neither provider nor recipient moves, but services are provided by post, fax, telephone, broadcast, etc.

This last situation arose in the instructive case of *Alpine Investments BV v Minister Van Financien* [1995] All ER (EC) 543, which concerned Dutch financial services laws banning the cold-calling of customers at home or abroad. The Dutch company prosecuted in this case argued that the law banning the cold-calling of foreign clients infringed Article 59 of the EC Treaty (now Article 49 EC). Clearly, the law in question did not discriminate against foreign service providers, but it still restricted the export of services because it directly affected access to the market in other States. Nevertheless, the restriction could be objectively justified in the general interest on grounds of consumer protection or the good reputation of the industry. Moreover, the restriction was proportional (the fact that other countries had no (or less strict) controls on cold-calling was considered irrelevant). It should be noted that, as in the *Cassis de Dijon* case (see **27.2.2**), restrictions like this, which apply without distinction to all service providers, could be justified on a wider range of grounds than those which appear in Article 46 EC.

26.8.3 Need to satisfy local conditions

Whether seeking establishment or providing services, the foreign national who tries to work abroad must satisfy local conditions for pursuit of the activity in question. However (according to *Gebhard*), these conditions:

(1) must be non-discriminatory;
(2) must be justified by imperative requirements in the general interest;
(3) must be suitable for securing the attainment of the objective which they pursue; and
(4) must not go beyond what is necessary to achieve it.

26.8.4 General approach to free movement under EU law

The approach of the ECJ in *Gebhard* is very similar to that already established by the ECJ in relation to goods (see the key case of *Cassis de Dijon* at **27.2.2**). It has been stressed that the approach is common to *all* cases of free movement. It thus applies in relation to workers under Article 48 of the EC Treaty (now Article 39 EC) (see *Bosman* [1996] All ER (EC) 97 at **25.2**), to establishment under Article 52 of the EC Treaty (now Article 43 EC) (*Gebhard*), and to services under Article 59 of the EC Treaty (now Article 49 EC) (*Alpine* [1995] All ER (EC) 543 at **26.8.2**).

26.9 FREE MOVEMENT OF PERSONS – IMMIGRATION RIGHTS

The EU citizen who seeks entry and residence in another State is subject to a bewildering range of different rules, depending on the category he falls into. The rules derive from the Treaty, Regulations, Directives and ECJ case-law. The table below is an attempt to summarise the rules which apply to the different categories of EC national in the UK. The EC Commission recognises that the current position is unsatisfactory and would like to codify the provisions in a single code.

Rights involve:

- free movement of workers (Article 39 EC);
- establishment (self-employed persons) (Article 43 EC);
- services (providers and recipients) (Article 49 EC);
- EU citizens (Directives).

Directives are implemented in the UK by:

- the Immigration (EEA) Order 1994;
- the Immigration Rules (HC 395).

Category	Nationality	Residence Right	Social Assistance/ Housing Education	Health/ NI Benefits
(A) 'EC workers', ie EC employees of UK firms	EU/EEA	Art 39 EC Regulation 1612/68 Directive: 68/360 5-year residence permit	1612/68 Arts 7, 9	Regulation 1408/71
(B) Jobseekers	EU/EEA	Art 39 EC Directive 48175 *Antonissen* [1991] 2 CMLR 373 a reasonable time to find work	Possibly	Yes (Subject to conditions)
(C) Family of 'EC workers'	Any	Regulation 1612/68 Directive 68/360 Residence permit as (A)	Yes	Yes
(D) Retired 'EC workers'	EU/EEA	Regulation 1251/70 permanent residence right in State where work done	Yes	Yes
(E) Family of retired 'EC workers'	Any	As above	Yes	Yes
(F) Self-employed workers in UK	EU/EEA	Art 43 EC Directive 73/148 5-year residence permit	Yes	Yes
(G) Family of self-employed	Any	Directive 73/148 Residence permit as above in (F)	Yes	Yes

Category	Nationality	Residence Right	Social Assistance/ Housing Education	Health/ NI Benefits
(H) Persons providing or receiving services (eg tourists)	EU/EEA	Directive 73/148 Duration of services	No	Yes? (Health)
(I) Families of above	Any	Directive 73/148	No	No?
(J) Retired EC self-employed	EU/EEA (Families: Any)	Directive 75/34 permanent	Yes	Yes
(K) Employees of firms providing services	Any	Duration of services (Article 49 EC) *Van der Elst* [1994] ECR I-3803	No?	No?
(L) Employees of EC firms	Any?	Temporary periods of secondment?	No?	No?
(M) Persons of independent means	EU/EEA	Art 14 EC Directive 90/364 5-year residence permit	No	No
(N) Retired persons (Not 'EC workers')	EU/EEA	Directive 93/365 5-year residence permit	No	No
(O) Students	EU/EEA	Directive 93/95 Duration of studies	No	No
(P) Family of above in (M), (N) and (O)	Any	Above Directives Same period	No	No

Chapter 27

FREE MOVEMENT OF GOODS

27.1 INTRODUCTION

The free movement of goods is one of the fundamental freedoms on which the EC is based. One of the most important aims of the EC Treaty was to create a single market in goods throughout all the Member States of the Community. Following amendments to the Treaty by the Single European Act 1986, this aim was intended to be achieved by 31 December 1992. Because of the importance of this freedom, the European Court has consistently interpreted the relevant Treaty provisions in such a way as to give maximum effect to this basic objective.

27.2 WHAT DOES THE EC TREATY PROVIDE?

The principal Treaty provision is Article 28 EC, which states that:

> 'Quantitative restrictions on imports and all measures having equivalent effect shall be prohibited between Member States.'

Article 29 EC makes similar provision in relation to exports, ie the requirement or refusal of an export licence.

27.2.1 What is meant by 'quantitative restrictions'?

Quantitative restrictions are limitations on the import of goods fixed by reference to quantitative criteria, ie amount or value ('quotas'). A complete ban on the import of a particular type of goods is also such a restriction (see *Commission of European Communities v Italy* [1961] ECR 317).

27.2.2 What is meant by a 'measure having equivalent effect'?

The phrase 'a measure having equivalent effect' is not defined in the EC Treaty itself but was defined by the European Court in *Dassonville* [1974] ECR 837. In that case, the phrase was said to extend to 'all trading rules enacted by Member States that are capable of hindering, directly or indirectly, actually or potentially, intra-Community trade'.

It is important to note the following about this definition:

(1) A measure having equivalent effect does not have to have an immediate or substantial effect on intra-Community trade. In particular, it is clear from *Re Prantl (Karl)* [1984] ECR 1299 that the European Court will not apply a de minimis principle here. This means that any legislation which is capable of affecting trade between Member States, even indirectly, because it is not the primary aim of the legislation, can infringe Article 28 EC. However, the case of *Criminal Proceedings Against Keck and Mithouard* [1995] 1 CMLR 101 shows that for 'selling arrangements' the measure must have the effect of putting the

imported goods at a disadvantage before it can be said to restrict imports. Contrary to the view expressed earlier in cases involving Sunday trading laws (*Torfaen Borough Council v B&Q plc* [1989] ECR 765), a restriction on volume of imports (ie the argument that with shops shut there will be fewer sales and therefore fewer imports) is not enough if domestic goods are at the same disadvantage.

(2) A measure having equivalent effect must be taken by an 'organ of the State'. Actions by private individuals, companies or other undertakings cannot fall within this definition. However, this requirement will be satisfied even if the Member State acts through another undertaking. In *Commission of European Communities v Ireland; Re 'Buy Irish' Campaign* [1982] ECR 4005, the Irish Government initiated a campaign to encourage Irish consumers to buy home-produced goods. The campaign was launched by an Irish Government Minister and was funded by the Government but was actually managed by a guarantee company set up for the purpose. The fact that it was not the Irish Government which was directly running the campaign did not prevent it being a measure having effect equivalent to a quantitative restriction. Likewise, other State bodies, for example local authorities, licensing authorities or courts, may see their 'measures' (eg injunctions) controlled in the same way.

(3) A measure having equivalent effect need not affect imported products alone, ie be 'distinctly applicable' to imports. It could be a measure applying to all goods, domestic and imported, without distinction ('indistinctly applicable'), for example national technical standards. The difference is that whereas the latter can be justified under the 'rule of reason' and so do not infringe Article 28 EC at all (see *Cassis de Dijon* below), the former are justifiable only under Article 30 EC. The following cases involved distinctly applicable measures. In *International Fruit Co NV v Produktschap voor Groenten en Fruit (No 3)* [1971] ECR 1107, a requirement that a licence be obtained before apples could be imported into France was struck down by the European Court as an infringement of Article 30 of the EC Treaty (now Article 28 EC). Similarly, in *Rewe-Zentralfinanz e GmbH v Landwirtschaftskammer* [1975] ECR 843, a requirement that apples had to be inspected before they could be imported into Germany was also held to breach Article 30 of the EC Treaty. Although these types of measure do not completely prevent the marketing of the product, they do result in delay and inconvenience for the importer which may lead to fewer such products being imported. In both these cases, the measures could not be justified under Article 36 of the EC Treaty (now Article 30 EC) which is restrictively interpreted.

Increasingly, the European Court has found measures to be within the *Dassonville* definition, and therefore caught by Article 28 EC, where the domestic product is also affected by the measure in question. The leading case is *Rewe Zentral v Bundesmonopolverwaltung fur Branntwein (Cassis de Dijon)* [1979] ECR 649. A German law required that spirits such as Cassis de Dijon should be of a stipulated alcoholic strength. Cassis was significantly less strong and therefore could not be sold on the German market. The European Court held that the German law fell within the *Dassonville* definition and was in breach of Article 30 of the EC Treaty (now Article 28 EC). The case is considered vital to the development of a single market in that it shows that imported products do not have to be changed to meet national technical standards unless the need to do so is justified. The case is considered further in **27.3.1**.

27.3 ARE THERE CIRCUMSTANCES IN WHICH ARTICLE 28 EC WILL NOT APPLY?

27.3.1 The 'rule of reason'

Although it is no answer to an Article 28 EC complaint to say that the measure in question affects the equivalent domestic product as well as the imported one, it is important to know whether or not this is the case. This is because only such a measure can benefit from the 'rule of reason' approach of the European Court in *Cassis de Dijon* referred to above. The Court recognised in that case that, if goods were lawfully manufactured in a particular way in a given Member State, they should ordinarily be entitled to move throughout the rest of the Community. However, where the EC itself had not imposed Community-wide standards, disparities between Member States' legislation could be acceptable. In the words of the Court, 'obstacles to movement within the Community resulting from disparities between the national laws relating to the marketing of products must be accepted in so far as those provisions are necessary in order to satisfy mandatory requirements relating in particular to the effectiveness of fiscal supervision, the protection of public health, the fairness of commercial transactions and the defence of the consumer'.

The list of mandatory requirements is not closed. The Court has since added to them the protection of the environment (see *Commission of European Communities v Denmark; sub nom Re Disposable Beer Cans* [1989] 1 CMLR 619), the protection of culture (eg the cinema from the threat of video cassettes in *Cinethèque v Federation Nationale des Cinemas Français* [1986] 1 CMLR B65) and employment in the Sunday trading cases. The list inevitably includes (but is much wider than) the list of justifications in Article 30 EC.

In order for a measure to be 'necessary' to satisfy a mandatory requirement, the aim of the measure in question must be justifiable in EC law and the measure taken must be *proportionate* to that aim. Therefore, if the aim could be achieved by a measure which was less restrictive of the free movement of goods, the measure taken will be held to be disproportionate. In *Cassis de Dijon*, the German Government successfully argued that the law in question was for the defence of the consumer, but the Court found that it was nevertheless disproportionate to its objective: the same aim could have been achieved by a law requiring that such spirits should be clearly labelled with their alcoholic strength.

27.3.2 The EC Treaty

Where a government measure is distinctly applicable (ie provides different conditions for imported goods), it can only be justified under the terms of the Treaty, ie Article 30 EC.

Article 30 EC provides a number of important exceptions to Article 28 EC. It states that:

> 'The provisions of Articles 28 to 29 shall not preclude prohibitions or restrictions on imports, exports or goods in transit justified on grounds of public morality, public policy or public security; the protection of health and life of humans, animals or plants; the protection of national treasures possessing artistic, historical or archaeological value; or the protection of industrial or commercial property.

Such prohibitions or restrictions shall not, however, constitute a means of arbitrary discrimination or a disguised restriction on trade between Member States.'

As this Article derogates from a fundamental principle of the EC, the Court construes it strictly; in particular, no further justifiable restrictions can be read into the list given above. Further, the burden of establishing that a measure does come within Article 30 EC will fall on the relevant Member State.

The following points should be borne in mind when considering the exceptions in Article 30 EC.

Public morality

The European Court will not seek to impose its own standards of morality; what is required in this area will be a matter for each Member State (see *DPP v Darby; DPP v Henn; DPP v Darby* [1979] ECR 3795). It is important to appreciate the significance of the final sentence of Article 30 EC, ie the measure taken by the Member State must not amount to arbitrary discrimination against the imported product nor to a disguised restriction on trade. In *Darby and Henn* the seizure of imported pornography by UK customs was not in breach of Article 30 of the EC Treaty (now Article 28 EC) as that type of pornography could not be lawfully sold in the UK. On the other hand, in *Conegate v Customs and Excise Commissioners* [1986] ECR 1007, the import of rubber dolls into the UK could not be prevented because if they had been produced in this country they could lawfully have been sold here.

Public policy

A Member State cannot invoke public policy whenever it is convenient to do so to avoid falling foul of Article 28 EC. The European Court has made it clear that this exception can be used only where there is a serious threat to a fundamental interest of society. See, for example, *R v Thompson (Brian Ernest)* [1978] ECR 2247 where it was applied to the right to mint coinage. Economic reasons, for example protection of industry from competition, are never, however, acceptable.

Public security

Similarly, public security cannot be readily called upon in defence of a breach of Article 28 EC. It seems clear only that it extends to the need to safeguard essential public services. Note *Campus Oil Ltd v The Minister for Industry and Energy* [1984] ECR 2727, where the Irish Government required importers of petrol to buy a percentage of their needs from an Irish refinery to ensure that the refinery remained viable. It seems that it can relate to the State's internal as well as external security (*Minister of Finance v Richardt* [1992] 1 CMLR 61).

Public health

In the absence of EC standards, Member States are entitled to decide what is appropriate for their own citizens in the field of public health. In the case of *Aragonesa de Publicidad v Departmamento de Sanidad y Seguridad Social de la Generalitat de Cataluna* [1991] OJ C220/8, the European Court upheld on public health grounds Spanish legislation which prohibited roadside advertisements for strong spirits. Despite the later case of *Keck and Mithouard* (below), this case may still involve a measure equivalent to quantitative restriction (MEQR) as it may be indirectly discriminatory against imported spirits not known to the Spanish public. It is clearly, however, justified.

Again, it is essential to pay close attention to the last sentence of Article 30 EC. For example, in *Commission of European Communities v United Kingdom; sub nom Re Imports of Poultry Meat* [1982] ECR 2793, where the UK Government prohibited the import of French poultry into the UK, ostensibly in order to avoid the spread of Newcastle Disease, the evidence indicated that the prohibition was unnecessarily restrictive and in reality was intended to protect the English poultry industry. It should be noted that in most areas there are now Directives laying down the minimum requirements for health or animal welfare. For example, EC Directives lay down minimum rules for the carriage of live animals and their stunning before slaughter. It is not a sufficient justification for the refusal of an export licence for live animals that these rules may be ignored in the importing State (see *R v Ministry of Agriculture, Fisheries and Food ex parte Hedley Lomas (Ireland) Ltd* [1996] All ER (EC) 493). The refusal will breach Article 29 EC.

The protection of national treasures

The exception for the protection of national treasures, although not yet used, is likely to be of value where a Member State wishes to impose an export ban on items representing part of its national heritage, ie in breach of Article 29 EC.

The protection of intellectual property rights

Intellectual property rights have posed difficulties for the European Court. In the absence of Community-wide regimes, such rights are granted by individual Member States and relate only to the territory of the State in question. This offers enterprises an opportunity to divide up the market on national lines. This is clearly contrary to the spirit of the Community. Because of this the European Court has been careful not to overextend the protection given to intellectual property rights in Article 30 EC.

Accordingly, the Court has distinguished between the existence and the exercise of intellectual property rights. Thus, measures (eg court injunctions keeping out imports of goods infringing a patent) are not caught by Article 28 EC even if their effect is to restrict imports (because of Article 30 EC).

In order to protect the existence of intellectual property rights, however, the Court has had to decide what the existence of each right amounts to. It has done this by developing the concept of the 'specific subject matter' of a right. Thus, for example, the specific subject matter of a patent is the exclusive right to use an invention for the manufacture of products and to be the first to market them (*Centrafarm BV and De Peijper v Sterling Drug Inc* [1974] ECR 1147). This means that once a company has marketed (or consented to the marketing of) a drug in, say, France it cannot thereafter purport to use its patent rights in, say, the UK, to prevent the import of the patented product. The products marketed in France could therefore be re-imported into the UK and the patent holder or UK court could not interfere with their free movement. The company's rights over that particular product were 'exhausted' when it consented to its marketing in France. The European Court has adopted a similar approach to trade mark rights and copyright. This protection of 'parallel imports' through exhaustion of rights applies only where the goods are marketed within the EU. The ECJ has ruled in *Silhouette International Schmied GmbH & Co KG v Hartlauer Handelsgesellschaft mbH* [1998] 3 WLR 1218 that following the harmonisation of trade mark rights through the 1994 Directive Member States' laws can no longer recognise a wider principle of world-wide exhaustion, ie through marketing outside the EU. Thus manufacturers can use their national trade marks to keep out goods which they authorised for sale only in countries outside the EU.

27.4 SUMMARY OF THE POSITION REGARDING TRADING MEASURES

The problem can be tackled by asking a series of questions.

(1) Is the measure an MEQR (Dassonville test)
To be an MEQR, the rule in question must affect the product itself, ie require some change, before it can be sold in the territory.

In general, rules about *selling arrangements* (ie the arrangements for selling the product once it is imported) for example Sunday trading, licensing hours, and prohibitions on selling at a loss (*Keck and Mithouard*), do not come within the *Dassonville* formula and thus (in the absence of discrimination) need no justification. Although they may restrict the volume of imports (if you sell less, you import less), these measures do not put imports at a disadvantage and thus cannot count as MEQRs).

Advertising restrictions, for example bans on leaflets (*GB-INNO-BM v Confédération du Commerce Luxembourgeoise Asbl* [1991] 2 CMLR 801) or comparative advertising (*Unwesen in den Wirtschaft eV v Yves Rocher GmbH* (1994) *Financial Times*, 9 June), may well put the imported product at a disadvantage because advertising is the most effective way for new imported products to penetrate a market. The rival domestic products may well be better known. It would, however, seem that restrictions on retailers advertising their sales (eg *Hünermund v Landespothekerkammer Baden-Württemberg* [1993] ECR 1-6787, where German pharmacists were prohibited from advertising off the premises or *Leclerc v TFI Publicité* [1995] ECR 1-179, where French retailers could not advertise at all on French television and thus were restricted in advertising their cheap foreign fuel) are to be treated as selling arrangements under *Keck and Mithouard*. By contrast, a blanket ban on advertising a particular product, for example alcoholic products or toys, would be seen, it is felt, as either a restriction to be justified under the 'rule of reason' in *Cassis de Dijon* or a case of indirect discrimination against imports which would have to be justified on similar objective criteria (see *Konsument-ombudsmannen (KO) v De Agostini (Svenska) Forlag AB; Konsument-ombudsmannen (KO) v TV-Shop I Sverige AB* (*De Agostini*) [1997] All ER (EC) 687).

The effect of *Keck and Mithouard* on the pre-existing case-law still has to be worked out but it does not seem to have affected the position of maximum and minimum selling prices. In *Van Tiggele* [1978] 2 CMLR 528, the fixing of minimum prices was held to be a measure in breach of Article 36 of the EC Treaty (now Article 30 EC) because more competitive foreign firms would find it harder to penetrate the market. Likewise, in *Tasca (Riccardo); Societa SADAM v Comitato Interministeriale dei Prezzi; Societa Fondaria Industriale Romagnola v Presidenza del Consiglio dei Ministri; Societa Romana Zucchero v Comitato Interministeriale dei Prezzi* [1977] 2 CMLR 183, the fixing of maximum selling prices was considered to breach Article 36 of the EC Treaty (now Article 30 EC) because importing firms with better quality products and higher overheads would also find it harder to penetrate the market.

These cases may now be regarded as examples of unjustified restrictions on selling arrangements which indirectly discriminate against imports. By contrast, a restriction on permissible profit margins (or even the restriction on selling at a loss in *Keck and Mithouard* itself) has no disciminatory effect and would not need to be justified.

The arrival of mail order and now e-commerce as an effective alternative to retail outlets will challenge many of the restrictions on selling arrangements. In Germany, for example, late shopping hours, Sunday trading and free gifts (eg 'two for one') are all prohibited. The mail order firm Lands End has been prosecuted for offering free gifts and extended guarantees with its products and the matter has been referred to the ECJ. Arguably, this restriction will affect the product itself if the product and the gifts are packaged together. Otherwise, it might be argued that such rules discriminated indirectly against distance sellers who are forced to revise their catalogues. E-commerce is now the subject of a number of proposals including one which will enable firms like Lands End to avoid German retailing restrictions by complying with the law of the place where it sets up its website. These proposals now appear in the E-Commerce Directive 2000, Art 3. They should be enacted in all Member States by December 2001. Once German retail restrictions are effectively bypassed in this way, it will be difficult to see them surviving.

(2) If it is an MEQR, does it apply only to imports (ie distinctly applicable measures) or directly discriminate (as selling arrangements)?

The best example of this is the French ban on British beef. This can only be justified under Article 30 EC (eg protection of public health) but needs to be 'proportional'. Thus, the ban on British beef might be justifiable as a measure protecting public health but is possibly not now proportional to the risks involved since the spread of mad cow disease can be prevented by rigorous policing of herds and slaughterhouses. If the ban was imposed not for reasons of public health but to boost confidence in European beef, this would probably not be justified as 'public policy', which must have a restrictive meaning.

Likewise, an injunction prohibiting the imports of goods said to infringe a national patent could only be justified under Article 30 EC (protection of IP rights).

(3) Does the measure apply to all products (ie indistinctly applicable measures) or (if a selling arrangement) indirectly discriminate?

Measures which apply to all goods (domestic and imported) without distinction will be caught by Article 28 EC only if they put the imported goods at a disadvantage compared with domestic goods. Thus, where the imported product has to be adapted before it can be sold on the domestic market it is prima facie at a disadvantage compared with domestic products which are made to domestic specifications. Here, because we are dealing with indirect discrimination, the measure infringes Article 28 EC unless it can be shown to be justified by a public interest objective (eg consumer protection, health, environment, etc – the list given in *Cassis de Dijon* is not exhaustive) which is proportional and takes precedence over the free movement of goods. If so justified, there is no Article 28 EC infringement. Measures falling into this category would be German measures on purity of spirits (*Cassis de Dijon*), sausages, beer, etc; packaging rules (eg Danish or German rules on recyclable bottles or containers – these may be justified on environmental protection grounds (see *Commission of European Communities v Kingdom of Denmark; sub nom Re Disposable Beer Cans* [1989] 1 CMLR 619)), rules on labelling, weight, trade marks, etc. In *Verband Sozialer Wettbewerb eV v Clinique Laboratories SNC and Estée Lauder Cosmetics* (Case C-315/92) , the cosmetic 'Clinique' could not be marketed under that mark in Germany because it was considered to suggest therapeutic properties which it did not have. Since the cosmetic had to be repackaged for sale in Germany, there was clearly an indirect restriction on imports which could not be justified on the basis of protecting consumers from confusion.

Since the effect of *Cassis de Dijon* is that Member States must mutually recognise different product standards which give equivalent protective effect, modern product standard Directives under the '1992' campaign (and after) have merely set a minimum level of protection ('the essential requirements') which different national products can satisfy. The obligatory Euro standard is a thing of the past, except for hazardous products like drugs and motor cars where full harmonisation of the specification requirements may be needed. In other areas, Euro standards are considered optional.

27.5 HOW TO USE ARTICLE 28 EC

Article 28 EC is directly effective; this means it can be relied upon before national courts and tribunals. It can therefore be used defensively, for example in response to a criminal prosecution for breach of trading standards in another Member State, or offensively, for example to challenge a 'buy national' campaign. In the latter case, the challenger must follow the most appropriate national procedure and claim the most effective national remedy. The European Court has made it clear that a Member State is under an obligation to provide an effective remedy for infringement of EC rights. Thus, a challenge to a government-sponsored 'buy national' campaign in the UK would be done by judicial review proceedings for a declaration that the Government was acting ultra vires accompanied by a claim for an injunction (see *R v Secretary of State for Transport ex parte Factortame (No 2)* (c-213/89) [1990] 3 WLR 818) or possibly damages (see *R v Secretary of State for Transport ex parte Factortame (No 4)* [1996] 2 WLR 506). The case of *Brasserie du Pêcheur* decided with *Factortame (No 4)* concerned a damages claim under Article 30 of the EC Treaty (now Article 28 EC) by beer importers who fell foul of Germany's purity laws. Since the particular restrictions (relating to a ban on additives) were not manifestly unlawful at the time, no damages were payable.

It should be noted that all new national rules on product standards have to be notified to Brussels under Directive 83/189. The failure to do so will invalidate the national law because Directive 83/189 has direct effect. (See *CIA Security International SA. v Signalson SA* [1996] 2 CMLR 781.) This, too, can be used as a defence.

Chapter 28

COMPETITION LAW

28.1 INTRODUCTION

The regulation of competition between businesses is as important to the Community as the attainment of the freedoms discussed in the previous chapters. It is of little use to provide that goods can move freely throughout the Community unless at the same time businesses are able to trade across frontiers without facing improper competition. Improper competition, particularly where it has the effect of dividing up markets along national lines, must be controlled. Thus, Article 3(1)(g) EC states that one of the activities of the Community is the institution of a system ensuring that competition in the common market is not distorted. This system is principally established in two Articles of the Treaty: Articles 81 and 82 EC. Article 81 EC controls anti-competitive agreements, while Article 82 EC regulates an abuse of a dominant position. It should be remembered that the object of any competition law is greater customer choice, either of manufacturers (different brands) or of dealers supplying the same brand. More competition equals more choice; this in turn compels competing manufacturers (or dealers) to cut costs and improve quality of goods or services.

28.2 ANTI-COMPETITIVE AGREEMENTS: ARTICLE 81 EC

28.2.1 What does Article 81 EC provide?

Article 81 EC provides that:

> 'The following shall be prohibited as incompatible with the common market: all agreements between undertakings, decisions by associations of undertakings and concerted practices which may affect trade between Member States and which have as their object or effect the prevention, restriction or distortion of competition within the common market …'

It then gives examples of the types of conduct which would be caught by this definition, such as fixing prices, controlling production and sharing markets. To discover what other practices may be within Article 81 EC, it is necessary to look at the Article in detail.

Agreements between undertakings

The term 'undertaking' is not defined in the Treaty but is taken to include any business enterprise, whatever legal form it may take. In particular, under English law it will include a company or a partnership, a sole trader or a trade association. A parent and a subsidiary company are usually taken to amount to a single undertaking for this purpose. Likewise, agreements between a company and its employees or agents are unlikely to be agreements 'between undertakings' as they lack the necessary independence.

Not only written agreements between two or more such undertakings but also less formal arrangements, such as a mere understanding or 'gentlemen's agreement', may breach Article 81 EC (see the *Quinine Cartel* case [1970] ECR 661). It was originally thought that Article 85 of the EC Treaty (now Article 81 EC) applied only to agreements between potential competitors, ie 'horizontal agreements' between undertakings at the same level of the production process, for example the traditional cartel where manufacturers meet in secret to carve up markets or fix prices. The agreement may, however, be a 'vertical' one, that is between undertakings involved at different stages of the manufacturing or trading process, for example an agreement between a wholesaler and a retailer. Even if the manufacturer is not involved in distribution itself, restrictions, eg on prices or exports, can affect competition between distributors (see, for example, *Consten SA and Grundig-Verkaufs-GmbH (Etablissements) v EEC Commission* [1996] CMLR 418 (ECJ)).

Decisions by associations of undertakings

The phrase 'decisions by associations of undertakings' would include, for example, decisions taken by a trade association, whether or not they were legally binding.

Concerted practices

An enterprise may breach Article 81 EC if it deliberately co-ordinates its behaviour with another business in the same market, for example if they agree to raise prices at the same time and by the same amount. It is not necessary to be able to prove an agreement that they should do so; the fact of synchronised activity may be enough, so that, in the words of the European Court in *Dyestuffs* [1972] ECR 619, 'the parties have substituted practical co-operation for the risks of competition'. It is important to appreciate that a business is entitled to respond to market conditions, including the behaviour of its competitors. This may well mean that enterprises operating within the same market do show similar behaviour without there being a 'concerted practice'.

How much of an effect does there have to be on trade between Member States?

Article 81 EC states that it is necessary that the agreement etc 'may' have an effect on trade. According to the European Court in *STM v Maschinenbau Ulm* [1966] ECR 235:

> 'it must be possible to foresee with a sufficient degree of probability on the basis of a set of objective factors of law or fact that the agreement in question may have an influence, direct or indirect, actual or potential, on the pattern of trade between Member States.'

Such an effect may result even where the parties to the agreement or concerted practice are based within one Member State if the effect is to distort competition elsewhere in the EC, for example because a company based in another Member State is unable to break into that market (see the *Dutch Cement* case [1972] ECR 977).

It can even occur where the parties are based outside the EC, provided the agreement or practice is implemented within it (*Re Wood Pulp Cartel* [1988] ECR 5193).

It has recently been held by the European Court of Justice that Article 81 EC can apply to exclusive distribution agreements in countries outside the EU (here Russia, Ukraine and Slovenia), which contain restrictions on exporting into the EU. Here, the distribution agreements for Yves St Laurent Perfumes were subject to French law and jurisdiction. The French courts therefore would be entitled to rule that the agreements were invalid under Article 81(2) EC (see *Javico v Yves St Laurent* (1998) *Financial Times*, 13 May (ECJ)).

This part of Article 81 EC therefore determines the jurisdiction of the EC competition authorities. But it also sets out clearly the policy of EC competition law, which is partly to create a single market. Agreements which have the effect of partitioning the single market (eg exclusive territories for dealers) are prima facie likely to infringe Article 81 EC.

'which have as their object or effect'

If, objectively, the parties intend the agreement or the practice to prevent, restrict or distort competition, there is no need to consider further what the effect of the agreement might be. On the other hand, if that is not the object, but it would be its effect, then Article 81 EC will still be breached.

'the prevention, restriction or distortion of competition'

The words 'the prevention, restriction or distortion of competition' are given their ordinary meaning. However, if the effect is likely to be minimal, Article 81(1) EC will not be breached (*Volk v Verwaecke* [1969] ECR 295). See further the Commission's Notice on Minor Agreements in **28.2.4**.

It should be remembered that even if the agreement has no effect on competition between the parties, it may still be prohibited by Article 81 EC if its effect is to restrict competition with third parties. This is the case with vertical agreements such as the exclusive distribution agreement which may restrict intra-band competition between the different dealers.

28.2.2 Can an undertaking apply for clearance that its arrangements are outside Article 81 EC?

Under Regulation 17/62, if the undertaking notifies its activities to the Commission (on a Form A/B) it can be granted 'negative clearance', that is confirmation that it is not in breach of this Article. To apply only for 'negative clearance' is, however, dangerous as there is no protection from fines if clearance is refused. For safety's sake, therefore, an application should always be made for an exemption in the alternative. It should be noted that (unlike exemptions) national courts, who ultimately have to rule on whether an agreement is enforceable, have jurisdiction to grant 'negative clearance', for example by a declaration that the agreement is not prohibited by Article 81(1) EC.

28.2.3 What is the result if there is a breach of Article 81 EC?

According to Article 81(2) EC, any agreement or decision prohibited by Article 81(1) EC is automatically void. This means that any agreement is unenforceable. It may be possible to sever offending clauses from the agreement and leave the rest of it standing. Whether this is possible depends on the domestic law to which the agreement is subject. Thus, under English law, such clauses can be severed if the remaining agreement still reflects accurately the agreement reached by the parties (*Chemidus Wavin v Société pour la Transformation et l'Exploitation des Resines Industrielles SA* [1978] 3 CMLR 514). Because Article 81(1) EC has been held to be directly effective, it seems that a party whose business interests are being or have been harmed by the anti-competitive agreement may seek an injunction to restrain operation of the agreement and may be able to claim damages (*Garden Cottage Foods v Milk Marketing Board* [1983] 3 WLR 143). In addition, the Commission has the power to levy fines upon the parties to an anti-competitive agreement, the size of the fine (up to a maximum of 10 per cent of turnover) being dependent on the degree of fault. In recent years, the size of the fine has been increased to provide an effective deterrent, however, especially against cartels of manufacturers in the chemical industry. The recent cement cartel case saw collective fines of over £200 million.

Because of limited resources, however, the Commission can make only 20 decisions per year. Most notifications are dealt with by 'comfort letters' closing the file.

The Commission is keen for national courts to take on the main role of safeguarding individuals from abuses of competition law, so that it can concentrate on implementing competition policy. In its Notice on Co-operation of February 1993 (93/C39/05), the Commission put forward the advantages of national courts. Importantly, they can award compensation to an injured party and grant interim relief more quickly than the Commission. If the national court needed and requested help, the Commission would be able to give an opinion on a point of law (not legally binding) and provide statistics on the relevant market to enable the national court to assess whether there had been a breach of Article 81 EC. If a legally binding ruling is required, the national court can always refer a question to the ECJ under Article 234 EC. Only the Commission can grant individual exemption within Article 81(3) EC. But where the parties have notified the agreement, the national court can take account of 'comfort letters' (and the Commission's opinion) in deciding whether a retrospective Commission exemption will be granted 'on the balance of probabilities'. The comfort letter is thus reasonably safe. See below for proposed changes to this system.

28.2.4 Are there any ways out for a business which seems to be at risk of breaching this Article?

There are primarily three ways in which a business may avoid breaching Article 81 EC.

The Notice on Agreements of Minor Importance

The Commission, which is responsible for implementing the Community's competition policy, has issued a Notice on Agreements of Minor Importance, which was radically amended in October 1997 (see [1997] OJ C372/13). According to this Notice, only agreements which have an appreciable effect on trade between Member States should be taken as breaching Article 85 of the EC Treaty (now Article 81 EC). It goes on to provide that this will be assumed not to be the case where the parties to the agreement have only a limited market share. If the parties are at the same level (horizontal agreement), the joint market share must not be more than 5 per cent. If the parties are at different levels, for example distribution or franchising (vertical agreements), the joint market share should be under 10 per cent. The relevant market here is determined in the same way as under Article 82 EC by looking at all the goods and services which the customer would take in substitute for those under the agreement. The firm's share of the market for such goods and services must not represent more than 5 per cent (or 10 per cent) of the total market for such goods in the area of the EC affected by the agreement. The more generous treatment of vertical agreements reflects the Commission's growing awareness that restrictions on intra-brand competition may be compensated by more inter-brand competition (see also the vertical restraints block exemption (below)).

The Notice does not give complete legal protection because:

(1) the market may be a very specialised one where even small companies (especially with patent protection) may have more than 5 (or 10) per cent; and

(2) account is to be taken of market share of other companies within the same group, or within the same distribution network and the fact that the share may increase; and

(3) account has to be taken of the overall effect of a network of similar agreements. For example, beer ties with smallish breweries may be caught by Article 81 EC since they are part of a network of similar ties with a substantial effect on competition (see *Delimitis v Henninger Braü* [1991] ECR 1-935); and

(4) in any event, the Commission admits that clauses which have the object of restricting competition by market sharing or price fixing are not necessarily de minimis. These, however, may be controlled by national competition authorities rather than the Commission.

Individual exemption

It may be possible to claim exemption from the effects of Article 81(2) EC for a particular agreement because of the operation of Article 81(3) EC. This provides for exemption for any agreement which:

(1) contributes to improving the production or distribution of goods or to promoting technical or economic progress; and

(2) allows consumers a fair share of the resulting benefit; and

(3) does not impose on the undertakings concerned restrictions which are not indispensable to the attainment of these objectives; and

(4) does not afford such undertakings the possibility of eliminating competition in respect of a substantial part of the products in question.

Thus, to satisfy Article 81(3) EC, the agreement must bring with it certain benefits while at the same time not including excessive restriction of competition.

To obtain an exemption for an individual agreement, the agreement must be notified to the Commission on a Form A/B. This requires a considerable amount of economic information to be supplied and is therefore not to be undertaken lightly. One advantage of notifying is that, if the Commission subsequently finds that the agreement does breach Article 81(1) EC and is not eligible for exemption, any fines levied can only relate to the period before notification. If, by contrast, the Commission decides to grant an exemption, this is backdated to the date of notification.

Rather than formally granting an individual exemption (or a negative clearance referred to above), however, the Commission will in most cases respond to the notification with a 'comfort letter' which indicates that it does not believe that the facts of the case require it to take any further action. Only a handful of cases every year are expressly given individual exemption under Article 81(3) EC. In 1999, the governing Regulation 19/65 was amended. The new Art 4(2) of the Regulation allows for retrospective exemption of vertical agreements so that effectively they need only be notified at the time of the agreement.

The Commission have issued a draft Regulation (COM (2000) 582) which proposes an overhaul of the Article 81(3) notification system. Under the proposed new rules, notification will no longer be made to the Commission. Instead, National Competition Authorities and national courts will be able to grant exemptions, leaving the Commission to concentrate on targeting serious breaches of competition law. This will lead to parties trying to decide for themselves whether they are within Article 81(3), thus providing them with a defence should they be sued for an alleged breach of Article 81(1). It is likely that the draft Regulation will not come into force until 2003, and until then the current system will remain in place.

Using a block exemption

The Commission in the early years of the Community was inundated with individual notifications and it was not unusual for years to go by without a reply being received from the Commission. To try to deal with this volume of agreements, the Commission began to introduce Block Exemptions (as Article 81(3) EC allows them) for particular categories of agreement which fulfil the conditions for an exemption. Several Regulations have now been issued by the Commission to deal with a range of different types of agreement. A considerable simplification took place in June 2000 when the vertical restraints block exemption (Regulation 2790/1999) came into effect. Covering all types of vertical agreement, this Regulation now replaces the three that appear in square brackets. The current block exemptions are thus:

> Regulation 2790/99 replacing –
> [Regulation 1983/83 on Exclusive Distribution Agreements]
> [Regulation 1984/83 on Exclusive Purchasing Agreements (including beer and petrol ties)]
> [Regulation 4087/88 on Franchising Agreements]
> Regulation 417/85 on Specialisation Agreements
> Regulation 418/85 on Research and Development Agreements
> Regulation 240/96 on Technology Licensing (ie patents and know-how)
> Regulation 1475/95 on Motor Vehicle Distribution Agreements.

The block exemptions are limited in time and mutually exclusive. Thus, for example, although concerned with vertical agreements, selective distribution for vehicles is not covered by the Regulation but by the more specific Regulation 1475/95, which expires only in 2005. Even if vertical patent licensing is covered by Regulation 240/96 rather than the broader vertical agreements exemption.

The older Regulations follow a similar pattern. They identify the benefits that can result from the kind of agreement in question. They then provide a list of permitted clauses which can properly be included in such an agreement (because they are presumed to be necessary to provide these benefits). They also identify prohibited clauses, the inclusion of any one of which will mean that the agreement cannot benefit from the exemption. The new Regulation on vertical restraints does not include an express permitted list but provides that all restraints in vertical agreements are exempted (Art 2) as necessary incentives for both parties provided there are no prohibited clauses (Art 4) and the supplier's turnover is under 30 per cent of the relevant market. This is the reverse of the old block exemption for exclusive distribution which had an express permitted list and impliedly prohibited all other restrictions. There is now an express prohibited list and all other restrictions are implicitly permitted. In the absence of prohibited clauses, the agreement would need an individual exemption only if the supplier's market share is over 30 per cent. If we take the example of a distribution agreement, it is accepted in the new Block Exemption (Regulation 2790/99) that providing dealers with an exclusive territory is a necessary incentive to taking on a dealership which itself improves distribution and gives consumers benefits (eg better choice, better prices). Moreover, the dealer can be required to concentrate his efforts on his own territory and not solicit (advertise for) customers in other dealers' territories. This, too, is a necessary incentive to prevent dealers 'free-riding' off other dealers' efforts. But a ban on 'passive sales', where the enterprising customer approaches the dealer unsolicited, is prohibited because this has the effect of partitioning the single market and is not a *necessary* incentive to take on the dealership. If an agreement comes within a block exemption, it is not necessary to notify the agreement individually. It is therefore highly desirable, if at all possible, for agreements which might be caught by Article 81(1) to be drafted with a view to their complying with the relevant block exemption. Some of the block exemptions, for example Regulation 240/96 on technology licensing, incorporate the 'opposition procedure'. This is to the effect that if the agreement contains restrictive clauses which are not contained in the permitted or the prohibited lists then the agreement should be notified individually. If it is so notified, it can be considered to be exempt if the Commission does not oppose its exemption within 4 months of the notification.

Note that since the Commission alone can give an exemption, severance by national courts would not be possible as the parties must stick to the terms of the block exemption before it can apply (see *Delimitis v Henninger Braü* [1991] ECR 1-935). Thus, firms which wish to have the certainty of a valid agreement must take particular care to draft their agreements to fit the relevant block exemption. If they include restrictions which are not allowed by the block exemption, the block exemption cannot apply and the national court cannot sever restrictions before applying the block exemption.

The only exception is the vertical restraints block exemption (Regulation 2790/99, Art 5) which allows for the severance of (inter alia) non-compete clauses including post-term restrictive covenants. If not within the block exemption, the agreement needs to be notified for individual exemption under Article 81(3) EC, but there is no real chance of justifying an agreement with prohibited clauses. Where the opposition procedure is available, as under the technology licensing block exemption 240/96, this is automatic if the Commission does not oppose within the 4 months. Where the agreement relates to vertical agreements, Art 4(2) of Regulation 17/65 now provides for notification of the agreement at any time, with the exemption back-dated to the agreement date. This will not protect from fines if they include prohibited clauses but may be useful if they are above the market share threshold.

28.2.5 The vertical restraints Regulation 2790/1999

This Regulation is a significant improvement on the previous regulations for exclusive distribution, exclusive purchasing (eg beer ties) and franchising. It now exempts Art 2(1) all vertical agreements (ie between two or more parties at different levels of the production or distribution chain). There are basically four things to check.

(1) Is it vertical?

Under the exemption in Art 2(1), they must be at different levels, but this would take in a number of different agreements involving goods or services such as exclusive distribution, selective distribution, franchises and exclusive purchasing. They would also cover exclusive supply agreements (eg where a large retailer persuades a supplier of parts to supply only him). Unlike previous block exemptions, it is no longer necessary to identify which type of vertical agreement one is dealing with.

The exemption can apply to multi-party agreements provided they are still vertical. Thus Art 2(2) specifically refers to agreements between a supplier and a trade association of small retailers. There is no reason why a British manufacturer wishing to distribute his product in France should not agree to supply the various retailers in such a trade association and achieve national retail coverage that way rather than supply an individual distributor.

It can also apply even though the chosen distributor is another manufacturer and thus a potential competitor. There is a danger here of the arrangements operating as a horizontal cartel but provided the arrangements are not reciprocal and the distributors' turnover limited the exemption will still apply (Art 2(4)).

The exemption does not apply to agreements, which are primarily concerned with licensing intellectual property rights, for example patent, trade mark, copyright or software licences (Art 2(3)). Thus, such agreements would normally need an individual exemption (if caught by Article 81 EC at all) although there is a block exemption for technology transfer licenses – patents and know-how. Obviously, the distribution agreement might include a trade mark license in it but this would be secondary and thus covered by the exemption. It is presumed that franchises are covered under the same principle even though the IP rights (trade mark and trade secrets – 'know-how') are considerably more important in such an agreement.

Finally, it should be remembered that the block exemptions are mutually exclusive (Art 2(5)) so that this exemption does not apply to vertical agreements (eg motor dealing) dealt with under other block exemptions.

(2) Prohibited list

Assuming that the agreement is vertical, then the exemption under Art 2(1) applies to all vertical restraints, otherwise prohibited by Art 81 EC, unless the agreement contains prohibited clauses. So, the second stage is to check the prohibited list in Art 4. Some of the prohibited clauses are directed to particular types of agreement so it may be helpful to see how this applies to exclusive distribution and selective distribution.

If it is **exclusive distribution** the clauses to avoid are as follows:

– Art 4(a) Price fixing. This includes minimum prices (which effectively prevents discounts) as well as fixed prices. It does not include maximum or recommended prices unless the price has become in practice fixed through pressure from the supplier. It may be worth considering why prices would be recommended – this may be more justified in selective distribution or franchising than in exclusive distribution.

– Art 4(b) **Restrictions on the buyer's resales to customers or into other territories**. It should be noticed that only restrictions on the buyer (the distributor) are prohibited; the block exemption would certainly cover restrictions on the supplier selling into the buyer's territory (the essence of course of exclusive distribution).

As far as restrictions on the buyer are concerned, it is permissible to prohibit the distributor from **actively** marketing the goods in territories reserved to the supplier or allocated to other distributors. Passive sales (where the customer approaches the dealer unsolicited) can, however, never be restricted. The enterprising customer must always be allowed to shop around the network to get the cheapest deal. With new methods of marketing over the internet, which knows no frontiers, the distinction between active and passive sales into other territories becomes a fine one. Fortunately, the Commission's guidelines make it clear that having a website is not actively selling outside the territory. A UK customer can thus check the websites of the dealers in, say, France, Germany and Italy and order from the cheapest. That is a passive sale and the agreement cannot prohibit the dealer from meeting that order without imperiling the validity of the agreement itself.

Although the agreement can stop the distributor from actively selling to a reserved territory or customer group, it cannot stop him from selling to a customer who would resell to such customers (see Art 4(b) first indent). This is the parallel importer (or exporter), the enterprising dealer who buys from the distributor with the cheapest prices with a view to reselling in those territories where prices are highest. Any restrictions on such sales would lose the block exemption.

If it is **selective distribution** the supplier must again avoid price fixing but he is even more restricted in the limitations he can put on dealers' customers.

The definition of selective distribution appears in Art 1(d). The dealers must be selected on the basis of specified criteria. These might be their qualifications to handle the product (eg computers or other hi-tech products) or give the right ambience to accord with the image of the brand (eg perfumes). The dealers in the network undertake, therefore, not to sell to unauthorised dealers, but other restrictions on sales are all black-listed. Thus dealers must be permitted to supply other selected dealers (Art 4(d)) and selected retailers cannot be prevented from supplying end-users, whether actively or passively (Art 4(c)). Thus, it is not possible to give selected dealers any territorial protection at all from other dealers, who will all compete, whether actively or passively, for the customers of each other.

(3) Market share

Once it is clear there are no prohibited clauses, the agreement (and all its restrictions) is covered by the exemption, but it is still necessary to check whether the supplier has more than 30 per cent of the relevant market. If he has, the block exemption cannot apply (Art 3). The rationale for this is that the Commission needs to be satisfied that the agreement does not substantially eliminate competition. Equally, the bigger the market share, the closer the firm comes to being dominant on that market, at which point many of the restrictions permitted under the block exemption would be seen as abuses under Article 82 EC. Thirty per cent has always been taken as the bottom line for dominance. So, even though most cases would be well over 40 per cent, the Commission would still want to vet these agreements individually to be sure. Under the new rules on notifications, however, this can be done when the dispute arises. Article 9 of Regulation 2790/1999 gives a definition of the relevant market but this is entirely in accordance with the tests applied under Article 82 EC (*United Brands* (Case 27/76) [1978] ECR 207– see **28.3.2**).

(4) Severable restrictions

This leaves one final step which is to check through Art 5 to see whether there are any severable restrictions in the agreement. These restrictions, which all concern non-compete obligations, do not destroy the exemption given to other vertical restraints. The national court is permitted to sever them from the agreement (assuming this is possible under its own national rules). The restrictions are:

(a) *Non-compete obligations (including exclusive purchase).* These must be for a fixed term under 5 years, although, for beer ties with tenanted pubs, the duration could be the length of the lease. Any indefinite exclusive purchase obligation will thus be void but severable. Article 1(b) defines such clauses to include those where the buyer has to take more than 80 per cent of his purchases from the supplier. Thus, in beer ties, the pub may well be taking a guest beer. If guest beers make up less than 20 per cent of the beer supply, the supplier needs to be wary of Art 5.

(b) *Post-term restrictive covenants.* As under English law, these are void if unjustified. But, under Art 5(b), they benefit from the exemption only if they are confined to the same premises, the same goods and a maximum duration of one year. Moreover, and most importantly, they can be justified only if they are there to protect trade secrets ('know-how'). It is unlikely that such covenants could ever be justified in exclusive distribution. There will however be trade secrets to protect in franchises and possibly in selective distribution.

(c) Finally, selective distribution dealers can never be prevented from selling competing goods, but such clauses are severable.

28.2.6 Agency agreements

The Commission has also issued a Notice on Agency Agreements [1962] L 39/2921 to the effect that such agreements will be outside Article 85 of the EC Treaty (now Article 81 EC) provided the agent accepts no financial risks and the principal is responsible for setting prices and terms. The point here is that such an agent is integrated into the principal's business and thus is not an independent undertaking. The Commission has now put the Notice in its new guidelines on vertical agreements.

28.2.7 Mergers

In principle, when two companies merge (eg one takes over the other), they cease to be independent undertakings and thus the agreement between then cannot be caught by Article 81 EC. Large-scale mergers at EC level are now controlled by DG Competition under Regulation 4064/89.

28.2.8 Pro-competitive agreements – the 'rule of reason'

The ECJ has indicated that some apparent restrictions on competition have such pro-competitive effects that they do not infringe Article 81(1) EC at all. Thus, post-contractual restrictive covenants on a sale of a business will not breach Article 81 EC if they are reasonable (in area and duration) for the protection of legitimate interests (ie the value of goodwill or trade secrets being sold as part of the business: see *Reuter (Gottfried) v BASF AG* (No 76/743/EEC) [1976] 2 CMLR D44, and *Nutricia* [1984] 2 CMLR 165).

Likewise, since goodwill and trade secrets are involved, a reasonable post-contractual restriction in a franchising agreement would be justified (see *Pronuptia de Paris GmbH Frankfurt am Main v Schillgalis* [1986] 1 CMLR 414). A similar restriction in a distribution agreement would not be justified since there are no legitimate interests to protect.

It is thought that the ECJ's view on this is much the same as the English common law on restrictive covenants, ie the 'restraint of trade' doctrine.

In a different context, the ECJ, in *Nungesser v EC Commission* [1982] ECR 2015, approved an exclusive plant breeder licence for maize seed since, without the exclusivity, the licensee would not have taken the licence and the new technology involved would not have reached the market.

Likewise, selective distribution, ie restricting dealers to those qualified to handle a product, for example hi-tech products, perfumes, etc, is not a breach of Article 81 EC if all qualified dealers are admitted to the network (see *Metro SB-Grossmarkte GmbH v Commission of the European Communities* [1978] 2 CMLR 44). Any restriction on numbers or supplies, however, needs an exemption under Article 81(3) EC, for example the block exemption for car dealers in Regulation 1475/95.

The Commission has always been suspicious of the 'rule of reason' because it is difficult to distinguish the criteria which would take an agreement outside Article 81(1) EC from those which the Commission must apply in any event to give an exemption under Article 81(3) EC. Thus, for example, the Commission's vertical agreements block exemption will not apply to a post-contractual restrictive covenant in excess of one year (although the Regulation does allow them to be severed). Likewise, under the technology licensing block exemption, an export ban preventing active selling by a patent licensee (ie *soliciting* customers in other licensed territories) is permitted so long as the patents are validly protected in those territories. But, in a refinement of *Nungesser*, a ban on passive selling into other licensed territories (ie meeting orders from unsolicited customers) is also permitted except where it exceeds 5 years from first marketing by any licensee. It is only in relation to licensing new technology that this *extra* protection is needed. Any longer protection will take the agreement outside the block exemption.

28.3 ABUSE OF A DOMINANT POSITION: ARTICLE 82 EC

28.3.1 What is the general effect of Article 82 EC?

Article 82 EC renders unlawful any behaviour which amounts to an abuse of its position by an undertaking which is dominant in its particular market. It will therefore be crucially important, when faced with a potential breach of Article 82 EC, to identify the relevant market; it will be seen that undertakings with quite small shares of one market can be dominant in a section of that market and so be at risk from Article 82 EC. It will also be seen that a distinction has to be drawn between an undertaking legitimately taking advantage of what may be a hard-won dominant position and an undertaking which illegitimately abuses that position.

28.3.2 What does Article 82 EC provide?

According to Article 82 EC:

'Any abuse by one or more undertakings of a dominant position within the common market or in a substantial part of it shall be prohibited as incompatible with the common market insofar as it may affect trade between Member States.'

The Article then goes on to give a non-exclusive list of the types of behaviour which might amount to such an abuse, for example an undertaking imposing unfair trading conditions, such as unfair prices.

What is a dominant position within the common market?

It is by no means essential for an undertaking to be in a monopoly position throughout the EC. The guiding principle here is that an undertaking is likely to be dominant where its economic strength allows it to behave independently of other operators within the market (*United Brands Co (New Jersey, USA) and United Brands Continentaal B (Rotterdam, The Netherlands) v EC Commission* [1978] ECR 207). An example of the principle is where a manufacturing company can set prices or conditions of supply to retailers of its product without regard to the prices or conditions imposed by its competitors. This is more likely to be the case where the undertaking has a larger market share. (In *Hilti v Commission of the European Communities* [1992] 4 CMLR 16, for example, an undertaking was held to be dominant with a 70–80 per cent share of its market.) However, a relatively low market share does not necessarily mean that the undertaking is not dominant. In *United Brands*, dominance was established although the company had a market share of only 40–45 per cent. A particularly important factor to take into account here is whether there are barriers to entry for other undertakings who might wish to enter the market. Does the allegedly dominant undertaking, for example, possess intellectual property rights which would create such a barrier? Whether or not an undertaking is dominant can only be considered in relation to a particular market. In order to identify the relevant market it is important to look at two things: the product market and the geographic market.

HOW IS THE PRODUCT MARKET RECOGNISED?

The key question in recognising the product market is 'what other product, if any, can be substituted for the product in question, given the nature of it, its price and its intended use?'. If a number of products are interchangeable, from the point of view of the user, it is arguable that they are all part of one market. On the other hand, if there is no acceptable alternative to the product in question then it can form a market on its own. In *United Brands*, the European Court found that bananas represented a single market because, in certain respects, bananas could not easily be replaced by another fruit. In particular, children and the elderly or the infirm might find it easier to digest bananas than any other fruit.

Similarly, in *Hugin Kassareregister AB and Hugin Cash Registers v EC Commission* [1979] ECR 1869, the European Court found that spare parts for Hugin cash registers represented a separate market in their own right because, once a customer had bought a Hugin machine, no other spare parts could be used. Clearly, if the product market is drawn so narrowly, an undertaking may find itself dominant even if its share of, say, the fruit market or the market for spare parts for cash registers generally is very small.

HOW IS THE GEOGRAPHIC MARKET RECOGNISED?

It is important to look at the geographic area within which the undertaking markets the product where the conditions of competition are the same. Here, too, the definition of the geographical scope of the market is based on substitutability; how far will customers look for their substitute product if the firm's product is unobtainable or too pricey. In many cases, this will be the whole of the single market, but factors such as cultural preferences, the personal nature of services contracts and the costs of transporting heavier goods may restrict the market to a particular region or country.

Article 82 EC applies where an undertaking is dominant in the common market or a substantial part of it. Dominance within a single Member State is likely to be within a substantial part of the common market.

What amounts to an abuse of a dominant position?

There are broadly two types of abusive behaviour: one affects competitors or potential competitors in the field; the other affects consumers. Abuse affecting competitors would include pricing the undertaking's products so low that those competitors are forced out of the market or requiring purchasers of one type of product to buy other products produced by the same undertaking in order to tie them in to a single supplier. Examples of abuses affecting consumers would be setting prices extortionately high or requiring the product to be sold in certain outlets only.

28.3.3 Are there any exceptions to Article 82 EC?

There is no equivalent in Article 82 EC of Article 81(3) EC (see **28.2.4**); the Commission cannot grant an individual exemption from Article 82 EC nor are there block exemptions. Even if an undertaking is entitled to claim the benefit of a block exemption under Article 81(3) EC for its activities, that does not necessarily mean that such activities do not amount to an abuse of a dominant position (*Tetra Pak Rausing SA v Commission of the European Communities* [1991] FSR 654). Negative clearance, however, can be applied for.

28.3.4 What are the sanctions for breach of Article 82 EC?

The Commission has the power to fine undertakings for breaches of Article 82 EC. As there is no possibility of exemption, there is no equivalent of notification to the Commission as a way of limiting potential fines. Behaviour in breach of Article 82 EC may also give rise to civil liability. It seems that under English law, an injunction can be granted to restrain breaches of Article 82 EC and it is arguable that damages could also be sought (see *Garden Cottage Foods* at **28.2.3**).

28.3.5 Supervision by national courts

Article 81(1) and (2) EC and Article 82 EC are directly effective and so can be relied on in national proceedings. National courts can therefore hold that an undertaking is in breach of Article 81 EC or Article 82 EC. National courts can award damages or grant an injunction (see **28.2.3**). If the undertaking has previously received a comfort letter from the Commission, that does not bind the national court, although the court may take the existence of the letter into account in reaching a decision. However, a national court has no power to grant an exemption under Article 81(3) EC; that is entirely a matter for the Commission. Likewise, only the Commission can impose a fine.

28.3.6 The role of national competition authorities

All EC States have national competition laws and national authorities are required to co-operate in the enforcement of EC competition law (see Commission Notice on Co-operation with National Competition Authorities [1997] OJ C313/3). The UK Competition Act 1998 brings UK competition law into line with Articles 81 and 82 EC and gives the Director General of Fair Trading (for the first time) powers to investigate and to fine. The statute will have to be interpreted in line with Articles 81 and 82 EC and relevant case-law of the ECJ, CFI and EC Commission.

The Competition Act 1998 came into force in March 2000, and replaces the form-based system of the Restrictive Trade Practices Act 1976 with general prohibitions in Chapter I (equivalent to Article 81 EC) and Chapter II (equivalent to Article 82 EC). Controversially, there will be a general exemption from Chapter I for all vertical agreements (subject to a basic blacklist (by order made under s 50)). Effectively, the only type of vertical agreement prohibited by the Act is one containing price fixing. The OFT argues that most of the problems with vertical agreements arise because of supplier pressure. If the supplier is dominant, arrangements such as unwanted ties, refusal to supply particular dealers and loyalty rebates would be seen as abuses under Chapter II. Even more controversially, the Director General of Fair Trading has announced that the de minimis threshold for appreciability under Chapter I will be set at 25 per cent joint market share. This guideline is not binding on the courts, which may consider (in line with the Commission and the ECJ) that a lower threshold applies. Ultimately, it is the courts which determine whether the agreement is prohibited and thus void.

By incorporating EC competition law (and the ECJ's case-law) into UK national law, the Competition Act 1998 compels all business lawyers to have a working knowledge of EC competition law.

Further details of EC competition law in practice, in particular the powers of the Commission, are contained in the LPC Resource Books *Business Law and Practice* (Jordans) and *Commercial Law and Practice* (Jordans).

28.4 SUMMARY

Article 82 EC cases are likely to be few and far between for most solicitors. Article 81 EC, however, is likely to be of much greater relevance.

In drafting commercial agreements such as licensing agreements for intellectual property rights, distribution agreements, joint ventures (or other arrangements with potential competitors), franchise agreements and exclusive purchasing arrangements (eg beer ties with public houses or solus agreements for petrol stations), the practitioner has to take Article 81 EC into account. He should consider in turn:

(i)   whether the restrictive agreement might affect trade between Member States, but remember that many agreements between UK parties have such potential;

(ii)   whether it is covered by the Notice on Agreements of Minor Importance (but this is only limited security as market share may change). The determination of the *relevant* market is as critical here as under Article 82 EC;

(iii) for full certainty that the agreement is valid, however, the parties must draft their agreement to fit the relevant block exemption Regulation;

(iv) if the parties wish to include clauses which are not permitted by a block exemption, the agreement is likely to be void under Article 81(2) EC and thus (subject to severance) unenforceable in the national courts;

(v) in which case, the parties must notify the agreement on form A/B to obtain an individual exemption (or, where applicable, exemption under the opposition procedure of some block exemptions). The procedure for doing this is set out in Regulation 3385/94 which contains in its annex form A/B, but for vertical agreements the parties need not notify in advance as they can notify retrospectively, for example at the time of the dispute (see Regulation 17/64, Art 4(2));

(vi) following notification, the receipt of a 'comfort letter' from the Commission can be relied on before national courts as evidence that the Commission will probably grant exemption. The Commission will co-operate with the national court in providing further evidence or advice. (See Notice on Co-operation [1993] OJ C39/05.)

The following is an illustration of how Article 81 EC might apply to an exclusive distribution agreement (based on *Consten SA and Grundig-Verkaufs-GmbH v EEC Commission* [1996] CMLR 418).

Example

Widgets Ltd, a UK manufacturer with 15 per cent of the EU widgets market, has a network of exclusive distributors at the wholesale level in France, UK and Germany (see diagram). It sells to its distributors at £5 per widget and they then mark the price up when selling on to retailers. The UK distributor (a wholly owned subsidiary) charges £10, whereas the German distributor charges only £6. To protect its position in the UK, therefore, Widgets Ltd imposes clauses on the German wholesaler which prevent it selling to customers outside its territory (export bars) and from selling to dealers in Germany who could resell outside (ie sales to parallel importers). Hopefully, it would thus have absolute territorial protection from competition on prices with its other EU distributors.

Such protection is, however, contrary to Article 81 EC and will attract fines, potential tort claims and void agreements. The block exemption on vertical agreements (Regulation 2790/99) *does* allow territorial exclusivity and a ban on active sales (advertising, etc) outside the territory but not a ban on passive sales (ie to unsolicited customers who place orders on their own initiative), nor a ban on sales to parallel exporters (see Art 4(b) first indent). Retailers across the EU are perfectly entitled to buy from the cheapest wholesaler in the network.

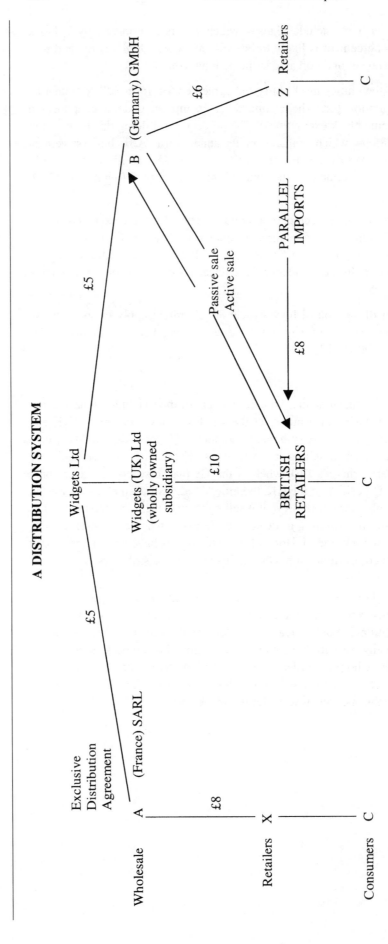

A DISTRIBUTION SYSTEM

Chapter 29

THE PRACTICAL IMPACT OF EC LAW

This brief chapter summarises the wide range of uses of EC law, underlining the fact that this is a pervasive subject.

29.1 EC LAW AND THE PRIVATE CLIENT

29.1.1 Immigration law

Consider the impact of:

- Article 39 EC (free movements of workers)
- Article 43 EC (establishment of self-employed person)
- Article 49 EC (ie free movement of services including tourists)
- Article 12 EC (discrimination)
- Migrant Workers Regulation 1612/68
- Social Security Regulation 1408/71
- Directives on residence rights and permits, for example Directive 68/360.

Example

Pancho, a Mexican national, is convicted before the Wombledon Magistrates' Court on charges of possessing cannabis. The magistrates are considering recommending deportation. Pancho's solicitor discovers that Pancho's wife, Sonia, is an Italian national working here as a nurse. He draws the magistrates' attention to the Treaty Article 39 EC and the Migrant Workers Regulation, Art 10 which protects Sonia's spouse even if of non-EC nationality. No deportation is possible unless there is a current threat to public security.

29.1.2 Employment law

(A) Sex discrimination and equal pay

Consider the impact of:

- Article 141 EC (guaranteeing equal pay including pensions),
- Directives on sex discrimination, ie
     equal treatment in employment (Directive 76/207);
     equal treatment in social security (Directive 79/7);
     equal treatment in pensions (Directive 86/378).

Examples

(1) Claims by part-timers for equal rights to full-timers

- Equal access to company pension schemes
- Equal rights to redundancy payment and unfair dismissal compensation (UK law in line 1995)
- Equal rights to share incentive schemes etc.

(NB: Claims are based on the Treaty, Article 141 EC (equal pay) or the Equal Treatment Directive 1976: see *Equal Opportunities Commission v Secretary of State for Employment* [1994] 1 All ER 910, HL.)

(2) Pension schemes giving women a pension at 60 while men have to wait until 65

- Men can claim an equal pension at 60 since that gives them equal pay (pensions) to women (but equality only required in relation to pensions resulting from employment since May 1990, the date of ECJ's ruling in *Barber v Guardian Royal Exchange Assurance Group* [1990] IRLR 240 (claims are based on Article 119 of the EC Treaty (now Article 141 EC))).
- Women are compulsorily 'retired' at 60 while men can remain employed until 65 (claims were based on the Equal Treatment Directive 1976, but only against a 'State' employer, see *Marshall v Southampton and West Hampshire Area Health Authority (Teaching)* [1986] 2 All ER 584). (The Sex Discrimination Act 1975 was brought into line from 1986.)

(3) Pregnancy dismissals

- Only recently considered sex discrimination under the Sex Discrimination Act 1975 (see *Webb v EMO Air Cargo (UK) (No 2)* [1995] 4 All ER 577 (HL)) (but for those with 'State' employers always considered a breach of the Equal Treatment Directive 1976, see Chapter 23 and **24.10**).
- New maternity rights (1994) give immediate protection from dismissal under Maternity Directive 1992 (No 92/85), in force from June 1994 and a right to maternity leave for *all* women employees (from October 1994).

(B) Other employment rights

(1) Workers' participation

The ECJ has ruled (*Commission of European Communities v United Kingdom* [1994] IRLR 392) that UK legislation must provide for obligatory recognition of workers' representatives to be consulted over transfers of undertaking (Acquired Rights Directive 1977/187) and collective redundancy (Directive 1975/129). UK law was brought into line on 1 March 1996.

Multi-national groups of companies must soon have European 'works councils' (EWCs) to be consulted over aspects of group policy (Directive 1994 OJ L254/64). The Directive is not yet binding on the UK (Social Chapter opt-out) but already affects UK companies with large subsidiaries in two other States. It came into force outside the UK in September 1996, but now that the Social Chapter is part of the EC Treaty (Article 137 EC), EWCs will apply to UK companies with a large subsidiary in another State from next year.

(2) Transfer of Undertakings Directive 1977/187

The ECJ considers the contracting out of government services as a 'transfer' where the existing employees must be protected (see *Schmidt (Christel) v Spar-und Leihkasse de Früheren Ämter Bordesholm, Kiel and Cronshagen* [1994] IRLR 302). This and many other rulings of the ECJ on the meaning of the Directive have been taken into account in the interpretation of the UK Regulations which implement them (Transfer of Undertakings (Exclusion of Implied Terms) Regulations 1981): see *Litster v Forth Dry Dock & Engineering Co Ltd* [1990] 1 AC 546.

(3) Protection in Insolvency Directive 1980/987

Enacted in the UK by Employment Protection (Consolidation) Act 1978, s 122, which provides for certain payments from the National Insurance Fund. It was this Directive which was at issue in *Francovich and Bonifacti v Italy* [1992] IRLR 84.

(4) Written Statements Directive 1991/533

Enacted in Employment Rights Act 1996, s 1, but, since this section gives no remedy for breach, it is arguably in breach of the Directive.

(5) Protection for Young People at Work Directive 1994/33

(C) Health and safety legislation

The Treaty, Article 138 EC allows the Council of Ministers to pass Directives in this area by qualified majority vote. A number of Directives have been passed protecting, inter alia:

- time off (Working Time Directive 93/104 (OJ L307)). This was implemented in the UK in November 1996;
- hearing damage (Noise Directive (86/247));
- eye strain and repetitive strain injuries for VDU users (VDU Directive (90/270));
- general health at the workplace (ie specifications as to ventilation, room dimensions, eating facilities, etc, under the Workplace Directive (89/654)).

These have resulted in substantial changes to UK health and safety legislation.

Those acting for victims of accidents at work (particularly those in the public sector) may have to consult the relevant Directive as well as the UK legislation.

29.1.3 Consumer protection

(A) Product liability

The Consumer Protection Act 1987 imposes strict liability for defective products in line with the EC Directive 1985 (85/374).

(B) Unfair contract terms

The Unfair Terms in Consumer Contracts Regulations 1994 (in force July 1995) make void a number of standard terms considered unfair in consumer contracts (implements EC Directive 93/13). The latest version of these Regulations allows for consumer associations to police trades' standard terms alongside the Office of Fair Trading.

(C) Door-step selling

UK Regulations introduced in 1987 (the Consumer Protection (Cancellation of Contracts Concluded Away From Business Premises) Regulations 1987, SI 1987/2117) implemented Directive 85/577 giving the right to a cooling-off period.

A new Directive adopted by the Council of Ministers on 23 January 1997 will give cooling-off rights under distance selling contracts (mail order, Internet, etc).

(D) Consumer credit

The Consumer Credit Act 1974 pre-dated the Consumer Credit Directive 87/102 by 12 years. The Directive echoes its provisions by providing for a uniform method of quoting (annual percentage rate (APR)), a cancellation right in certain circumstances and the right to enforce consumer claims against credit card companies. The Directive is confined to consumers so the Government is considering reducing the Act's protection which is currently given to business debtors as well as consumers.

(E) Package travel

UK Regulations introduced in January 1993 (the Package Travel Regulations 1992, SI 1992/2643) implemented the Directive of 1990 (90/314) which makes the tour operator liable for the contents of its brochure and the providers of services contained in the package. There is provision for a guarantee fund in case of insolvency. An EC Regulation (2409/92) provides for fixed compensation for delays due to double-booking of flights originating in the EU.

(F) Protection of tourists

Provisions which discriminate against tourists (eg by not allowing tourists access to criminal injuries compensation schemes or requiring them always to have a locally qualified guide) can be attacked under Articles 12 EC and 49 EC (services). See further Chapter 26.

29.2 EC LAW AND THE BUSINESS CLIENT

29.2.1 Import/export

(A) Where the problems lie with local legislation consider the impact of:

- Article 28 EC (free movement of goods)
- Article 43 EC (establishment)
- Article 49 EC (services)
- Directives harmonising product standards, services, etc.

(B) Where problems lie with restrictive agreements (eg local dealers subject to export bans or price fixing imposed by manufacturers) or monopolies (eg dominant firm abusing its position by refusing to deal etc), consider the impact of:

- Article 81 EC (restrictive agreements)
- Article 82 EC (abuse of a dominant position).

29.2.2 Marketing arrangements

Consider the impact of Article 81 EC and the various block exemptions when choosing the right sales medium:

- *Agency arrangements* – not caught by Article 81 EC because agent not a separate (ie independent) undertaking but extensive statutory protection in each Member State under Commercial Agents Directive 1986/653 (implemented in the UK by Commercial Agents Regulations 1993, SI 1993/3053 – see the LPC Resource Book *Business Law and Practice: Legislation Handbook* (Jordans)).
- *Exclusive distribution agreement* – caught by Article 81 EC but (if properly drafted) covered by block exemption 2790/99.

- *Patent licensing agreement* (ie giving a manufacturer exclusive production rights within its territory) – is also prohibited by Article 81 EC but (if properly drafted) covered by block exemption on technology licensing.
- *Joint-venture* – for example, A and B jointly agree to pool their resources to produce new products through a jointly owned subsidiary. Likely to be caught by Article 81 EC with no specific block exemption, therefore should notify for individual exemption.
- *Merger* – only large (Community-size) mergers need to be cleared by Brussels (DG IV) under Regulation 4064/89. Other mergers are subject to national controls only under the principle of 'subsidiarity'.
- *Subsidiary* – subject to rules on mergers, the acquisition of a subsidiary company does not involve EC competition problems.

29.2.3 Company law

Consider the impact of:

- Article 43 EC (establishment);
- company law Directives (approximately 15 per cent of English company law derives from Directives, which should be referred to as an aid to interpretation);
- the European Economic Interest Grouping (EEIG) – a non-profit making entity for cross-border co-operation between companies and firms (often used by networks of European law firms) (see Regulation 2137/85, OJ 1985 2 119/1);
- banking, financial services, insurance (a number of Directives are concerned with harmonising the rules on protection for consumers with a view to encouraging free movement, for example by ensuring the capital adequacy of banks).

29.2.4 Public Procurement Directives

Government (and local government) contracts above a certain size must be put out for tender throughout the EC. Damages can be awarded to firms that lose contracts because the government favours a local supplier (discrimination). The rules apply to contracts for public works and the supply of goods or services. Similar rules apply to supply contracts with public utilities (telecommunications, gas, etc). The relevant Directives are 71/305 (public works), 77/62 (supply of goods), 90/351 (utilities), 92/50 (services), and 89/665 (remedies).

29.2.5 Tax law

Consider the impact of:

- Article 90 EC, ie discrimination (whether direct or indirect) resulting from national rules for taxing goods (eg VAT, car tax, tobacco, fuel tax, etc).
- Article 12 EC (discrimination) and the other rules on free movement. Thus, discriminatory direct taxes (eg corporation tax, National Insurance contributions or income tax) which deter free movement of persons by offering tax incentives only to nationals are likely to be unlawful (see *Finanzamt Koln-Alstadt v Schumacker* [1995] All ER (EC) 319).
- The VAT Directives, especially the 6th Directive 77/388. Value Added Tax is an EC tax imposed on all Member States by Directives. Thus, national tax laws cannot impose VAT in cases where the Directive does not allow it. Each year, scores of cases involving EC law are referred by VAT tribunals to Luxembourg.

29.2.6 Product standards/consumer protection/health and safety at work/employment protection

Hundreds of Directives in these areas have a bearing on business (see **29.1**, and the chapters referring to free movement).

29.2.7 The environment

Directives on the quality of bathing water, drinking water, car and factory emissions, waste disposal, environmental assessments, etc, may all have an impact on business, planning law and other areas.

29.2.8 Intellectual property rights

Consider the impact of:

* Articles 28/30 EC – Can I use my UK IP rights (eg patent or trade marks etc) to stop imports? Yes, if the product was marketed in the other EC State without my consent (eg because I had no IP protection in that State). No, if I had consented to the marketing in that State (eg by licensee or distributor) because I would then have exhausted my rights which protect my right to first marketing within the EC;
* *Harmonisation Directives* – ie Directives which try to harmonise protection to prevent distortion of the single market, for example the harmonised copyright protection Directive (Directive 93/98) in force from July 1995 extends copyright protection to 70 years (previously 50);
* the European Patent Office (Munich) can issue a bundle of patents (ie for each EU State). There is as yet no single Community patent;
* the rules on competition (Articles 81 EC, 82 EC) and the technology licensing block exemption;
* the European Trade Marks Office (Alicante). An EC Regulation 40/94 has created the Community trade mark (CTM) which can be registered as a mark for the whole EU.

See, further, the LPC Resource Book *Commercial Law and Practice* (Jordans).

29.2.9 E-commerce

This new area of practice, which has caught the public attention, with .com companies reaching giddy heights on the stock exchange, represents something of a challenge for lawyers. There are a number of related problems.

First, which law should the internet supplier comply with – his own law or that of all the countries in which he supplies the goods. As we have seen from *Keck and Mithouard* (C-267/91 and C-268/91) [1995] 1 CMLR 101 (see **27.4**), restrictions on selling arrangements will not in themselves represent restrictions in breach of either Article 49 EC (services) or Article 28 EC (goods). In Germany. it is unlawful to offer free gifts or special deals ('two for one'), additional guarantees or discount books. There are restrictions on shop hours and Sunday shopping. A recent case involving Lands End, the mail order and e-commerce company, highlighted some of the difficulties for e-commerce companies which typically offer such deals but run the risk of prosecutions in Germany for unfair competition under rules dating back to the 1930s. The Commission has proposed a bold solution: their E-commerce Directive

2000, adopted by Council and Parliament in May 2000, says that the seller need only comply with law of the country where the website is sited, ie where it goes on-line. Thus, a British supplier of goods or services can offer packages to Germans in accordance with UK law and at any hour of the day or night. This will be a significant improvement when this becomes law. The rules governing formation and the contract generally will equally be those of the country of origin, but consumers will still be able to rely on statutory protection in their own country.

This development will go hand-in-hand with a revision of the Brussels and Rome Conventions which deal with jurisdiction and applicable law respectively. Both Conventions are already subject to the jurisdiction of the ECJ in preliminary references, but it is sensible to make the amended texts into regulations directly applicable in every member State. One obvious change is to remove the requirement for writing for a jurisdiction clause as an electronic communication in e-commerce ought to be sufficient. There is a general requirement in the draft framework directive on e-commerce to be neutral between electronic and written messages.

This, however, raises the question of security in e-commerce and particularly electronic signatures. National laws will often require written contracts duly signed by the parties. The move to e-commerce requires that electronic signatures be given similar recognition to written ones. However, the scope for fraud being greater, the electronic signatures Directive requires that the signature be certified by an accredited third party. The UK is already passing legislation to implement this.

There still remains, though, the problem of consumer protection. In general, under the Brussels Convention and Rome Convention, the consumer who is solicited in his own country can sue in his own courts and use his own local law. This is presumably the case with the Internet, although some clarification may be needed in the forthcoming regulations. In the meantime, the wave of consumer protection Directives will continue to harmonise this protection. The one directly aimed at distance selling will require the consumer to be given a 7-day cooling-off period (just as with doorstep selling). All other consumer laws will have to be complied with, for example the Directive on Unfair Contract Terms. However, in the pipeline and still to be implemented by January 2002, are consumer guarantees (Directive 1999/44). Legislation must, of course, be neutral between written and electronic contracts, but there is no question of it being more generous to e-commerce.

Another area of concern to the community is privacy or, more particularly, the protection of personal data. The data protection Directive deals with this (implemented in the UK by the Data Protection Act 1998).

Finally, it should be obvious to anyone buying on the net that the only real way of paying is with a credit card. The Consumer Credit Directive 87/102 allows a claim against the supplier for non-conformity or non-delivery to be enforced directly against the credit card company, thus leaving the credit card company to recover the claim from the supplier. The UK legislation (Consumer Credit Act 1974) goes further in allowing all claims to be enforced in this way, at least where the goods cost more than £100.

29.3 EC LAW FOR LAWYERS AND LITIGATORS

29.3.1 Lawyers

Consider the impact of:

- Article 43 EC (establishment) and the Directive on mutual recognition of diplomas;
- Article 49 EC (free movement of services) and the Directive on legal services (77/249) which allows a lawyer to provide legal services by representing a client before the courts of other EC countries. For example, a solicitor representing a client has a right of audience before a French High Court (Tribunal de Grande Instance) whereas his rights are more restricted in England. A German lawyer from Hamburg may represent his client before the English High Court whereas his rights in other parts of Germany were (until recently) more restricted.

29.3.2 Litigators

Consider the impact of:

(a) Article 12 EC (non-discrimination) when combined with Article 49 EC (services). Thus, national rules requiring security for costs from non-resident plaintiffs may be unlawful (*Hubbard v Hamburger* (Case C-20/92) [1993] ECR I-3777). Likewise, allowing a plaintiff to obtain a freezing injunction freezing the assets of a non-resident defendant might be unlawful if local defendants would not be subject to such orders in the same circumstances. In *Philip Alexander Securities v Bamberger* [1997] Eu LR 63, the Court of Appeal ruled that provisions of the Consumer Arbitrations Agreement Act 1988 which confine the Act's protection to domestic consumer contracts (thus excluding international contracts) were contrary to Articles 12 EC and 49 EC. The Act makes void contract clauses which oblige consumers to submit their disputes to arbitration rather than going to court. Bamberger's contract for financial services was made under English law, but as a German he was entitled to the protection of the Act and thus to the right to bring his case before his local German courts under the Brussels Convention (see (b) below). The limitation in the Act to domestic contracts was contrary to Article 12 EC (as it discriminated against other EU consumers) and restricted services under Article 49 EC and Bamberger and others might be discouraged from seeking services in the UK because of this lack of protection.

(b) The Brussels Convention on Civil Jurisdiction and Enforcement of Judgments 1968. This must be referred to whenever litigation involves an EC element, as the Convention determines the national courts which have jurisdiction over the dispute. Suing in the wrong courts can be an expensive error for the client and can lay the solicitor open to negligence actions. Under the Convention, judgments obtained in one EC State can be enforced against the defendant's assets in other EC States. The Convention has been extended to other EFTA States by the Lugano Convention. It does not apply to arbitration agreements. Many questions involving the Convention are referred to the ECJ each year under a referral system similar to Article 234 EC. The existence of this 'single market for judgments' was a crucial factor in both the *Hamburger* and *Bamberger* cases.

(c) The Rome Convention 1980. This provides for a uniform set of rules as to the law which should apply to the contract to determine disputes. In general, the parties can choose, but (in some circumstances) cannot contract out of mandatory legal protection by choosing foreign law. In the absence of choice, the applicable law under Article 4 EC is presumed to be that of the party whose performance is characteristic of that contract, for example seller, agent, distributor. Appeal courts can also refer questions to the ECJ.

(d) There is no convention on the law applicable to tort cases. UK rules on this were substantially revised by the Private International Law Act 1995.

29.4 CONVERSION TABLE FOR THE EC TREATY AS AMENDED BY THE TREATY OF AMSTERDAM

The old numbers will still be relevant when consulting ECJ judgments and other sources.

Post-Amsterdam	Pre-Amsterdam
Article 1	Article 1
Article 2	Article 2
Article 3	Article 3
Article 4	Article 3a
Article 5	Article 3b
Article 6	Article 3c
Article 7	Article 4
Article 8	Article 4a
Article 9	Article 4b
Article 10	Article 5
Article 11	Article 5a
Article 12	Article 6
Article 13	Article 6a
Article 14	Article 7a
Article 15	Article 7c
Article 16	Article 7d
Article 17	Article 8
Article 18	Article 8a
Article 19	Article 8b
Article 20	Article 8c
Article 21	Article 8d
Article 22	Article 8e
Article 23	Article 9
Article 24	Article 10
Article 25	Article 12
Article 26	Article 28
Article 27	Article 29
Article 28	Article 30
Article 29	Article 34
Article 30	Article 36
Article 31	Article 37
Article 32	Article 38
Article 33	Article 39
Article 34	Article 40
Article 35	Article 41

Post-Amsterdam	Pre-Amsterdam
Article 36	Article 42
Article 37	Article 43
Article 38	Article 46
Article 39	Article 48
Article 40	Article 49
Article 41	Article 50
Article 42	Article 51
Article 43	Article 52
Article 44	Article 54
Article 45	Article 55
Article 46	Article 56
Article 47	Article 57
Article 48	Article 58
Article 49	Article 59
Article 50	Article 60
Article 51	Article 61
Article 52	Article 63
Article 53	Article 64
Article 54	Article 65
Article 55	Article 66
Article 56	Article 73b
Article 57	Article 73c
Article 58	Article 73d
Article 59	Article 73f
Article 60	Article 73g
Article 61	Article 73i
Article 62	Article 73j
Article 63	Article 73k
Article 64	Article 73l
Article 65	Article 73m
Article 66	Article 73n
Article 67	Article 73o
Article 68	Article 73p
Article 69	Article 73q
Article 70	Article 74
Article 71	Article 75
Article 72	Article 76
Article 73	Article 77
Article 74	Article 78
Article 75	Article 79
Article 76	Article 80
Article 77	Article 81
Article 78	Article 82
Article 79	Article 83
Article 80	Article 84
Article 81	Article 85
Article 82	Article 86
Article 83	Article 87
Article 84	Article 88
Article 85	Article 89

Post-Amsterdam	Pre-Amsterdam
Article 86	Article 90
Article 87	Article 92
Article 88	Article 93
Article 89	Article 94
Article 90	Article 95
Article 91	Article 96
Article 92	Article 98
Article 93	Article 99
Article 94	Article 100
Article 95	Article 100a
Article 96	Article 101
Article 97	Article 102
Article 98	Article 102a
Article 99	Article 103
Article 100	Article 103a
Article 101	Article 104
Article 102	Article 104a
Article 103	Article 104b
Article 104	Article 104c
Article 105	Article 105
Article 106	Article 105a
Article 107	Article 106
Article 108	Article 107
Article 109	Article 108
Article 110	Article 108a
Article 111	Article 109
Article 112	Article 109a
Article 113	Article 109b
Article 114	Article 109c
Article 115	Article 109d
Article 116	Article 109e
Article 117	Article 109f
Article 118	Article 109g
Article 119	Article 109h
Article 120	Article 109i
Article 121	Article 109j
Article 122	Article 109k
Article 123	Article 109l
Article 124	Article 109m
Article 125	Article 109n
Article 126	Article 109o
Article 127	Article 109p
Article 128	Article 109q
Article 129	Article 109r
Article 130	Article 109s
Article 131	Article 110
Article 132	Article 112
Article 133	Article 113
Article 134	Article 115
Article 135	Article 116

Post-Amsterdam	Pre-Amsterdam
Article 136	Article 117
Article 137	Article 118
Article 138	Article 118a
Article 139	Article 118b
Article 140	Article 118c
Article 141	Article 119
Article 142	Article 119a
Article 143	Article 120
Article 144	Article 121
Article 145	Article 122
Article 146	Article 123
Article 147	Article 124
Article 148	Article 125
Article 149	Article 126
Article 150	Article 127
Article 151	Article 128
Article 152	Article 129
Article 153	Article 129a
Article 154	Article 129b
Article 155	Article 129c
Article 156	Article 129d
Article 157	Article 130
Article 158	Article 130a
Article 159	Article 130b
Article 160	Article 130c
Article 161	Article 130d
Article 162	Article 130e
Article 163	Article 130f
Article 164	Article 130g
Article 165	Article 130h
Article 166	Article 130i
Article 167	Article 130j
Article 168	Article 130k
Article 169	Article 130l
Article 170	Article 130m
Article 171	Article 120n
Article 172	Article 130o
Article 173	Article 130p
Article 174	Article 130r
Article 175	Article 130s
Article 176	Article 130t
Article 177	Article 130u
Article 178	Article 130v
Article 179	Article 130w
Article 180	Article 130x
Article 181	Article 130y
Article 182	Article 131
Article 183	Article 132
Article 184	Article 133
Article 185	Article 134

Post-Amsterdam	Pre-Amsterdam
Article 186	Article 135
Article 187	Article 136
Article 188	Article 136a
Article 189	Article 137
Article 190	Article 138
Article 191	Article 138a
Article 192	Article 138b
Article 193	Article 138c
Article 194	Article 138d
Article 195	Article 138e
Article 196	Article 139
Article 197	Article 140
Article 198	Article 141
Article 199	Article 142
Article 200	Article 143
Article 201	Article 144
Article 202	Article 145
Article 203	Article 146
Article 204	Article 147
Article 205	Article 148
Article 206	Article 150
Article 207	Article 151
Article 208	Article 152
Article 209	Article 153
Article 210	Article 154
Article 211	Article 155
Article 212	Article 156
Article 213	Article 157
Article 214	Article 158
Article 215	Article 159
Article 216	Article 160
Article 217	Article 161
Article 218	Article 162
Article 219	Article 163
Article 220	Article 164
Article 221	Article 165
Article 222	Article 166
Article 223	Article 167
Article 224	Article 168
Article 225	Article 168a
Article 226	Article 169
Article 227	Article 170
Article 228	Article 171
Article 229	Article 172
Article 230	Article 173
Article 231	Article 174
Article 232	Article 175
Article 233	Article 176
Article 234	Article 177
Article 235	Article 178

Post-Amsterdam	Pre-Amsterdam
Article 236	Article 179
Article 237	Article 180
Article 238	Article 181
Article 239	Article 182
Article 240	Article 183
Article 241	Article 184
Article 242	Article 185
Article 243	Article 186
Article 244	Article 187
Article 245	Article 188
Article 246	Article 188a
Article 247	Article 188b
Article 248	Article 188c
Article 249	Article 189
Article 250	Article 189a
Article 251	Article 189b
Article 252	Article 189c
Article 253	Article 190
Article 254	Article 191
Article 255	Article 191a
Article 256	Article 192
Article 257	Article 193
Article 258	Article 194
Article 259	Article 195
Article 260	Article 196
Article 261	Article 197
Article 262	Article 198
Article 263	Article 198a
Article 264	Article 198b
Article 265	Article 198c
Article 266	Article 198d
Article 267	Article 198e
Article 268	Article 199
Article 269	Article 201
Article 270	Article 201a
Article 271	Article 202
Article 272	Article 203
Article 273	Article 204
Article 274	Article 205
Article 275	Article 205a
Article 276	Article 206
Article 277	Article 207
Article 278	Article 208
Article 279	Article 209
Article 280	Article 209a
Article 281	Article 210
Article 282	Article 211
Article 283	Article 212
Article 284	Article 213
Article 285	Article 213a

Post-Amsterdam	Pre-Amsterdam
Article 286	Article 213b
Article 287	Article 214
Article 288	Article 215
Article 289	Article 216
Article 290	Article 217
Article 291	Article 218
Article 292	Article 219
Article 293	Article 220
Article 294	Article 221
Article 295	Article 222
Article 296	Article 223
Article 297	Article 224
Article 298	Article 225
Article 299	Article 227
Article 300	Article 228
Article 301	Article 228a
Article 302	Article 229
Article 303	Article 230
Article 304	Article 231
Article 305	Article 232
Article 306	Article 233
Article 307	Article 234
Article 308	Article 235
Article 309	Article 236
Article 310	Article 238
Article 311	Article 239
Article 312	Article 240
Article 313	Article 247
Article 314	Article 248

PART IV

HUMAN RIGHTS

Chapter 30

THE EUROPEAN CONVENTION ON HUMAN RIGHTS

30.1 INTRODUCTION TO HUMAN RIGHTS

Since the Human Rights Act 1998 (HRA 1998) came into force, the subject of human rights has been treated as a pervasive topic on the Legal Practice Course. Perhaps more than any other pervasive topic, its reach is long and already it has begun to make its presence felt in almost every area of law and practice. As a distinct area of law within the United Kingdom it is in its infancy. But there is a substantial body of case-law developed by the European Court of Human Rights in Strasbourg upon which the British judiciary will draw.

This part of this book is intended to provide a brief introduction to human rights. This chapter introduces you to the European Convention and some of the most important Convention rights. Chapter 31 deals with the mechanism by which the HRA 1998 makes those rights enforceable in the UK.

30.2 INTRODUCTION TO THE CONVENTION

The UK was instrumental in drafting the European Convention for the Protection of Human Rights and Fundamental Freedoms 1950 (European Convention on Human Rights) (ECHR). The Convention was drafted by members of the Council of Europe (a body unrelated to the European Community) in the aftermath of the Second World War and the human rights abuses which took place during it. The UK was one of the original signatories on 4 November 1950. The Convention came into force on 3 September 1953. However, unlike many of the other signatories, the UK did not incorporate the Convention into its own legal system. The government believed that incorporation was unnecessary because the rights contained in the Convention already flowed from British common law.

The original ECHR contained the civil and political rights to be found in classical liberal thought, such as freedom of expression, freedom of religion and freedom from interference with privacy. A series of protocols, some of which have been ratified by the UK, deal with certain matters including the right to education and the right to peaceful enjoyment of private property (First Protocol) and the prohibition of the death penalty (Sixth Protocol).

The most imaginative feature of the ECHR was that it imposed an international judicial system for the protection of human rights on Europe. It is the most developed of regional systems for the protection of human rights.

30.3 THE RELATIONSHIP BETWEEN THE ECHR AND ENGLISH LAW

The ECHR is a treaty and, as such, is legally binding on the UK as a matter of international law. The UK must comply with the rulings of the European Court of Human Rights (ECtHR) to which any aggrieved person can present a petition. However, the English legal system is 'dualist': it regards international legal obligations and domestic law as being two distinct matters. Because prior to 2000, the Convention was not incorporated into English law, it operated only on the plane of international law and was not enforceable in domestic courts. There were a few cases (most notably *R v Secretary of State for the Home Department ex parte Brind* [1991] 1 AC 696) in which judges were prepared to take indirect account of the Convention. But, overall, Strasbourg jurisprudence had made few inroads into English law.

This, of course, is no longer the case. The HRA 1998 (which came into force in October 2000) has bridged the gap between the domestic and international planes so far as the Convention is concerned. Domestic English courts are now empowered to enforce Convention rights. Exactly how they may do so will be discussed in Chapter 31.

30.4 THE RELATIONSHIP BETWEEN THE ECHR AND THE EC

While there is a close relationship between the EC and the ECHR, the two are distinct and should not be confused. In particular, bear in mind the following differences.

(1) Far more countries are signatories to the ECHR than are members of the EC.
(2) The EC's concern with human rights has traditionally been limited. Some rights are protected. Article 141 EC, for example, deals with sex discrimination.
(3) The ECHR confers rights on everyone within the jurisdiction of a State which is party to the Convention, and not just those who are nationals of the State in question. This is important for asylum seekers, for example. EC law is usually concerned only with the rights of nationals of member states.
(4) The ECHR has its own institutions and procedures, in particular the ECtHR which sits in Strasbourg, not Luxembourg or Brussels.

For some years there has been concern that the EC (itself a 'superstate') is outside the reach of the ECHR. There have been suggestions since 1977 that the EC might become a party to the ECHR. So far, this has not happened, and indeed the ECJ has ruled that the Council has no power to accede to the ECHR under the Treaty as currently drafted (see *Opinion No 2/94* [1996] ECR I-1759, 28 March 1996). But the ECJ has said that EC law will draw upon the jurisprudence of the ECHR because it represents the common traditions of the EC member states in the field of human rights. In the context of the European Union, the Maastricht Treaty makes an express reference to human rights and in particular to the ECHR: see the Recitals and TEU Article 6.

Aside from the ECHR, there are currently moves afoot to create an EU Charter of Fundamental rights. This idea was proposed by the German EU presidency in early 1999. At the time of writing, a draft Charter is under consideration, but a timetable for its implementation is still uncertain. For more information see *Human Rights in the EU: the Charter of Fundamental Rights* (House of Commons Research Paper 00/32, http://www.parliament.uk/commons/lib/research/rp2000/rp00-032.pdf).

30.5 THE SUBSTANTIVE LAW OF THE ECHR

30.5.1 The Convention rights

These are the main rights protected by the Convention:

(1) right to life (Article 2);
(2) prohibition of torture (Article 3);
(3) prohibition of slavery and forced labour (Article 4);
(4) right to liberty and security (Article 5);
(5) right to a fair trial (Article 6);
(6) no punishment without lawful authority (Article 7);
(7) right to respect for family and private life (Article 8);
(8) right to freedom of thought, conscience and religion (Article 9);
(9) right to freedom of expression (Article 10);
(10) right to freedom of assembly and association (Article 11);
(11) right to marry (Article 12);
(12) prohibition of discrimination (Article 14);
(13) right to peaceful enjoyment of possessions (First Protocol, Article 1);
(14) right to education and right of parents to educate children in accordance with religious and philosophical convictions (First Protocol, Article 2).

The most important of these rights are described below (**30.5.3–30.5.8**).

30.5.2 Some general considerations when dealing with Convention rights

Drafting

The Convention is drafted in quite a different way from a United Kingdom statute. In the UK, legislative drafting tends to be very tight and exhaustive. The rights in the Convention are deliberately left open-ended and the Strasbourg organs do not interpret the Convention in the same way as English judges interpret domestic legislation. Lawyers in the UK will have to become used to this different way of working.

Absolute and limited rights

Some of the Convention rights are absolute. For example, the right to freedom from torture: the Convention allows no circumstances in which torture could be legitimate. But most of the rights are subject to limitations and qualifications. For example, the right to freedom of expression can be interfered with where the matters being expressed are defamatory or harmful to national security. Much of the argument in Convention cases turns not on whether there has been an interference with Convention rights, but whether that interference is justifiable. In considering the interference, the ECtHR has invented a number of tools with which UK lawyers will need to become familiar.

Judicial method

Once it has been established that a Convention right has been interfered with, the court must consider whether the interference is justified (unless the right is one which is absolute, in which case no interference is allowed).

There are four key concepts which the ECtHR uses.

(A) THE RULE OF LAW

No matter how desirable the end to be achieved, any interference with a Convention right must be based on some ascertainable law, and not on an arbitrary executive decision. Without detailed authorisation by law, any interference, however justified, will violate the Convention. For example, telephone tapping by the police in the 1970s was regulated by nothing more than an internal police guidance note which was not available to the public. The interference with the right to respect for correspondence (Article 8) was not therefore justified by law and was contrary to the Convention (*Malone v United Kingdom* (1984) 7 EHRR 14).

(B) LEGITIMATE AIMS

The defendant must say why the right is being interfered with, and the reason must be a legitimate one. Many of the Articles (eg Articles 8, 9, 10 and 11) set out what sorts of aims are legitimate, for example the interests of public safety, national security or the protection of the rights and freedoms of others. For example, if a prisoner's correspondence is being read by the prison authorities then the prevention of disorder or crime within the prison would be a legitimate reason for the interference with Article 8 if there was a genuine belief that there was a risk. But the routine reading of mail would not be legitimate (*Campbell v United Kingdom* (1992) 15 EHRR 137).

(C) PROPORTIONALITY

The cliché usually used to describe the doctrine of proportionality is that the State cannot use a sledgehammer to crack a nut. In the more formal language of the court, any restriction on a right must be 'necessary in a democratic society' or based on some 'pressing social need'. For example, it has been held that the criminalisation of buggery between consenting gay men in Northern Ireland was disproportionate to what at that time was considered the legitimate aim of protecting vulnerable members of society (*Dudgeon v United Kingdom* (1981) 4 EHRR 149, para 60).

Judicial review judges in the UK have already toyed with the concept of proportionality which has filtered into our legal system from the EC. The Human Rights Act will give proportionality a much higher profile here.

(D) MARGIN OF APPRECIATION

This is the Strasbourg equivalent of what in Brussels is called subsidiarity. It means that the states which are party to the Convention are allowed a degree of leeway out of sensitivity to their own political and cultural traditions. For example, the case of *Handyside v United Kingdom* (1976) 1 EHRR 737 concerned the publication in England in 1971 of *The Little Red School Book*, a children's book including a section on sex. The publisher had been convicted under the Obscene Publications Act 1959. The ECtHR had to consider the UK government's argument that the interference with the publisher's right to freedom of expression was necessary for the purpose of the 'protection of morals'. The court accepted that such a matter was within the competence of national authorities and a standard could not be imposed by an international body:

> 'By reason of their direct and continuous contact with the vital forces of their countries, state authorities are in principle in a better position than the international judge to give an opinion.' (para 48)

The majority of commentators agree that, by its nature, the doctrine of the margin of appreciation will not be relevant to cases decided under the HRA 1998 by UK courts. The doctrine exists to take account of the geographical and cultural gaps between an international court and the various countries it supervises. Within a unitary domestic legal system it will serve no purpose.

30.5.3 Article 5: The right to liberty and security

> '1. Everyone has the right to liberty and security of person. No one shall be deprived of his liberty save in the following cases and in accordance with a procedure prescribed by law:
>
> (a) the lawful detention of a person after conviction by a competent court;
> (b) the lawful arrest or detention of a person for non-compliance with the lawful order of a court or in order to secure the fulfilment of any obligation prescribed by law;
> (c) the lawful arrest or detention of a person effected for the purpose of bringing him before the competent legal authority on reasonable suspicion of having committed an offence or when it is reasonably considered necessary to prevent his committing an offence or fleeing after having done so;
> (d) the detention of a minor by lawful order for the purpose of educational supervision or his lawful detention for the purpose of bringing him before the competent legal authority;
> (e) the lawful detention of persons for the prevention of the spreading of infectious diseases, of persons of unsound mind, alcoholics or drug addicts or vagrants;
> (f) the lawful arrest or detention of a person to prevent his effecting an unauthorised entry into the country or of a person against whom action is being taken with a view to deportation or extradition.
>
> 2. Everyone who is arrested shall be informed promptly, in a language which he understands, of the reasons for his arrest and of any charge against him.
>
> 3. Everyone arrested or detained in accordance with the provisions of paragraph 1(c) of this Article shall be brought promptly before a judge or other officer authorised by law to exercise judicial power and shall be entitled to trial within a reasonable time or to release pending trial. Release may be conditioned by guarantees to appear for trial.
>
> 4. Everyone who is deprived of his liberty by arrest or detention shall be entitled to take proceedings by which the lawfulness of his detention shall be decided speedily by a court and his release ordered if the detention is not lawful.
>
> 5. Everyone who has been the victim of arrest or detention in contravention of the provisions of this Article shall have an enforceable right to compensation.'

Article 5 is the most lengthy of the Convention rights. It is of particular importance to criminal litigation practitioners, especially in challenging arrests and detentions.

Its overall purpose is to ensure that no one is deprived of his or her liberty in an arbitrary fashion (*Engel v Netherlands* (1976) 1 EHRR 647, para 58).

The article has two distinct limbs. Paragraph (1) prohibits interference with liberty or security of person except in certain well-defined circumstances. No distinction tends to be made in Strasbourg jurisprudence between the two concepts of liberty and security of person. Paragraphs (2) to (5) provide a set of procedural rights for detainees.

Lawful detention

Paragraph 1 insists in particular that any detention must be 'lawful' (the word is used in each of subparagraphs (a)–(f)). This requires that the domestic law upon which a detention is based must be accessible and precise. The paragraph also requires that the detention be 'in accordance with a procedure prescribed by law'. This calls for a consideration of how the detainer has gone about detaining the individual rather than why. Where there is no procedure prescribed by domestic law, or where the detainer has failed to follow it, Article 5 will have been breached.

Reasons

Paragraph 2 provides a right for those placed under arrest to be given reasons. These do not need to be in writing, and formal notification is not necessary if the reasons are made clear during the arrest (*X v Netherlands* 5 YB 224 at 228).

Judicial supervision

Paragraph 3 requires that the person under arrest be brought promptly before a judge (usually a magistrate in the UK). In *Brogan v United Kingdom* (1988) 11 EHRR 117 detention for 4 days and 6 hours in police custody before being taken before a court was a violation of Article 5(3). The paragraph also provides for trial within a reasonable time, or release pending trial (ie bail). There is a presumption that bail will be granted unless there are good reasons not to grant it (for example, because there is a risk that the accused will fail to appear at the trial, *Stögmüller v Austria* (1969) 1 EHRR 155).

Challenge and review

Paragraph 4 requires that a speedy procedure must be available by which detention can be challenged. The habeas corpus procedure in the UK fulfills this requirement, so long as it concludes swiftly. In *Zamir v United Kingdom* (1983) 40 DR 42 it was held that a delay of 7 weeks between an application for habeas corpus being made and the hearing taking place violated Article 5(4). The ECtHR has also held that where the circumstances of detention vary over time a regular reviewing procedure must exist. For example, in *Curley v United Kingdom* (Application No 32340/96) (2000) unreported, 28 March, the ECtHR held that it was a breach of Article 5(4) for a life prisoner to be held for 10 years after the expiry of his tariff with no review of his detention by a body capable of ordering his release.

Compensation

Paragraph 5 provides a right to compensation for any interference with Article 5 rights. In practice, this is unlikely to add anything to the availability of damages (and possibly exemplary damages) in tort for wrongful arrest or unlawful detention.

30.5.4 Article 6: The right to a fair trial

'1. In the determination of his civil rights and obligations or of any criminal charge against him, everyone is entitled to a fair and public hearing within a reasonable time by an independent and impartial tribunal established by law. Judgment shall be pronounced publicly but the press and public may be excluded from all or part of the trial in the interest of morals, public order or national security in a democratic society, where the interests of juveniles or the protection of the private life of the parties so require, or to the extent strictly necessary in the opinion of the court in special circumstances where publicity would prejudice the interests of justice.

2. Everyone charged with a criminal offence shall be presumed innocent until proved guilty according to law.

3. Everyone charged with a criminal offence has the following minimum rights:

(a) to be informed promptly, in a language which he understands and in detail, of the nature and cause of the accusation against him;

(b) to have adequate time and facilities for the preparation of his defence;

(c) to defend himself in person or through legal assistance of his own choosing or, if he has not sufficient means to pay for legal assistance, to be given it free when the interests of justice so require;

(d) to examine or have examined witnesses against him and to obtain the attendance and examination of witnesses on his behalf under the same conditions as witnesses against him;

(e) to have the free assistance of an interpreter if he cannot understand or speak the language used in court.'

Article 6 is arguably the most important, and certainly the most utilised, of all the Convention rights. It provides for a right to fair criminal and civil trials, and lays down certain procedural standards. It is of direct importance to all litigators, and therefore indirectly to all lawyers.

Determination of civil rights

Paragraph 1 lays down the basic 'due process' standards for the determination of civil and criminal matters. The phrase 'in the determination of his civil rights' needs some explanation. It does not simply cover any issue which might be the subject of a trial in civil law as an English lawyer would understand that expression. The Strasbourg case law on this is complex. All proceedings between private individuals and private bodies are included. Not all proceedings involving public authorities are, and here further research may be necessary. Broadly, a distinction is made between those decisions of public bodies which affect private law rights (which are within the scope of the article) and those affecting public law rights (which are not). For example, planning decisions affect property rights and are included. Actions to sue public authorities for compensation will be included, because private law rights in tort or contract are involved. But decisions of public authorities affecting education involve public law, not private law rights, and are not subject to Article 6 requirements (*Simpson v United Kingdom* (1989) 64 DR 188). For the same reason decisions on the categorisation of prisoners for security purposes are not covered (*Brady v United Kingdom* (1979) 3 EHRR 297). For a fuller discussion of this see Starmer, *European Human Rights Law* (The Legal Action Group, 1999), paras 12.9–12.47.

A fair trial

Paragraph 1 sets out the minimum requirements for a fair trial. They are:

- a fair and public hearing;
- an independent and impartial tribunal;
- trial within a reasonable period;
- public judgment (with some exceptions); and
- a reasoned decision.

As the most litigated article, a great deal of case-law has grown up around these requirements. The approach of the ECtHR in interpreting and applying Article 6(1) is generous to applicants, and the court reaches its decisions 'bearing in mind the prominent place which the right to a fair trial holds in a democratic society' (*Delcourt v Belgium* (1979–80) 1 EHRR 355). Not only have these decisions built on the requirements expressly contained in the paragraph set out above, they have read other rights into the paragraph. These include:

- the right of access to a court (eg *Osman v United Kingdom* (2000) 29 EHRR 245: police immunity a denial of the right of access to a court);
- equality of arms (*Dombo Beheer BV v Netherlands* (1994) 18 EHRR 213); and
- the right to participate effectively in proceedings (*Stanford v United Kingdom* (Case A/282) (1994) *The Times*, March 8: poor court room acoustics).

Furthermore, in civil litigation, paragraph 1 has been held to require a right to legal aid should the circumstances of the case demand it, especially 'by reason of the complexity of the procedure of the case' (*Airey v Ireland* (Case A/32) (1979) 2 EHRR 305). (Article 6(3) expressly requires legal aid in criminal litigation.)

Presumption of innocence

Paragraph 2 provides for the presumption of innocence in criminal trials. 'Reverse onus' provisions, which place the burden of proof upon a defendant to demonstrate his innocence have been held not necessarily to violate Article 6(2) (*Lingens v Austria* (1981) 26 DR 171, also *R v DPP ex parte Kebilene* [1999] 3 WLR 972, the first HRA case to reach the House of Lords). In *Murray v United Kingdom (Right to Silence)* (1996) 22 EHRR 29, the ECtHR ruled that the drawing of adverse inferences from the exercise by the accused of his right to silence did not violate the article either. However, in *Saunders v United Kingdom* (1996) 23 EHRR 313, the use of statements obtained by compulsion by inspectors exercising statutory powers under the Companies Act 1985 was held to be a violation of Article 6(2).

Procedural safeguards in criminal trials

Because of the serious nature of criminal litgation, paragraph 3 provides specific procedural rights in this context. These are rights:

- to be informed promptly of the accusation against him;
- to have adequate time and facilities to prepare his defence;
- to choose his legal representative and to receive legal aid if necessary;
- to call witnesses and to cross-examine witnesses against him; and
- to have free access to an interpreter if necessary.

Again, these rights have caused a great deal of litigation. Reference to the case-law or to a specialist work is needed to understand them fully.

30.5.5 Article 8: The right to respect for private and family life

'1. Everyone has the right to respect for his private and family life, his home and his correspondence.

2. There shall be no interference by a public authority with the exercise of this right except such as is in accordance with the law and is necessary in a democratic society in the interests of national security, public safety or the economic well-being of the country, for the prevention of disorder or crime, for the protection of health or morals, or for the protection of the rights and freedoms of others.'

Article 8 has been used creatively by lawyers and judges. Its essential object is to protect the individual against arbitrary action by public authorities (*Kroon v Netherlands* (1994) 19 EHRR 263). It has been used in cases where it might seem quite at home, such as those involving phone tapping, or interference with prisoners' mail. But it has also been used in contexts which might come as a surprise to those who drafted it, such as the rights of transexuals to have official records amended to recognise their status, the right to an environment unpolluted by noise and chemicals, and the right to practise ones sexuality freely.

Private life

This encompasses:

- noise pollution issues (*Rayner v United Kingdom* (1986) 47 DR 5);
- pollution by waste (*López Ostra v Spain* (1994) 20 EHRR 277);
- sexual orientation (*Smith and Grady v United Kingdom* (2000) 29 EHRR 548);
- the unauthorised disclosure of confidential data to third parties (*MS v Sweden* (1999) 28 EHRR 313);
- surveillance by the security services (*Harman and Hewitt v United Kingdom* (1989) 67 DR 88); and
- the monitoring by an employer of office telephone calls without warning (*Halford v United Kingdom* (1997) 24 EHRR 523).

Family life

It is disruption of the family unit which is most likely to offend against this aspect of Article 8. This might include, for example, a situation in which the state wishes to take a child into care. It is also an extremely important issue for immigration lawyers, as immigration controls may often result in families being broken up.

'Family' clearly includes those with blood and marital links, but has also been extended by the ECtHR to include other emotional ties. In *K v United Kingdom* (1986) 50 DR 199, the ECtHR said 'the question of the existence or non-existence of "family life" is essentially a question of fact depending upon the real existence in practice of close personal ties'. However, it does not extend to homosexual relationships (*S v United Kingdom* (1986) 47 DR 274). Such relationships do have protection under the private life principle above, although this would offer no help in circumstances where, for example, the couple is being broken up by one of them being removed.

Home

Clearly, there is some overlap between privacy, family life and home life. This element of Article 8(1) specifically protects the right to occupy one's home without harassment or interference. Noise nuisance can violate this right (*Arrondelle v*

United Kingdom (1982) 26 DR 5). So can entry by the police to search or for other purposes. In *McLeod v United Kingdom* (1999) 27 EHRR 493, the police accompanied an estranged husband into the former matrimonial home. As there was little risk of disorder the ECtHR held that this was a disproportionate interference with the applicant's right to home life. In the context of housing law, the article does not extend to the right to have a home (*Buckley v United Kingdom* (1996) 23 EHRR 101).

Correspondence

It was under this provision that the *Malone* case was brought sucessfully challenging telephone tapping by the police without statutory authority. This resulted in the enactment of the Interception of Communications Act 1985 to grant the police statutory powers. Similar issues were raised in the *Halford* case. The Regulation of Investigatory Powers Act 2000 is an important piece of legislation in this area which now, amongst other things, governs the interference with communications by employers. As for interference with written correspondence, most of the case law concerns prisoners' rights. Broadly they may correspond freely with their lawyers, but prison authorities may interfere with other correspondence so long as this is justified (*Golder v United Kingdom* (1975) 1 EHRR 524, *Silver v United Kingdom* (1983) 5 EHRR 347).

Justification for interference

Article 8 is not absolute. Paragraph 2 sets out reasons which may justify interference with paragraph 1 rights. The principle of proportionality requires that the interference must be the minimum necessary to achieve the legitimate aim (for example, see the *McLeod* case above).

30.5.6 Article 10: The right to freedom of expression

'1. Everyone has the right to freedom of expression. This right shall include freedom to hold opinions and to receive and impart information and ideas without interference by public authority and regardless of frontiers. This Article shall not prevent States from requiring the licensing of broadcasting, television or cinema enterprises.

2. The exercise of these freedoms, since it carries with it duties and responsibilities, may be subject to such formalities, conditions, restrictions or penalties as are prescribed by law and are necessary in a democratic society, in the interests of national security, territorial integrity or public safety, for the prevention of disorder or crime, for the protection of health or morals, for the protection of the reputation or rights of others, for preventing the disclosure of information received in confidence, or for maintaining the authority and impartiality of the judiciary.'

The ECtHR has described this right as 'one of the essential foundations of a democratic society and one of the conditions of its progress' (*Handyside v United Kingdom* (1979) 1 EHRR 737). It is particularly useful to the press and broadcast media, as well as other publishers and political organisations. The right extends to receiving as well as imparting information. However, this does not oblige public authorities to disclose information against their will (*The Gaskin Case* [1990] 1 FLR 167, no right of access to fostering records held by a local authority). It merely prohibits restrictions on the receipt of information, for example information about abortion in Ireland (*Open Door Dublin Well Women v Ireland* (1992) 15 EHRR 244).

Where there is an interference with Article 10 rights, it will be incompatible with the Convention unless:

- it is prescribed by law;
- it pursues a legitimate aim (see paragraph 2);
- it is necessary in a democratic society; and
- it is proportionate.

Defamation

The ECtHR recognises that individuals have a right to have their reputations protected. But defamation actions are an interference with article 10 rights and so must be justified using the criteria above on a case-by-case basis. In *Tolstoy Miloslavsky v United Kingdom; Lord Aldington v Watts*, for example, the Court found that a damages award of £1.5 million was excessive ((1995) 20 EHRR 442).

The Court has also recognised, however, that criticism of public figures, especially politicians, is more easily justifed under Article 10. In *Lingens v Austria* (1986) 8 EHRR 407 the Court said:

'The limits of acceptable criticism are ... wider as regards a politician as such than as regards a private individual. Unlike the latter, the former inevitably and knowingly lays himself open to close scrutiny of every word and deed by both journalists and the public at large, and he must consequently display a greater degree of tolerance.' (para 42)

Prior restraint

The use of injunctions to prevent publication of material in advance is viewed with suspicion by the ECtHR. In the *Spycatcher* case (*Guardian Newspapers v United Kingdom* (1992) 14 EHRR 153) it said:

'the dangers inherent in prior restraint are such that they call for the most careful scrutiny ... News is a perishable commodity and to delay its publication, even for a short period, may well deprive it of all its value and interest.' (para 60)

The concern which the Strasbourg court has is reflected in s 12 of the HRA 1998.

30.5.7 Article 11: The right to freedom of assembly and association

'1. Everyone has the right to freedom of peaceful assembly and to freedom of association with others, including the right to form and to join trade unions for the protection of his interests.

2. No restrictions shall be placed on the exercise of these rights other than such as are prescribed by law and are necessary in a democratic society in the interests of national security or public safety, for the prevention of disorder or crime, for the protection of health or morals or for the protection of the rights and freedoms of others. This Article shall not prevent the imposition of lawful restrictions on the exercise of these rights by members of the armed forces, of the police or of the administration of the State.'

This Article contains two distinct rights, freedom of peaceful assembly and freedom of association.

Freedom of peaceful assembly

This extends to anyone who intends to organise a peaceful march or static assembly. The possibility of violence arising because of the intentions of counter-demonstrators or extremist infiltrators does not affect the right (*Christians Against Racism and Facism v United Kingdom* (1980) 21 DR 138).

The sorts of restrictions which paragraph 2 envisages include limitations on the location of a demonstration or the route of a march.

Freedom of association

This covers the right of individuals to join together, especially in organisations like political parties and trade unions. It also extends to the right *not* to join such organisations. For example, compulsory membership of a union (a 'closed shop') will usually be contrary to the Convention (*Young, James and Webster v United Kingdom* (1982) 4 EHRR 38).

The right does not extend to a right to negotiate with employers via collective bargaining (*Swedish Engine Drivers' Union v Sweden* (1976) 1 EHRR 617). Nor does it include a right to strike (*Schmidt and Dahlstrom v Sweden* (1979) 1 EHRR 632).

30.5.8 Article 14: The prohibition on discrimination

> 'The enjoyment of the rights and freedoms set forth in this Convention shall be secured without discrimination on any ground such as sex, race, colour, language, religion, political or other opinion, national or social origin, association with a national minority, property, birth or other status.'

Article 14 is not as important as it may at first appear. It is vital to realise that the right not to be discriminated against cannot be relied upon on its own. It may only be invoked in conjunction with another Convention right.

A claimant relying on Article 14 must first establish that a substantive Convention right is in issue. There need not necessarily have been a breach of that right. It must only be shown that the facts fall within the ambit of that provision. The next step is to ask whether there is a difference in treatment between different sorts of people. Finally one must examine whether that difference has a legitimate aim.

An example is the case of *Abdulaziz v United Kingdom; Cabales v United Kingdom; Balkandali v United Kingdom* (1985) 7 EHRR 471, an immigration case. The exclusion of spouses of new entrants from the UK in certain circumstances was held not to breach Article 8. However, the admission of the spouses of male entrants but the exclusion of spouses of female entrants breached Article 14.

30.5.9 Protocol 1, Article 1: The right to peaceful enjoyment of possessions

> 'Every natural or legal person is entitled to the peaceful enjoyment of his possessions. No one shall be deprived of his possessions except in the public interest and subject to the conditions provided for by law and by the general principles of international law.
>
> The preceding provisions shall not, however, in any way impair the right of a State to enforce such laws as it deems necessary to control the use of property in

accordance with the general interest or to secure the payment of taxes or other contributions or penalties.'

'Possessions' in this article has a wide meaning. It includes amongst other things land, money, shares and goodwill.

The Article contains two distinct rights:

- the right not to be deprived of possessions, subject to certain conditions; and
- the right not to have the state control possessions, subject to certain conditions.

Deprivation covers situations in which title is transferred or extinguished, for example the creation of a presumption of title in land in favour of the State (*Holy Monasteries v Greece* (1994) 20 EHRR 1). Control covers situations falling short of this, for example limiting the amount of rent which a landlord may charge, placing restrictions upon developing property and rules restricting rights of inheritance.

In both cases interference with the right is permissible in the public interest or the general interest (a distinction which is of little importance). The guiding principle is one of fair balance between individual and community interests. In striking this balance regard must always be had to the principle of proportionality (see **30.5.2**).

30.6 PETITIONING THE COURT IN STRASBOURG

30.6.1 Introduction

Despite the Human Rights Act 1998, there will be situations where an individual is denied a remedy under UK law, for example because primary legislation is clearly incompatible or because there is some gap in the legislation which cannot be filled by the common law. In such cases, the individual can petition the ECtHR in Strasbourg. This, however, will be the last resort as the Convention requires the applicant to exhaust domestic remedies (including the HRA 1998) before going to Strasbourg. The ECtHR consists of judges from all the Member States of the Council of Europe together with a staff of over 40 lawyers. Inevitably, the ECtHR will, in future, find an increaing caseload from Eastern Europe and particularly Russia. The fact that British complaints (statistically, Britain is one of the worst offenders) are now likely to be dealt with at home must be something of a relief for the ECtHR.

30.6.2 Procedural law of the ECHR

Initially, it was envisaged that the primary mechanism for enforcing the ECHR would be applications by other Member States. It was felt that, if this had been possible in the 1920s and 1930s, fascist atrocities and the Second World War might have been avoided. Such applications have been made several times; for example, cases were brought by Scandinavian countries against Greece during the regime of the Colonels between 1967 and 1973. They have also been brought against the UK, including by Ireland in respect of interrogation and other techniques used in Northern Ireland in the early 1970s. The ECHR in Article 25 included a unique new mechanism: the possibility that individuals might petition the Commission direct. This can be done only if the State concerned has accepted this option. The UK did so in 1966 and has reviewed this declaration every 5 years, most recently in 1996.

Until November 1998, the complaint was directed to the Commission of Human Rights, which carried out an initial check on admissibility. That body has now, however, been abolished (or effectively merged into the Court) so that the complaint will be addressed to the Secretary of the Court of Human Rights. The initial complaint does not need to be on a special form, although one would have to be completed eventually. Under the new rules made under the Eleventh Protocol, a chamber of the court will determine admissibility. As in the days of the Commission, it is likely that 90% of complaints will be ruled inadmissible, usually because of failure to exhaust domestic remedies or because they are 'manifestly ill-founded' or because they fail to meet the time-limit of 6 months from the exhaustion of the final remedy. The initial decision on admissibility will be taken by a committee of three.

Once the committee has judged a complaint admissible, the ECtHR will try to reach a friendly settlement with the government concerned, which must include the reform of any offending rules. Failing a settlement, there will be further submissions including an oral hearing at which, as well as the parties, relevant organisations like Liberty or Justice may be represented. The ECtHR (usually a chamber of seven but exceptionally a grand chamber of seventeen) may award compensation as part of its judgment but the judgment itself does not change the law in the UK. That is a matter for the UK Government. There is also a new right of appeal to the Grand Chamber on issues of general importance (subject to the leave of the first chamber). This is a little like obtaining leave to appeal to the House of Lords. The new rules of Court were published on 4 November 1998.

Chapter 31

THE HUMAN RIGHTS ACT 1998

31.1 INTRODUCTION

The Human Rights Act 1998 (HRA 1998) has been described by the former Home Secretary, Jack Straw, as 'the most significant statement of human rights in domestic law since the 1689 Bill of Rights'. Even allowing for political hyperbole, it is difficult to overestimate the potential importance of this piece of legislation. Part III of this book describes the effect which EC law has had on our legal system over the course of nearly 30 years. The effect of the HRA will ultimately be more pervasive: it is not limited in scope to certain areas of law in the same way that the EC law is. It will also be more immediate: there is a sense of pent-up demand amongst lawyers for the opportunity to use Convention rights.

HRA 1998 was a central plank of the Labour Party's programme of constitutional reform. It was based on the ideas contained in the White Paper *Rights Brought Home* published on 24 October 1997, 6 months after the new government's election. For many years previously, a number of senior members of the judiciary had in extra-judicial writings and speeches called for incorporation of the ECHR. The counter argument, that the ECHR merely encapsulates rights which are adequately protected by the common law, was widely believed to be discredited.

In brief, the effect of the Act is to make it possible for litigants in the UK to rely on Convention rights in our own domestic courts without the delay and expense incurred by taking the case to the ECtHR in Strasbourg. The constitutional issues which are raised by this are potentially momentous. Giving the judiciary a yardstick against which they can measure UK legislation and find it to be wanting has obvious impacts on the traditional conception of parliamentary supremacy. The HRA 1998 attempts to defuse this by the device of the declaration of incompatibility. It also shifts power towards the judiciary, giving them greater scope to determine difficult, perhaps emotive and politically charged questions. This raises questions about the accountability of our judges. Citizens of the United States of America are accustomed to their courts deciding such issues, but their judiciary is appointed in a very different way from our own. Might we need to modify our procedure for the selection of judges?

The HRA 1998 came into force on 2 October 2000. From this date, all lawyers in the UK will need to bear Convention rights in mind. Those rights will have much more impact in some areas of law than others. For example, criminal law and immigration practitioners will need to have regard to HRA 1998 on a day-to-day basis. However, the HRA 1998 requires that all legislation be read in accordance with Convention rights and that all public authorities make their decisions in accordance with them: any lawyer who makes use of legislation or who has dealings with organs of the State now does so against the backdrop of the HRA 1998.

Chapter 31 contents
Introduction
Convention rights
The mechanisms of the Act
Procedure for using the Act

31.2 CONVENTION RIGHTS

The concept of Convention rights is central to the HRA 1998. They are certain rights from the ECtHR which are listed in Sch 1 to the HRA 1998. The most important are those discussed in Chapter 30.

Section 2 requires that any court or tribunal determining a Convention right must take into account any decision of the Strasbourg institutions, in particular judgments of the ECtHR. Notice that these decisions are not binding in the same way that decisions of higher courts within the UK are, or even decisions of the ECJ in the context of EC law. They must only be taken into account. Clearly, they will be highly persuasive, but, should a UK court feel the need to decide the matter differently (perhaps because public opinion on the point has changed with time), then it is free to do so.

Decisions on the meaning to be given to Convention rights may involve UK courts and lawyers looking further afield than Strasbourg. The House of Lords has already accepted that it is appropriate to look to case-law from other jurisdictions in determining such matters (*R v Khan* [1997] AC 558). Most other countries have an established constitutional human rights document with a well-developed jurisprudence. We can expect to see overseas judgments being cited in our courts, especially those from common law jurisdictions such as New Zealand and Canada.

31.3 THE MECHANISMS OF THE ACT

31.3.1 Introduction

The HRA 1998 seeks to give Convention rights effect in UK law through two pathways. Whenever legislation is relevant lawyers will be able to rely on a new rule of statutory interpretation that legislation should be read in line with Convention rights. Even where there is no legislation in issue, all public authorities have an obligation to act in accordance with Convention rights.

31.3.2 The interpretative obligation

Section 3(1) reads:

> 'So far as it is possible to do so, primary legislation and subordinate legislation must be read and given effect in a way which is compatible with the Convention rights.'

This interpretative obligation applies whether the legislation is question was passed before or after HRA 1998.

This new rule goes far beyond the principle in *R v Secretary of State for the Home Department ex parte Brind* [1991] 1 AC 696 that the Convention can be used as an aid to statutory construction in cases of ambiguity. Now all legislation *must* be read in such a way as to be compatible with Convention rights, even if it is unambiguous, so long as the wording will bear such an interpretation. How far the courts will be prepared to distort the round blocks provided by legislators to make them fit the square holes of the Convention remains to be seen. Our judges are certainly becoming accustomed to the purposive approach to statutory construction which is required by EC law. For example, in *Litster v Forth Dry Dock & Engineering Co Ltd*

[1990] 1 AC 546, the House of Lords was prepared to read delegated legislation as if it contained words which were not there in order to make it comply with an EC directive. Section 3 extends the purposive approach beyond those pieces of legislation which implement EC law to all legislation.

Notice that this principle applies whether the other party is public or private. So long as a litigant can find a piece of legislation to which the Convention right can be pinned the status of their opponent does not matter.

Section 19 gives judges an extra spur to find a construction which is compatible with Convention rights. It provides that all Bills introduced into Parliament from November 1999 onwards must be accompanied by statement from the sponsoring Minister on the compatibility or otherwise of the Bill with Convention rights. Clearly, Ministers will almost invariably make statements of compatibility: were a Minister to stand up and state that a Bill did not comply with Convention rights, some very good reasons why it should be enacted in spite of this would have to be provided. The doctrine in *Pepper v Hart* [1993] AC 59 allows the courts to look to such ministerial statements in Hansard as evidence of parliamentary intention. Equipped with such evidence, courts may feel especially justified in straining legislative wording where necessary to give it a meaning compatible with Convention rights.

31.3.3 Declarations of incompatibility

Section 4 applies to higher courts (the High Court, Crown Courts, the Employment Appeals Tribunal and above). It empowers them to make declarations of incompatibility. This provides a fallback for situations in which a court recognises that legislation does not comply with Convention rights but, because of the clear words used by the legislator, does not feel that it is possible to give it a purposive interpretation.

These declarations are a compromise between the need to provide a remedy in such cases and the attachment of the UK to the doctrine of parliamentary supremacy which prevents courts from striking down acts of Parliament. They flag up the incompatibility but provide no further redress. They do not affect the continuing operation of the offending legislation (s 4(6)).

Clearing up the aftermath of such a declaration is left to the politically accountable organs of state: the government and Parliament. Section 10 and Sch 2 allow Ministers to amend an incompatible act by a 'fast track' procedure rather than having to put amending legislation through the full process in both houses of Parliament. Broadly speaking, this allows Ministers to lay before Parliament a 'remedial order' amending the offending legislation. The order will take effect after 120 days, so long as no objections are made by either house. In emergencies the remedial order can take effect immediately, but will automatically cease to have effect if not given positive approval by both houses within 120 days.

However, remedial action is optional. The HRA 1998 places no obligation on Ministers to do anything after a declaration of incompatibility is made. Even if they decide to take action, they do not have to do so via the fast track. Remember, though, that the road to Strasbourg is not closed. If a UK court declares legislation to be incompatible with Convention rights and the UK Government does not take adequate steps to put matters right, then a judgment could be sought in the ECtHR. The government would then have an obligation in international law to act.

Declarations of incompatibility are reserved in the main for primary legislation, that is acts of Parliament. Delegated or subordinate legislation (usually made by ministers under an enabling power in an Act of Parliament) is more easily attacked. Striking out such subordinate legislation does not offend against the principle of parliamentary supremacy. In fact by ensuring that Ministers only use enabling powers in an appropriate way it reinforces the will of Parliament. Because of this, courts have never shied away from ruling subordinate legislation to be ultra vires and therefore inoperative. They will continue to do so in circumstances in which subordinate legislation is incompatible with Convention rights and it is not possible to place a purposive interpretation upon it in accordance with s 3.

31.3.4 Public authorities

Public authorities may find themselves challenged because the statutory framework within which they operate gives rise to the indirect application of Convention rights via the interpretative obligation as described in **31.3.2**. However, in addition, and unlike their private counterparts, the Convention can be applied directly to their activities: it is not necessary for a litigant first to find a legislative provision to interpret purposively. Section 6(1) provides simply:

> 'It is unlawful for a public authority to act in a way which is incompatible with a
> Convention right.'

Section 6 does not fully define public authority, but does say that it includes 'any person certain of whose functions are functions of a public nature'. The dividing line between public and private bodies is a difficult one to draw. The question has exercised the minds of judicial review lawyers for some time because only public bodies are susceptible to judicial review (eg *R v Panel on Takeovers and Mergers ex parte Datafin plc* [1987] QB 815). It has also been an issue for EC lawyers because of the important distinction between the horizontal and vertical effect in EC law (eg *Foster v British Gas* (C-188/89) [1990] ECR I-3313). For the purposes of HRA 1998 there is no doubt that the departments of central government are public authorities, nor that local government is. Large companies which exercise quasi-public regulatory authorities are likely to be regarded as public authorities when exercising their public functions (eg Railtrack plc). But there are many grey areas which will doubtless be a fertile ground for litigation. It is likely that the courts will draw on the developed case-law from the fields of judicial review and EC law, and that they will try to develop one unified body of jurisprudence which can be applied across these areas of public law.

So, for example, the BBC is certain to be regarded as a public authority under the HRA 1998. When it takes a decision not to broadcast certain matter it must have regard to Art 10, the right to freedom of expression. Similarly, the police, when they exercise their powers at common law to arrest to prevent a breach of the peace, must have regard to Art 5, the right to liberty and security of the person.

Sometimes a public authority will attempt to argue that it had no choice but to act in the way it did because it was merely obeying obligations imposed by another Act of Parliament. In such cases there are two possibilities. The court may use the interpretative obligation in s 3 to read the offending legislation in such a way that the public authority was not restricted as it thought; in such a case, the public authority will be regarded as having made an error of law and an appropriate remedy will be awarded against it. Alternatively, the court may agree with the public authority's reading of the legislation, which may be so clear that it cannot be purposively interpreted in line with Convention rights. In this case, the public authority will have the defence that as a result of the legislation in question it could not have acted differently (s 6(2)) and the other party will have to content themselves with a declaration of incompatibility against the legislation.

31.4 PROCEDURE FOR USING THE ACT

The s 3 interpretative obligation can be raised in any court or tribunal hearing in which the meaning of a legislative provision needs to be construed.

Many HRA points will be raised in criminal proceedings by defendants. This may be on the basis that an Act upon which the prosecution seeks to rely does not bear the meaning which the prosecution attributes to it when s 3 is applied. Alternatively, it may be that the defence wish to raise a 'freestanding' HRA point, not linked to any legislation, that the police or the Crown Prosecution Service have acted contrary to Convention rights and therefore have broken s 6.

The other procedure which will commonly be used to raise Convention rights against public authorities is judicial review under RSC Ord 53. Under this procedure, the Divisional Court is well accustomed to scrutinising the decisions of public authorities and measuring them against a variety of standards of legality and procedural fairness. The HRA 1998 will add another string to the bow of judicial review lawyers.

The HRA 1998 introduces some special procedural rules for s 6 challenges to public authorities. Section 7(1) introduces a new locus standi test for such challenges. The claimant must be a 'victim' of the unlawful act. Existing Strasbourg case-law on this expression says that to qualify a person must be actually and directly affected by the act or omission which is the subject of the complaint. This is a narrower gateway than the usual judicial review test of 'sufficient interest'.

Section 6 challenges are also subject to a one year limitation period from the date on which the offending act took place (s 7(5)). This can be extended if the court thinks it equitable to do so. However, it is also subject to any stricter time-limit imposed by the particular procedure being used. If judicial review is used, an application must usually be made 'promptly and in any event within three months' (RSC Ord 53).

The s 3 interpretative obligation is not subject to these special provisions for locus standi or limitation period. The usual rules will apply for whatever procedure is chosen.

Section 8 provides for remedies in s 6 challenges to public authorities. It empowers courts to award such remedies within its powers as it considers just and appropriate. This will include injunctions to restrain breaches of Convention rights and damages. In awarding damages under this provision, UK courts must take account of the principles applied by the ECtHR in awarding compensation under Article 41. In practice, this means that awards of compensation are likely to be low.

Claims which introduce Convention rights indirectly via the interpretative obligation are not subject to s 8. If they are civil claims, they will have available whatever remedies are available for the cause of action being used (eg tort).

PART V

PROBATE AND ADMINISTRATION

Chapter 32

SUCCESSION TO PROPERTY ON DEATH: THE BACKGROUND LAW

32.1 WHAT PROPERTY PASSES BY THE WILL OR THE INTESTACY RULES?

When an individual dies, he may have provided for the disposition of his property on death by leaving a valid will. A will can operate to dispose of most types of property which an individual may own on death. A gift in a valid will of 'all my estate to my son, John' would include property held in the sole name of the testator at the time of his death in a variety of different forms, such as cash, money in bank and building society accounts, stocks and shares and other investments, land and chattels. If an individual does not dispose of such property by will, it passes on his death according to the intestacy rules.

However, there are some types of property which pass on death independently of the terms of the will or the intestacy rules.

32.1.1 Joint property

Where property is held by more than one person as joint tenants in equity, on the death of one joint tenant his interest passes by survivorship to the surviving joint tenant(s).

> *Example*
> George makes a will leaving all his estate to a charity. He and his brother Harry have a joint bank account and own a house as joint tenants in equity. On George's death his interests in the house and the bank account pass automatically to Harry, not to the charity under the terms of George's will.

This principle does not apply to land held on a tenancy in common. The share of each tenant in common passes on his death under his will (or under the intestacy rules).

32.1.2 Nominated property

Where an individual has deposited money with certain particular institutions, he may, exceptionally, dispose of the property on death by means of a nomination. A nomination is a direction to the institution to pay the money in the account, on the death of the investor, to a chosen ('nominated') third party. The statutory provisions which permit these disposals apply to deposits not exceeding £5,000 in certain trustee savings banks, friendly societies and industrial and provident societies.

If an individual has an account to which these provisions apply and has made a nomination, on his death the property passes to the chosen nominee regardless of the terms of the will (if any) or intestacy rules. If no nomination has been made, the money in the account will pass under the will or intestacy in the usual way.

32.1.3 Insurance policies

Where a person takes out a simple policy of life assurance, the benefit of that policy belongs to him. On his death, the policy matures and the insurance company will pay the proceeds to his PRs who will distribute the money according to the terms of his will or the intestacy rules.

However, a life assurance policy may be taken out for the benefit of specified individuals. This may be done under the terms of the Married Women's Property Act 1882, s 11. Under this section, a person taking out a life assurance policy on his own life may express the policy to be for the benefit of his spouse and/or children. This creates a trust in favour of the named beneficiaries. Alternatively, the policy may be expressly written in trust for named beneficiaries. In either case, the benefit of the policy does not belong to the life assured. On death, the policy matures and the insurance company will pay the proceeds to the named beneficiaries (or to trustees for them) regardless of the terms of the deceased's will.

32.1.4 Pension benefits

Many pension schemes provide for the payment of benefits if an employee dies 'in service'. Commonly, a lump sum calculated on the basis of the employee's salary at the time of his death is paid by the trustees of the pension fund at their discretion to members of his family. Such a scheme usually allows the employee to indicate to the trustees which people he would like to benefit. The employee's choice is not binding on the pension fund trustees, but they will normally abide by his wishes.

Such pension benefits do not belong to the employee during his lifetime and pass on his death independently of the terms of his will.

32.2 IS THERE A VALID WILL?

In order to create a valid will, a testator must have the necessary capacity and intention and must observe the formalities for execution of wills laid down in the Wills Act 1837. Once the will is made, it can be revoked by marriage, by destruction or by later will.

32.2.1 Capacity

In order to make a valid will, an individual must be aged 18 or over (with certain limited exceptions) and must have the requisite mental capacity. This testamentary capacity was defined in *Banks v Goodfellow* (1870) LR 5 QB 549 as 'soundness of mind, memory and understanding'. The testator must understand:

(1) the nature of his act and its broad effects;
(2) the extent of his property (although not necessarily recollecting every individual item); and
(3) the moral claims he ought to consider (even if he decides to reject such claims and dispose of his property to other beneficiaries).

Proof and presumptions

Initially, the burden of proving that the testator had testamentary capacity at the time he executed the will falls on the propounder of the will (ie the person who seeks to prove after the testator's death that the will is valid). However, there are two presumptions which may affect the burden of proof.

(1) If the will appears rational (ie reads sensibly) then the presumption is that the testator did have testamentary capacity. Consequently, the propounder can shift the burden of proof. The will is admitted to probate by the registrar unless any person alleging that the will is invalid can provide enough evidence to rebut this presumption of capacity, in which case the propounder will actually have to prove testamentary capacity.

(2) Mental states are presumed to persist. If a person who does not ordinarily have testamentary capacity (eg through mental illness) makes a will, the presumption is that he still lacked testamentary capacity at the relevant time and the propounder of the will must actively prove that the testator had in fact recovered testamentary capacity (either temporarily or permanently) at the time he made the will.

32.2.2 Intention

When he signs the will, the testator must have both general and specific intention. This means that he must intend to make a will (as opposed to any other sort of document), and he must also intend to make the particular will now being executed (ie he must know and approve its contents).

Proof and presumptions

As with testamentary capacity, the burden of proving the testator's knowledge and approval falls on the propounder of the will, but there is one presumption which will usually assist.

A testator who has capacity and has executed his will is presumed to have the requisite knowledge and approval (particularly where he has previously read the text or had it read over to him). However, this presumption does not apply in the situations listed below.

TESTATOR BLIND/ILLITERATE/NOT SIGNING PERSONALLY

The presumption that the testator knew and approved the contents of his will does not apply if the testator was blind or illiterate or another person signed the will on his behalf (eg because he had an injured hand).

In these cases, the probate registrar will require evidence to prove knowledge and approval.

SUSPICIOUS CIRCUMSTANCES

Similarly, the presumption of knowledge and approval does not apply if there are suspicious circumstances surrounding the drafting and/or execution of the will (eg the will has been prepared by someone who is to be a major beneficiary under its terms or is the close relative of a major beneficiary).

In such cases, because the presumption does not apply, the propounder of the will must remove the suspicion by proving that the testator did actually know and approve the will's contents.

Proving absence of knowledge and approval

If the presumption of knowledge and approval applies, then any person who wishes to challenge the will (or any part of it) on these grounds must prove absence of knowledge and approval in order to prevent some or all of the document from being admitted to probate. This can be done by proving one or more of the following:

FORCE, FEAR, FRAUD OR UNDUE INFLUENCE

The testator made his will (or part of it) as a result of force or fear (through actual or threatened injury); or fraud (eg after being misled by some pretence); or undue influence (where the testator's freedom of choice was overcome by intolerable pressure, even though his judgement remained unconvinced).

MISTAKE

All or part of the will was included by mistake. Any words included without the knowledge and approval of the testator will be omitted from probate. In this respect, it is important to distinguish between actual mistake (ie absence of knowledge and approval) and misunderstanding as to the true legal meaning of words used in the will.

32.2.3 Formalities for execution

Section 9 of the Wills Act 1837 (as substituted by Administration of Justice Act 1982, s 17) provides:

> 'No will shall be valid unless—
>
> (a)   it is in writing, and signed by the testator, or by some other person in his presence and by his direction; and
>
> (b)   it appears that the testator intended by his signature to give effect to the will; and
>
> (c)   the signature is made or acknowledged by the testator in the presence of two or more witnesses present at the same time; and
>
> (d)   each witness either—
>
> > (i)   attests and signs the will; or
> > (ii)   acknowledges his signature,
> >
> > in the presence of the testator (but not necessarily in the presence of any other witness),
>
> but no form of attestation shall be necessary.'

Proof and presumptions

If the will includes an attestation clause which recites that the s 9 formalities were observed, a presumption of due execution is raised. The will is valid unless there is proof that the formalities were not observed.

If the will does not contain an attestation clause, the district judge (or registrar) must require an affidavit of due execution from a witness or any other person who was present during the execution or, failing that, an affidavit of handwriting evidence to identify the testator's signature, or refer the case to a judge (all of which involve time and expense).

Witnesses

There are no formal requirements relating to the capacity of witnesses, although they must be capable of understanding the significance of being the witness to a signature.

If either of the witnesses is a beneficiary under the will or is the spouse of a beneficiary, the witnessing remains valid but the gift to the witness or to the witness's spouse fails (Wills Act 1837, s 15; see **32.3.3**).

32.2.4 Revocation

A testator can always revoke his will during his lifetime provided he has testamentary capacity. There are three ways of revoking a will.

(1) By a later will or codicil

Under the Wills Act 1837, s 20, a will can be revoked in whole or in part by a later will or codicil. Normally, a will contains an express clause revoking all earlier wills and codicils.

If a will does not contain an express revocation clause, it operates to revoke any earlier will or codicil by implication to the extent that the two are inconsistent.

Exceptionally, the court may decide that a testator's intention to revoke his earlier will by an express revocation clause was conditional upon a particular event (eg the effectiveness of a gift in the new will). If that condition is not satisfied, the revocation may be held to be invalid so that the earlier will remains effective (the doctrine of 'dependent relative revocation').

(2) By marriage

For wills executed after 31 December 1982, the basic rule is that, if the testator marries after executing a will, that marriage automatically revokes the will (Wills Act 1837, s 18, as substituted by the Administration of Justice Act 1982). The rule does not apply where a testator makes a will prior to and in anticipation of his forthcoming marriage if it appears from the will that he does not intend that marriage to revoke the will (s 18(3)).

If the testator makes a will and is later divorced (or the marriage is annulled or declared void) then, under the Wills Act 1837, s 18A (amended by the Law Reform (Succession) Act 1995 with effect from 1 January 1996):

(1) provisions of the will appointing the former spouse as executor or trustee take effect as if the former spouse had died on the date on which the marriage is dissolved or annulled; and

(2) any property, or interest in property, which is devised or bequeathed to the former spouse passes as if the former spouse had died on that date.

This means that substitutional provisions in the will which are expressed to take effect if the testator's spouse predeceases him will also take effect if the marriage is dissolved or annulled.

(3) By destruction

A will can be revoked by 'burning, tearing or otherwise destroying the same by the testator or by some person in his presence and by his direction with the intention of revoking the same' (Wills Act 1837, s 20). Physical destruction without the intention to revoke is insufficient; a will destroyed accidentally or by mistake is not revoked. If its contents can be reconstructed (eg from a copy) an order may be obtained allowing its admission to probate as a valid will.

Physical destruction is required; symbolic destruction (eg simply crossing out wording or endorsing 'revoked' across the will) is not sufficient, although if a vital part (eg the signature) is destroyed, this partial destruction may be held to revoke the entire will. If the part destroyed is less substantial or important, then the partial destruction may revoke only that part which was actually destroyed.

Occasionally, the court may apply the doctrine of dependent relative revocation to save a will, on the basis that the testator's intention to revoke his will by destruction was conditional upon some future event (eg upon his later execution of a new will). If that event did not in fact take place, the original will may be valid even though it was destroyed. The contents of the original will may be reconstructed from a copy or draft.

32.2.5 Alterations

If a will has been altered, the basic rule is that the alterations are invalid unless it can be proved that they were made before the will was executed or unless the alterations are executed like a will (the initials of the testator and witnesses in the margin beside the alteration are sufficient).

If a will includes invalid alterations, the original wording will stand if the original words are 'apparent': ie can still be read. If the original words have been obliterated in such a way that they can no longer be read, those words have effectively been revoked by destruction. The rest of the will remains valid, and takes effect with the omission of the obliterated words.

Again, the court may decide that the testator's intention to revoke the obliterated words was conditional only. This inference is most likely where the testator attempted to replace the obliterated words with a substitution. The implied condition is that the testator only intended to revoke the original words if the substitution was effective. As it is not, the original words remain valid and if they can be reconstructed (eg from a copy or draft) they will take effect.

32.3 WHAT IS THE EFFECT OF THE WILL?

When a testator dies, the PRs must decide (usually with the help of a solicitor) the effect of the will in the light of the circumstances at the date of the testator's death. They will need to consider what property the testator owned when he died and which of the people named in the will have survived the testator in order to decide the effect of the gifts.

32.3.1 What property passes under the gifts in the will?

As seen in **32.1** above, certain types of property may pass independently of the will either because they have their own rules of succession (eg joint property) or because the testator did not own them beneficially when he died (eg life assurance policies written in trust). When the PRs have decided what property is capable of passing under the will, they must apply the terms of the will to the property.

Basic rule

The basic rule is stated in the Wills Act 1837, s 24 which provides:

> '... every will shall be construed, with reference to the real estate and personal estate comprised in it, to speak and take effect as if it had been executed immediately before the death of the testator, unless a contrary intention shall appear by the will.'

This means that a gift of 'all my estate' or 'all the rest of my estate' takes effect to dispose of all property the testator owned when he died, whether or not he owned it when he made the will.

Ademption

A specific legacy, ie a gift of a particular item or group of items of property, will fail if the testator no longer owns that property when he dies. The gift is said to be 'adeemed'. Ademption usually occurs because the property has been sold, given away or destroyed during the testator's lifetime.

Example

In her will Ellen gives 'my diamond bracelet' to her sister Grace and the rest of her estate to her husband Harry. Ellen no longer owns the bracelet when she dies. Grace receives nothing: her legacy is adeemed. All Ellen's estate passes to Harry under the residuary gift.

Problems may arise where the asset has been retained but has changed its nature since the will was made. For example, where the will includes a specific gift of company shares, the company may have been taken over since the will was made so that the testator's shareholding has been changed into a holding in the new company. In such a case, the question is whether the asset is substantially the same, having changed merely in name or form, or whether it has changed in substance. Only if there has been a change in substance will the gift be adeemed.

Another area of potential difficulty occurs where the testator disposes of the property described in a specific gift but before his death acquires a different item of property which answers the same description; for example a gift of 'my car' or 'my piano' where the original car or piano has been replaced since the will was made. It has been held that the presumption in such a case is that the testator meant only to dispose of the particular asset he owned at the date of the will so that the gift is adeemed. By referring to 'my' car or piano, the testator is taken to have shown a contrary intention to s 24. It has been suggested that this construction may vary according to the circumstances and that the respective values of the original and substituted assets may be taken into account.

32.3.2 Has the beneficiary survived the testator?

Basic rule

A gift in a will fails or 'lapses' if the beneficiary dies before the testator. If a legacy lapses, the property falls into residue. If a gift of residue lapses, the property passes under the intestacy rules, unless the testator has provided for the possibility of lapse by including a substitutional gift in the will. Where no conditions to the contrary are imposed in the will, a gift vests on the testator's death. This means that provided the beneficiary survives the testator, for however short a time, the gift takes effect. If the beneficiary dies soon after the testator the property passes into the beneficiary's estate.

LPA 1925, s 184

The principle outlined above means that if the deaths of the testator and beneficiary occur very close together, it is vital to establish who died first. The law of succession does not accept the possibility that two people might die at the same instant. If the order of their deaths cannot be proved, s 184 provides that the elder of the two is deemed to have died first. If the testator was older than the beneficiary, the gift takes effect and the property passes as part of the beneficiary's estate.

Survivorship clauses

Commonly, gifts in wills are made conditional upon the survival of the beneficiaries for a specific period of time, such as 28 days. These survivorship provisions both prevent s 184 from applying if there is no evidence of the order of deaths of testator and beneficiary, and also prevent a gift from taking effect where the beneficiary only survives the testator for a relatively short time. As with any other contingent gift, if the beneficiary fails to satisfy the contingency the gift fails.

Lapse of gifts to more than one person

A gift by will to two or more people as joint tenants will not lapse unless all the donees die before the testator. If a gift is made 'to A and B jointly' and A dies before the testator, the whole gift passes to B. If the gift contains words of severance, for example to A and B in equal shares, this principle does not apply. If A dies before the testator, his share lapses and B takes only his own share.

If the gift is a class gift (eg 'to my children in equal shares') the membership of the class is determined at the date of the testator's death and there is no lapse unless all the members of the class predecease the testator.

Wills Act 1837, s 33: gifts to children and remoter issue

This section applies to all gifts by will to the testator's children or remoter issue unless a contrary intention is shown in the will and its effect is to incorporate an implied substitution provision into such gifts. It provides that, where a will contains a gift to the testator's child or remoter descendant and that beneficiary dies before the testator, leaving issue of his own who survive the testator, the gift shall not lapse but shall pass instead to the beneficiary's issue. The issue take 'according to their stock, in equal shares' the gift their parent would have taken.

> *Example*
>
> Tom's will includes a gift of £40,000 to his daughter Caroline. Caroline and her daughter Sarah both die before Tom, but Caroline's son James and Sarah's children Emma and Daniel all survive him. Under s 33, the legacy is saved from lapse. James takes half the gift (£20,000) while Sarah's half passes to her own children equally. Thus, Emma and Daniel take £10,000 each.

Section 33 does not apply if the will shows a contrary intention. This is usually shown by including an express substitution clause.

32.3.3 Does the gift fail for any other reason?

Divorce

Under the Wills Act 1837, s 18A (as substituted by the Law Reform (Succession) Act 1995), where after the date of the will the testator's marriage is dissolved or annulled or declared void, 'any property which, or an interest in which, is devised or bequeathed to the former spouse shall pass as if the former spouse had died' on the date of the dissolution or annulment of the marriage.

> #### *Example*
> Fiona makes a will in which she leaves all her estate to her husband Simon with a substitutional provision that, if Simon dies before her, the property should pass to her children equally. Fiona and Simon are later divorced but Fiona does not change her will. She dies, survived by Simon and the children. Under s 18A, the gift to Simon fails. Even though Simon in fact survived Fiona, the substitutional gift takes effect and Fiona's estate passes to the children.

Beneficiary witnesses will

Under the Wills Act 1837, s 15, a gift by will fails if the beneficiary or his spouse witnesses the will.

Disclaimer

A beneficiary need not accept a gift given to him by will. He can disclaim the gift, which will then fall into residue or, in the case of disclaimer of a gift of residue, pass on intestacy. Once a beneficiary has received a benefit from a gift (eg a payment of income) he is taken to have accepted the gift and may no longer disclaim.

32.4 INTESTACY

The intestacy rules contained in the Administration of Estates Act 1925 (AEA 1925) apply to decide who is entitled to an individual's property when he dies without disposing of it by will.

This may occur because the deceased has died intestate (ie without a will) or because his will failed to dispose of all his estate (partial intestacy).

The intestacy rules only apply to property which is capable of being left by will (see **32.1**).

> #### *Example*
> Laura dies intestate, survived by her husband Michael and their two children. Laura and Michael own their house as beneficial joint tenants. Laura has taken out a life assurance policy for £100,000 which is written in trust for the children and she owns investments worth £150,000. The intestacy rules do not affect Laura's share of the house (which passes to Michael by survivorship) or the life policy (which passes to the children under the terms of the trust). Only the investments pass under the intestacy rules.

32.4.1 Statutory trust for payment of debts, etc

The intestacy rules impose a trust over all the property (real and personal) in respect of which a person dies intestate (AEA 1925, s 33). This trust is similar to the usual express trust found in a will and includes a power of sale: it provides that the PRs must pay the funeral, testamentary and administration expenses and any debts of the deceased. The balance remaining (after setting aside a fund to meet any pecuniary legacies left by the deceased in the will) is the 'residuary estate' to be shared among the family under the rules of distribution set out in s 46 of the AEA 1925. The PRs have power under s 41 to appropriate assets in or towards satisfaction of a beneficiary's share (with the beneficiary's consent).

32.4.2 Spouse and issue

Definition

Under the intestacy rules, a spouse is the person to whom the deceased was married at his death, whether or not they were living together. A divorced spouse is excluded.

The term 'issue' includes all direct descendants of the deceased: ie children, grandchildren, great grandchildren, etc. Adopted children (and remoter descendants) are included, as are those whose parents were not married at the time of their birth.

Entitlements

Where the intestate is survived by both spouse and issue, the 'residuary estate' (as defined in **32.4.1**) is distributed as follows:

(a)   The spouse receives the personal chattels absolutely. 'Personal chattels' are defined in s 55(x) of the AEA 1925:

> '"Personal chattels" mean carriages, horses, stable furniture and effects (not used for business purposes), motor cars and accessories (not used for business purposes), garden effects, domestic animals, plate, plated articles, linen, china, glass, books, pictures, prints, furniture, jewellery, articles of household or personal use or ornament, musical and scientific instruments and apparatus, wines, liquors and consumable stores, but do not include any chattels used at the death of the intestate for business purposes nor money or securities for money'.

(b)   In addition, the spouse receives a 'statutory legacy' of £125,000 free of tax and costs plus interest from death until payment. The rate of interest payable is determined from time to time by statutory instrument. If the residuary estate, apart from the personal chattels, is worth less than £125,000, the spouse receives it all (and the issue receive nothing).

(c)   The rest of the residuary estate (if any) is divided into two equal funds. One fund is held on trust for the spouse for life with remainder to the issue on the statutory trusts. The other fund is held for the issue on the statutory trusts.

For deaths after 1 January 1996, the entitlement of the intestate's spouse is conditional upon the spouse surviving the intestate for 28 days. Under the Law Reform (Succession) Act 1995, where the intestate's spouse dies within 28 days of the intestate, the estate is distributed as if the spouse has not survived the intestate.

Applying the statutory trusts

The statutory trusts determine membership of the class of beneficiaries, and the terms on which they take, as follows:

(a) The primary beneficiaries are the children of the intestate who are living at his death. Remoter issue are not included unless a child has died before the intestate.

(b) The interests of the children are contingent upon attaining the age of 18 or marrying under that age. Any child who fulfils the contingency at the intestate's death takes a vested interest. If a child dies after the intestate but without attaining a vested interest, his interest fails and the estate is redistributed.

(c) If any child of the intestate has predeceased him, any children of the deceased child (grandchildren of the deceased) who are living at the intestate's death take their deceased parent's share equally between them, contingently upon attaining 18 or earlier marriage. Great grandchildren would be included only if their parent had also predeceased the intestate. This form of substitution and division is known as a 'per stirpes' distribution.

Example

Joanne dies intestate survived by her husband, Kenneth, and their children, Mark (who has a son, Quentin) and Nina. Their daughter, Lisa, died last year. Her two children, Oliver and Paul, are living at Joanne's death.

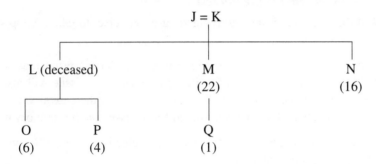

Joanne's estate consists of her share in the house, held as joint tenants with Kenneth, and other property worth £440,000 after payment of debts, funeral and testamentary expenses. This figure includes personal chattels worth £15,000.

DISTRIBUTION
Joanne's share in the house passes to Kenneth by survivorship. The rest of her estate passes on intestacy.

£	
15,000	personal chattels to Kenneth
125,000	statutory legacy to Kenneth
150,000	(Fund A) on trust for Kenneth for life remainder issue on the statutory trusts
150,000	(Fund B) for issue on the statutory trusts
440,000	

The statutory trusts apply to both funds of £150,000 to determine the distribution between Joanne's issue.

The primary beneficiaries under the statutory trusts are Mark and Nina, Joanne's children living at her death. However, Lisa's share is held for her children, Oliver and Paul in equal shares. The interests of Nina, Oliver and Paul are contingent upon attaining 18 or earlier marriage.

Thus, Mark has a vested interest in one-third of each fund. He is entitled to £50,000 on Joanne's death, and to one-third of Fund A when Kenneth dies. If Mark should die shortly after Joanne, his share in both funds would form part of Mark's estate on death. Quentin has no entitlement under Joanne's intestacy.

Nina has a contingent interest in one-third of each fund, which will vest when she is 18 or if she marries before 18. If Nina should die under the age of 18 and unmarried her interest would fail. One half of Nina's share would pass to Mark and the other half would be held for Oliver and Paul equally. This result would follow even if Nina had a child who survived her. The substitution of grandchildren applies only where a child of the intestate dies before him, whereas Nina was alive at the date of Joanne's death.

Oliver and Paul have contingent interests in one-sixth of each fund, which will vest at 18 or earlier marriage. If Oliver should die under the age of 18 and unmarried, his share would pass to Paul (and vice versa). If both Oliver and Paul were to die under the age of 18 and unmarried, their shares would be divided equally between Mark and Nina.

Spouse's right to redeem the life interest

Under s 47 of the AEA 1925, the surviving spouse may elect to take a lump sum in place of the life interest.

This means that the half of the residue which would, under the provisions outlined above, be held on trust for the spouse for life with remainder to issue will instead be divided between the spouse and issue. The spouse receives the capital value of the life interest immediately and the balance is held for the issue on the statutory trusts.

The spouse must give written notice of his or her election to the PRs within 12 months of the grant of representation.

Spouse's right to require appropriation of the matrimonial home

If the matrimonial home forms part of the estate passing on intestacy, the surviving spouse can require the PRs to appropriate the matrimonial home in full or partial satisfaction of the spouse's absolute interest in the estate (including the capitalised value of the life interest in residue) (Intestates' Estates Act 1952, s 5).

If the property is worth more than the spouse's entitlement, the spouse may still require appropriation provided he or she pays the difference, 'equality money', to the estate.

The election must be made in writing to the PRs within 12 months of the grant of representation.

32.4.3 Spouse and parents, brothers or sisters or their issue

Where the intestate leaves a surviving spouse but no issue, the distribution of the estate depends on whether any other close relatives survive. If the intestate is survived by either or both parents, by brothers or sisters of the whole blood or by issue of deceased brothers and sisters, the following rules apply.

Entitlement of spouse

From the 'residuary estate' (as defined in **32.4.1**) the spouse receives:

(a)   the personal chattels absolutely (as in **32.4.2**);

(b)   a statutory legacy of £200,000 free of tax and costs plus interest from the date of death until payment. If the residuary estate apart from the personal chattels is worth less than £200,000, the spouse receives it all (and the parents receive nothing);

(c)   half the rest of the residuary estate absolutely (ie no life interest arises in this case).

For deaths on or after 1 January 1996, the spouse's entitlement is conditional upon surviving the intestate for 28 days. If the spouse dies within 28 days of the intestate, the intestate's estate is distributed as if the spouse had not survived him.

Distribution of remainder

If the intestate is survived by either parent, that parent receives the rest of the estate absolutely. If both parents survive, the rest of the estate is shared equally between them. If both parents have predeceased the intestate, the rest of the estate is divided between the intestate's brothers and sisters of the whole blood on the statutory trusts. The terms of the statutory trusts are the same as those for issue (see **32.4.2**). The substitution provision means that if a brother or sister of the intestate has predeceased him leaving issue, such issue (nephews and nieces of the intestate) take their parent's share.

Example

Irene dies intestate. Her estate passing on intestacy is worth £350,000 (including personal chattels of £10,000). She is survived by her husband, Henry, and brother Brian and sister Susan. She has no issue and both her parents are dead.

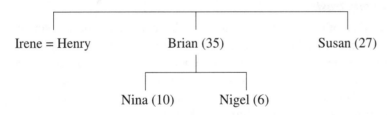

Irene = Henry	Brian (35)	Susan (27)
	Nina (10) Nigel (6)	

Henry receives:

£	
10,000	personal chattels
200,000	statutory legacy
70,000	one half of the residue absolutely

(Again, if Irene dies on or after 1 January 1996, Henry will be entitled as above only if he survives Irene for 28 days.)

The remaining £70,000 is held for the brothers and sisters on statutory trusts. This means that it is divided equally between Brian and Susan, who both have vested interests because they are over 18.

If Brian had predeceased Irene, his share (£35,000) would be held for his children, Nina and Nigel, equally, contingently upon attaining the age of 18 or earlier marriage.

Spouse's right to require appropriation of the matrimonial home

As described in **32.4.2**, the surviving spouse may elect to take the matrimonial home in full or partial satisfaction of his interest in the estate.

32.4.4 Intestate survived by spouse and no other close relatives

Where the intestate leaves a surviving spouse but no issue, parent, brother or sister of the whole blood or issue of a deceased brother or sister, the whole estate, however large, passes to the spouse absolutely. More distant relatives, such as half brothers and sisters, grandparents and cousins are not entitled.

If the intestate died on or after 1 January 1996, the spouse's entitlement is conditional upon surviving the intestate for 28 days. If the spouse died within that period, the estate is distributed as if the spouse had not survived the intestate.

32.4.5 Distribution where there is no surviving spouse

Where there is no surviving spouse (or, for deaths after 1 January 1996, where the spouse dies within 28 days of the intestate), the 'residuary estate' is divided between the relatives in the highest category in the list below:

(1) issue on the 'statutory trusts' (see **32.4.2**), but if none,
(2) parents, equally if both alive, but if none,
(3) brothers and sisters of the whole blood on the 'statutory trusts', but if none,
(4) brothers and sisters of the half blood on the 'statutory trusts', but if none,
(5) grandparents, equally if more than one, but if none,
(6) uncles and aunts of the whole blood on the 'statutory trusts', but if none,
(7) uncles and aunts of the half blood on the 'statutory trusts', but if none,
(8) the Crown, Duchy of Lancaster, or Duke of Cornwall (bona vacantia).

The statutory trusts

Each category other than parents and grandparents takes 'on the statutory trusts'. This means that members of the specified class share the estate equally (children under 18 take their interest contingently upon attaining 18 or marrying earlier), and that issue of a deceased relative may take that relative's share. This means that relatives not mentioned in s 46 (eg nephews, nieces and cousins) may inherit on intestacy if their parents died before the intestate.

> *Example 1*
> Tom dies intestate. He was not married to his partner, Penny, although the couple have a son, Simon, aged 13, Tom's only child. Tom's parents predeceased him but he is survived by his only sibling, his brother Bob, aged 40.
>
> Tom's estate is held on trust for Simon, contingently upon attaining 18 or marrying earlier. If Simon dies before the contingency is fulfilled, Tom's estate passes to Bob absolutely.

> *Example 2*
> Vera, a widow aged 80, is cared for by her step-daughter Carol (the child of her deceased husband's first marriage). Her only living blood relatives are cousins, the children of her mother's brothers and sisters. Vera dies intestate. Her estate

is divided 'per stirpes' between her cousins (and the children of any cousins who predeceased her). Carol receives nothing from Vera's estate.

Adopted and illegitimate children

Adopted children are treated for intestacy purposes as the children of their adoptive parents and not of their natural parents. If a person who was adopted dies intestate without spouse or issue, his estate will be distributed between the closest relatives in the adoptive family. An adopted child may also inherit on the intestacy of any member of his adoptive family.

Similarly, the intestacy rules are applied regardless of whether or not a particular individual's parents were married to each other. However, on the intestacy of an individual whose parents were not married to each other, it is presumed that the individual has not been survived by his father or by any person related to him through his father unless the contrary is shown (Family Law Reform Act 1987, s 18(2)). This presumption avoids any necessity for the PRs to make awkward enquiries where the identity or whereabouts of the father is unknown.

Example

Jessica, whose parents did not marry, dies intestate. Her only known relative is a half brother, the child of her mother's later marriage. Nothing is known of Jessica's father or any other children he may have had. Jessica's PRs may distribute her estate to her half brother, relying on the presumption in s 18(2).

Bona vacantia

Where an estate passes bona vacantia, the Crown, Duchy of Lancaster or Duke of Cornwall has a discretion to provide for dependants of the intestate or for other persons for whom the intestate might reasonably have been expected to make provision.

32.5 THE INHERITANCE (PROVISION FOR FAMILY AND DEPENDANTS) ACT 1975

The Inheritance (Provision for Family and Dependants) Act 1975 (I(PFD)A 1975) allows certain categories of people who may be aggrieved because they have been left out of a will, or are not inheriting on an intestacy, to apply for a benefit from the estate following the testator's or intestate's death. The I(PFD)A 1975 can also be used by a person who has received some benefit under the will or intestacy but is dissatisfied with the amount of the inheritance.

Section numbers below refer to the I(PFD)A 1975 unless otherwise stated.

32.5.1 When should a claim be made?

An application must be brought within six months of the date of issue of the grant of representation to the deceased's estate (s 4). The court has a discretion to extend this time-limit.

32.5.2 Who can make a claim?

The following persons can make a claim (s 1(1)):

(1) the spouse of the deceased;
(2) a former spouse of the deceased who has not remarried (except where, on the granting of the decree of divorce or nullity, the court made an order barring the former spouse from making a claim);
(3) a child of the deceased (whatever the child's age);
(4) any person treated by the deceased as a child of the family in relation to any marriage of the deceased (eg a step-child);
(5) any person who, immediately before the death of the deceased, was being maintained by him either wholly or in part. A person is 'maintained' if 'the deceased, otherwise than for full valuable consideration, was making a substantial contribution in money or money's worth towards the reasonable needs of that person' (s 1(3));
(6) any person who, during the whole of the period of two years ending immediately before the date when the deceased died, was living:

  (a) in the same household as the deceased, and
  (b) as the husband or wife of the deceased (this category was added by the Law Reform (Succession) Act 1995).

32.5.3 What must the applicant prove?

The only ground for a claim is that 'the disposition of the deceased's estate effected by his will or the law relating to intestacy, or a combination of his will and that law, is not such as to make reasonable financial provision for the applicant'. Section 1(2) sets out two standards for judging 'reasonable financial provision':

(1) 'the surviving spouse standard' which allows a surviving spouse such financial provision as is reasonable in all the circumstances 'whether or not that provision is required for his or her maintenance' (s 1(2)(a)); and
(2) 'the ordinary standard' which applies to all other categories of applicant and allows 'such financial provision as it would be reasonable in all the circumstances ... for the applicant to receive for his maintenance' (s 1(2)(b)).

32.5.4 What factors does the court take into account?

Section 3 contains guidelines to assist the court in determining whether the will and/or intestacy does make reasonable financial provision for the applicant. Some matters should be considered for every claimant (ie the common guidelines). There are also special guidelines for each category of applicant.

The common guidelines in s 3(1) are:

(1) the financial resources and needs of the applicant, other applicants and beneficiaries of the estate now and in the foreseeable future;
(2) the deceased's moral obligations towards any applicant or beneficiary;
(3) the size and nature of the estate;
(4) the physical or mental disability of any applicant or beneficiary;
(5) anything else which may be relevant, such as the conduct of the applicant.

The special guidelines vary with the category of applicant. For example, where the applicant is the surviving spouse, the court takes into account the applicant's age and contribution to the welfare of the family, the duration of the marriage and the likely financial settlement if the marriage had ended in divorce rather than death. On an application by a child of the deceased the applicant's education or training requirements are considered. (The courts have shown a reluctance to award financial provision to adult, able-bodied children.)

When considering the common and special guidelines, the court takes into account:

(1) the facts at the date of the hearing (s 3(5)); and
(2) with regard to the financial resources and needs of the applicant:

   (a) his earning capacity; and
   (b) his financial obligations and responsibilities (s 3(6)).

32.5.5 What orders can the court make?

The court has wide powers to make orders against the 'net estate' of the deceased, including orders for periodical payments, lump sum payments or the transfer of specific property to the applicant.

The 'net estate' against which an order can be made includes not only property which the deceased has, or could have, disposed of by will or nomination, but also the deceased's share of joint property passing by survivorship if the court so orders and provided the application was made within 6 months of the grant.

In making an order, the court will declare how the burden of the order is to be borne, ie which beneficiary is to lose part or all of the property he would otherwise have taken.

For IHT purposes, the altered disposition of the estate is treated as taking effect from death.

If the order alters the amount passing to the deceased's spouse, the amount of any IHT payable on the estate will be affected.

32.5.6 Protecting the PRs

PRs should be advised not to distribute the estate until 6 months have elapsed from the issue of the grant. In any event, they must not distribute once they have notice of a possible claim. If PRs do distribute within the 6-month period and an applicant subsequently brings a successful claim, the PRs will be personally liable to satisfy the claim if insufficient assets remain in the estate. Where a court permits an application out of time, the PRs will not be liable personally if they have distributed the estate, but the claimant may be able to recover property from the beneficiaries.

Chapter 33

PROBATE PRACTICE AND PROCEDURE

33.1 INTRODUCTION

This chapter considers the events immediately following the death of a person. That person may have been the client of the solicitor. Whether or not that is the case, the solicitor's clients at this stage are the deceased's PRs. The solicitor himself (or his firm) may be acting as PR (or one of several PRs). In either case, the practice and procedure will be substantially the same.

33.2 WHO ARE THE PRs?

The PRs will be either the deceased's executors or intended administrators.

The executors

If the will is valid and contains an effective appointment of executors of whom one or more is willing and able to prove the deceased's will, a grant of probate will be issued to him or to them (see **33.9**).

Administrators with the will annexed

If there is a valid will but there are no persons willing or able to act as executors, then the next persons entitled to act are administrators with the will annexed who should be appointed in accordance with r 20 of the Non-Contentious Probate Rules 1987 (NCPR 1987) (see **33.10**).

Administrators (simple administration)

If a deceased left no will, or no valid will, the estate will be administered in accordance with the law of intestacy by administrators appointed by the application of NCPR 1987, r 22 (see **33.11**).

Number of PRs required

One executor may obtain a grant and act alone. This is so, even if the estate contains land which may be sold during the administration, because a receipt for the proceeds of sale from one executor is sufficient for the purchaser. This is in contrast to the position of trustees where, if a good receipt for the proceeds of sale of land is to be given to a purchaser, it must be given by at least two trustees (or a trust corporation).

In the case of administrators (with or without the will), it will often be sufficient for one to act in the administration of the estate. However, where the will or intestacy creates a life or minority interest, two administrators are normally required.

Authority of PRs before the grant

An executor derives his authority to act in the administration of an estate from the will. The grant of probate confirms that authority. Although he has full power to act from the time of the deceased's death, the executor will be unable to undertake certain transactions (eg sale of land) without producing the grant as proof of authority.

An administrator (with or without the will) has very limited powers before a grant is made because his authority stems from the grant which is not retrospective to the date of death.

33.3 FIRST STEPS AFTER RECEIVING INSTRUCTIONS

Following a person's death, a number of matters will require the immediate attention of the solicitor who is to act for the PRs, including those set out below.

33.3.1 The deceased's will

Ascertain whether the deceased made a will. If so, ensure the executors named in the will receive copies of it.

33.3.2 Directions as to cremation etc

Give immediate consideration to the terms of the will to ascertain any special directions by the deceased as to cremation or the use of his body for medical research or other purposes.

33.3.3 Details of assets and liabilities

Obtain details of the deceased's property and of any debts outstanding at the date of death, by asking the PRs for building society passbooks, share certificates and details of bank accounts, etc. Enquiries should be made of the deceased's bank manager as to whether the bank holds in safe custody any share certificates or other property owned by the deceased (the bank manager will require sight of the death certificate before giving such information).

From these details, the solicitor will be able to begin to evaluate the size of the deceased's estate, and the amount of any liability to IHT.

33.3.4 Details of the beneficiaries

From the deceased's will (if any), the solicitor must establish the identity of the beneficiaries, and the nature and extent of their entitlement (eg whether as legatee or as residuary beneficiary). If specific legacies have been given, it is important to ascertain whether the property given by those specific gifts is part of the estate (if not the gift(s) will have adeemed) (see **32.3.1**). If the deceased has died intestate, it is necessary to establish which members of the family have survived so that the basis of distribution of the estate may be established in accordance with the rules discussed at **32.4**.

33.3.5 Missing and/or unknown creditors and beneficiaries

The position as PR carries with it responsibility to administer the deceased's estate correctly and failure by a PR to carry out his duties can give rise to personal liability. PRs may be faced with the problem that persons entitled under the will or intestacy rules have disappeared or are unknown to them (eg because they were children born outside the deceased's marriage but whose identity he did not disclose). In addition, the PRs may not be sure that they have identified all the deceased's debtors and creditors.

PRs can obtain statutory protection by advertising for claims in accordance with the Trustee Act 1925, s 27.

The following procedure should be followed.

Early advertisement

In view of the minimum notice period of 2 months, PRs should advertise as early as possible in the administration. If they are executors, they may advertise at any time after the death; if they are administrators they have power to advertise at any time after obtaining their grant.

Placing the advertisement

The PR should give notice of the intended distribution of the estate, requiring any person interested to send in particulars of his claim whether as a creditor or as a beneficiary by:

(1) advertisment in the *London Gazette*;
(2) advertisement in a newspaper circulating in the district in which land owned by the deceased is situated; and
(3) 'such other like notices, including notices elsewhere than in England and Wales, as would, in any special case, have been directed by a court of competent jurisdiction in an action for administration'.

A court would normally order the placing of advertisements as are appropriate in the particular circumstances of the case. Printed forms for the advertisements can be obtained from law stationers.

Time for claims

Each notice must require any person interested to send in particulars of his claim within the time specified in the notice, which must not be less than two months from the date of the notice.

Searches in case of land

The PRs should also make searches which the prudent purchaser of land would make in the Land Registry, Land Charges Register and Local Land Charges Registry as appropriate. The purpose of these searches is to reveal the existence of any liability in relation to the deceased's ownership of an interest in land, for example a second mortgage.

Distribution after notices

When the time-limit in the notice has expired, the PRs may distribute the deceased's estate, taking into account only those claims of which they have actual knowledge, or which they discover as a result of the advertisements. The PRs are not personally liable for any other claim, but a claimant may pursue the claim by following the assets into the hands of the beneficiaries who have received them from the PRs.

33.4 NECESSITY FOR A GRANT OF REPRESENTATION

A grant enables the PRs to prove their authority to deal with the deceased's property which passes under the will or the intestacy rules. However, it is not always necessary to obtain a grant of representation. This can be particularly useful where the deceased's family needs funds immediately for IHT or other purposes.

A grant may not be required in the three situations which follow.

33.4.1 Assets which may pass to the PRs without a grant

Administration of Estates (Small Payments) Act 1965

Orders made under this Act permit payments to be made under various statutes and statutory instruments to persons appearing to be beneficially entitled to the assets without formal proof of title. This facility is restricted, in that it is not available if the value of the asset exceeds £5,000; in addition, as the payments are made at the discretion of the institutions concerned, it is not possible for PRs to insist that payments should be made. Payment is often refused where the estate is of substantial overall value, leaving the PRs in a position where they must obtain a grant before the asset can be collected. Subject to these points, payments can be made in respect of, for example:

(1) money in the National Savings Bank and Trustee Savings Bank (but not in other bank accounts);
(2) National Savings Certificates and Premium Bonds; and
(3) money in building societies and friendly societies.

Chattels

Movable personal property such as furniture, clothing, jewellery, and cars can normally be sold without the PRs having to prove formally to the buyer that they are entitled to sell such items.

Cash

Normally, the PRs do not require a grant when taking custody of any cash found in the deceased's possession (ie found in the home of the deceased as opposed to deposited in a bank or other account).

33.4.2 Assets not passing through the PR's hands

Joint property

On death, any interest in property held by the deceased as joint tenant in equity with another (whether it is an interest in land or personalty, eg a bank account) passes by survivorship to the surviving joint tenant. As it does not pass via the PRs, any grant is irrelevant. The survivor has access to the property and can prove title to the whole of it merely by producing the deceased's death certificate. Since it is common for married couples to own property jointly, there are many occasions where a grant is not required for this reason.

(Conversely, if the property is held by persons as beneficial tenants in common, the share of each tenant in common passes on his death to his PRs for distribution.)

33.4.3 Property not forming part of the deceased person's estate

The deceased may have insured his own life, but in such a way that the policy and its proceeds are held in trust for others. This trust may be established by writing the policy under the Married Women's Property Act 1882, s 11 ('a Married Women's Property Act policy') for the spouse or children of the deceased, or by making a separate declaration of trust for those or other beneficiaries. On death, the policy money is payable to the trustees of the policy on production of the death certificate. A grant is not required since the money does not form part of the estate. As the deceased had no beneficial interest in the policy or its proceeds (because of the trust) no IHT will be payable on the proceeds. Such a policy is particularly advantageous, as the proceeds make tax-free provision for dependants of the deceased and can be collected in immediately following the death.

Pension benefits

Death in service benefits under a pension scheme are generally payable at the discretion of the pension fund trustees. Payments are made to the beneficiaries on production of the death certificate. A grant is not required, since the pension benefits do not form part of the deceased's estate. This is another method of making tax-free provision for dependants, and such provision can also be collected in immediately following the death.

33.5 APPLICATION FOR GRANT

Where a grant is required, it is necessary to apply to the Principal Registry of the Family Division or a district probate registry. The application is made by lodging such of the following documents as are appropriate to the particular case:

(1) Inland Revenue Form D18 confirming payment of any IHT;
(2) the deceased's will and codicil, if any, marked by the executors (or administrators if there are no proving executors) and the solicitor before whom the supporting oath is sworn or affirmed;
(3) the oath, sworn or affirmed by the executors or administrators;
(4) any affidavit evidence which may be required (see **33.5.2**);
(5) probate court fees (an administration fee based on the value of the net estate passing under the grant).

33.5.1 Admissibility of will to probate

In view of the necessity to lodge the deceased's will with the application, the solicitor must ascertain at an early stage that it is admissible to probate. If it is not, application will be made instead for a grant of simple administration.

To ensure that the will is admissible, the solicitor should check the following:

(1) the will is the last will of the testator;
(2) that it has not been validly revoked;
(3) that it is executed in accordance with the Wills Act 1837, s 9; and
(4) that it contains an attestation clause which indicates that the will was executed in accordance with the requirements of the Wills Act 1837 and raises a presumption of 'due execution'.

33.5.2 The registrar's additional requirements

If the application is in order, the registrar will issue the original grant, sealed with the court seal and signed by him. In some cases, before issuing the grant, the registrar may require further evidence.

Affidavit of due execution

If there is no attestation clause, if the clause is in some respect defective, or if there are doubtful circumstances about the execution of the will, the registrar will require affidavit evidence, usually by an attesting witness, to establish that the will has been properly executed. The evidence is provided by means of an affidavit of due execution. If there is doubt about the mental capacity of the testator to make the will, the affidavit of a doctor may be necessary. In such cases, the doctor should have been asked to examine the testator to ascertain whether he had sufficient capacity at the time the will was made.

Affidavit as to knowledge and approval

It may appear to the registrar that there is doubt as to whether the testator was aware of the contents of the will when he executed it. This may arise through blindness, illiteracy or frailty of the testator, or because of suspicious circumstances, for example where the person who prepared the will for the testator benefits substantially by its terms.

In any of these circumstances, the attestation clause should be suitably adapted, ideally by indicating that the will was read over to the testator or was independently explained to him. In the absence of this, the registrar will require to be satisfied that the testator had knowledge and approval of the contents of the will. The evidence is provided by means of an affidavit of knowledge and approval of contents made by someone who can speak as to the facts. Normally, this will be one of the attesting witnesses, but it could be an independent person who explained the provisions of the will to the testator.

Affidavit of plight and condition

If the state of the will suggests that it has been interfered with in some way since execution, the registrar will require further evidence by way of explanation. This may arise:

(1) where the will has been altered since its execution;
(2) where there is some obvious mark on it indicating a document may have been attached to it (eg the marks of a paper clip raising a suggestion that some other testamentary document may have been attached); or
(3) where it gives the appearance of attempted revocation.

Generally, the explanation required will take the form of an affidavit of plight and condition made by some person having knowledge of the facts.

Lost will

A will which was known to have been in the testator's possession but which cannot be found following the death is presumed to have been destroyed by the testator with the intention of revoking it.

However, if the will has been lost or accidently destroyed, probate may be obtained of a copy of the will, such as a copy kept in the solicitor's file, or a reconstruction. In such a case, application should be made to the registrar, supported by appropriate affidavit evidence from the applicant for the grant of probate.

33.6 COMPLETING THE INLAND REVENUE ACCOUNT

33.6.1 Purpose of an Inland Revenue account

One of the first steps towards obtaining the grant of representation is the preparation of the appropriate Inland Revenue account and the calculation of any IHT payable.

If the estate is an 'excepted estate', the PRs do not need to complete and submit an Inland Revenue account. In other cases, they will prepare account form IHT 200 and relevant supplementary pages (see **33.7**).

The Inland Revenue account is an inventory of the assets to which the deceased was beneficially entitled and of his liabilities, and is the form for claiming reliefs and exemptions and calculating the IHT payable. It should usually be delivered within 12 months of the end of the month in which the death occurred. Usually PRs aim to deliver the account within 6 months to comply with IHT time-limits. Until the account is submitted no grant of representation can be issued.

IHT is payable on all property to which the deceased was beneficially entitled immediately before his death whether or not such property vests in his PRs. Certain types of property qualify for tax relief, for example business or agricultural property, or an exemption may apply because of the identity of the beneficiary (ie the surviving spouse or a charity) (see **4.6.3**).

Paying the IHT

IHT on property without the right to pay by instalments (see **4.6.8**) must be paid within 6 months of the end of the month in which the death occurred. For example, if a person dies on 10 January, IHT is due on 31 July, or on delivery of the Inland Revenue account if this is earlier. Until this tax has been paid, no grant can issue to the deceased's estate.

Where there is property which qualifies for the right to pay the tax by instalments, none of the tax on that property is due until the expiry of the 6-month period. If the option is exercised, only the first instalment of one-tenth must then be paid. In an estate where it is not possible to deliver the Inland Revenue account within that period, all tax on non-instalment option property plus the appropriate number of instalments on property with the option and interest must be paid on delivery of the account. Interest runs on all tax not paid on the due date.

33.6.2 Valuations

General principles

Assets in the estate are valued at 'the price which the property might reasonably be expected to fetch if sold in the open market' immediately before the death (s 160 of IHTA 1984).

Jointly owned assets

There is a special valuation rule where the deceased was the co-owner (as tenant in common or as beneficial joint tenant) of land at his death. The market value at the date of death may be discounted to reflect the virtual impossibility of selling a part interest in property. The probate value of the deceased's interest is the discounted market value at the date of death divided proportionately between the co-owners. A discount of 10–15 per cent is normally considered reasonable.

> #### Example 1
> Mary and Nellie owned a house as joint tenants. The value of the house at Mary's death was £100,000. Apply a 10% discount.
>
> The discount is £100,000 × 10% = £10,000
>
> and her half share £100,000 – £10,000 = £90,000 ÷ 2 = £45,000.
>
> The probate value of Mary's share is £45,000.

The discount is not available where the co-owners are husband and wife because of the related property rules (see **4.3.2**) nor where the co-ownership is of an asset other than land. For such assets, for example bank and building society accounts, the probate value is the account balance as at the date of death (plus interest) divided proportionately between the joint owners.

33.6.3 Funding the IHT

Where there is IHT to pay on delivery of an Inland Revenue account, the PRs must arrange for the appropriate amount of money to be sent to the Inland Revenue with the account. When this tax is paid, receipted Form D18 and other documents (see **33.5**) are sent to the appropriate Registry so that the grant can issue. Funding the tax bill may be problematic as all the deceased's assets vesting in the PRs are 'frozen', and therefore untouchable, until the grant issues giving the proof of title to the PRs.

The options which may be available to raise funds to pay the IHT are set out below.

The deceased's building society account or life assurance

If there is sufficient cash in a building society account or policy of insurance on the deceased's life, the institution holding the funds may be willing to release funds to pay the IHT. If so, the funds will generally be paid directly to the Inland Revenue and not to the PRs or their solicitors.

Assets realisable without production of the grant

By applying the Administration of Estates (Small Payments) Act 1965 (see **33.4.1**), assets may, in some cases, be realised without production of a grant. The maximum value of any one asset that may be realised is £5,000. The Act gives discretion to the institution to allow assets to be realised in this way. Where an estate is reasonably large or complex, this discretion will often not be exercised. In such cases, a grant must first be obtained and produced to release the asset concerned.

Loans from beneficiaries

Wealthy beneficiaries may be prepared to fund the IHT from their own resources, on condition that they will be repaid from the deceased's estate once the grant issues. Alternatively, beneficiaries may already have received assets as a result of the death which they are prepared to use to pay the tax, such as money from a jointly held bank account or the proceeds of a life policy vested in them under the Married Women's Property Act 1882. However, it is likely that the deceased arranged for such assets to provide financial assistance for that beneficiary while his estate was being administered and the beneficiary may not be able to afford to make a loan.

Bank borrowing

Banks will usually lend against an undertaking to repay the loan given by the PRs. A bank may also require an undertaking from the solicitor to repay the loan from the proceeds of the estate. Whether or not the solicitor is a PR, any undertaking should be limited to 'such proceeds as come into the solicitor's control'. Undertakings to pay money should be carefully worded so as to ensure payment is not due from the solicitor personally.

While it is often the only viable option, bank borrowing is expensive, because the bank will charge an arrangement fee and interest on the amount borrowed. Money borrowed should be repaid at the earliest opportunity so as to honour any undertaking and to stop interest running. Income tax relief is available to the PRs for interest paid on a separate loan account in respect of IHT payable on personalty vesting in them.

National Savings

Payment of tax may also be made from National Savings Bank accounts or from the proceeds of National Savings Certificates, any Government stock held on the National Savings register or any other National Savings investment.

33.7 THE REQUIREMENT FOR AN INLAND REVENUE ACCOUNT

33.7.1 Excepted estates

If the estate is an excepted estate, there is no need for an account to be submitted, although the Inland Revenue can demand an account within 35 days of the date of issue of the grant of representation. If an estate which initially appears to be excepted is subsequently found not to be so, the PRs must submit the appropriate account within 6 months of the discovery.

To qualify as an excepted estate, the estate must fulfil five criteria. If any criterion is not satisfied an account will be required. The criteria for deaths on or after 6 April 2000 are as follows:

(1) the deceased must have died domiciled in the UK; and
(2) the deceased must not have made any chargeable transfers within 7 years of his death other than transfers consisting only of cash, quoted shares or quoted

securities with an aggregate value not exceeding £75,000 (PETs made more than 7 years before the death are not chargeable); and

(3) the total value of any assets outside the UK owned by the deceased must not exceed £50,000; and

(4) the only assets owned by the deceased immediately before his death pass as a result of the death by will/intestacy and/or survivorship and/or nomination; and

(5) the combined value of the gross IHT estate and the value transferred as in (2) above must not exceed £210,000.

Example

Adam has just died. His will leaves his estate to his wife Brenda and daughter Clare in equal shares. He is UK-domiciled and has made no lifetime transfers.

His estate consists of:

House owned jointly with Brenda (half share)	£50,000
Building society a/c (sole name)	£10,000
Personal chattels	£2,000
Debts (funeral bill and Access a/c)	£1,800

Adam's estate satisfies the criteria and it has an IHT value of £62,000 gross (note that IHT exemptions and reliefs are ignored when ascertaining the gross IHT estate).

This is an excepted estate and no Inland Revenue account is required. This fact will also be noted on the oath.

33.7.2 Form IHT 200

Form IHT 200 must be used whenever the deceased dies domiciled in the UK and his estate is not an 'excepted' estate.

Reduced IHT 200

In some cases, broadly those cases where IHT is not payable, a 'reduced' form IHT 200 can be delivered to the Inland Revenue instead of the full form. Only some parts of the IHT 200 need be filled in where the deceased died domiciled in the UK and either of the following conditions is satisfied:

(1) the entire estate passes to an 'exempt beneficiary', ie:

 – a UK-domiciled spouse or a UK-registered charity (in either case, by way of outright gift or gift into trust);

 – a gift for national purposes to a body listed in IHTA 1984, Sch 3, eg the British Museum or The National Trust; or

(2) the gross value of the assets (before liabilities, exemptions and reliefs) passing by will or intestacy other than to 'exempt beneficiaries', plus:

 – other chargeable assets, eg property passing by survivorship, trust property and property subject to reservation of benefit; and

 – chargeable transfers within 7 years of death (after deducting exemptions and reliefs)

is less than the IHT threshold (nil rate band = £242,000 for 2001/02).

If a 'reduced' form IHT 200 can be used, only the following pages of the form need be completed.

Page 1. Complete in full.

Page 2. Answer all the questions.

> 'Yes' answers. Questions D1–D6 – complete the relevant supplementary pages (estimated values may be used where assets pass to an 'exempt beneficiary').

> Questions D7–D16 – the relevant supplementary pages are not required where *all* of the assets pass to an 'exempt beneficiary'.

Pages 3–5. Fill in the relevant boxes (again, giving only estimated values where assets pass to 'exempt beneficiaries'.

Pages 6 and 7. No IHT will be payable. Complete Form IHT(WS) and copy the figures to these pages.

Page 8. Complete in full (but not Box L3 where assets pass to 'exempt beneficiaries').

Note: under the 'reduced' account form conditions, PRs can include their own estimate of value for assets passing to 'exempt beneficiaries' so avoiding the need for a formal (and costly) valuation. If, subsequently, the estate is found not to meet the conditions, an open market value of the assets will be required.

33.8 OATHS: THE BACKGROUND LAW

33.8.1 Types and purpose of oaths

Every application for a grant of representation must be supported by the appropriate form of oath. The three most common types of oath are as follows:

(1) oath for executors;
(2) oath for administrators with will annexed;
(3) oath for administrators.

The oaths differ from each other in detail but they have a common purpose, namely:

(1) to give details of the deceased;
(2) to set out the basis of the applicant's claim to take the grant;
(3) to require the applicant to swear that he will administer the estate correctly;
(4) in the case of oaths for executors and oaths for administrators with the will annexed, to identify and exhibit the will and any codicils.

Unless the appropriate oath is accurately completed and submitted to the probate registry by, or on behalf of, those PRs who may properly make an application, no grant of representation will be issued.

33.8.2 Swearing or affirming the oath

Before the oath is submitted to the probate registry, the PRs must swear or affirm the truth of its contents. This must be done before a commissioner for oaths or a solicitor holding a current practising certificate, neither of whom is connected with the firm of solicitors acting for the PRs. PRs may prefer to affirm in which case they say 'I do solemnly sincerely and truly declare and affirm that …'. A PR who swears the oath will be required to hold the New Testament or Bible whilst saying 'I swear by Almighty God that …'.

Once the oath has been sworn or affirmed it should be sent to the probate registry with any will, Inland Revenue account and the appropriate probate court fees.

33.9 OATH FOR EXECUTORS

33.9.1 Entitlement to act

The oath for executors will lead to a grant of probate where they have been appointed by a valid will. One executor may obtain a grant and act alone.

> *Example 1*
> Alex by his will appoints Brian and Colin to be his executors and leaves his entire estate to a named charity.
>
> Brian and/or Colin can apply for a grant of probate by lodging an oath for executors, and the will, with the probate registry.

The appointment is not affected by the fact that the will may fail to dispose of some or all of the deceased's estate.

> *Example 2*
> Diana has just died. Her will appoints Eric as her executor and leaves her entire estate to Freda. Freda died before Diana whose estate will therefore be distributed according to the intestacy rules. Eric is alive and prepared to act as executor. Eric will apply for a grant of probate by swearing an executors oath.

33.9.2 Capacity to act

Capacity to act as executor is judged at the time of the application for the grant.

Mental incapacity

A person appointed as an executor by the will but who, at the testator's death, is suffering from mental incapacity may not act as executor or apply for the grant.

Minors

There is no prohibition on a testator naming a minor as his executor. However, if the executor is still a minor at the testator's death he cannot act as an executor nor obtain a grant of probate until he attains majority.

Where one of several executors is a minor, the other(s) being adults, probate can be granted to the adult executor(s) with power reserved to the minor (for an explanation of 'power reserved', see **33.9.4**). If the administration of the estate has not been completed by the time the minor attains 18 years he can then apply for a grant of double probate to enable him to act as executor alongside the other proving executor(s).

Example

George dies appointing his wife, Ingrid and his son Harry (aged 16) as his executors.

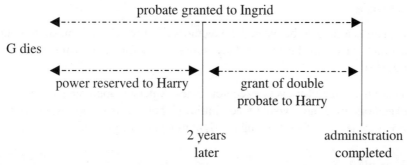

Where the minor is the only executor appointed by the will (or the adult executors are not able or willing to act), the testator's estate cannot be left unadministered until the executor reaches 18 years. A grant of letters of administration with will annexed for the use and benefit of the minor will be made, usually to the parent(s) or guardian(s) of the minor, until the minor attains 18 years. On obtaining majority the executor may apply for a cessate grant of probate.

The former spouse

If the testator appointed his spouse as his executor and the marriage subsequently ended in divorce, that appointment will fail unless the testator has shown a contrary intention in the will (Wills Act 1837, s 18A: see **32.2.4**).

If the spouse was one of several executors, the others may apply for the grant of probate without her. If she was the sole executrix, application should be made for a grant of letters of administration with will annexed. In either case, the oath to lead to the appropriate grant should cite the fact and date of the divorce.

33.9.3 Renunciation

Any person appointed as an executor may renounce his right to take the grant, provided that he has not intermeddled in the estate. A person has intermeddled when he has done tasks a PR might do, for example notifying the deceased's bank of the death. Once an executor has intermeddled, he must take the grant.

Provided there has been no intermeddling, the executor who does not wish to act can renounce his right. His rights as executor then cease and the administration of the estate proceeds as if he had never been appointed.

The renunciation must be made in writing, signed by the person renouncing (the signature must be witnessed) and the renunciation must be filed at the probate registry. This is normally done by the PRs who are applying for a grant when they lodge their application at the probate registry.

33.9.4 Power reserved

There is no limit on how many executors can be appointed by the will, but probate will be granted to only a maximum of four executors. Power may be reserved to the other(s) to take out a grant in the future if a vacancy arises.

Example 1

Alan's will appoints B, C, D, E and F to be his executors. All are willing and able to act. Probate is granted to C, D, E and F. 'Power is reserved' to B. If F dies before the administration is complete, B can then apply for a grant. It is not automatic.

If there is a dispute between the exectuors as to which of them should apply for a grant, this may be resolved by summons before a registrar (NCPR 1987, r 27(6)).

There is no need for every executor to act. A person appointed as one of several executors may not wish to act initially, but he may not want to take the irrevocable step of renouncing his right to a grant of probate.

Example 2

Alan appoints Ben and Charles as his executors. When Alan dies, Ben is working in Germany but is due to return to England in 12 months' time. Ben does not feel that he should act as executor whilst abroad and is happy to leave everything to Charles, but he does want to help in the administration if it has not been completed by the time he returns to England.

Charles should apply for the grant 'with power reserved to Ben'.

33.10 OATH FOR ADMINISTRATORS WITH WILL ANNEXED

33.10.1 Entitlement at act

As the title of this oath suggests, it is used in an estate where there is a valid will but no executor willing and able to apply for a grant of probate.

There may be no executor because:

(1) the will fails to appoint executors; or
(2) the appointment was of the testator's spouse and has failed as a result of the testator's divorce (Wills Act 1837, s 18A; see **32.2.4**);
(3) the executor has predeceased the testator;
(4) the executor has died after the testator but before taking the grant; or
(5) the executor has renounced.

33.10.2 NCPR 1987, r 20

The order of priority of the person(s) entitled to a grant of letters of administration with will annexed is governed by NCPR 1987, r 20. The rule states as follows:

'Where the deceased died on or after 1 January 1926 the person or persons entitled to a grant in respect of a will shall be determined in accordance with the following order of priority, namely—

(a) the executor...;
(b) any residuary legatee or devisee holding in trust for any other person;
(c) any other residuary legatee or devisee (including one for life) or where the residue is not wholly disposed of by the will, any person entitled to share in the undisposed of residue (including the Treasury Solicitor when claiming bona vacantia on behalf of the Crown), provided that—

(i) unless a registrar otherwise directs, a residuary legatee or devisee whose legacy or devise is vested in interest shall be preferred to one entitled on the happening of a contingency, and

(ii) where the residue is not in terms wholly disposed of, the registrar may, if he is satisfied that the testator has nevertheless disposed of the whole or substantially the whole of the known estate, allow a grant to be made to any legatee or devisee entitled to, or to share in, the estate so disposed of, without regard to the persons entitled to share in any residue not disposed of by the will;

(d) the personal representative of any residuary legatee or devisee (but not one for life, or one holding in trust for any other person), or of any person entitled to share in any residue not disposed of by the will;

(c) any other legatee or devisee (including one for life or one holding in trust for any other person) or any creditor of the deceased, provided that, unless a registrar otherwise directs, a legatee or devisee whose legacy or devise is vested in interest shall be preferred to one entitled on the happening of a contingency;

(f) the personal representative of any other legatee or devisee (but not one for life or one holding in trust for any other person) or of any creditor of the deceased.'

Clearing off

Each applicant is listed in priority. When applying for the grant, any person falling in categories (b) and below must explain on the oath why there is no applicant from a higher-ranked category. This is called 'clearing off'. A person in a lower-ranked category may apply only if there is nobody in a higher category willing and able to take the grant.

The categories will now be considered in detail with examples of clearing off.

'(a) the executor…'

NCPR 1987, r 20 in fact provides the 'order of priority for grant where deceased left a will'. This covers both grants of probate and letters of administration with the will annexed. If an executor has been appointed in the will and is able and willing to act then he has first right to a grant.

The remaining categories assume that, for whatever reason, no executor is available.

'(b) any residuary legatee or devisee holding in trust …'

Example

Arthur has died leaving a will. Although he failed to appoint executors, he left his residue to Brian and Claire on trust for Debbie. Brian and Claire are the residuary legatees (or devisees, depending on the type of trust property) and so they have first right to a grant. Clearly, Arthur was happy for them to deal with his property otherwise he would not have appointed them as trustees. They will have to state that 'no executor was appointed in the will'.

'(c) any other residuary legatee or devisee ...'

Example 1

Amanda has died leaving a will appointing Boris as her executor and giving the residuary estate to Carol, ie Carol is the residuary legatee and devisee.

Carol can apply for a grant only if Boris is unable or unwilling to act. She must 'clear off' Boris by saying, 'the executor named in the will has [renounced probate] or [predeceased the deceased]' or as the case may be.

Note: strictly it is also necessary to clear off trustees of residue (ie 'any residuary legatee or devisee holding on trust for any other person'). However, unless such trustees were specifically appointed in the will this is often not done. Such practice is acceptable to the probate registrars.

Example 2

The facts are the same as in Example 1, but Boris was appointed 'executor and trustee' and the residue was given to Carol for life.

Carol must clear off Boris in both capacities by saying, 'the executor and trustee named in the will has [renounced probate] etc ...'.

'... or ... any person entitled to share in the undisposed of residue'

If a partial intestacy arises because the will fails to dispose of all or part of the residuary estate, those people entitled to the residue by virtue of the intestacy rules (see **32.4**) may apply for a grant under NCPR 1987, r 20 but they must show why they are entitled to the grant by clearing off all persons in higher-ranked categories.

Example

Damien's will appoints Errol to be his sole executor and residuary beneficiary. Errol died last month and Damien has just died. Damien's closest living relative is his mother, Florence.

As the sole residuary beneficiary has predeceased the deceased (and the gift is not saved by any substitutional gift), the residue is undisposed of and will be distributed according to the intestacy rules. Damien has left no spouse, nor issue but is survived by his mother, Florence, who is next entitled to the property.

Florence will apply for a grant of letters of administration with will annexed by clearing off the executor. She must also establish her entitlement to the undisposed of property and, therefore, to the grant. She will say 'the executor and residuary legatee and devisee has predeceased the deceased [and the deceased died a bachelor without issue] ...'.

'(d) the PR of a deceased residuary legatee or devisee ...'

Where there is no proving executor and, for example, the residuary beneficiary survives the testator to take a vested interest in the estate but then dies without having taken the grant, that beneficiary's PR may apply for the grant. This is because the gift under the will forms part of the beneficiary's estate and needs to be collected by his PR.

Example

Gloria died last week leaving a will appointing Honor as executrix and giving the residuary estate to Ian absolutely. Honor has predeceased Gloria and Ian died yesterday. Ian's will appoints Janice as his sole executrix and beneficiary.

Janice may apply for a grant of letters of administration with will annexed to Gloria's estate. To do so the oath must clear off Honor and Ian by saying, 'the sole executrix predeceased the deceased and the sole residuary legatee and devisee named in the said will survived the deceased and has since died without having proved the said will'.

'(e) any other legatee or devisee...or any creditor of the deceased ...'

This category covers any other beneficiary under the will, for example, a specific devisee who has been left the deceased's house or a general legatee who has been left £5,000 by the deceased. It also covers creditors of the deceased.

'(f) the PR of any other legatee or devisee ... or of any creditor ...'

This category works on the same principles as category (d) above.

Beneficiary with vested interest preferred

Where there is more than one person of equal rank but one has a vested and one a contingent interest in the estate, the court generally prefers an application by the beneficiary with the vested interest.

Example

Keri's will leaves her residuary estate to her two children, Lisa and Matthew, contingent on their attaining 25 years of age. There is no executor appointed in the will and at Keri's death Lisa is 30 years old and Matthew 23 years old.

Lisa and Matthew can make a joint application but if they were to apply separately the court would prefer Lisa because Matthew's interest is still contingent.

33.10.3 Minors

A minor cannot act as administrator with will annexed, nor can he apply for a grant. His parent(s) or guardian(s) may apply for a grant 'for his use and benefit' on his behalf. The grant is limited until he attains the age of 18.

If there is a person not under a disability who is entitled in the same degree as the minor then that person will be preferred to the guardian of the minor (NCPR 1987, r 27(5)).

33.10.4 The number of administrators

Maximum number

If there are several people entitled to act as administrators, the grant will not issue to more than four of them (Supreme Court Act 1981, s 114). It is not possible for an administrator to have power reserved to him.

If a person is entitled to act as administrator but does not obtain a grant (eg because there are four other applicants), this does not affect that person's beneficial entitlement to the estate.

Number in the same category

Subject to the provisions of s 114 of the Supreme Court Act 1981 (see **33.14.1** below), where two or more people are entitled in the same degree, a grant can be made on the application of any one of them without notice to the other or others (NCPR 1987, r 27(4)).

> *Example*
>
> Jane dies leaving her residuary estate by will to her two adult brothers Ken and Larry. Jane's will does not appoint an executor. Larry does not wish to act.
>
> Ken can apply for a grant alone. This does not affect Larry's beneficial entitlement to half the estate.

Need for two administrators

If there is a valid will but no executor and the will does not dispose of all the estate, the appropriate grant is still letters of administration with will annexed. The property undisposed of by the will is distributed according to the intestacy rules (see **32.4**).

Where the will or intestacy rules create a life interest or pass property to an infant (whether the interest is vested or contingent) the court normally requires a minimum of two administrators to apply for the grant (Supreme Court Act 1981, s 114). The court may dispense with this and allow a single administrator in special limited circumstances.

> *Example 1*
>
> Max has just died leaving a valid will which:
>
> (1) appoints Nora his executor;
> (2) gives £1,000 to Olive (aged 6);
> (3) gives the residue of his estate to Peter and Paul.
>
> Nora renounces probate.
>
> Both Peter and Paul must apply for the grant because there is a minority interest, ie the legacy to Olive.

> *Example 2*
>
> Quentin's will fails to appoint an executor. He leaves his estate to his wife Rose for life, remainder to his adult son, Sam.
>
> Both Rose and Sam must apply for the grant because of Rose's life interest.

> *Example 3*
>
> Tim's will leaves his residuary estate to his friend Una, whom he has also appointed executrix. Una has predeceased Tim. Tim is divorced and has three children, Victor (21), Wendy (19), and Zena (15).
>
> Tim therefore dies partially intestate. By virtue of the intestacy rules his children take the residuary estate on the statutory trusts.

Victor and Wendy must both apply for the grant because part of the estate goes to Zena who is a minor.

33.10.5 Renunciation

Any person entitled to apply for a grant of letters of administration with will annexed can renounce in the same way as an executor, except that an administrator does not lose the right to renounce by intermeddling. Renunciation does not affect his beneficial entitlement.

33.11 OATH FOR ADMINISTRATORS

33.11.1 Entitlement to act

This oath is required if the deceased has died totally intestate.

The person or persons entitled to the grant are listed in NCPR 1987, r 22 as follows:

'(1)   Where the deceased died on or after 1 January 1926, wholly intestate, the person or persons having a beneficial interest in the estate shall be entitled to a grant of administration in the following classes in order of priority, namely—

    (a)   the surviving husband or wife;

    (b)   the children of the deceased and the issue of any deceased child who died before the deceased;

    (c)   the father and mother of the deceased;

    (d)   brothers and sisters of the whole blood and the issue of any deceased brother or sister of the whole blood who died before the deceased;

    (e)   brothers and sisters of the half blood and the issue of any deceased brother or sister of the half blood who died before the deceased;

    (f)   grandparents;

    (g)   uncles and aunts of the whole blood and the issue of any deceased uncle or aunt of the whole blood who died before the deceased;

    (h)   uncles and aunts of the half blood and the issue of any deceased uncle or aunt of the half blood who died before the deceased.

(2)   In default of any person having a beneficial interest in the estate, the Treasury Solicitor shall be entitled to a grant if he claims bona vacantia on behalf of the Crown.

(3)   If all persons entitled to a grant under the foregoing provisions of this rule have been cleared off, a grant may be made to a creditor of the deceased or to any person who, notwithstanding that he has no immediate beneficial interest in the estate, may have a beneficial interest in the event of an accretion thereto.'

Some of the descriptions of relations may require further explanation as follows.

'Children'

On an intestacy, no distinction is drawn between those who have been born legitimate, or have been adopted, or whose parents were not married.

The one exception is where a child whose parents were not married dies intestate. In such circumstances, it is presumed that his natural father and all relatives of his natural father predeceased him (Family Law Reform Act 1987, s 18(2)). This presumption can be rebutted, for example where both parents are living together or the father maintains contact with his child.

Equally entitled with the deceased's children are the children or grandchildren of any child who predeceased the deceased.

'Brothers and sisters'

Brothers and sisters of the deceased are also known as 'siblings'. A sibling is of the 'whole blood' where they share both parents in common with the deceased, and of the 'half blood' where they have only one common parent.

Example

Susan has been married twice. By Tom she had two children, Una and Victoria and by Tony she had a daughter, Wendy.

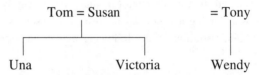

Una and Victoria are sisters of the whole blood.

Wendy is their sister of the half blood.

'Uncles and aunts'

Uncles and aunts of 'the whole blood' are the children of both grandparents of the intestate. Aunts and uncles of the 'half blood' are the children of only one of the deceased's grandparents.

Example

David has died recently and his closest living relations are his uncles, Ben and Charles. Ben and David's mother, Ann, were children of the same parents; Charles was the son of David's grandfather, Fred, and Fred's mistress, Joan.

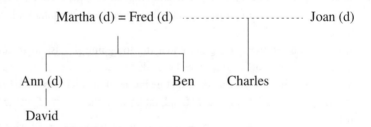

Ben is David's uncle of the whole blood.

Charles is David's uncle of the half blood.

33.11.2 Clearing off

Each category is listed in priority in NCPR 1987, r 22. Like the applicant under NCPR 1987, r 20 (see **33.10.2**), an applicant under r 22 must explain on the oath why nobody in a higher category is able to apply for the grant (again, this is called 'clearing off').

Where there is a surviving spouse and he or she is applying for the grant either alone or with others, there is nobody with a higher priority to clear off and therefore there is no need to add any clearing off words to the oath.

Where there is no surviving spouse, this fact must be stated by saying that the deceased died intestate, 'a bachelor', or 'a spinster', or 'a widower', or 'a widow', as the case may be.

Where the applicant needs to clear off categories of relation in addition to the spouse he will do so by stating that the deceased died intestate 'without issue' or 'parents' or 'brothers and sisters of the whole blood' or 'their issue' etc.

Example 1

Alice has died intestate survived by her son. Her husband died 5 years ago.

The oath will read:

INTESTATE a widow.

Example 2

Brian who never married has just died intestate aged 92 years. He is survived by his two brothers.

The oath will read:

INTESTATE a bachelor without issue or parents.

33.11.3 The need for a beneficial interest in the estate

Unless the applicant is the Treasury Solicitor or a creditor, he must have a beneficial interest in the estate (or would have such an in interest if there was an accretion to the estate) by virtue of the intestacy rules; hence there is a similarity of entitlement under NCPR 1987, r 22 and under AEA 1925, s 46 (see **32.4**).

Example 1

Clara dies intestate survived by her mother and one brother.

Only the mother can apply for the grant because she is solely and absolutely entitled to Clara's estate under the intestacy rules.

Example 2

David dies intestate survived by his wife Eve and father Fred. David's estate is valued at £300,000.

As Eve and Fred share the estate by virtue of the intestacy rules, Fred can apply for the grant if Eve does not, although Eve ranks in priority and must be cleared off if Fred applies for the grant.

Example 3

The facts are the same as in Example 2 but David's estate is £90,000. Prima facie, Fred would seem to have no interest and would therefore be unable to apply for a grant if Eve failed to do so. But Fred can apply in these circumstances on the basis that if additional assets were found in David's estate Fred would then share the estate with Eve. It is irrelevant that David's estate never actually increases above £90,000. Again, Eve ranks in priority.

33.11.4 Minors

A minor cannot act as administrator nor can he apply for a grant. The same rule as that discussed at **33.10.3** above should be applied.

33.11.5 Renunciation

A person entitled to a grant under NCPR 1987, r 22 can renounce his right to the grant in the same way as an administrator with the will annexed. If he is the only relative of the deceased with a beneficial entitlement, the grant will be made to a creditor of the deceased. Renunciation does not affect the beneficial entitlement.

Example

Graeme dies intestate survived by one brother, Henry and an uncle, Jack. Graeme owes Kirsty £100.

Henry has priority over Jack under r 22. As Jack has no beneficial interest in the estate, under the intestacy rules he cannot apply for the grant if Henry fails to do so. In that event Kirsty should apply for the grant of letters of administration.

It is common for a creditor to take the grant if the estate is insolvent.

33.11.6 The number of administrators

The rules applying to the number of administrators with will annexed apply equally to administrators of a totally intestate estate.

Maximum number

The grant will issue to a maximum of four administrators. If there are more than four people with an equal entitlement, it is not possible to have 'power reserved' to a non-proving administrator.

Number in the same category

Where two or more people are entitled in the same degree, a grant can be made on the application of any one of them without notice to the other(s).

Need for two administrators

A minimum of two administrators is generally required where the intestacy creates a life interest in favour of the surviving spouse and/or minority interests through property being held for minors on the 'statutory trusts'. The court may dispense with the need for two administrators in special circumstances.

Example 1

Grace dies intestate with an estate with a net value for probate purposes of £250,000. She is survived by her husband, Henry and her adult daughter, Ingrid.

The grant must be taken by Henry and Ingrid because the intestacy rules give Henry a life interest in part of the estate.

Example 2

John dies intestate with a net estate for probate purposes of £300,000 and is survived by his wife, Karen and children, Laura (20) and Mike (16).

Karen and Laura must take the grant. Two administrators are needed because the intestacy creates a life interest and a minority interest. Mike cannot be an administrator because he is a minor.

Example 3

Nigel dies intestate, a bachelor without issue. Both his parents are dead.

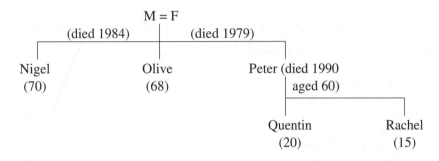

His sister and the issue of his deceased brother are equally entitled to apply for the grant as they share the estate under the intestacy rules. Both Olive and Quentin must apply because Rachel is a minor.

33.12 EFFECT OF GRANT

33.12.1 Grant of probate

A grant of probate confirms the authority of the executor(s) which stems from the will and arises from the time of the testate's death (see **33.2**).

The grant provides conclusive evidence of the title of the executor(s) and of the validity and contents of the will.

33.12.2 Grant of administration (with or without will)

A grant of administration (with or without will annexed) confers authority on the administrator and vests the deceased's property in the administrator. Until the grant is issued, the administrator has no authority to act and the deceased's property is vested in the President of the Family Division.

The grant provides conclusive evidence of the administrator's title and of the validity and contents of any will (or intestacy). Normally, the grant is not retrospective to the date of the deceased's death.

33.13 LIMITED GRANTS

A grant of representation is normally general, ie it is expressed to relate to 'all the estate which by law devolves to and vests in the PRs of the deceased'.

When necessary, a grant may be limited; for example, it may be:

(1) limited as to a specified part of the deceased's property. For example, a novelist might appoint literary executors to administer his literary estate; general executors would be responsible for his general estate;

(2) limited to settled land. Any settled land vested in the deceased is usually excepted from a general grant if the land remains settled after his death. The trustees of the settlement will submit an oath limited to the settled land;

(3) limited to a special purpose. For example, if the person entitled to apply for a grant is a minor, then application should be made by his parent(s) or guardian(s) for a grant for his use and benefits. The practice in making such grants is governed by NCPR 1987, r 2.

33.14 THE CHAIN OF REPRESENTATION AND GRANT DE BONIS NON ADMINISTRATIS

33.14.1 Introduction

If there are several proving PRs administering an estate and one dies after taking the grant but before the administration has been completed, the surviving PRs continue to act. The continuing PRs' powers remain unaffected. Where the death leaves a sole surviving PR, the court may exercise its powers to appoint an additional PR. This might happen, for example, where there is a life or minority interest and the court prefers a minimum of two PRs (Supreme Court Act 1981, s 114).

If a person entitled to be the PR (either as the executor under a will, or by virtue of NCPR 1987, r 20 or r 22) survives the deceased but then dies himself without taking out a grant of representation, AEA 1925, s 5 provides that his rights concerning the grant die with him (unless it is an exceptional case where his PR may apply for a grant under NCPR 1987, r 20).

Example 1
David dies, appointing Elizabeth as his executrix and leaving his estate to Richard. Elizabeth dies a few days after David and without having proved his will. Richard should apply for a grant of letters of administration with will annexed to David's estate.

The position is more complicated on the death of a sole or sole surviving PR if the administration is incomplete.

Example 2
Anthony died 6 months ago, appointing Edward as his sole executor.

Edward obtained a grant of probate to Anthony's estate and had begun to deal with the assets when he died. The house is on the market but unsold and the final IHT assessment cannot be agreed because tax is being paid on the house by instalments. The administration is therefore incomplete. What happens?

33.14.2 Chain of representation

The office of executor is personal to the executor appointed by the testator in his will. Because it is an office of personal trust an executor cannot assign that office (although he can appoint an attorney). However, AEA 1925, s 7 provides for the automatic transmission of that office on the death of a proving executor: 'an executor of a sole or last surviving executor of a testator is the executor of that testator'.

Unbroken chain

The chain of representation is applicable only where there is an unbroken sequence of proving executors.

> *Example*
> Colin died, leaving a will appointing Diane as his executrix.
>
> Diane proved the will and obtained a grant of probate.
>
> Diane died before she had completed the administration of Colin's estate.
>
> Diane's will appointed Eric to be her executor. If Eric applies for probate of Diane's will he automatically becomes executor of Colin's estate.
>
> It is not possible to accept the office of executor to Diane's estate and refuse to be executor by representation of Colin's estate.

AEA 1925, s 7

Section 7 provides that an executor by representation:

(1) has the same rights in respect of the testator's estate as if he was the original executor; and
(2) is, to the extent to which the testator's estate has come into his hands, answerable as if he was the original executor.

Broken chain

If for any reason there are not successive executors, the chain of representation will be broken.

> *Example 1*
> Fiona appointed Graham to be her executor. Graham obtained probate to Fiona's estate. Graham then died intestate. Graham's PR under NCPR 1987, r 22 is Ian, who obtains a grant of letters of administration to Graham's estate. Ian will not become the executor of Fiona's estate.

> *Example 2*
> John died intestate and Kelly obtained a grant of letters of administration to his estate. Kelly died leaving a will appointing Louise to be her executrix. Louise proved Kelly's will and obtained probate. Louise does not become the executrix of John's estate.

33.14.3 Grant de bonis non administratis

In situations where the chain of representation cannot apply because there are not successive proving executors, a grant de bonis non administratis must be obtained to the original estate (usually known as a 'grant de bonis non'). The grant de bonis non may be one of administration with the will or one of simple administration, depending on the circumstances.

It is issued in estates where the sole, or sole surviving, PR has died after obtaining the grant but without having completed the administration and it relates only to the unadministered part of the estate. Two requirements apply:

(1) there must have been a prior grant of probate or letters of administration to a PR who has now died; and
(2) the chain of representation must not apply.

The grant de bonis non will issue to the person who would have been entitled had the original PR never taken the grant. The order of priority will depend on NCPR 1987, r 20 or r 22 as appropriate.

33.15 CAVEATS AND CITATIONS

Caveats and citations are available under the NCPR 1987 to assist in the event of a dispute over the right to take out a grant of representation to an estate. They are designed to resolve disputes without the expense and delay of contentious proceedings.

33.15.1 Caveats (NCPR 1987, r 44)

The effect of a caveat is to prevent the issue of a grant of representation. The person lodging or entering a caveat is called a 'caveator'. A caveat might be used, for example where a beneficiary believes the executor named in the will lacks the mental capacity to act or where the validity of the will is questioned.

> *Example 1*
> The will appoints Eric as executor, gives a legacy to Ann and the residue to Ben.
>
> Eric wants to act as executor but Ann challenges his capability. Ann should enter a caveat before a grant of representation is issued so that the court can decide who should act as PR.

> *Example 2*
> On Dan's death a homemade will is found appointing Edward as executor and sole beneficiary. Freda would be entitled to Dan's estate under the intestacy rules and Freda believes the will is invalid. She should enter a caveat to prevent any grant of representation issuing until the court has decided the validity or otherwise of the will.

33.15.2 Citations (NCPR 1987, r 46)

Only executors or persons specified under NCPR 1987, r 20 or r 22 can take a grant of representation. If the person initially entitled to take the grant refuses to do so and also refuses to renounce, the estate remains unadministered and the beneficiaries are left waiting indefinitely for their inheritance. In such circumstances, a citation provides a remedy.

There are several types of citation which can be issued by the probate registry at the request of a beneficiary ('the citor').

Citation to take probate

A citation to take probate may be used where an executor has lost his right to renounce probate by intermeddling in the estate (eg by advising the deceased's bank of his death, see **33.9.3**) but has not applied for a grant of probate within 6 months of the testator's death and shows no signs of so doing. Once cited, the executor must proceed with an application for a grant of probate. If he does not (without good reason) the citor can apply to the court for an order allowing the executor to be passed over and a grant of letters of administration with will annexed to issue to the person(s) entitled under NCPR 1987, r 20.

Citation to accept or refuse a grant

A citation to accept or refuse a grant is the standard method of clearing off a person with a prior right to any type of grant who has not applied, and shows no intention of applying, for a grant. If the person cited does not take steps to take out the grant, a grant may be issued to the citor.

> *Example*
> Adam's will appoints Bert his executor and Clare the residuary beneficiary. Bert takes no steps towards administering the estate or proving the will. Clare may cite Bert to act and, if Bert does nothing, Clare may apply by virtue of NCPR 1987, r 20 for a grant of letters of administration with will annexed.

Chapter 34

ADMINISTRATION OF AN ESTATE

34.1 THE ADMINISTRATION PERIOD

Having obtained the grant of representation, the PRs have full power to undertake the administration of the estate. The work involved in administering an estate is broadly the same whether the deceased left a will or died intestate. However, in the latter case, the beneficiaries will be ascertained by application of the law of intestacy rather than from construction of the will.

The administration of an estate may be divided conveniently into five elements or stages as follows:

(1) considering the duties of and powers available to the PRs in carrying out their task;
(2) collecting the deceased's assets;
(3) paying the deceased's funeral and testamentary expenses and debts;
(4) distributing the legacies; and
(5) completing the administration and distributing the residuary estate.

All five of the above elements in the administration occur within the 'administration period'. This is the period which commences at the moment immediately following the death and ends when the PRs are in a position to vest the residue of the estate in the beneficiaries, or the trustees if a trust arises under the will or the intestacy law.

34.2 DUTIES OF THE PRs

The Administration of Estates Act 1925 (AEA 1925), s 25 (as substituted by AEA 1971, s 9) states that the PRs of a deceased person shall be under a duty to 'collect and get in the real and personal estate of the deceased and administer it according to law'. The duties to be undertaken by a PR are generally said to be onerous. A PR who accepts office by taking a grant of representation, or acting as executor, is personally liable for loss to the estate resulting from any breach of duty he commits as PR (although he is not generally liable for breaches committed by a co-PR). A breach of duty can occur in a number of ways, for example, failure to take appropriate steps to preserve the value of assets and, in consequence, the estate; or using assets to pay creditors or beneficiaries other than in accordance with the order provided by statute or by the deceased's will.

Although personally liable, the Trustee Act 1925 (TA 1925), s 61 gives the court power at its discretion to relieve a PR from liability for breach of duty if satisfied that the PR 'has acted honestly and reasonably and ought fairly to be excused for the breach'. Alternatively, an executor may be able to rely on a clause in the deceased's will providing protection from liability for mistakes made in good faith.

34.3 PROTECTION AGAINST LIABILITY

Failure to pay an unknown creditor or beneficiary is a breach of duty by the PR. As a positive step, a PR should be advised to obtain protection against personal liability to creditors or beneficiaries of whom he is unaware. This can be achieved by complying with the statutory advertisement provisions of the TA 1925, s 27, discussed at **33.3.5**.

34.4 MISSING BENEFICIARIES

Breach of duty will also arise if PRs, being aware of the existence of a beneficiary, fail to take him into account when distributing the estate. TA 1925, s 27 (mentioned above) will not provide protection for the PRs in these circumstances.

PRs should, therefore, be advised to obtain protection by application to the court for a *Benjamin* Order (*Re Benjamin* [1902] 1 Ch 723) permitting them to distribute the deceased's estate on a given basis. This will normally permit distribution on the assumption that the missing beneficiary predeceased the testator leaving no issue. If the person concerned is later proved to have survived the deceased, he, or his PRs, may recover his share of the estate from the other beneficiaries; however, the PRs are protected from personal liability on the basis of the order.

Before making an order, the court will require evidence that the fullest possible enquiries were made to trace the missing person. If the court considers the advertisements made in addition to the TA 1925, s 27 are insufficient it will direct that further enquiry be made.

34.5 INHERITANCE (PROVISION FOR FAMILY AND DEPENDANTS) ACT 1975

PRs will be personally liable where an applicant under the I(PFD)A 1975 successfully obtains an order for 'reasonable financial provision' from the estate. They can protect themselves against such liability by distributing the estate more than 6 months following the date of the grant of representation. If earlier distribution is required, PRs should ensure they retain sufficient assets to satisfy an order should an applicant be successful within 6 months of the grant.

34.6 ADMINISTRATIVE POWERS OF PRs

34.6.1 Statutory powers of PRs and trustees

PRs have a wide range of powers which they may exercise in carrying out the administration of an estate. These powers are largely conferred on them by statute. The AEA 1925 gives some powers specifically to PRs. TA 1925 and the Trustee Act 2000 (TA 2000) confer powers on trustees for use in administering a trust. Since 'trustee' in the TA 1925 and TA 2000 includes a 'personal representative', PRs (executors and administrators) have these powers as well.

The TA 2000, modifies in various ways powers previously available to PRs and trustees. The main purpose of the Act is to remedy certain deficiencies by bringing the law into line with what has been regarded as good drafting practice for some years.

The TA 2000 deals with powers to invest trust property, appoint agents and nominees, remuneration of trustees (and PRs) and to insure trust property. A duty of care requires trustees (and PRs) when exercising many of their powers under the Act to exercise the skill and care reasonable in the circumstances, having regard to any special knowledge or expertise of the trustee.

The main changes made by the TA 2000 are noted in context in the paragraphs which follow.

34.6.2 Powers granted by a will

Modification of statutory powers

Many of the statutory powers may be modified by express provision contained within a will. If there are no executors who prove the will but the will is proved by administrators with the will annexed, they also have these modified powers available to them.

Additional powers

In addition to modification of statutory powers, a will often grants powers which are not available at law, for example power to advance capital to a surviving spouse to whom a life interest has been given, or to lend capital to such a person; in the absence of any such express power, the executors have no implied power to advance or lend capital to the surviving spouse.

Will drafting

The desirability of modification or extension of implied powers, and the provision of further express powers, will have been considered when drafting the will. It is good drafting practice for a will to set out in full all the powers of the executors so that the position is clear on the face of the will, thus avoiding the possibility of a particular power available at law being overlooked. Whether the following powers are available to the PRs at all, or in modified form, will depend on the terms of the particular will and the circumstances of the estate.

34.6.3 Provisions concerning the administration of the estate

The provisions which follow may be included in the will to simplify the administration of the estate. However, if the terms of the will are short and simple, the draftsman may have decided not to extend the executors' statutory powers.

Power to appropriate assets without consent of beneficiary

THE STATUTORY PROVISIONS

AEA 1925, s 41 gives PRs the power to appropriate any part of the estate in or towards satisfaction of any legacy or any other interest or share in the estate provided that the appropriation does not prejudice any specific beneficiary. Thus, if the will gives a pecuniary legacy to a beneficiary, the PRs may allow that beneficiary to take chattels or other assets in the estate up to the value of his legacy, provided that these assets have not been specifically bequeathed by the will. The section provides that the beneficiary (or his parent or guardian if he is a minor) must consent to the appropriation.

SPECIMEN CLAUSE

> **Power to exercise the power of appropriation conferred by s 41 of the Administration of Estates Act 1925 without obtaining any of the consents required by that section.**

This provision is commonly included in order to relieve the PRs of the duty to obtain formal consent. Nevertheless, the PRs would informally consult the beneficiaries concerned.

Power to insure

THE STATUTORY PROVISION

TA 1925, s 19 (as substituted by TA 2000, s 34) gives PRs and trustees power to insure trust property against any risks, to the full value of the property and to pay premiums out of either capital or income.

SPECIMEN CLAUSE

> **Power to insure any asset of my estate on such terms as they think fit and to pay premiums at their discretion out of income or capital and to use any insurance money received either to restore the assets or as if it were the proceeds of sale.**

Power to accept receipts from or on behalf of minors

THE STATUTORY PROVISION

Under the general law, an unmarried minor cannot give a good receipt for capital or income. A married minor can give a good receipt for income only (LPA 1925, s 21). AEA 1925, s 42 gives PRs the power to appoint trustees to hold a legacy for a minor who is absolutely entitled under the will. The receipt of the appointed trustees (who could be the child's parents or guardians) discharges the PRs from further liability. This power does not apply where the child has a contingent interest.

EXTENDED STATUTORY POWER

Where a specific or pecuniary legacy is left to a minor, the will may include a clause allowing the PRs to accept the receipt of the child's parent or guardian or of the child himself if over 16 years old. Such a provision avoids the need for a formal appointment of trustees under s 42. The provision may be incorporated into the legacy itself or may be included in a list of powers in the will.

34.6.4 Provisions concerning the administration of a trust

At the end of the administration of an estate, the PRs may be able to distribute the residue to the beneficiaries, thus completing their task. However, in some cases distribution will be delayed and the PRs will hold the residue (or part of it) as trustees. This may happen:

(1) where the beneficiary is a minor, and so cannot give a valid receipt to the PRs;

(2) where the beneficiary has a contingent interest, and so cannot be given the property until the interest vests; or

(3) where the interests in the property are divided, for example between income and capital.

In any of these cases, the statutory powers of the trustees may also be extended.

Power to invest trust funds

THE STATUTORY PROVISION

Under general law, trustees have a duty to invest trust money. TA 2000, s 3 gives trustees a 'general power of investment' enabling them to invest as if they were absolutely entitled to the trust property themselves. This wide power excludes investment in land, other than by mortgage, but further powers in relation to land are contained in s 8 (see below). In exercising this power, trustees are required to take proper advice and to review investments of the trust from time to time. They must have regard to the standard investment criteria, namely the suitability to the trust of any particular investment and to the need for diversification of investments of the trust.

SPECIMEN CLAUSE

> **My trustees shall have power to invest trust money and to transpose investments with the same unrestricted freedom in their choice of investments as if they were an absolute beneficial owner.**

Power to purchase land

THE STATUTORY PROVISIONS

TA 2000, s 8 gives trustees power to acquire freehold or leasehold land for 'investment, for occupation by a beneficiary or for any other reason'. When exercising their power, the trustees are given 'all the powers of an absolute owner in relation to the land'.

SPECIMEN CLAUSE

> **My trustees may apply trust money in the purchase or improvement of any freehold or leasehold dwelling-house and may permit any such dwelling-house to be used as a residence by any person with an interest in my residuary estate upon such terms and conditions as my trustees may think fit.**

This clause gives trustees an express power to use trust money to buy or improve land for use as a residence by the beneficiaries. It leaves the question of responsibility for the burden of repairs and other outgoings to the discretion of the trustees.

Power to sell personalty

Trustees holding land in their trust have the power to sell it under their powers of an absolute owner (see above). However, there is some doubt whether trustees who do not hold other assets on an express trust for sale have power to sell personalty. Before 1996, it was usual to impose an express trust for sale over residue because otherwise, if residue included land, the Settled Land Act 1925 could apply to the land and a strict settlement could arise. Since 1 January 1996, no new strict settlements can be created. This means the main reason for creating an express trust for sale has gone, leaving the doubt about trustees' power to sell personalty. For this reason, some wills may continue to impose an express trust for sale over residue. The alternative solution is to include power in the will (among the administrative provisions) giving the trustees express power to sell personalty.

SPECIMEN CLAUSE

Power to sell mortgage or charge any asset of my estate as it they were an absolute beneficial owner.

Power of maintenance

THE STATUTORY PROVISIONS

Where trustees are holding a fund for a minor beneficiary, TA 1925, s 31 gives them power to use income they receive for the minor's maintenance education or benefit.

TA 1925, s 31 (as amended by TA 2000) states (inter alia):

'(1) Where any property is held by trustees in trust for any person for any interest whatsoever, whether vested or contingent, then, subject to any prior interests or charges affecting that property—

(i) during the infancy of any such person, if his interest so long continues, the trustees may, at their sole discretion, pay to his parent or guardian, if any, or otherwise apply for or towards his maintenance, education, or benefit, the whole or such part, if any, of the income of that property as may, in all the circumstances, be reasonable, whether or not there is—

(a) any other fund applicable to the same purpose; or

(b) any person bound by law to provide for his maintenance or education; and

(ii) if such person on attaining the age of eighteen years has not a vested interest in such income, the trustees shall thenceforth pay the income of that property and of any accretion thereto under subsection (2) of this section to him, until he either attains a vested interest therein or dies, or until failure of his interest:

Provided that, in deciding whether the whole or any part of the income of the property is during a minority to be paid or applied for the purposes aforesaid, the trustees shall have regard to the age of the infant and his requirements and generally to the circumstances of the case, and in particular to what other income, if any, is applicable for the same purposes; and where trustees have notice that the income of more than one fund is applicable for those purposes, then, so far as practicable, unless the entire income of the funds is paid or applied as aforesaid or the court otherwise directs, a proportionate part only of the income of each fund shall be so paid or applied.

(2) During the infancy of any such person, if his interest so long continues, the trustees shall accumulate all the residue of that income by investing it, and any profits from so investing it, from time to time in authorised investments, and shall hold those accumulations ... .

(3) This section applies in the case of a contingent interest only if the limitation or trust carries the intermediate income of the property ... .'

APPLICATION OF SECTION 31

Example – Trust 1

The trustees are holding £100,000 for Mary (16) who has a vested interest in the capital. Under s 31(1), the trustees have the power to pay all or part of the income to Mary's parent or guardian or 'otherwise apply' it for Mary's maintenance, education or benefit. This could include paying bills (eg school fees) directly.

The power is limited to so much of the income as is 'reasonable'. The proviso directs the trustees to take into account various further points such as Mary's age and requirements and whether any other fund is available for her maintenance.

Section 31(2) directs the trustees to accumulate any income not used for maintenance and invest it.

Example – Trust 2

The trustees are holding £100,000 for Dora (14) who has a contingent interest in the capital. They may pay or apply the income for Dora's maintenance, education or benefit in the same way as the trustees of Trust 1.

The trustees are holding £100,000 for Charles (19) who also has a contingent interest in the capital. Section 31(1)(ii) directs them to pay all the income to Charles until his interest vests (ie until he is 21) when he will receive the capital, or fails (ie if he dies before he is 21). The same will apply to the income from Dora's share from her 18th birthday onwards.

Example – Trust 3

The trustees are holding £200,000 for Henry for life with remainder to Stephen (10). They have no power to use the income for Stephen's benefit as Henry is entitled to it. If Henry dies while Stephen is still a minor, s 31 will apply to allow the trustees to apply income for Stephen's maintenance etc during the period from Henry's death until Stephen is 18 (when they will transfer the capital to Stephen).

EXTENDING SECTION 31 – SPECIMEN CLAUSE

Section 31 of the Trustee Act 1925 shall apply to the income of my estate as if the words 'as the trustees shall in their absolute discretion think fit' were substituted for the words 'as in all the circumstances be reasonable' in paragraph (i) of subsection (1) thereof and the proviso to subsection (1) had been omitted and as if the age of 21 years were substituted for all references to the age of 18 wherever they occur in s 31 (references to 'infancy' being construed accordingly).

The clause begins by removing the 'reasonable' limitation in s 31. It gives the trustees complete discretion over whether to pay or apply income for minor beneficiaries and over how much income they pay or apply.

Secondly, it removes the right for a contingent beneficiary to receive all the income from the age of 18. The trustees' discretion under s 31 to pay or apply income for maintenance or to accumulate any surplus will continue until the beneficiary is 21. Thus in Trust 2 the trustees would have a discretion over the payment of income to Charles even though he is over 18.

Power to advance capital

THE STATUTORY PROVISIONS

TA 1925, s 32 allows trustees in certain circumstances to permit a beneficiary with an interest in capital to have the benefit of part of his capital entitlement sooner than he would receive it under the basic provisions of the trust.

Section 32 states:

'(1) Trustees may at any time or times pay or apply any capital money subject to a trust, for the advancement or benefit, in such manner as they may, in their absolute discretion, think fit, of any person entitled to the capital of the trust property or of any share thereof, whether absolutely or contingently on his attaining any specified age ... and whether in possession or in remainder or reversion ...

Provided that—

(a)   the money so paid or applied for the advancement or benefit of any person shall not exceed altogether in amount one-half of the presumptive or vested share or interest of that person in the trust property; and

(b)   if that person is or becomes absolutely and indefeasibly entitled to a share in the trust property the money so paid or applied shall be brought into account as part of such share; and

(c)   no such payment or application shall be made so as to prejudice any person entitled to any prior life or other interest, whether vested or contingent, in the money paid or applied unless such person is in existence and of full age and consents in writing to such payment or application.'

APPLICATION OF SECTION 32

Example – Trust 1

Mary has a vested interest in the £100,000 capital. Section 32 allows the trustees to release some of the capital for Mary's benefit. 'Benefit' is widely construed: money could be used to pay educational or living expenses. The amount the trustees may advance is limited to one half of Mary's entitlement, ie £50,000.

Example – Trust 2

Charles and Dora have contingent interests in the capital, their presumptive shares being £100,000 each. Section 32 applies to allow the trustees to release up to £50,000 for the benefit of either beneficiary. The trustees could give money directly to Charles as he is old enough to give a valid receipt. The power applies even though the interests of Charles and Dora are contingent. If either beneficiary dies before the age of 21 there is no right to recover any advance even though that beneficiary's interest in capital has failed.

Section 32(1)(b) requires advances to be brought into account on final distribution. If the trustees give £50,000 to Charles now, he will receive £50,000 less than Dora when the fund is finally distributed to them.

Example – Trust 3

Henry has only an interest in income and s 32 does not permit the release of capital to him. The section does apply to Stephen's vested interest in remainder, and permits the trustees to apply up to £100,000 (half his interest) for Stephen's benefit.

Such an advance would prejudice Henry since his income would be substantially reduced. Section 32(1)(c) provides that no advance may be made without Henry's written consent.

EXTENDING SECTION 32 – SPECIMEN CLAUSE 1

Power to apply for the benefit of any beneficiary as my trustees think fit the whole or any part of the share of my residuary estate to which that beneficiary is absolutely or presumptively entitled and I leave it within the discretion of my trustees whether and to what extent the beneficiary shall bring into account any payments received under this clause.

This clause extends the limit in s 32(1)(a) to the full amount of the beneficiary's share. Up to £100,000 could be advanced for Mary (in Trust 1) or for Charles and Dora (in Trust 2). In Trust 3, the whole fund could be advanced for Stephen provided that Henry consents.

The second part of the clause supersedes s 32(1)(b) and means that, if in Trust 2 £50,000 was advanced to Charles, the trustees could on distribution still divide the remaining fund equally between Charles and Dora.

EXTENDING SECTION 32 – SPECIMEN CLAUSE 2

Power to pay or apply capital money from my residuary estate to any extent to or for the benefit of my husband.

Power to advance capital money from my residuary estate to my husband by way of loan to any extent upon such terms and conditions as my trustees may in their absolute discretion think fit.

These provisions would permit the trustees in Trust 3 to give or lend capital from the fund to Henry even though he has only an interest in income, not capital. Such a clause may be included to give more flexibility in case the income proves insufficient for Henry's needs. Henry still remains dependent on the discretion of the trustees.

Power to accept receipts from and on behalf of minors

THE STATUTORY PROVISIONS

Where a trust arises in favour of a beneficiary who is a minor, the trustees have statutory powers of maintenance and advancement under ss 31 and 32 of the TA 1925. Section 31 specifically allows the trustees to pay income to the child's parent or guardian or 'otherwise apply' it for the child's maintenance, education or benefit. Similarly, s 32 empowers the trustees to pay 'or apply' capital for the beneficiary's advancement or benefit. Thus the trustees will have no difficulty in obtaining a good receipt when exercising these powers.

EXTENDING THE STATUTORY POWER – SPECIMEN CLAUSE

Power in any case where my trustees have an obligation or discretion under the provisions of my will or under the general law to pay income or capital to or for the benefit of a minor to make payment either to a parent or guardian of the minor or to the minor personally if at least sixteen years old so that their respective receipts shall be a full discharge to my trustees who shall not be required to see to the application of any income or capital so paid.

If the testator wishes to give the trustees a wider power, a general provision may have been included in his will, which may even allow them to make payments to the child himself.

This clause would apply to any specific or pecuniary legacies to minor beneficiaries as well as to the interest of any minor under a trust.

Control of trustees by beneficiaries

TLATA 1996, s 19 provides that, where beneficiaries are sui juris and together entitled to the whole fund, they may direct the trustees to retire and appoint new trustees of the beneficiaries' choice. This means that in a case where the beneficiaries could by agreement end the trust under the rule in *Saunders v Vautier* (1841) 4 Beav 115, they now have the option of allowing the trust to continue with trustees of their own choice. The provision may be expressly excluded by the testator. If, under the terms of the trust, the position could arise where all the beneficiaries are in existence and aged over 18 but the trust has not ended, the testator may wish to prevent the beneficiaries from choosing their own trustees.

SPECIMEN CLAUSE

> **The provisions of section 19 of the Trusts of Land and Appointment of Trustees Act 1996 shall not apply to any trust created by this will so that no beneficiary shall have the right to require the appointment or retirement of any trustee or trustees.**

Trusts of land

The TLATA 1996 gives special powers (see below) to a beneficiary under a trust of land who has an interest in possession. If, under the terms of the will, a trust with an interest in possession could arise the will may amend those powers. The Act does not define 'interest in possession', so it presumably has its usual meaning; a beneficiary has an interest in possession if he is entitled to claim the income of the fund as it arises (normally either because he has a life interest or because he is over 18 and entitled to claim income under TA 1925, s 31).

DUTY TO CONSULT BENEFICIARIES

Trustees exercising any function relating to the land must consult any beneficiary who is of full age and beneficially entitled to an interest in possession in the land and, so far as consistent with the 'general interest of the trust', give effect to the wishes of any such beneficiary (TLATA 1996, s 11). The duty to consult may be excluded by the will.

SPECIMEN CLAUSE

> **The provisions of section 11 of the Trusts of Land and Appointment of Trustees Act 1996 shall not apply so that it shall not be necessary for my trustees to consult any beneficiaries before carrying out any function relating to land.**

BENEFICIARY'S RIGHTS OF OCCUPATION

A beneficiary with a beneficial interest in possession, even if not of full age, has the right to occupy land subject to the trust if the purposes of the trust include making the land available for occupation by him or if the trustees acquired the land in order to make it so available (TLATA 1996, s 12). There is no power to exclude s 12, but a declaration that the purpose of the trust is not for the occupation of land may be included in the will.

SPECIMEN CLAUSE

> **The purposes of any trust created by this will do not include making land available for occupation of any beneficiary [although my trustees have power to do so if they wish].**

The apportionment rules

One of the duties of trustees is to ensure that a fair balance is kept between the interests of the beneficiaries. This is particularly important where different beneficiaries are entitled to income and capital, for example where property is left on trust for X for life with remainder to Y as in Trust 3 above. The trustees must ensure that the investments they choose produce a reasonable income for X, the life tenant, and preserve the capital reasonably safely for Y, the remainderman.

THE EQUITABLE RULES

The equitable rules to preserve a fair balance between the life tenant and the remainderman derive from *Howe v Dartmouth* (1820) 7 Ves 137 and *Allhusen v Whittell* (1867) LR 4 Eq 295. Although the even-handed result of applying these rules may be desirable, in practice the calculations required by the rules are complex and the time and expense involved is rarely justified. Thus it is usual to exclude the rules when drafting life interest trusts.

APPORTIONMENT ACT 1870

The Apportionment Act 1870, s 2 provides that income such as rent and dividends is to be treated as accruing from day to day and apportioned accordingly. Thus, where assets in the estate produce income (such as dividends on shares) which is received after death but relates to a period partly before and partly after death, the income must be apportioned. The part accruing before death is capital, while that accruing after death is income. In addition, the Apportionment Act 1870 applies to any specific gift of an income-producing asset, and to a contingent gift where the beneficiary is entitled to income but dies before the contingency is fulfilled.

These apportionments are very inconvenient where an estate or trust includes many shareholdings paying dividends in relation to different periods and so it is usual to exclude the Act, particularly in wills which create life interest trusts.

EXCLUDING THE APPORTIONMENT RULES – SPECIMEN CLAUSE

> **Power to treat as income all the income from any part of my estate whatever the period in respect of which it may accrue and to disregard the Apportionment Act 1870 [and the rules of equity relating to apportionment including those known as the rules in *Howe v Dartmouth* and *Allhusen v Whittell* in all their branches].**

This clause is appropriate in a will which creates a life interest trust. It is intended to exclude the application of all the apportionment rules described above. In a will containing a specific gift of an income-producing asset or a contingent gift of residue, the clause could be included with the omission of the words in square brackets.

34.6.5 Miscellaneous additional powers

Charging clause

BACKGROUND LAW

The rule of equity that a trustee may not profit from his trust applies both to trustees and executors. Its effect is that an executor or trustee may claim only out-of-pocket expenses and may not charge for time spent in performing his office.

TA 2000, ss 28–31 have made various changes to the general rule of law governing the remuneration of 'professional' trustees, including the following.

The common law rule requiring an express charging clause to be strictly construed against the trustee is reversed by TA 2000, s 28(2). Previously, only if the remuneration clause so provided could a professional trustee charge and be paid for services which a lay person could have provided personally.

In any case where a professional executor or trustee is appointed such as a bank, a firm of solicitors, an individual solicitor or an accountant, a power to charge should be included in the will.

POWER TO CHARGE – SPECIMEN CLAUSE

> **Any of my trustees being a solicitor or other person engaged in any profession or business may charge and be paid his usual professional charges for work done by him or his firm in the administration of my estate and the trusts arising under my will including acts which a trustee not engaged in any profession or business could have done personally.**

POWER TO APPOINT A TRUST CORPORATION – SPECIMEN CLAUSE

> **Power to appoint a trust corporation to be the sole trustee or one of the trustees of my will upon such terms and conditions in all respects as may be acceptable to the corporation so appointed.**

Provision of this latter kind is not commonly included in practice. Its purpose is to ensure that, if individual trustees wish to retire and no substitutes can readily be found, a bank (or other trust corporation) may be appointed even though there may be minor beneficiaries who are unable to give the required consent to the bank's usual terms and conditions, particularly in relation to charging.

TA 2000, s 29 implies a charging clause into non-charitable trusts where no express provision exists for the remuneration of the trustees. Trust corporations and other professional trustees are entitled to receive 'reasonable remuneration' (defined by TA 2000, s 29(2)) for services provided by them. However, this entitlement is not available to a sole professional trustee and, in other cases, depends on the agreement in writing of the co-trustees.

POWER TO CARRY ON BUSINESS

Where an estate includes a business which was run by the deceased as a sole (unincorporated) trader, the powers of the PRs to run the business are limited. For example, they may only run the business with a view to selling it as a going concern and may use only those assets employed in the business at the date of death. These powers may be extended by will, although in practice PRs are unlikely to wish to involve themselves in the detailed running of a business. It may be preferable to bequeath the business by specific legacy.

POWER TO EMPLOY AGENTS

TA 2000, ss 11–15 replace in similar but clearer terms the provisions of TA 1925, s 23(1) by allowing non-charitable trustees to delegate to agents any or all of their 'delegable functions'. Functions personal to the trustees which cannot be delegated include:

- decisions on distributing trust property to beneficiaries;
- allocation of fees or payments to income or capital;
- appointment of trustees;
- appointment of nominees or custodians of trust assets.

Only in the case of delegation of their asset management function is agreement in writing required.

A trustee who satisfies the duty of care in TA 2000, s 1 in relation to the appointment and subsequent review of the appointment of an agent is not liable for the acts and defaults of the appointee. Typically, this power will be used by PRs to employ estate agents, stockbrokers or bankers to carry out executive functions in relation to the administration. For example PRs may instruct estate agents to sell the deceased's house or stockbrokers to value shares for IHT purposes.

DELEGATION BY POWER OF ATTORNEY

TA 1925, s 25, as substituted by the Trustee Delegation Act 1999, s 5, allows trustees and PRs to delegate by power of attorney the exercise of any of the powers and discretions vested in them for a period not exceeding 12 months. However, in this case, the PRs remain liable for the acts of the delegate as if they were their own acts.

This provision is often used by PRs who, having obtained their grant, find that they are unable to be involved personally in the administration for some temporary reason, such as absence abroad on business or on holiday. If, before taking out the grant, a long absence is anticipated, the better course of action would be for the PR to renounce his right to a grant or for others to take a grant reserving power to any absentee executor. It is too late to renounce or reserve power if the grant has already been obtained and, in particular, if the PR has intermeddled in the estate.

34.7 COLLECTING THE DECEASED'S ASSETS

34.7.1 Property devolving on the PRs

At law, the real and personal estate to which a person is entitled at death devolves on the PRs. It is this property which the PRs should collect and administer for the beneficiaries. In order to collect the property, the PRs generally produce their grant of representation to whoever is holding the various assets, for example to the deceased's bank or building society. If the bank manager is holding share certificates or documents of title to land, these also will be handed over to the PRs once the grant has been produced. In most cases, an office copy grant will be accepted as evidence of title.

In some cases, a grant is not required to collect certain assets. As explained at **33.4.1**, it may be possible to realise assets without production of a grant under the Administration of Estates (Small Payments) Act 1965.

382 Pervasive and Core Topics

Property not passing to the PRs passes on the death according to its own rules of succession, as described below.

34.7.2 Property not devolving on the PRs

The following examples illustrate types of property which do not devolve on the PRs and which therefore will not pass under any will or under the intestacy law.

Life interest

> *Example*
> Terry died some years ago having by his will left property to Henry and Ian on trust for sale 'for Andrew for life, remainder for Ben'. Andrew has recently died. Assuming Ben is sui juris, Henry and Ian will transfer the property to him in accordance with the terms of Terry's will.

Joint tenancy

> *Example*
> Alan and Brian own property as beneficial joint tenants at law and in equity. On Alan's death his interest passes by operation of the right of survivorship to Brian the surviving joint tenant.

Policy held in trust for others

As explained at **33.4.3**, any proceeds of an insurance policy written in trust for third parties, or written under the Married Women's Property Act 1882, s 11 for the benefit of the deceased's spouse and/or children, will be paid to the trustees of the policy on proof of death, usually by production of the death certificate. The trustees will then distribute the proceeds among the beneficiaries in accordance with the trusts of the policy.

Pension schemes

Lump sums payable at the discretion of trustees under a pension scheme (eg death in service benefits payable under an occupational pension scheme established by the deceased's former employers) do not devolve on the deceased's PRs and do not form part of his estate for succession purposes. In exercising their discretion as to payment, the trustees will have regard to any 'letter of wishes' given to them by the deceased person during his lifetime; however, they are not bound to give effect to these wishes (see **33.4.3**).

34.8 PAYING THE DECEASED'S FUNERAL AND TESTAMENTARY EXPENSES AND DEBTS

34.8.1 Preliminary considerations

Immediate sources of money

As soon as monies can be collected from the deceased's bank or building society, or realised through insurance policies etc, the PRs should begin to pay the deceased's outstanding debts and the funeral account. Administration expenses, for example estate agents' and valuers' fees, will arise during the course of administration of the estate and will have to be settled from time to time while the administration is proceeding.

Repayment of loan to pay IHT

It may be necessary to raise money to repay a loan from the deceased's bank to pay IHT to obtain the grant. If an undertaking has been given to the bank in connection with the loan, it will probably be a 'first proceeds' undertaking. This means that the PRs must use money first realised by them during the administration to repay the bank. Failure to do so will be a breach of the terms of the undertaking.

Which assets to sell?

The PRs must take considerable care when deciding which assets they will sell to raise money for payment of the various outgoings from the deceased's estate. A number of points must be addressed when making their decision including the matters set out below.

PROVISIONS OF THE DECEASED'S WILL

The will may direct from which part of the deceased's estate the debts, funeral account, testamentary and administration expenses should be paid; usually they will be paid from the residue. In the absence of such direction, the PRs must follow the statutory rules for the incidence of liabilities as outlined below. In any event, it will be generally incorrect for PRs to sell property given specifically by will (eg a gift of the testator's valuable stamp collection to his nephew) unless all other assets in the estate have been exhausted in payment of the debts etc.

THE BENEFICIARIES' WISHES

Where possible, the wishes of the beneficiaries of the residuary estate should be respected by the PRs. Although the PRs have power to sell any assets in the residuary estate, it is clearly appropriate that the residuary beneficiaries should be consulted before any sale takes place. Generally, beneficiaries have clear views as to which assets they desire to be retained for transfer to them; other assets may be sold by the PRs to raise the necessary money, possibly following receipt of professional advice as to particular sales.

TAX CONSEQUENCES

Before selling assets, the PRs should consider the amount of any capital gains (or losses) likely to arise as a result of the sale, and the availability of any exemptions, etc. Full use should be made of the annual exemption for CGT. If assets are to be sold for a loss (compared to their value at the date of death) CGT loss relief may be available for the PRs, as may 'loss relief' for IHT purposes. An explanation of these reliefs is contained at **34.10.6**.

Financial Services Act 1986

To decide whether a particular activity by the PRs, for example, advice on sales of assets to raise money to pay debts and funeral expenses, gives rise to investment business within the Financial Services Act 1986, three questions must be considered.

(1) Is the asset an 'investment'?
(2) Is the solicitor carrying on a listed activity?

(3) Does an exclusion apply?

34.8.2 Funeral and testamentary expenses and debts

Funeral expenses

Reasonable funeral expenses are payable from the deceased's estate. In all cases, it is a question of fact what funeral expenses are reasonable.

Testamentary expenses

The phrase 'testamentary and administration expenses' is not defined in the AEA 1925, but through case-law it is generally considered to mean expenses incident to the proper performance of the duties of a PR. The phrase will include:

(1) the costs of obtaining the grant;
(2) the costs of collecting in and preserving the deceased's assets;
(3) the costs of administering the deceased's estate, for example solicitors' fees for acting for the PRs, valuers' fees incurred by PRs in valuing the deceased's stocks and shares or other property; and
(4) any IHT payable on death on the deceased's property in the UK which vests in the PRs (IHTA 1984, s 211).

34.8.3 Administration of assets: solvent estate

The rules applying to the payment of funeral and testamentary expenses and debts depend on whether the estate is solvent or insolvent. The insolvent estate is considered at **34.8.5**.

AEA 1925, s 34(3)

Section 34(3) of the AEA 1925 states:

> 'Where the estate of a deceased person is solvent his real and personal estate shall, subject to rules of court and the provisions hereinafter contained as to charges on property of the deceased, and to the provisions, if any, contained in his will, be applicable towards the discharge of the funeral, testamentary and administration expenses, debts and liabilities payable thereout in the order mentioned in Part II of the First Schedule to this Act.'

AEA 1925, s 34(3) has an important bearing on the payment of funeral and testamentary expenses and debts from any estate. The following points can be established:

'PART II OF THE FIRST SCHEDULE'

Part II of the First Schedule lays out an order which the PRs must follow when deciding which part of the deceased's estate should be used for the purposes of payment of the funeral and testamentary expenses and debts. Under the order generally, assets forming part of the residue are to be used before using property given to specific legatees.

'SUBJECT ... TO'

However, the effect of the proviso 'subject to' is that the operation of s 34(3) is expressly subject to two important rules or provisions, as follows:

(1) AEA 1925, s 35, which deals with secured debts, ie debts owing by the deceased which are charged on particular items of property, for example a loan secured by legal mortgage on the deceased's house. The effect of this rule is that the property passes under the will to the beneficiary subject to the charge which is thus not paid from residue.

(2) Any provisions in the deceased's will which have the effect of varying the provisions implied by AEA 1925, ss 34(3) and/or 35. Clearly, no contrary provision is possible where the deceased has died intestate. In such cases the terms of ss 34(3) and 35 should be followed by the administrators when administering the assets of the intestate's estate.

34.8.4 Contrary provision in the will

Clauses showing contrary provision

Before paying the debts and expenses, the PRs must construe the will to ascertain whether the testator has indicated the necessary contrary intention to oust AEA 1925, ss 34(3) and 35.

EXTRACT FROM TOM SMITH'S WILL – SPECIMEN CLAUSES

> **3. I GIVE all my freehold property situate at and known as 3 Tunsgate Weyford aforesaid to my sister Susan absolutely and I DIRECT that any and all taxes payable by reason of my death in respect of such property and also any mortgage debt or charge affecting such property or any part thereof at the time of my death shall be paid out of the residue of my estate in exoneration of the said property.**
>
> **4. I GIVE all my estate both real and personal whatsoever and wheresoever not hereby or by any codicil hereto otherwise specifically disposed of (hereinafter called 'my residuary estate') unto my trustees UPON TRUST to raise and discharge thereout my debts and funeral and testamentary expenses and all legacies given hereby or by any codicil hereto and any and all taxes payable by reason of my death in respect of property given free of tax and subject thereto UPON TRUST to pay and divide the same equally between....**

Effect of the clauses

Clauses 3 and 4 provide adequate express instructions from Tom Smith as to the payment of debts etc. All outgoings are to be paid from the fund of general residue described as 'my residuary estate' and ss 34(3) and 35 will not apply. The operation of such a clause is illustrated in the following example.

> *Example*
>
> Tom's will includes the clauses mentioned above. His sister Susan inherits 3 Tunsgate and his children inherit residue.
>
> His house is worth £200,000 (subject to a mortgage of £50,000). Debts, funeral and testamentary expenses (including IHT on 3 Tunsgate) amount to £100,000. Residue is £500,000.

Distribution of the estate

	£	£		Beneficiary
House		<u>200,000</u>	to	Susan
Residue		500,000		
less: mortgage	50,000			
debts etc	<u>100,000</u>			
		<u>(150,000)</u>		
		350,000	to	children

Other clauses showing contrary provision

Clause 4 quoted above contains a trust of the residuary estate with a direction for the payment of outgoings before distribution to the beneficiaries. A will which leaves the residuary estate to a beneficiary 'subject to' or 'after payment of' the funeral and testamentary expenses and debts (but without creating a trust) would also be construed as providing contrary intention varying the implied provisions.

34.8.5 The insolvent estate

Meaning of insolvency

An estate is insolvent if the assets are insufficient to discharge in full the funeral, testamentary and administration expenses, debts and liabilities. In such cases, the creditors will not be paid in full (or at all) and the beneficiaries under the will or the intestacy provisions may receive nothing from the estate. In doubtful cases, the PRs should administer the estate as if it is insolvent. Failure to administer an insolvent estate in accordance with the statutory order is a breach of duty by the PRs.

In the case of an insolvent estate which is being administered by the deceased's PRs out of court (this being the most common method of administration), the order of distribution in the Administration of Insolvent Estates of Deceased Persons Order 1986 should be followed.

Secured creditors, for example those holding a mortgage or charge over the deceased's property, are in a better position than unsecured creditors in that they may (inter alia) realise the security, ie sell the property by exercising a power of sale as mortgagee or chargee.

34.9 PAYING THE LEGACIES

34.9.1 Introduction

Once the funeral, testamentary and administration expenses and debts have been paid, or at least adequately provided for by setting aside sufficient assets for the purpose, the PRs should consider discharging the gifts arising on the death, other than the gifts of the residuary estate. They may also consider making interim distributions to the residuary beneficiaries on account of their entitlement.

34.9.2 Specific legacies

It is unusual for property given by specific bequest or devise to be needed for payment of the deceased's funeral and testamentary expenses and debts. Once the

PRs are satisfied that the property will not be so required, they should consider transferring it to the beneficiary, or to trustees if a trust arises, for example if the property is given to a beneficiary contingently on attaining a stated age and the beneficiary has not yet reached that age.

The method of transferring the property to the beneficiary or trustee will depend on its particular nature. For example, the legal estate in a house or flat should be vested in a beneficiary by a document known as an assent. If the specific legacy is of company shares, a stock transfer form should be used.

In the case of specific gifts only, the vesting of the asset in the beneficiary is retrospective to the date of death, so that any income produced by the property, for example dividends on a specific gift of company shares, belongs to the beneficiary. He is not entitled to the income as it arises but must wait until the PRs vest the property in him. As the beneficiary is entitled to the income he will be liable to be assessed for any income tax due on that income since the death.

Any costs of transferring the property to a specific legatee, and the cost of any necessary insurance cover taken to safeguard the property are the responsibility of the legatee who should reimburse the PRs for the expenses incurred (subject to any contrary direction in a will indicating that such expenses should be paid from residue).

34.9.3 Pecuniary legacies – provision by will for payment

An example of a clause expressly for the payment of pecuniary legacies is clause 4 of Tom Smith's will, first mentioned in connection with the payment of debts in **34.8.4**.

The clause reads as follows:

> **I GIVE all my estate both real and personal whatsoever and wheresoever not hereby or by any codicil hereto otherwise specifically disposed of (hereinafter called 'my residuary estate') unto my trustees UPON TRUST to raise and discharge thereout my debts and funeral and testamentary expenses and all legacies given hereby or by any codicil hereto and any and all taxes payable by reason of my death in respect of property given free of tax and subject thereto UPON TRUST to pay and divide the same equally between … .**

There is clear intention shown by the testator to pay the pecuniary legacies from the fund of general residue described as 'my residuary estate'. If instead, the clause gave the residuary estate 'subject to' or 'after payment of' the pecuniary legacies the effect would be the same, that is, the legacies should be paid from the fund of residue before the division of the balance between the residuary beneficiaries.

34.9.4 Incidence of pecuniary legacies – no provision by will for payment

Example

A will leaves a legacy of £5,000 to Dawn. There is no direction as to payment of the legacy. Residue consisting of personalty and realty is given by the will to 'Edward if he shall survive me by 28 days'. He does so survive the testator, and residue is, therefore, fully disposed of. The PRs should pay the legacy from the personalty, with the proceeds of the realty being used afterwards if necessary.

If a partial intestacy arises, for example where part of a gift of residue fails because one of the beneficiaries dies before the testator, it is often unclear as a matter of law which is the appropriate part of the estate for the payment of the pecuniary legacies.

34.9.5 Time for payment of pecuniary legacies

The executor's year

The general rule is that a pecuniary legacy is payable at the end of 'the executor's year', ie one year after the testator's death. AEA 1925, s 44 provides that PRs are not bound to distribute the estate to the beneficiaries before the expiration of one year from the death. It is often difficult to make payment within the year and, if payment is delayed beyond this date, the legatee will be entitled to interest by way of compensation. The rate of interest will either be 6 per cent per annum or the rate prescribed by the testator's will. If the testator stipulates that the legacy is to be paid 'immediately following my death', or that it is payable at some future date, or on the happening of a particular contingency, then interest is payable from either the day following the date of death, the future date or the date the contingency occurs, as may be appropriate.

Interest payable from the date of death

There are four occasions when, as an exception to the normal rule, interest is payable on a pecuniary legacy from the date of the death. These occur when legacies are:

(1) payable in satisfaction of a debt owed by the testator to a creditor;
(2) charged on realty owned by the testator;
(3) payable to the testator's infant child (historically this was so that provision was made for maintenance of the child, and interest is not payable under this provision if other funds exist for the child's maintenance); or
(4) payable to any child (not necessarily the child of the testator) where the intention is to provide for the maintenance of that child.

34.10 COMPLETING THE ADMINISTRATION AND DISTRIBUTING THE RESIDUARY ESTATE

34.10.1 Introduction

Once the PRs have paid the deceased's funeral, testamentary expenses and debts and any legacies given by the will, they can consider distribution of the residuary estate in accordance with the will or the intestacy rules.

The PRs may have made interim distributions to the residuary beneficiaries on account of their entitlements, at the same time ensuring that they have retained sufficient assets to cover any outstanding liabilities, particularly tax.

Before drawing up the estate accounts and making the final distribution of residue, the PRs must deal with all outstanding matters. Such matters relate mostly to IHT liability, but there will also be income tax and CGT to consider.

34.10.2 Adjusting the IHT assessment

Adjustment to the amount of IHT payable on the instalment and non-instalment option property in the estate may arise for a number of reasons including:

(1) discovery of additional assets or liabilities since the Inland Revenue account was submitted;

(2) discovery of lifetime transfers made by the deceased within the 7 years before death;

(3) agreement of provisionally estimated values, for example with the shares valuation division of the Inland Revenue (in the case of shares in private companies) or the district valuer (in the case of land). The shares valuation division and the district valuer are official agencies established for the formal agreement of valuations on behalf of the Inland Revenue with PRs and others. Especially in the case of private company shares, but also in the case of land, valuations may require long negotiations and can often delay reaching a final settlement of IHT liabilities;

(4) agreement between the PRs and the Inland Revenue of a tax liability or repayment, in relation to the deceased's income and capital gains before the death;

(5) sales made by the PRs after the deceased's death which have given rise to a claim for IHT 'loss relief'.

IHT loss relief

Where 'qualifying investments' are sold within 12 months of death for less than their market value at the date of death (ie 'probate value'), then the sale price may be substituted for the market value at death and the IHT liability adjusted accordingly (IHTA 1984, ss 178–189). 'Qualifying investments' include shares or securities which are quoted on a recognised stock exchange at the date of death and also holdings in authorised unit trusts.

If the PRs make several sales of qualifying investments in the 12-month period, the aggregate of the sale proceeds over the whole period must be taken into account when determining whether there has been a loss (or gain) on sale (IHTA 1984, s 179).

There are similar provisions relating to the sale of land within 4 years of a death at a loss (IHTA 1984, ss 190–198).

34.10.3 PRs' continuing IHT liability

IHT by instalments

The PRs may have opted to pay IHT by instalments on the property in the deceased's estate attracting the instalment option. Depending on the time taken to administer the estate, possibly only one of the 10 instalments will have been paid, leaving a continuing liability for the following 9 years. As the PRs are liable to pay this outstanding amount, it is essential that they decide how their liability is to be discharged, for example by retaining sufficient assets in the estate. Details of the instalment option facility are discussed at **4.3.7**. If any instalment option property is sold, any outstanding IHT on the property sold becomes due immediately.

IHT on lifetime transfers

If the deceased dies within 7 years of making either a potentially exempt transfer (PET), or a chargeable transfer, IHT (if a PET) or more IHT (if a chargeable transfer) may become payable. Although the general rule is that the donees of lifetime transfers are primarily liable for the tax, the PRs of the donor's estate may become liable if the tax remains unpaid by the donees 12 months after the end of the month in which the donor died. However, the PRs' liability is limited to the extent of the deceased's assets which they have received, or would have received in the administration of the estate, but for their neglect or default.

In addition, if the deceased gave away property during his lifetime but reserved a benefit in that property, such property is treated as part of his estate on death (see **4.3.1**). The donee of the gift is primarily liable to pay the tax attributable but, if the tax remains unpaid 12 months after the end of the month of death, the PRs become liable. Again the PRs should consider how they can protect themselves in case this liability materialises.

34.10.4 Inland Revenue corrective account

Corrective account

When all variations in the extent or value of the deceased's assets and liabilities are known, and all reliefs to which the estate is entitled have been quantified, the PRs must report all outstanding matters to the Inland Revenue (Capital Taxes) (IR(CT)). This report is made by way of a corrective account on Form Cap D3, although, in a case where there are only minor adjustments to be made, a letter will generally suffice. The form is signed by the PRs as disclosing all matters relevant to the IHT position of the estate, but it does not require self-assessment of IHT by the PRs, unlike the original Form IHT 200. Submission of the form results in the IR(CT) issuing the final IHT assessment. The assessment should be checked carefully. If it is correct the PRs should arrange to pay any further IHT which is due or seek a repayment of any overpaid IHT.

34.10.5 IHT clearance certificate

Certificate of discharge

The last step for the PRs to take in relation to IHT is to obtain from the IR(CT) a certificate of discharge from any further claim to IHT. If the IR(CT) is satisfied that IHT attributable to a chargeable transfer has been, or will be made, they can and, if the transfer is one made on death they must, give a certificate. The effect of the certificate is to discharge all persons, thus in particular the PRs, from further liability to IHT (unless there is fraud or non-disclosure of material facts). The same certificate also extinguishes any Inland Revenue charge imposed on the deceased's property for the IHT.

IHT Form Cap 30

To obtain the certificate of discharge the PRs complete an application in duplicate on IHT Form Cap 30. This form briefly summarises all particulars relating to the deceased, his estate and the Inland Revenue accounts already submitted, and the PRs' request for a formal certificate of discharge. The IR(CT) will return the form with the certificate endorsed on it.

In cases where the estate is an 'excepted estate', a certificate is not required because automatic discharge from liability is generally given within 35 days of issue of the grant.

A full certificate of discharge cannot be issued to the PRs if they are paying the IHT by instalments. However, it is possible in such cases for the PRs to obtain a full certificate of discharge 'save and except' the IHT payable on the instalment option property; once all the IHT has been paid, the PRs should apply for a full certificate.

34.10.6 Income tax and CGT

The deceased's liability

Immediately following the death, the PRs must make a return to the Inland Revenue of the income and capital gains of the deceased for the period starting on the 6 April before the death and ending with the date of death. Even though the deceased died part way through the income tax year, the PRs, on his behalf, may claim the same reliefs and allowances as the deceased could have claimed had he lived throughout the whole year. Any liability to tax must be paid by the PRs during the administration, and it will represent a debt due at death deductible by them when calculating the amount of IHT. Alternatively, if a refund of tax is obtained, this will represent an asset, so increasing the size of the estate for IHT purposes.

The administration period

For each income tax year (or part) during the administration period, the PRs must make a return to the Inland Revenue of the income they receive on the deceased's assets, and any gains they make on disposals of chargeable assets for administration purposes, for example to raise money to pay IHT or the pecuniary legacies. These returns for the estate are distinct from the PRs' returns of their own income and capital gains.

Income tax

RATE OF TAX

The rates at which PRs pay income tax depends on the type of income they receive. For 2001/2002, this is:

dividends	10%	(Schedule F ordinary rate)
interest	20%	(lower rate)
other (gross) income	22%	(basic rate)

PRs do not pay income tax at any higher rate(s).

In many cases, the PRs will have no tax to pay since income is often received after bearing income tax at the relevant rate. This applies to interest received (20%) and to dividends (non-recoverable 10% tax credit). If gross income is received, PRs will be assessed to tax at 22%.

CALCULATION OF PRs' LIABILITY

In calculating any income tax liability on the income of the administration period, the PRs may be able to claim relief for interest paid on a bank loan to pay IHT. If the PRs use this loan to pay the IHT on the deceased's personal property in the UK which devolves on them in order to obtain the grant, income tax relief is generally available to them.

Example

PRs' only income is gross interest of £4,000 for a tax year in the administration period. They pay £1,000 interest to the bank on a loan to pay IHT to obtain their grant.

Gross income	£4,000
Less: interest paid	£1,000
Taxable income	£3,000
Less: lower rate (20%)	£600
Net income for the beneficiaries	£2,400

BENEFICIARY'S INCOME TAX LIABILITY

Once the PRs' tax position has been settled, the remaining net income will be paid to the beneficiary. The grossed up amount of this income should be included by the beneficiary in his return of income for the income tax year to which it relates.

Example

PRs have completed the administration of an estate and there is bank deposit account interest which, after payment of tax at 20% by the PRs, amounts to £800. That sum is paid by the PRs to the residuary beneficiary.

When the beneficiary makes his return of income he must declare the estate income grossed up at lower rate (20%), ie $£800 \times \dfrac{100}{80} = £1,000$.

The PRs will supply the beneficiary with a certificate of deduction of tax, on Form R185, which the beneficiary should send to his own inspector of taxes as evidence of the payment of the tax by the PRs.

CGT

NO DISPOSAL ON DEATH

On death, there is no disposal for CGT purposes, so that no liability to CGT arises. The PRs acquire all the deceased's assets at their probate value at death. This has the effect of wiping out gains which accrued during the deceased's lifetime so that these gains are not charged to tax. Although there is no disposal, the probate value becomes the PRs' 'base cost' of all the deceased's assets for future CGT purposes.

CALCULATION OF PRs' LIABILITY

If the PRs dispose of chargeable assets during the administration of the deceased's estate to raise cash (eg to pay IHT or other outgoings or legacies), they are liable to CGT on any chargeable gains that they make. PRs pay CGT at the rate of 34 per cent (2001/2002) whatever the size of the gains made.

In addition to deducting their base cost (probate value), the PRs may deduct from the disposal consideration the incidental costs of disposal (eg stockbroker's commission on sale of shares). In addition, they may deduct a proportion of the cost of valuing the deceased's estate for probate purposes. Calculations may be based either on a scale published by the Inland Revenue or on the actual expenditure incurred if this is higher.

The indexation allowance and taper relief apply in the same way as for individuals.

The PRs may claim the annual exemption for disposals made in the tax year in which the deceased died and the following 2 tax years only (if the administration lasts this long). The exemption is the same as for an individual (ie £7,500 for 2001/02). Maximum advantage will be taken from this exemption if the PRs plan sales of assets carefully so that gains are realised in stages in each of the 3 tax years for which it is available.

Example

PRs need to raise £50,000 to pay administration expenses. The investments they are advised to sell will realise a net gain of £10,000. They have no unused losses. Ignore indexation and taper.

(1) If all sales occur in the same tax year, their CGT position is as follows:

		£	
gain		10,000	
annual exemption		7,500	
taxable		2,500	at 34% = £850

(2) If the sales are spread evenly over 2 tax years, their CGT position is as follows:

		£
Year 1	gain	5,000
	annual exemption	7,500
	taxable	nil
Year 2	gain	5,000
	annual exemption	7,500
	taxable	nil

SALES AT A LOSS

If the PRs sell assets for less than their value at death, an allowable loss for CGT will arise. This loss may be relieved by setting it against gains arising on other sales by the PRs in the same, or any future tax year, in the administration period. Any loss which is unrelieved at the end of the administration period cannot be transferred to the beneficiaries. In view of this limitation, the PRs should plan sales carefully to ensure they can obtain relief for all losses which they realise. If there is a possibility of losses being unused, the PRs should either plan sales of other assets or consider transferring the assets worth less than their probate value to the beneficiaries (see below).

TRANSFER OF ASSETS TO THE 'LEGATEES'

If, instead of selling assets, the PRs vest them in the 'legatees', ie in the beneficiaries or trustees if a trust arises, no chargeable gain arises. The beneficiary or trustee is assumed to acquire the asset transferred at its probate value. This 'base cost' of the asset will be relevant to the CGT calculation on a future disposal.

Example 1

A testator by will leaves his residuary estate to Phil. Among the assets forming residue are 1,000 shares in XYZ plc. Probate value of these was £5,000. Since death they have risen to £10,000. Five years after death Phil sells them for £15,000.

Disposal consideration	£15,000
Less: base cost (probate value)	£5,500
Gain	£9,500
Less: annual exemption	£7,500
Chargeable gain	£2,000

Example 2

If he sells the shares for £2,000 less than their probate value his position would be as follows:

Disposal consideration	£3,000
Less: base cost (probate value)	£5,000
Loss	(£2,000)

The loss of £2,000 is available to Phil to set against chargeable gains he may have in the same, or any future, tax year.

34.10.7 Transferring assets to residuary beneficiaries

Interim distributions

Once the outstanding tax, legal costs and other matters have been disposed of, PRs should consider transferring any remaining assets to the residuary beneficiaries. In doing so they must remember that payments may have been made already to the beneficiaries as interim distributions on account of their entitlement. If so, these will be taken into account when determining what and how much more should be transferred to those beneficiaries. These interim distributions will also be shown in the estate accounts.

Adult beneficiaries

If the beneficiaries are adults, and have a vested entitlement to property in the residuary estate, their entitlement can be transferred to them. If they have a contingent entitlement, the property cannot be transferred to them but will instead be transferred to trustees to hold on their behalf until the contingency is satisfied.

Minor beneficiaries

If any beneficiaries are under 18 years of age, whether the interest enjoyed is vested or contingent, the property will usually be held in trust for them until the age of majority is reached or the contingency is satisfied. If a minor beneficiary has a vested interest the PRs may be able to transfer his entitlement to him or to other persons in the manner set out below. If these options are not available for any reason, or if the beneficiary's interest is contingent, the PRs will retain the property (as trustees) for the beneficiary.

INFANT RECEIPT CLAUSE IN A WILL

The PRs may be able to transfer the property to the beneficiary personally if the will contains an appropriate infant receipt clause. Generally, a clause of this type will only permit transfer by the PRs if the beneficiary has attained the age of 16 years.
In addition, it may permit transfer of the property to the beneficiary's parent or guardian from whom the PRs can receive an appropriate receipt.

AEA 1925, s 42

Under the AEA 1925, s 42 the PRs may transfer property to which the beneficiary has a vested entitlement to two trustees, or a trust corporation, to hold until the beneficiary attains majority. Often, this provision is used to transfer the property to the beneficiary's parents, providing the PRs with a full discharge.

Transferring property to the residuary beneficiaries

The manner in which the property is transferred to residuary beneficiaries, or to trustees of their behalf, will depend on the nature of the property remaining in the estate.

PERSONAL PROPERTY

The PRs indicate that they no longer require property for administration purposes when they pass title to it by means of an assent. Generally, no particular form of assent is required in the case of personalty so that often the property passes by delivery. The beneficiary's title to the property derives from the will; the assent is merely the manner of giving effect to the gift by the PRs. Company shares are transferred by share (stock) transfer form. The PRs must produce their grant to the company as proof of title to the shares. They, as transferors, transfer the shares 'as PRs of X deceased' to the beneficiary (the transferee) who then applies to be registered as a member of the company in place of the deceased member.

FREEHOLD OR LEASEHOLD LAND

PRs vest the legal estate in land in the person entitled (whether beneficially or as trustee) by means of an assent which will then become a document of title to the legal estate. If PRs are to continue to hold property in their changed capacity as trustees under trusts declared by the will, or arising under the intestacy law, an assent will again be appropriate. The PRs should formally vest the legal estate in themselves as trustees to hold for the beneficiaries.

By the AEA 1925, s 36(4), an assent must be in writing, it must be signed by the PRs, and it must name the person in whose favour it is made. It then operates to vest the legal estate in the named person. A deed is not necessary to pass the legal estate but PRs may chose to use a deed, for example if they require the beneficiary to give them the benefit of an indemnity covenant. If the title to the land is registered, the assent must be in the form specified by the Land Registration Rules 1925.

Any person in whose favour the PRs make an assent or conveyance may require notice of it to be endorsed on the original grant of probate or administration. In view of this entitlement, it is good practice that the endorsement should be made by the PRs, or solicitors on their behalf, as a matter of routine at the same time as the assent is given. Indeed, if the PRs have made an assent where the title is unregistered in favour of a beneficiary, endorsement is essential for that beneficiary's protection in view of the provisions of AEA 1925, s 36(6) benefitting any later purchaser from the PRs.

If the title to the land is registered, two options are open to the PRs:

(1) they can apply to be registered as proprietor in place of the deceased, in which case they must produce the grant of representation when making the application; or

(2) they can transfer the property by assent without being registered as proprietor themselves, in which case the beneficiary must be given a certified copy of the grant of representation so that he can present it with his application for registration.

As the register is conclusive as to title, the provisions in the AEA 1925 regarding endorsements on the grant are of no relevance.

34.10.8 Estate accounts

Purpose of the accounts

The final task of the PRs is usually to produce estate accounts for the residuary beneficiaries. Their task will be considerably eased if they have kept full records of all transactions affecting the estate during the course of its administration. The purpose of the accounts is to show all the assets of the estate, the payment of the debts, administration expenses and legacies, and the balance remaining for the residuary beneficiaries. The balance will normally be represented by a combination of assets transferred to the beneficiaries in specie, and some cash. Approval of the accounts is shown by signature of the residuary beneficiaries on the accounts. In the absence of fraud or failure to disclose assets, their signatures will also release the PRs from further liability to account to the beneficiaries.

Presentation of the accounts

There is no prescribed form for estate accounts. Any presentation adopted should be clear and concise so that the accounts are easily understood by the residuary beneficiaries. If interim distribution payments were made to the residuary beneficiaries during the administration period, these must be taken into account and shown in the estate accounts.

VERTICAL PRESENTATION

Estate accounts may be presented vertically, disclosing assets less liabilities, etc, and a balance for the beneficiaries, or on a double-sided basis, disclosing receipts opposite the payments. It is customary to use the probate values of the assets for accounting purposes.

NARRATIVE INTRODUCTION

The accounts generally start with a narrative statement of the date of death, the date of the grant of representation, a summary of the will or succession under the intestacy law and the value of the deceased's gross and net estate. All this information is provided to make the understanding of the accounts easier for the beneficiaries.

CAPITAL AND INCOME ACCOUNTS

Normally accounts show capital assets, and income produced by those assets during the administration period, in separate capital and income accounts. In small estates this may not be necessary so that one account showing both capital and income will be sufficient. However, it is always necessary to prepare separate accounts if the will (or the intestacy rules) creates a life or minority interest, since the different interests of the beneficiaries in the capital and income need to be distinguished throughout the period of the trust, and when it ends.

INDEX

References are to paragraph and Appendix numbers.